£32.50

RESTAURANT DESIGN

RESTAURANT DESIGN
NINETY-FIVE SPACES THAT WORK

SUSAN COLGAN of
RESTAURANT AND HOTEL *Design*

THE ARCHITECTURAL PRESS: LONDON

Entrance to Twenty/Twenty in New York City (frontispiece). The architects were Haverson/Rockwell Architects, P.C. Photography: © Timothy Hurlsly.

First published in Great Britain in 1987 by
The Architectural Press,
9 Queen Anne's Gate, London SW1H 9BY

All rights reserved. No part of this publication may be reproduced, stored in a retrieval system, or transmitted, in any form or by any means—electronic, mechanical, photocopying, recording, or otherwise, without the prior permission of the publishers. Such permission, if granted, is subject to a fee depending on the nature of the use.

Copyright © 1987 by Restaurant and Hotel Design

ISBN 0-85139-971-1

Manufactured in U.S.A.

First printing, 1987

1 2 3 4 5 6 7 8 9 / 92 91 90 89 88 87

ACKNOWLEDGMENTS

I would like to give special thanks to Mary Jean Madigan, editor in chief of *Restaurant and Hotel Design*, and to the magazine's staff: Rachel Long, managing editor; Maureen Picard, associate editor; John Lenaàs, art director; Dion Birney, assistant editor; Karen Rifkin, special projects coordinator; Michael Webb, West Coast editor; and Adriana Spazzoli, Italian correspondent. Thanks also are due to *Restaurant and Hotel Design*'s contributing writers, Kim Johnson Weiss, Jill Fox, and Richard Sasanow, as well as to production director Barbara Devlin and assistant production manager, Valentina Chiofalo, who has borne the brunt of my relentless search for the *right* picture. I am also indebted to former staffers and contributors Jerry Cooper, Mark Kristal, Barbara Knox, Deborah Dietsch, Philip Mazzurco, Justin Henderson, Diana Aceti, Barry H. Slinker, Florence Bruin, Teresa Byrne-Dodge, Betsy Lippy, and Jay Pridmore. For a specific list of their contributions—too numerous to include here—see the source and credit listing beginning on page 248.

To Paul Weintraub, publisher of *Restaurant and Hotel Design* magazine, deep appreciation for his continuing efforts in conceiving and promoting this project and helping to guide it over many potentially rocky shoals.

Special thanks goes to the staff at the Whitney Library of Design: Julia Moore, senior editor; Victoria Craven-Cohn, associate editor; Bob Fillie, designer; and Ellen Greene, production manager.

And finally, I thank all the designers and photographers whose works appear here. Their creativity has truly given this project life.

CONTENTS

INTRODUCTION by M. J. Madigan	8
1. DESTINATION RESTAURANTS	14
2. CAFES, GRILLES, AND BRASSERIES	34
3. FAST FOOD ESTABLISHMENTS	64
4. CHAIN RESTAURANTS	84
5. THEMATIC DESIGNS	108
6. ETHNIC RESTAURANTS	134
7. EAT-IN/TAKE-OUT ESTABLISHMENTS	158
8. RESTAURANTS IN HOTELS	180
9. NIGHTSPOTS	196
10. CAFETERIAS	214
11. RESTAURANTS WITH VIEWS	222
12. ADAPTIVE USE DESIGNS	232
SOURCES AND CREDITS	248
INDEX	253

INTRODUCTION

Philip Johnson's and John Burgee's controversial ovoid "lipstick building" in New York City is the site of Toscana Ristorante, an establishment conceptualized by veteran restaurateur Sergio Bitici and his three brothers. Italian architects Piero Sartogo and Nathalie Grenon designed the restaurant's 50-seat bar and grill room and the 100-seat formal dining room, both luxuriously lined with pearwood veneer and Carrara marble. Toscana's logo and graphics were created by designers Lella and Massimo Vignelli. Emery Roth & Sons were the architects.

A BOOK SUCH AS THIS one could not have been conceived a generation ago, when the primary measure of any restaurant's success was its reputation for serving good food.

The menu still matters, of course, but today's sophisticated diners expect far more than mere gustatory satisfaction when they select a place to dine. They are seeking an "experience"—a sensory envelope of sight, sound, taste, smell, and touch that matches a mood or reinforces an image of self. As the mood and the image vary, so does the restaurant experience: It can be funky or formal, casual or opulent, low key or charged with drama.

To create this experience takes the talents of a cadre of professionals that range from the restaurateur—who generally is responsible for the overall concept—to the architect, interior designer, and contractor. Often, special consultants are engaged to design the kitchen, lighting plan, sound system, and graphics elements of the project.

It was not always so. The idea of restaurant as experience or as theater engaging the creative talents of a team of professional designers is a contemporary phenomenon, a concept that did not come fully into its own until the 1980s, when changes in the American social fabric were beginning to affect the foodservice industry in the United States. The increase in two-wage-earner families, for example, has meant that people have fewer hours to devote to home cooking, but more discretionary income to spend on meals purchased outside the home. The upward price push for urban housing has shoehorned many young couples into apartments with little space for cooking or dining in comfort, let alone entertaining friends. Restaurants, especially commodious ones, have became places to stretch one's body and spirit, places to socialize, and to see and be seen.

The eighties has also seen the coming of age of the Baby Boomers—that sophisticated and materialistic generation raised in a postwar period of unprecedented prosperity. They constitute a new breed of consumer, relentless in their pursuit of perceived value, willing to spend heavily for self-gratification. They are the first generation of American restaurant patrons to expect—and to get—an experience along with lunch or dinner.

Well traveled, the Boomers find traditional theme and ethnic restaurants to be hackneyed imitations of the real thing. Well educated, they demand eating places that will expand their cultural horizons with art, music, exotic food, and wine. Status-conscious, they want restaurants that will deliver the panache of cuisine by a top-name chef in an environment created by an architect or interior designer of note. The Boomers have been fond of "restaurant collecting"—seeking out trendy new establishments for the prestige of simply having been there.

This crowd of new-generation restaurant-goers, though enthusiastic, has proven itself fickle. Trendy spots are born quickly and die quickly. According to industry statistics, the average lifespan of a big-city restaurant is just three years. In such a competitive atmosphere, restaurateurs have pulled out all the stops to ensure that their establishments, which often

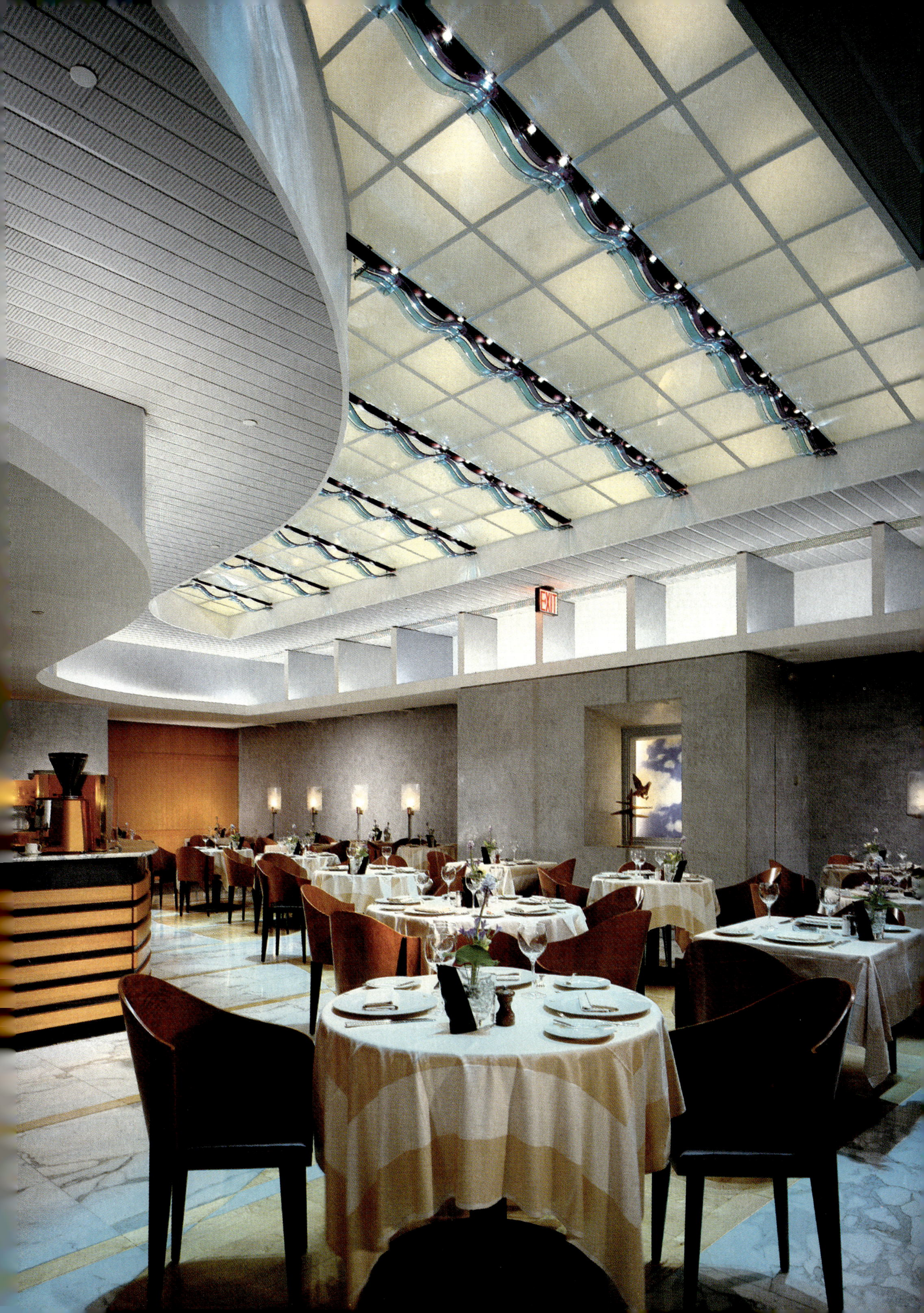
EXIT

cost well into seven figures, produce as much revenue as possible during their predictably short lives.

In so doing, today's restaurant operators have created a thriving market for imaginative architects and interior designers who specialize in this field, as well as for kitchen consultants and experts in lighting and acoustics. Manufacturers and suppliers, in turn, have responded to the designers' demand for market-specific products for the restaurant industry. Never before has there been such a wide selection of furniture, fabrics, finishes, and fixtures available to enhance a project's visual appeal, while meeting strict sanitary and fire codes, standing up to hard daily wear, and offering ease of maintenance.

While traffic patterns, back-of-house planning, and other functional considerations are certainly critical to the success of any restaurant, during the past decade aesthetics has assumed an important almost without precedent in the industry. In part, this reflects the renaissance of design consciousness that began in the late 1970s, cutting across many levels of society.

Few would dispute that restaurants are indeed products of their times. A glance backward shows that the very first restaurants were inns that sprang up at crossroads during the Middle Ages, when people first began to journey away from home and hearth. These medieval travelers were grateful for simple respite from the dangers of the road; for a loaf and a haunch and something spirited with which to wash them down. This crude standard of hospitality remained fairly constant over the next five centuries: Coaching inns and public houses—quite literally, road houses—were places where one dined while en route from one place to another because the rough circumstances of travel allowed no other choice.

The restaurant as we know it—an eating facility not necessarily connected with a lodging place—came into its own in the second half of the nineteenth century, hard on the heels of the Industrial Revolution and the urbanization it brought. There evolved a new class of worker, one who spent days not on a farm, but in a city factory, shop, or office too far from home to permit returning for "dinner," the substantial meal then customarily served at midday. Those who could afford not to carry a "dinner bucket" provided a ready market for the private clubs and public eating houses that proliferated in cities everywhere. As the business day extended beyond sunset, these establishments began to serve evening meals as well as the noontime repast.

By the 1890s, the lunch room, the drugstore soda fountain, the tea room, and the railway station restaurant all emerged as viable foodservice operations. The very first chain restaurant was born in America when entrepreneur Fred Harvey opened his pioneering rail depot restaurant in Topeka, Kansas, in 1876, to serve travelers in the West. It became the prototype for other Harvey Houses along the Atchison, Topeka and Santa Fe rail line. Although some were embellished with motifs and artifacts of the Southwest, they were notable primarily for their white tablecloths and air of respectable formality—civilized oases in the midst of what was then a rough frontier. In the best and most pragmatic American fashion, the focus of the Harvey Houses was not on the experience of eating, but on the food itself, served by efficient young women in reassuringly sanitary surroundings that reminded the weary traveler of home.

Shortly after the turn of the century, the "eat and run"

Small but exquisite touches distinguish Toscana's interiors: In the bar and grill room, custom-designed Murano glass ashtrays have the shape of the restaurant's logo. The marble bar itself was crafted in Italy and shipped completely assembled. The award-winning disymmetrical burlwood and leather Tuscana chairs, designed by Sartogo and Grenon, are commercially available. Fitted together in pairs, the chairs form a loveseat.

A gracefully curved pearwood veneer wall sheaths the wine display area housed between Toscana's bar and the entrance to the main dining room. In strongly angular contrast to the curvilinear soffited ceiling, blocks of Carrara marble flooring alternate with strips of pale wood. The plaster walls of the dining room were given a glowing faux marbre finish. Photography: © Milroy/McAleer.

approach, so much in tune with the accelerating pace of industrial America, gave rise to the concept of fast food. As decade followed decade in the first half of the twentieth century, fast food—served in lunchrooms, cafeterias, automats, and finally, as automobiles proliferated, in drive-in restaurants—became a uniquely American, taken-for-granted dining option.

Moreso than in formal restaurants, where the anonymous, white-tablecloth aesthetic stayed much the same from one decade to the next, America's quick-service restaurants paraded a succession of styles: Art Deco facades of glass tile with artful signage distinguished storefront eateries of the twenties and thirties. Diners of the forties, having evolved from streetcars turned into lunch wagons, were "streamlined" with rounded corners and metallic finishes. McDonald's and similar freestanding roadside restaurants of the early fifties boasted futuristic parabolic arches and eye-catching pylons to pull customers off the freeways. In the sixties, as fast food chains spread into residential neighborhoods, they abandoned these flashy pylons for the discreet camouflage of red "Georgian" brick. By the seventies, the fern-bar concept with its ceiling of live hanging plants and its "natural" finishes had become the dominant mode of decoration in fast food and other chain restaurants.

Virtually all such quick-service restaurants were "designed"; some by their individual owners, many more in replication of a prototype dictated by the operator or franchisor of a specific chain. Invariably, however, such designs were inspired by purely pragmatic motives: to attract customers to an attention-getting facade; to provide an efficient, easy-to-care-for kitchen, and a dining area that would speed customers in and out quickly—nothing too comfortable, lest the restaurant's turnover be slowed and its margin of profit reduced.

On the other hand, the so-called white tablecloth, or formal, restaurants, including the ones situated in hotels, tended until the late 1970s to be undesigned—conceived by their owners, and decorated to whatever standard of comfort and "good taste" prevailed among their target group of customers. All too often, that meant flocked red wall covering and crystal chandeliers.

This was the design climate in the foodservice industry in late 1978, when *Restaurant and Hotel Design* began publication as *Restaurant Design* magazine, a quarterly offshoot of the restaurant operator's journal, *Restaurant Business*. (*Restaurant Business* had itself grown up with the industry, starting life early in the century as *Soda Fountain*.) *Restaurant Design*'s publishers sensed a growing demand among operators and owners for information specific to design. They felt that a new magazine, directed to architects and interior designers as well as to restaurant owners, would function as an industry catalyst, bringing together the two groups in pursuit of the common goal of improved restaurant design.

Their timing could not have been better: Design consciousness was on the rise, and the hospitality industry was booming. The new magazine was well received, and by 1986, had increased its frequency to twelve issues a year. Along the way, it became *Restaurant and Hotel Design*, in acknowledgment of the fact that many architects and designers of restaurants are also engaged in the planning of lodging facilities.

As the magazine has grown, so has the seemingly insatiable demand for case study information on restaurants. It was the desire to provide such information in a concise, easy-to-use format that ultimately inspired the publication of this book. The ninety-five successful restaurant projects that follow have been selected because—individually and as a group—they offer a comprehensive overview of the state of the art in restaurant design today. The objective is to show how hundreds of design professionals responded to the briefs of their various clients—however extreme or demanding. Thus, each case is announced with its design imperative.

As with all attempts at classification, the effort to divide these diverse and often unique projects into specific categories has been to some extent arbitrary. But given the number of restaurants covered, it seemed a logical way to proceed. Here, under chapter headings organized by type, you will find ethnic and theme restaurants, restaurants in hotels, fine "destination" restaurants, nightspots, cafeterias, adaptive use designs, fast food facilities, chain establishments, and more.

Each chapter opens with a concise introduction by Susan Colgan, who is special projects editor for *Restaurant and Hotel Design*. Her deft summaries trace the evolution of each project category, placing each type of restaurant within its social and historical context. Drawing from material researched by staff writers and other contributors to the magazine, Colgan has edited their descriptive texts to provide the most informative essentials, and she has selected exciting photographs that telegraph important visual data about each project.

Here then is the story of successful restaurant design in the 1980s, told through nearly a hundred outstanding projects conceived by designers and architects all over the world. Whether your interest in restaurant design is personal or professional, we are confident you will profit from the cases detailed in these pages.

MARY JEAN MADIGAN
Editor in Chief
Restaurant and Hotel Design

1. DESTINATION

RESTAURANTS

A destination restaurant is a special place to go. It has an excellent reputation: The food is *au point* and the atmosphere usually combines elegance and restraint. Such a restaurant has no single "look." It may be suffused with warm, peachy light, it may have gauzy white curtains falling from 20-foot ceilings, it may offer views stretching for miles, or it may be smooth and curved and mellow with no windows at all. It may have a clean, sharp, modern edge; it may be stately and traditional. With a destination restaurant, the owners, the designers, and the chef have done the same thing: created an outstanding experience for those who seek it out.

The food is known for its quality. The service is usually formal and European. The price range is high-end. Invariably, the kitchen is run by a chef of some repute who has a following. Because a considerable amount is invested in the chef and his or her training, the owners will not put a lot of money into a trendy design that is unlikely to age well. Such a restaurant will be designed to last; it will often become a classic. New York's Four Seasons Restaurant is probably the quintessential destination restaurant.

This chapter includes a variety of destination restaurants. Each one offers its patrons a special atmosphere and dining experience. The guiding elements in the design of these establishments are as varied, of course, as the spaces they occupy. Arcadia, shown on the page opposite, has a chic Manhattan address and a typical New York space: long, narrow, and windowless. Architect Randolph Croxton opened up the space by creating windowlike screens, commissioning landscape murals, and subtly adjusting the ceiling level with a lip of indirect light. Historic Bryan Homes's architect, Randolph Henning, has united two waterfront houses, while the architect of Le Triangle, Stanley Felderman, has converted an early twentieth-century factorylike space into a two-level extravaganza of postmodern design.

TRANSFORM A REINFORCED CONCRETE STRUCTURE
AN ELEGANT SKYLIT DINING SPACE IS CREATED ON TWO LEVELS

The space of Le Triangle—composed of the Cafe du Triangle, on the lower level, and the formal Max au Triangle restaurant above—is fractured dramatically by classic arches, one upended, sending the eye soaring upward to the vaulted ceiling. A skylight here spills light into the mezzanine level's more formal dining area as well as into the piazzalike café.

"CREATE A JEWELLIKE restaurant, set in a garden," the backers of Le Triangle told designer Stanley Felderman. From a reinforced concrete structure built in 1906, Felderman wrested an airy, elegant restaurant meeting specifications and exceeding expectations. The result is unique. The idiosyncrasies of the space are used to heighten its elegance and work to create a true destination restaurant in a city of razzle-dazzle and glitz.

The low structure was stripped down, revealing an elaborate metal ceiling support as dramatic as any massive nineteenth-century warehouse. Felderman had the supports painted white, leaving them exposed above a graceful suspended ceiling of gold mesh that ties together the different areas of the restaurant and its adjacent lounge.

An unusual atrium provides a focus around which Felderman's plan unfolds. The atrium is an irregular 15,000-square-foot wedge shape with a formal restaurant on the mezzanine level overlooking a piazza-like café.

Anchoring the Cafe du Triangle are two classical arches of plaster washed and textured to suggest stone. One is upended like a reflection of the other, below skylights that are framed by a complex layered geometry of openings with every line and plane springing away at a different angle.

From the ground level of Cafe du Triangle, an elevator and wraparound staircase lead up to the formal restaurant, Max au Triangle, which seats 120 in generously proportioned armchairs. Max's end wall is paneled in mirrored glass; its side walls are also mirrored and screened in bright white trellis.

Here light pours down from the skylight and from overhead spots. The airy feeling is enhanced by the view over the brass-railed parapet into the piazza-like space below. Max's reception area is defined by a handsome etched and tinted glass panel and by touches of lime green and mauve. The dining room is divided by blue-gray columns, draped with white gauze to suggest open windows.

Max au Triangle's bar has a chic, sharp-edged elegance. Windows are angled; one frames the nearby Beverly Wilshire Hotel. The faceted black granite bar projects into the room at a right angle. The chairs are covered with a mock zebra fabric.

Throughout both restaurant and café, quality shows in all the details. Draped fabric is echoed in plaster folds around the reception area. The freestanding elevator shaft is inlaid and accented with marble, and in the café, thin marble sheets are fretted and backed with mirror glass to highlight the serving area. The blonde wood frames of the black and gray armchairs have a lustrous sheen. Even the menu is die-cut in the shape of a fan. Everywhere forms that are current and fashionable have been used in an original way. The spaces are spatially well sequenced and detailing is superb.

LE TRIANGLE	*Beverly Hills, California*
Owners:	*Beverly Rodeo Passage*
Interior Design:	*Felderman & Associates (Stanley Felderman)*
General Contractors:	*Buckeye Construction*
Budget:	*$1.5 million*
Photography:	*© David Glomb*

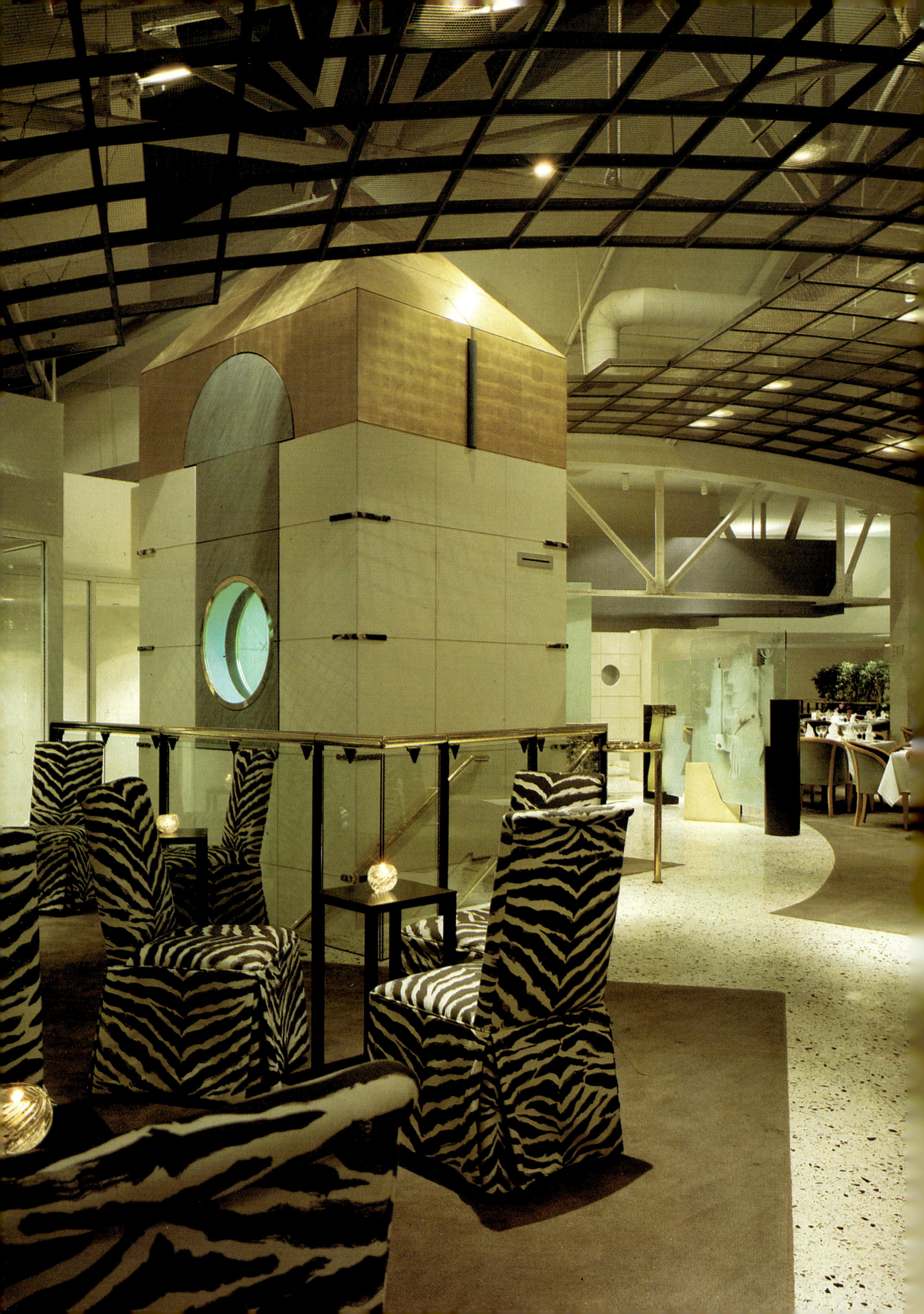

Max's lounge, opposite, is tucked between the obelisklike elevator and angled window wall. Note the elegant use of terrazzo, inlaid carpet, the zebralike upholstery, and the brass railings—all contributing to the overall quality and polish of the space. In Max's dining room (right), the truly formal part of the restaurant, Felderman reiterates the gridwork of the gold mesh ceiling in the wall trellises. Adding warmth is the sleek wood-paneled room divider and the blonde wood frames of the black and gray armchairs. The floorplan shows how the staircase and elevator lead up into the mezzanine level.

19

FIND THE RIGHT LOCATION
AN AMBIENCE-RICH RESTAURANT UTILIZES A WATERFRONT SITE

A gently curving walk leads visitors to the Historic Bryan Homes Restaurant through a broad front yard abutting New River Canal (left). Inside, a series of intimate spaces are appointed with period antiques, original works of art, and a warm color scheme. In the Reed Bryan house (opposite), designers chose to retain exposed stone block walls and to keep the warmth of the natural wood surfaces.

CREATING A FINE restaurant with just the right ambience sometimes takes more than time, money, and a good designer. For Anthony Gillette—experienced chef, former faculty member of the Culinary Institute of America, and independent foodservice consultant—the search for the right location took him from Palm Beach to Coconut Grove before he settled on a waterside site on the New River Canal in downtown Fort Lauderdale.

What he found—a pair of dilapidated turn-of-the-century houses offered for lease by the city—didn't necessarily sing out "restaurant." But these unimpressive houses, built in 1904 by Fort Lauderdale pioneer Phileman Bryan for his sons, offered a good downtown location that promised steady, year-round clientele.

It was the start of a healthy operation for Gillette. Having settled on a site, he negotiated a complicated lease with the city and began the process of sympathetic renovation/restoration. Much of the approximately $1.2 million renovation was financed by the city as part of a comprehensive urban renewal scheme for the downtown business district.

With architect Randolph C. Henning, AIA, and designers Wendy Costa and Paula Kline (Costa and Kline Interiors, Fort Lauderdale) Gillette converted the freestanding buildings into one efficient restaurant. This required three major structural changes. First, the houses (which stand about eight feet apart) had to be connected; then a first-rate kitchen facility—capable of servicing the restaurant as well as an anticipated catering operation—had to be built; finally, verandas and a porch on the two houses had to be enclosed.

HISTORIC BRYAN HOMES RESTAURANT
Fort Lauderdale, Florida

Owner: *Anthony Gillette*

Architecture: *Randolph C. Henning*

Interior Design: *Costa & Kline Interiors (Wendy Costa, Paula Kline)*

Budget: *$1.2 million*

Time: *2 years*

Photography: *© Martin Fine (Forer Inc.)*

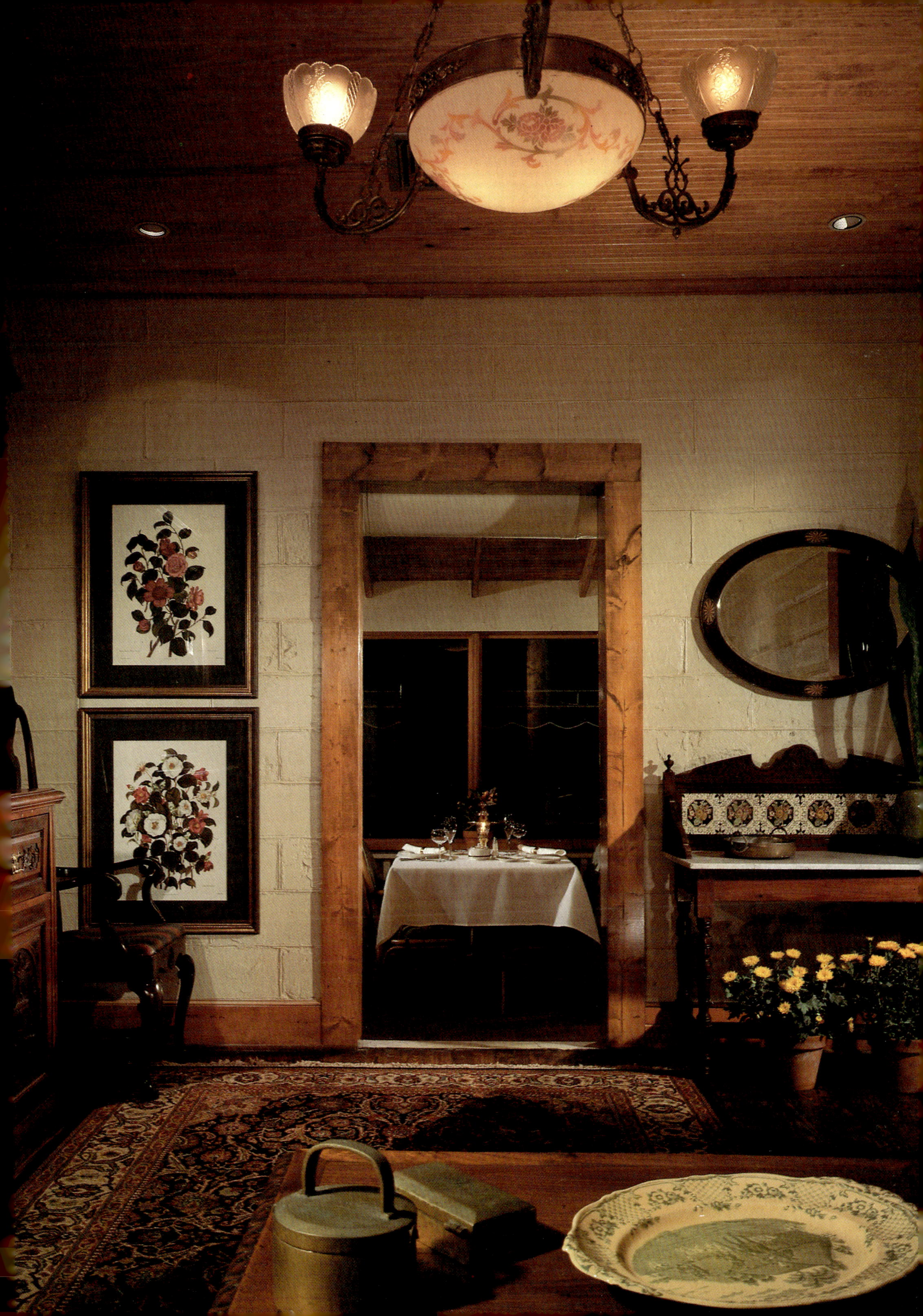

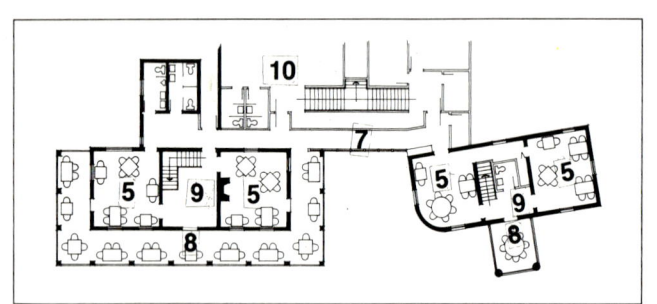

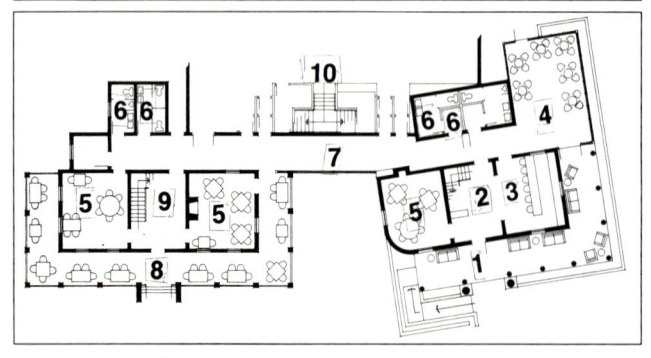

Connecting the houses and adding the kitchen became one comprehensive effort. For Henning, it was important that the two houses "still be seen as separate structures." So he designed a two-story, glass-faced connector at the rear of the two houses, then located the massive kitchen addition, also two stories high, behind that.

The connecting section serves to unify the two houses visually and to join the two spaces in an orderly, function-related flow through the series of small rooms and porches from house to house and floor to floor. To best integrate the new kitchen with the existing structures, Henning specified exterior materials and a silhouette sympathetic to those of the old homes.

He used a concrete veneer similar to the irregular hand-painted concrete blocks of the original homes. The tallest part of the kitchen was placed against the two-story houses, stepping down to a one-story element and camouflaging mechanical equipment within the roof structure.

Enclosing the verandas on the Reed Bryan house to the west and a porch on the Tom Bryan house to the east—the object being additional seating with views of lawns and canal within temperature-controlled comfort—was in some ways the most delicate alteration because it addressed the structures themselves.

On the Reed Bryan house, casement-style windows were installed, slightly recessed from existing columns to allow the original scale and materials to continue to predominate. The Tom Bryan house porch was enclosed with a structural roof and plate glass.

Inside, designers Costa and Kline worked to retain the houses' original character and form, keeping any required alteration of structure or aesthetic details to a minimum. Since they were working with a historic site, they were fairly limited as to what could be changed; for the most part they were dealing with finishes.

Costa and Kline found that though the houses were built at the same time by the same man, there were important differences. The Tom Bryan house, with smooth walls and handsome moldings, was a bit more refined than the adjacent Reed Bryan house with its interior walls of exposed stone blocks. In keeping with the mood of each, the former was decorated to a more elegant standard, while the roughhewn Reed house had been left pretty much intact.

Unifying the small rooms and lending to the quality of the space are the color scheme, the antiques, the commissioned art, and the textures and fabrics. The warm color scheme centers on red, hunter green, and camel, complementing the warm wood tones of the beams and the furnishings. A massive, vintage-1895 mahogany bar was purchased and customized for the restaurant. Commissioned art includes "Old Florida" themes in keeping with the overall historic aspect of the structures and the site.

Gillette's persistence in searching to find the right location paid off. He created a space for a restaurant with an ambience charged with history and commanding graceful waterfront views.

Traditional furnishings, warm colors, and soft lighting unify various spaces—from cozy dining rooms (above), to glass-enclosed verandas (opposite). Floorplan: porch main entrance (1); maitre d' entrance hall (2); bar (3); lounge (4); dining rooms (5); restrooms (6); loggia (7); verandas (8); entrance halls (9); kitchen (10).

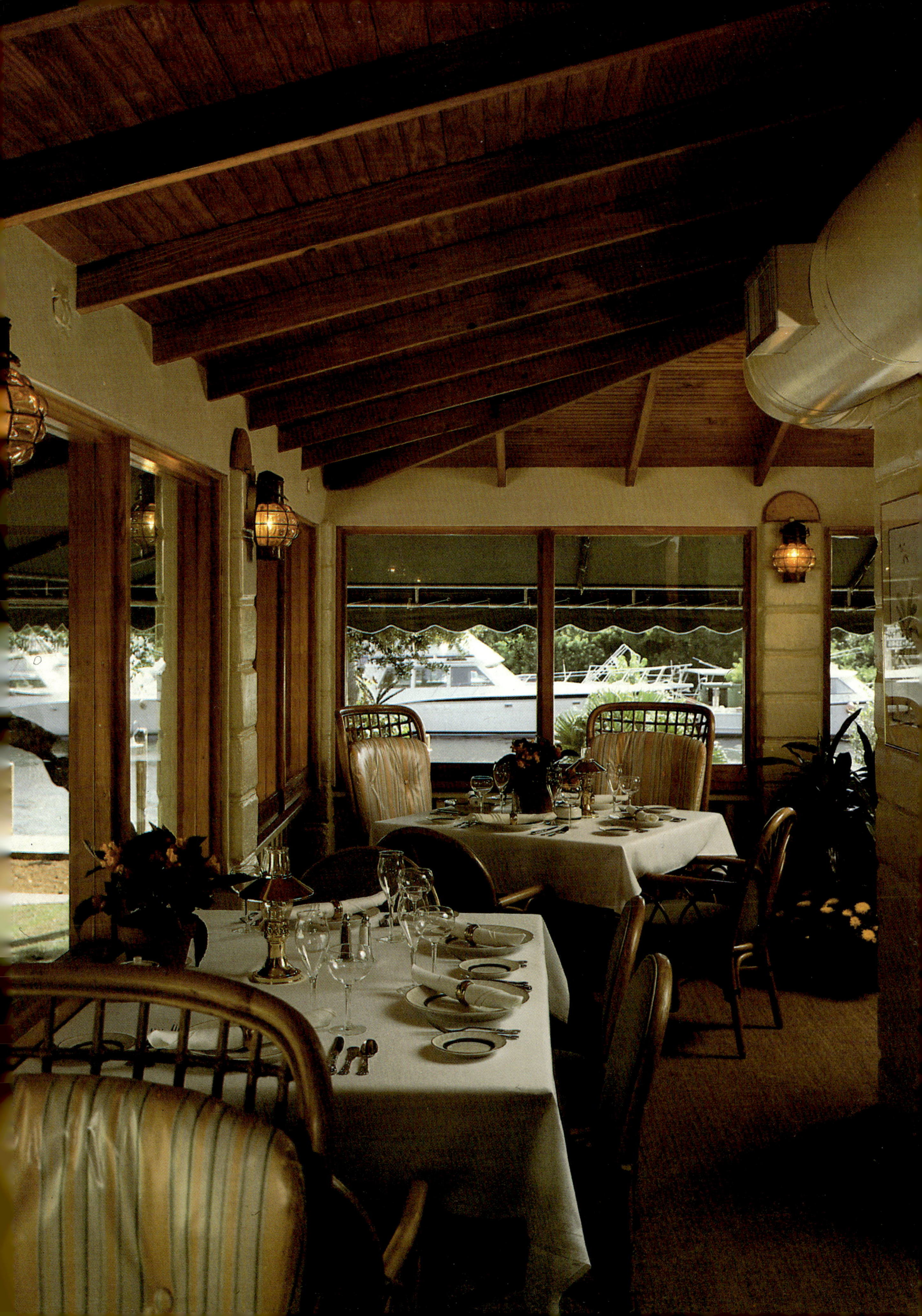

CREATE A VIEW IN A SHOEBOX
MURALS MAKE A HAVEN FROM THE CITY

A seat anywhere in Arcadia gives patrons a look at the view, the mural that wraps the space (opposite). A classic windowpane screen divides the bar and dining areas and repeats the design of the restaurant's facade. Architect Randolph Croxton fashioned Arcadia's bar, above, to be a standing piece of sculpture that patrons see as soon as they enter. The floorplan shows how hard lines and edges of the dining room were rounded and softened, enhancing the luxurious, cocoonlike atmosphere.

THE SPATIAL AND STRUCTURAL challenges were distinctly urban in nature, and the site was classically New York: a deep, dark, narrow, space. With a structure more than a century old, possessed of a disastrous kitchen and in need of all new utilities, the owners and their architect, Randolph Croxton, were interested in the idea of looking "out and beyond." They wanted something small, luxurious, and elegant.

An artistic solution was required. It began with Croxton's design of a classic windowpane in mahogany and beveled glass with segments of the bow line lifted to create a more complex version of the wood screen. This became the thematic element that defines the restaurant's entire facade and repeats in the screen dividing the bar and the dining room. The simple arch is also evident in the rounded edges and top of the large handmade mahogany bar.

Through the windowpanes, the restaurant's "view"—actually a mural that wraps the perimeter of the seating area—is inviting. Before settling on the mural's theme, Croxton researched images of America from the turn of the century. Ultimately, inspiration came from owner Ken Aretsky's country house, which overlooks the Hudson River. Arcadia's co-owner and chef, Anne Rosenzweig, concurred and research shifted to the Hudson River School of painters. Arcadia emerged when artist Paul Davis rendered what Croxton describes as "a concept of the river in its many states."

In the dining room, the challenge was to draw the eye away from the 8-foot 6-inch ceilings and toward the panoramic mural that flows around the room. Croxton did so by creating a lip of indirect lighting that, while actually lowering the ceiling at its edges to roughly standing height, emphasizes the mural's picture-window appearance and makes it seem less a work of art and more an idyllic vista.

The muted rose color of the banquettes and carpet complements the mahogany, yet keeps all the active color changes in the mural. The space was further enhanced by the elimination of hard edges and lines. This included rounding the room's four corners to create an elegant cocoon.

What pleases the owners is the quality of the space: it is friendly and warm; people feel comfortable and look good.

ARCADIA New York City

Owners: *Anne Rosenzweig, Ken Aretsky*

Interior Design/Architecture: *Croxton Collaborative, Architects (Randolph R. Croxton, principal; John Obelenus, project architect)*

Seating: *52*

Photography: *© Otto Baitz*

25

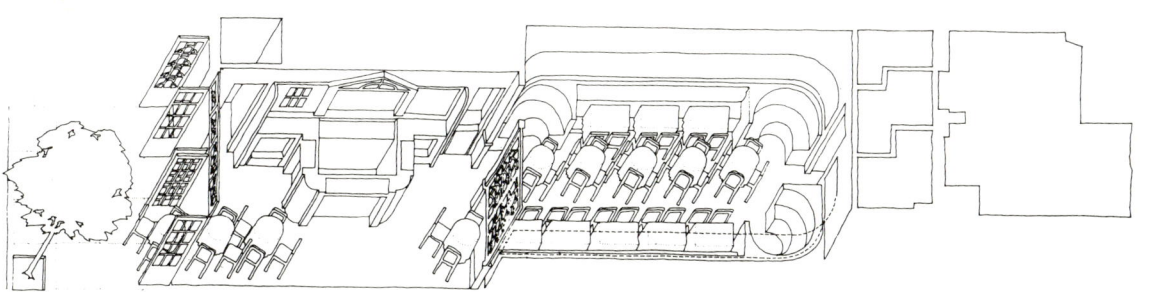

LET MUSIC GUIDE THE DESIGN
A MINIATURE OPERA HOUSE IS OUTFITTED FOR DINERS

BERNARD AND SHEILA SEGAL wanted an understated performance space with unobstructed views of a stage. They wanted a place where live opera could be performed. They wanted a large bar area to encourage patrons to drop by regularly and enjoy the music for the price of a drink. They wanted, in short, a restaurant where music would be the inspiration and the guiding spirit. From this vision, a complex, elegant, and lucid design emerged.

The Segals found a landmark building in Santa Monica—previously used as a mortuary—and hired the inventive local architectural firm of Morphosis to convert it. Thom Mayne and Michael Rotondi stripped the arcaded facade of superfluous ornament, painted it dark red, and built a ramp behind the arches (to provide wheelchair access to the raised entrance), creating the look of a miniature opera house.

Inside, they excavated part of the main floor by three feet to create a sunken dining area. A half-closed upper dining room to the left of the entrance balances the elevated stage in the rear. Straight ahead is the bar, and two rows of small tables flank an axial, pitch-vaulted corridor that leads past the kitchen.

Morphosis' main concern was to create a sense of hierarchy, subtly defining and interrelating the subsidiary spaces that surround three sides of the main dining area. The shifts in floor and ceiling height, and the alternation between openness and enclosure, offer a feeling of intimacy, give everyone a privileged view, and allow service to continue during the three evening performances.

Ceiling vaults and wall surfaces are treated as relief sculpture modeled by soft-hued lighting concealed behind moldings. Walls are painted off-white; the upholstery is a dusky rose; the carpet dark gray. The effect is serene yet precise, a triumph of sensitive lighting and imaginative spatial geometry.

Murals painted by David Schorr are an integral element of the design. The Segals had long admired his cartoons in the *New Republic*, and particularly a series entitled "My Verdi." He painted a frieze of scenes from *Aida* around the upper dining room; portraits of Rigoletto, Othello, and Azucena in the main dining room; and behind the bar, an animated ball scene from *La Traviata*. The soft colors and vibrant lines of these murals soften the architecture and help sustain the mood of the performances.

An axial corridor (3 on floorplan) is an important element in the complex interrelating of various spaces, joining rear and front sections of Verdi. Floorplan: entrance (1); bar (2); corridor (3); main dining area (4); stage (5); raised dining (6); kitchen (7); restrooms (8); rear entrance (9).

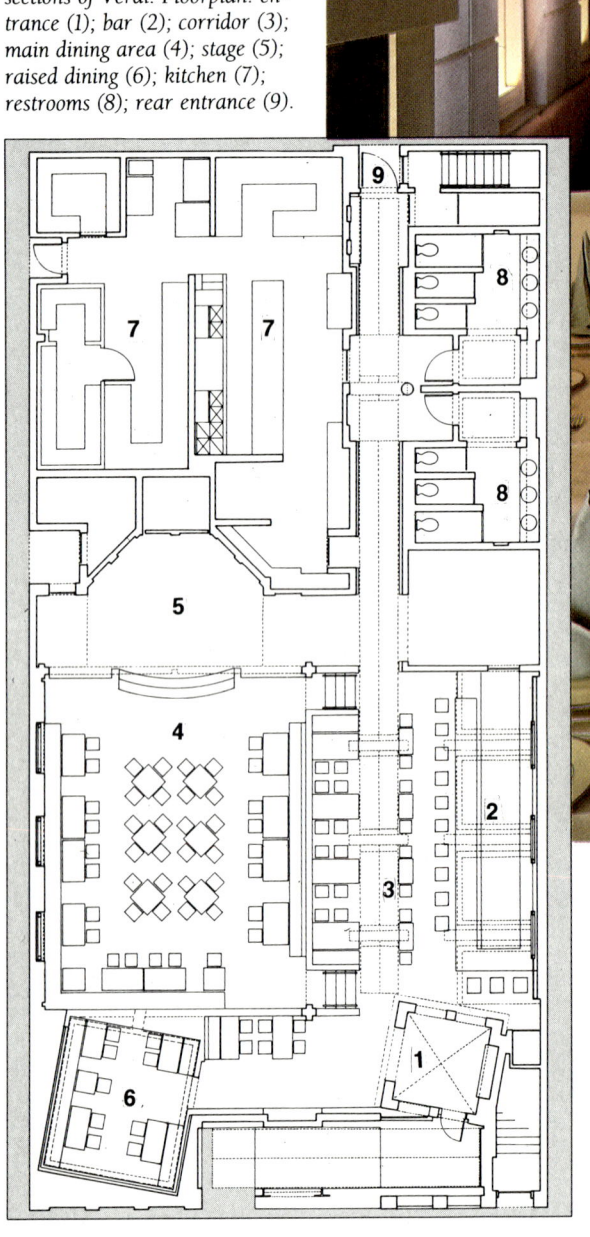

VERDI	*Santa Monica, California*
Owners:	*Bernard and Sheila Segal*
Architecture:	*Morphosis (Thom Mayne, Michael Rotondi)*
Design Team:	*Ben Caffey, Judith Newmark*
Structural Engineer:	*Erelyi Mezey*
Mechanical Engineer:	*Sullivan & Associates*
Lighting Consultant:	*Saul Goldin*
Foodservice Consultant:	*Tony Singaus*
Seating:	*135 plus 26 at bar*
Photography:	*© Marvin Rand*

More than a mere aesthetic theme, music and its performance is an integral part of the Verdi design. A platform stage dominates the lowered main dining room. To accommodate views from all quarters, subtle changes in floor levels and ceiling heights have been carefully planned, allowing service during performances as well.

ACCOMMODATE THIRTY-FOUR-FOOT WINDOWS
A PROBLEM SPACE IS UNIFIED AROUND THE VIEW

JOSEPH MEISEL HAS CREATED many restaurants for the Levy organization; at Spiaggia he worked closely with the Levys to make a supremely functional, visually unified restaurant out of a grand but problematic multilevel space dominated by 34-foot windows.

The address for Spiaggia is as compelling as the space: One Magnificent Mile, the highrise designed by Skidmore, Owings & Merrill at the juncture of Michigan Avenue and Oak Street, midway between Chicago's most affluent residential areas and its top hotels.

Bearing this in mind the owners worked on the premise that the space could generate at least $4.5 million a year and budgeted close to $4 million for the design and construction, including $2.9 million for hard construction, $500,000 for interior millwork and furniture, and $400,000 for kitchen equipment.

It was Louis Levy's love of Italian cooking that gave rise to the theme for the restaurant, as well as its name. "Spiaggia" is Italian for beach; it also takes into account the restaurant's view of nearby Oak Street Beach. The design for the restaurant evolved over time, according to Meisel, who traveled to California with the owners to tour upscale restaurants. They wanted an open kitchen, they wanted to utilize the view, and they wanted a café that would open into the adjacent department store on the second floor of the building.

Taking space from his original—and larger—kitchen plan, Meisel was able to shoehorn 66 seats into the Café Spiaggia, which is not visible from the luxe, formally tiered 150-seat dining room of Spiaggia itself. Later, plans were implemented for private dining rooms on a mezzanine level overlooking the main dining area.

To lend importance to Spiaggia's entrance and set the tone for the interior, Meisel designed a postmodern rusticated facade with a keystoned arch and pillars of veined black marble. Inside, he used a marble colonnade to define the upper dining level and bar area, suggesting an airy portico. His deft arrangement of seating and mirrors gives most diners a view of the beach and of each other.

Enhancing the luxury, Meisel selected such softly textured materials as leather, suede, mohair, and silk in flattering tones of rose and plum, offset by teal. These rich textures play off the shiny hardness of the marble, lacquered wood, and tile that are used throughout the restaurant. Decorative lighting sconces repeat the keystone motif which is Spiaggia's postmodern design signature.

SPIAGGIA	*Chicago, Illinois*
Owner:	*The Levy Corporation*
Building Architecture:	*Skidmore, Owings & Merrill*
Restaurant Architecture/Design:	*Meisel Associates, Ltd. (Joseph A. Meisel III)*
Budget:	*$4 million*
Seating:	*150 in dining room, 66 in café*
Photography:	*© Barry Rustin*

Twilight glimmers through Spiaggia's windows (opposite, top). Seating is arranged in tiers (above) to take full advantage of the view. On the topmost level is a bar, not visible here, and an open kitchen, glimpsed between the Italian marble columns (right foreground). With postmodern eloquence, the glass-enclosed entrance (opposite, bottom) assures guests that they've arrived.

CONVERT A FIVE-STORY BROWNSTONE TO A TWO-STORY RESTAURANT
SCHEME MOVES DINERS EFFORTLESSLY UPWARD

Le Cygne's foyer opens onto a tightly designed lobby area, which includes a two-seat black lacquered bar (left) and a coatroom, as well as three separate staircases. The main stairwell (opposite) is the undisputed focal point of the restaurant. Rising 44 feet to a vaulted ceiling, this dramatic stair links the two-story space and articulates the architects' desire to make the approach to Le Cygne's dining areas theatrical.

THE SET OF CIRCUMSTANCES that launched Le Cygne is as intrinsic to the end result as the design process itself. Having already established a restaurant of stellar reputation, Le Cygne owners Michel Crouzillat and Gerard Gallian found in 1980 that they would lose their lease; the building was coming down to make way for a tower complex on Madison Avenue.

After much negotiation, the owners were able to sign an agreement to move next door into a five-story brownstone. It was an unusual situation. While the original Le Cygne continued to operate, architects Voorsanger & Mills of New York worked to create a new home for the haute cuisine establishment.

Their plan was to keep the restaurant in human scale, but also to take the great vertical space and make it a strong element in the design scheme. Consequently, each of the dining areas is comfortably scaled while the lobby/stairwell soars 44 feet to a vaulted pinnacle. The stairwell itself is almost exactly a double cube, measuring 18 by 20 by 44 feet.

The architects wanted to let the restaurant become a theater of arrival, progression, and destination. From the moment of entrance, the restaurant exudes a certain mysterious quality that heightens the experience from foyer to table.

A tiny two-seat bar sits directly inside the entrance. Within the small lobby space, the designers had to create a bar, a coat room, and a main staircase. It is within the vertical stairway that patrons truly feel a sense of mystery. As Voorsanger noted, "nobody really wants to climb up a flight of stairs to get to their table. We had to make the experience of the stairwell

LE CYGNE	*New York City*
Owners:	*Michel Crouzillat, Gerard Gallian*
Architecture:	*Voorsanger & Mills Associates*
Interior Design Consultant:	*Savany Associates*
Lighting Consultants:	*Paul Marantz, Jules Fisher*
Budget:	*$700,000*
Time:	*2 years*
Photography:	*© Peter Aaron (ESTO)*

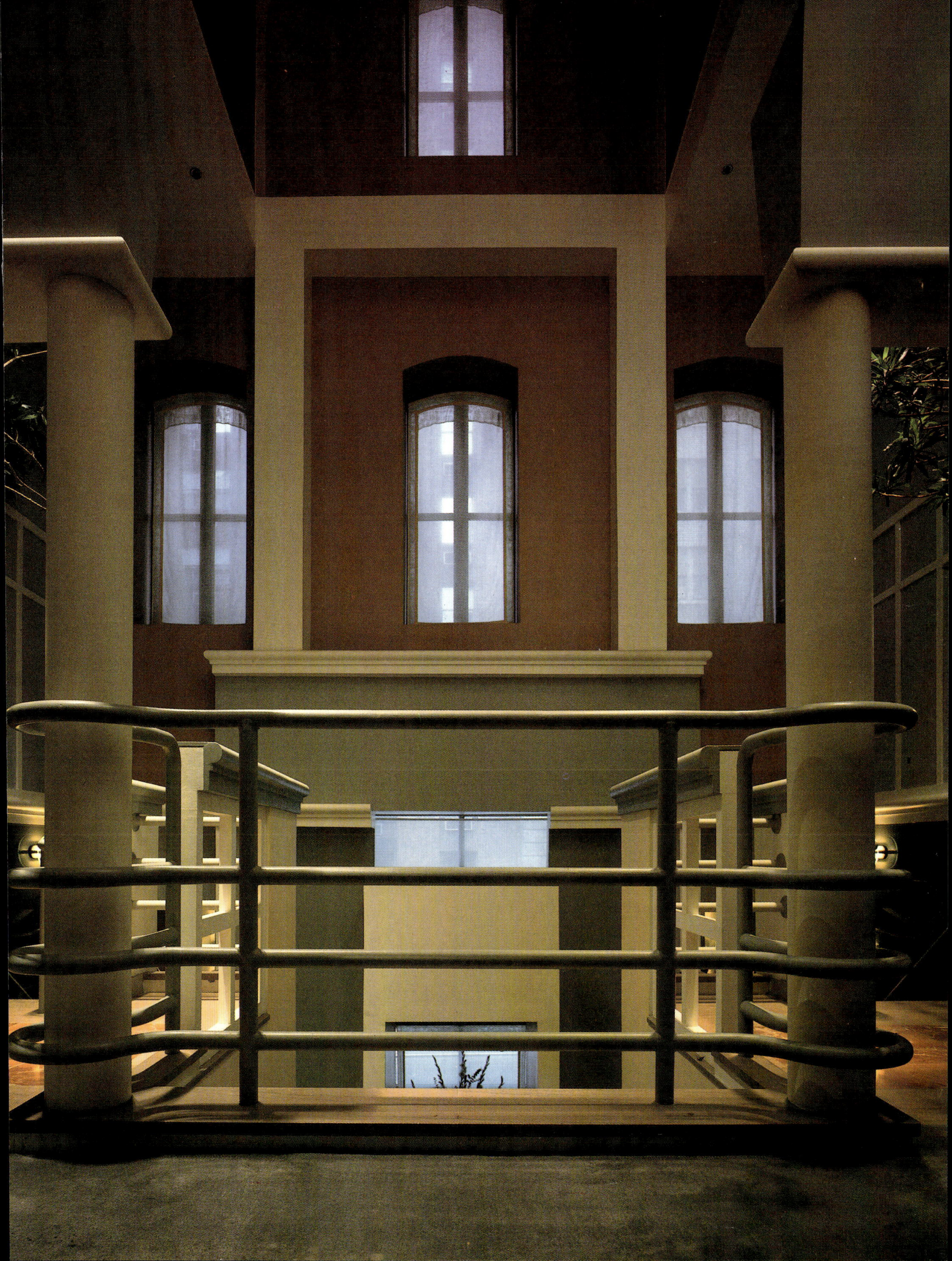

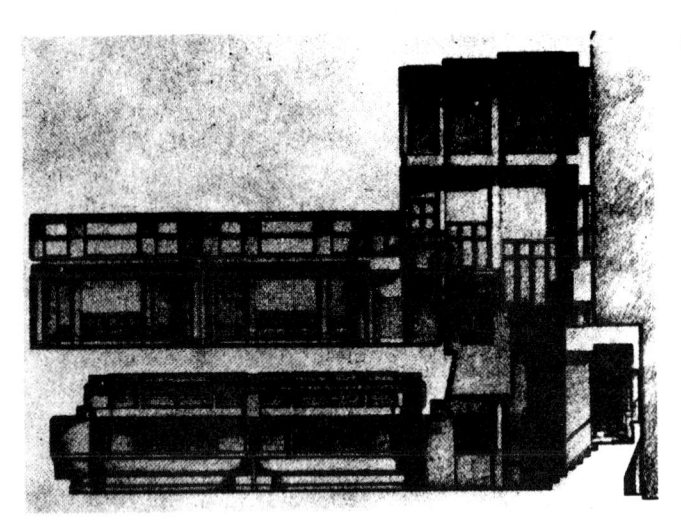

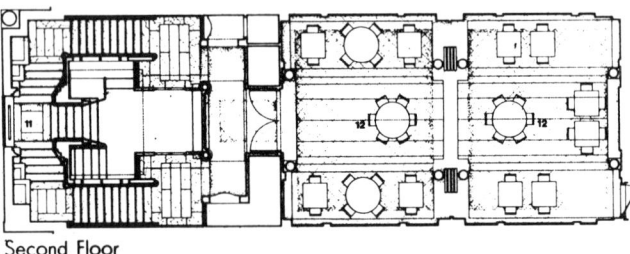

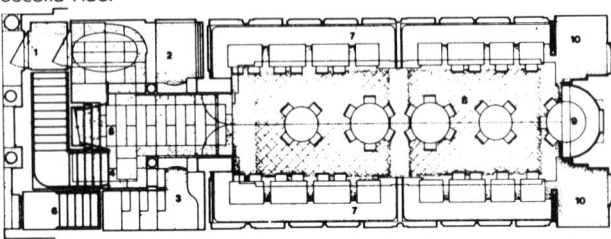

Project architect Richard Velsor's technical drawings of Le Cygne reveal the intricacies of design, particularly in the stairwell. Floorplan: entry (1); bar (2); coatroom (3); stair down (4); main stair up (5); service stair (6); banquette seating (7); first-floor dining (8); exedra (9); to kitchen (10); stairwell (11); second-floor dining (12).

strong enough so that patrons never realize how far they are climbing."

All along the ascent are interesting things to look at as well as choices to be made. At the first landing the single staircase branches to either side, continuing up to the second floor. This adds to the mystery, says Voorsanger; people can wonder which way to go.

In addition to the connecting link of the stairs, both light and color work to unify the restaurant space. Natural light is limited and skylights were not an option the owners favored; therefore artificial light is filtered throughout the space. Using Impressionist colors and light, the first floor, with its pale blues, blue-grays, pinks, and lavenders, evokes morning. The lobby/stairwell, through its sheer architectural strength and strong natural light, simulates midday, and the upstairs dining room, toned with warmer pinks, oranges, and ochres, recalls the evening.

Furthering the illusion, the architects commissioned original murals for both dining rooms. Flower garden murals by Barbara Goodwin, set into panels and offset on either side by mirrors, represent the windows that could not physically exist. This motif repeats upstairs with landscape murals by Mikhaill Ivanetsky.

Because light was as essential as color in the overall design, the architects manipulated interior architectural details to supply appropriate effects. In the main dining room, a backlit, louvered clerestory provides the morning light, with supplemental cove lighting above the flower garden mural panels. The light orchestration also works to give this typically narrow New York space (20 feet wide) a feeling of additional width.

Upstairs the evening light comes through the impressive barrel-vaulted ceiling. Much like a theatrical scrim, white mesh screen inlays are lit from behind, filling the room with soft light. "It was important to light the second floor from above," according to Voorsanger, "so that people would know they were on the top floor."

Since the second floor was also conceived as a banquet space, the architects designed folding partition walls that pull out of the permanent wing walls in the room's center. When closed, they blend perfectly with existing architecture, creating two discrete rooms. The barrel vault unites the two spaces when the doors are open but the four-columnar system used resolves each room when the doors are closed.

Although the new Le Cygne cost nearly double the projected budget, the owners had no regrets.

CAST A ROSY GLOW
CUSTOM-DESIGNED FIXTURES BATHE A LUXURIOUS RESTAURANT IN THE WARM LIGHT OF DAWN

Subtle lighting, comfortable leather armchairs, and spaciously arranged tables lend a casual sophistication to the restaurant Joe Baum envisioned as "simply comfortable."

WITH THE FOUR SEASONS and Windows on the World on his list of credits, Joe Baum's wish to create the perfect restaurant was no idle fantasy. For Baum, who has masterminded many classics, a comfortable restaurant serving superb food could be nothing less than perfect.

To accomplish this, Baum lined up some experts: architect Philip George as general consultant for the project, graphic designer Milton Glaser, and tabletop expert Barbara Kafka. Finding the right spot in midtown Manhattan was more difficult. Finally, a spot on the ground floor of an office building opened up off Park Avenue.

One diner likened the completed restaurant, which is embellished with the bubble motif throughout, to "being under water." The pink glow of dawn emanates from bubble-shaped pendant lamps above the bar, while underfoot, deep sea-green carpets are awash with "bubbles." The dinner plates, custom designed (like the carpets) by Glaser, are also imprinted with bubbles. And the salt stand set in the middle of each white table is topped by a small rosy glass globe.

Named for the goddess of dawn, the restaurant needed a statue of Aurora; she is ensconced in a niche above the welcoming bar, just opposite the entrance. The sinuous curves of the bar, which facilitate comfortable conversation and set the gracious tone of the restaurant, are emphasized by the bar rail. Banquettes that flank the entrance are also curved, as is the point of juncture between the tile flooring and rich carpet.

The room is spacious and the widely spaced tables contribute to the comfortable, clubby atmosphere created by subtle use of wood paneling and generously proportioned leather chairs and banquettes.

But the piece de resistance at Aurora is the lighting. A profusion of layered bowl chandeliers cast circular blooms of light on the ceiling, while along the paneled walls, sconces shaped like scallop shells emit a soft glow. The room's blush of light feels at once intimate and elegant.

AURORA   *New York City*

Owner: *The Joseph Baum, Michael Whiteman and Dennis Sweeney Company*

Interior Design: *Milton Glaser*

Tabletop Consultant: *Barbara Kafka*

Photography: *© Mark Jenkinson*

2. CAFES, GRILLES,

AND BRASSERIES

In the jargon of the trade, cafés, grilles, and brasseries are informal eating facilities. The terms are often interchangeable, because the facilities tend to be similar—serving fresh, simply prepared food in a relatively casual atmosphere that is conducive to people-watching. The emphasis is on conviviality and on easy social interplay.

America has wholeheartedly embraced the idea of the café, loosely patterned on the cafés of Paris, where a light meal and coffee are the order of the day and the atmosphere is one of bustle, open space (indoors and out), and *noise*. Every summer, more big-city restaurants seem to spill out onto adjacent sidewalks, taking advantage of the weather and the rent-free space. In urban/industrial areas, large spaces once occupied by lofts, showrooms, and factories are being converted into dining spots inspired by European prototypes. Like cafés, grilles (literally, where grilled food is served) and brasseries (unpretentious restaurants serving simple food and brew) are enjoying a vogue.

People and their movements are often integral to the design of such establishments. Haverson/Rockwell Architects, who created the New York restaurant Twenty/Twenty (opposite), were asked to make the atmosphere theatrical, to put people on stage. Similarly, at Casual Quilted Giraffe, New York architect J. Woodson Rainey of McDonough Nouri Rainey & Associates has also made people integral to the design scheme by using brushed metal, gray granite, and glass to create a space virtually without color, "the better to let people and flowers and food provide color of their own."

But there are no fast rules; the definitions have become arbitrary. All three—cafés, grilles, and brasseries—take advantage of current trends; all respond to what the market wants: healthful food in an atmosphere that reinforces the patron's self-image as a person of sophistication and taste.

LET PEOPLE PROVIDE THE COLOR
A CLASSIC RESTAURANT SHIMMERS WITH METALLIC NEUTRALS

Terrazzo bar (opposite) presents a handsome front to passersby. Waiter's cabinet (left) centers a wall of service windows. Floorplan: kitchen (1); elevator to prep (2); waiter's cabinet (3); coats (4); bar (5); wine storage (6).

ALTHOUGH THE AMBIENCE of Casual Quilted Giraffe may be informal, its architectural concept is not: This is an intellectual exercise in what architect J. Woodson Rainey likes to call "cosmic geometries." Explaining it he says, "It is a very educated floorplan: axial, with the diligence of a classic church, involving science and mathematics. Every placement relates to everything else." Just as the church's nave, aisles, and altar bear a certain proportion to one another, so do the elements of the floorplan in Casual Quilted Giraffe.

A restaurant that anchors the arcade level of such a powerful architectural statement as Philip Johnson's AT&T Building has a lot to live up to and more so when that restaurant is the informal counterpart of one of New York's exclusive, expensive dining spots.

The Wines wanted to maintain the level of quality they'd achieved in the original Quilted Giraffe in an environment

CASUAL QUILTED GIRAFFE	New York City
Owners: Barry and Susan Wine	
Architecture: McDonough Nouri Rainey & Associates (J. Woodson Rainey Jr., partner in charge; William A. McDonough, Hamid R. Nouri, Michael Neal, senior designers; Mark Rylander, Andreas Hausler, Lee Dunnette, Burt Tyson, designers)	
Contractor: F. J. Sciame & Company	
Mechanical Engineer: Cosentini Associates	
Structural Engineer: James Weisenfeld	
Lighting Consultant: Jerry Kugler & Associates	
Seating: 90	
Construction Period: 8½ months	
Photography: © Nathaniel Lieberman	

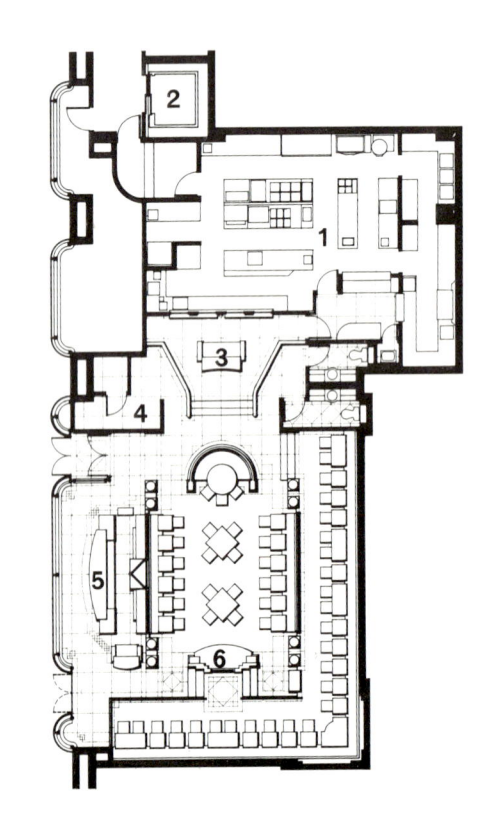

"the CASUAL Quilted Giraffe"

The "nonhierarchical" dining room is laid out on two levels. A wine storage vault and circular banquette, plus eight standing lamps, modulate the spaces. The pattern on the dinner plates adds color and features the graphic signature of the restaurant: a reduction of the famous broken pediment surmounting the AT&T Building, in which the restaurant is housed.

that would offer their usual customers a change of pace, a certain ease. New York architects McDonough Nouri Rainey & Associates obliged with a restaurant that is, in Rainey's words, "not a bistro, not a café. It's like no other spot in the city."

"Searching for the right palette, we turned to the AT&T Building itself, and cracked it open like a geode," Rainey says. The interior is a hard/soft shimmer of brushed metals, etched glass, gray granite, and terrazzo—"without color, the better to let people and flowers and food provide color of their own."

Ten-foot double-window bays, flanked by entrance and exit doors, modulate the organization of the interior spaces. A handsome convex granite bar is centered on these windows, facing outward. Backed with a row of banquettes, it defines one side of the ground-level dining area, which is bracketed by a wine storage console and a large semicircular booth—the closest thing to a power seat in Rainey's "nonhierarchical layout." Cornering the central dining space are pairs of aluminum standing lamps with hemispherical martelè reflectors. Several steps above the main level, a lustrous leather banquette wraps two sides of the room below walls clad in stainless steel panels that are perforated to soften sound.

The main kitchen—which with the basement prep kitchen accounts for sixty percent of the floorspace—is also stepped up a couple of feet to allow for proper plumbing drainage. The architects turned this "overlook" to good advantage, placing a handsome waiter's cabinet beneath four kitchen service windows that glow above the long axis of the dining room with a distinctly altarlike effect. ("It has a proscenium quality," Rainey says of the service area.) A multizone dimming system ensures that the room can be "staged" for various times of the day and the year.

Design-conscious diners can have fun discovering clues to this cerebral layout. Mechanical vents in the ceiling reiterate the room's geometry, and its floorplan is inlaid in iridescent titanium in the granite bartop—the architect's sole concession to color. "Susan Wine reminded me there's something celebratory about going out to dinner. So just for the hell of it, we took fifty different titanium 'jewels' by Tamiko Ferguson and set them at random into the tabletops. Titanium has moving, electric color," Rainey observes. "It adds joy."

Historical references abound in the restaurant's decorative elements. Overall, the mood is deco, but square grids and metal spheres on the railings, the waiter's cabinet, and the ice buckets recall Wiener Werkstätte design. Rainey's custom lighting fixtures suggest towers atop deco skyscrapers. The restaurant's signature graphic, a reduction of the famous broken pediment surmounting the AT&T Building, is used on the elegant ceramic dinner plates, the coasters, and the matchbooks.

Although the budget for a 5,500-square-foot, 90-seat restaurant was a "decent" $1.5 million, Rainey points out that "when the figures were established, we had not yet completed the detailing. To be sure we could get what we wanted, we depended on a network of craftspersons, many of them in Vermont, to fabricate the metalwork and other elements to our specification."

The construction period for the Casual Quilted Giraffe was eight-and-a-half months, once plans and contracts were in place.

UNIFY TWO SPACES FOR ARCHITECTURAL DRAMA
A BILEVEL RESTAURANT IS VISUALLY INTEGRATED

Architect Charles Boxenbaum's facade (left) creates the illusion of a separate structure for Ancora on upper Broadway in New York City. The chimney is both striking and functional; it provides an outlet for heat from the tiled pizza oven inside. Closely spaced balustrades in the railing along the upper dining space (opposite) permit diners to glimpse action on the floor below. This facilitates the integration of the levels as Boxenbaum intended.

ANCORA, DESIGNED BY ARCHITECT Charles Boxenbaum, appears to be a freestanding building on New York's Upper West Side. In fact, Boxenbaum combined spaces formerly occupied by a children's clothing store and a bowling alley, both contained within a two-story commercial block. The resulting restaurant is fronted with a bold facade of melon-colored stucco, surmounted by a lattice sun screen and pediment. A focal chimney element, rising from the restaurant's pizza oven, is carried inside to define two spacious levels of dining and join both together in a bustling, open format.

"I wasn't interested in fashionably styling a restaurant, but in creating a basic architectural order that would orient the diner," explains Boxenbaum. "My idea was that if the finishes

---
ANCORA New York City
Owner: *Ancora Restaurant, Inc.*
Architecture: *Charles Boxenbaum Architect (David Norris, Ole Lokensgaard)*
Lighting Consultants: *CHA Design (Carl Hillman, Don Leithauser)*
Structural Engineer: *Robert Silman Associates*
General Contractor: *Bronx Store Construction*
Photography: *© Norman McGrath*

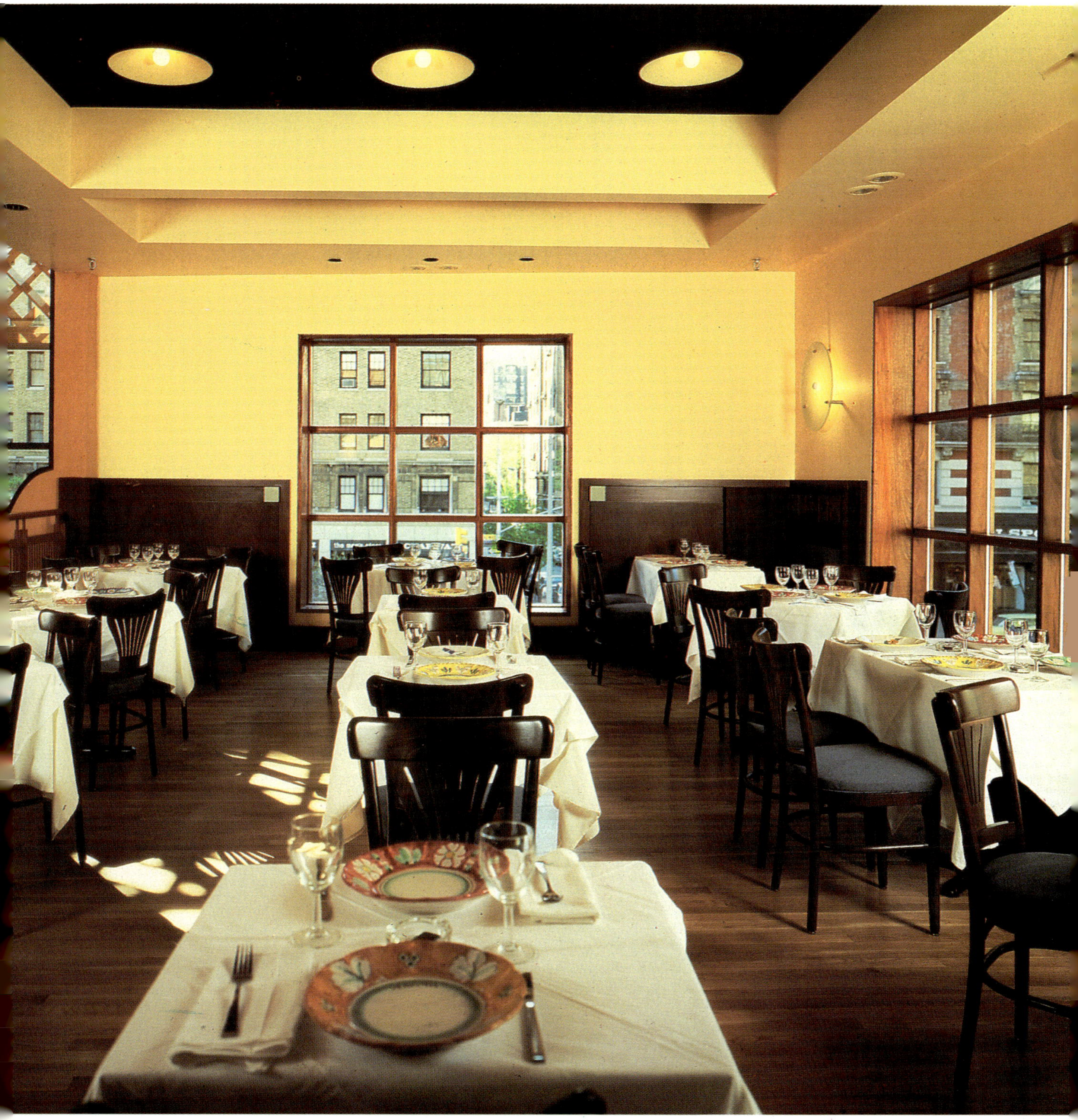

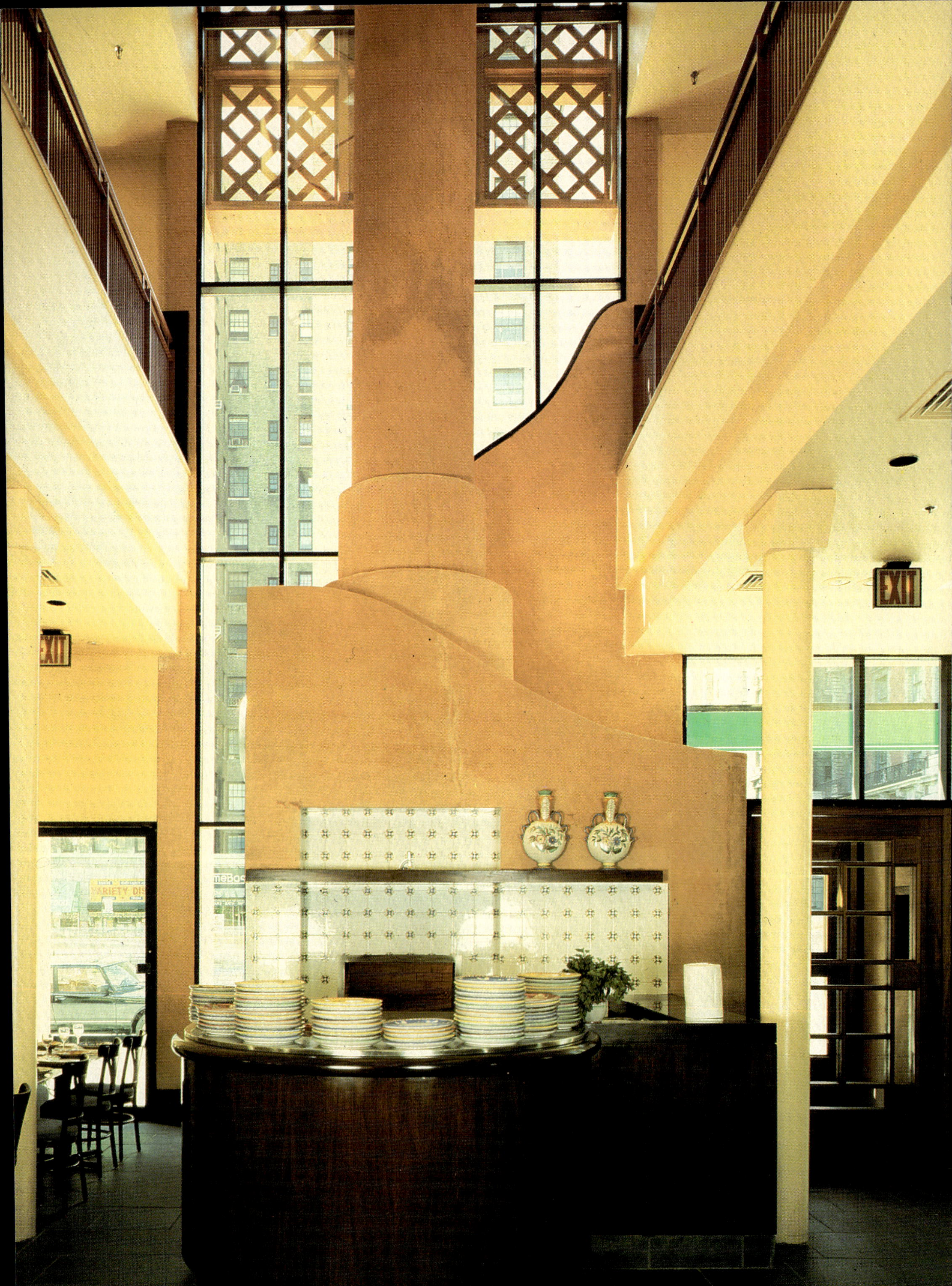
EXIT
EXIT

were to change, they would serve to unify the space." His plan revolves around a double-height central space that terminates at either end with the towering oven chimney and a central steel staircase that leads to the second-floor dining room.

Placed on axis with one another, these primary formal elements of the restaurant's interior create a vertical thrust that "drives the space upward," according to the architect. They visually connect the 1,750-square-foot ground floor café and bar to the 3,250-square-foot dining room above. "The upper floor of a two-story restaurant can really turn into Siberia, if it's not immediately seen," states Boxenbaum. "Nobody wants to sit away from the action."

To promote continuous interchange between levels, the central staircase divides into two runs above the landing, creating a ceremonial procession opportunity, with views directed down to the ground floor. The upper dining level is visible through its steel railing and the closely spaced balustrades that enclose the opening between floors.

Views throughout Ancora's interior invariably focus on the chimney and tiled pizza oven that wraps around the stucco of the exterior side. Patrons enter alongside the oven into a stucco vestibule with views of the ground floor bar, café dining, and pizza preparation area at the circular counter in front of the oven. From here the more intimate second-floor dining room is also visible.

Stylistically, Ancora combines the cool formality of the slate floors and counters, mahogany woodwork, frosted glass partitions, and precisely grid-patterned surfaces with the informality of stucco curves, warm paint colors, and brightly decorated tiles and dinner plates. Infusing the design are elements that recall the work of Charles Rennie Mackintosh—especially in the upward thrust of the central core and the square-paned windows, the latticework and the wooden banisters and railings that gracefully rise and surround the upper dining area. Boxenbaum notes, too, that the banquettes are decorative devices inspired by Frank Lloyd Wright.

"I juggled different materials to create a tension between them, to break down the scale within the space, and to give a sense of texture," says Boxenbaum. Filtering through the space is a plentitude of natural light during the day and, in the evening, an inventively arranged lighting system that comprises wall sconces, shaded incandescent bulbs over the second story, and downlights over the bar and café.

Just as the architectural elements of stair and chimney define a vertical emphasis within the restaurant, light is used to layer spaces horizontally. Both devices achieve a functional and visual integration between dining levels, promoting an exchange of excitement that, in the words of the architect, "makes you feel like you're dining in both places at once."

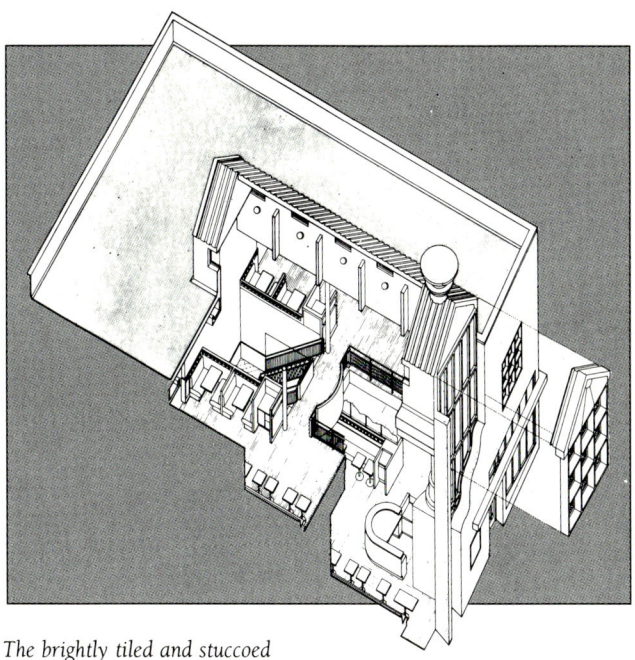

The brightly tiled and stuccoed oven and chimney (opposite) ascend through the central atrium to draw the eye upward and help unify the separate dining levels. Corresponding to this at the opposite end of the room is the staircase (top) linking the separate spaces as well. This interconnection of levels is crucial to the design and functioning of the space. The axonometric drawing (above) shows the relationship of the upper level to the floor it overlooks.

ANIMATE WITH LIGHT AND COLOR
A RESTAURANT COMES ALIVE AFTER DARK

WHEN ROCK STARS Nick Ashford and Val Simpson—together with co-owners Bobby and Caroline Ochs—decided to open a restaurant, they wanted the atmosphere to be theatrical. They wanted to put people on stage; they wanted elegance and funk. Haverson/Rockwell Architects of New York complied, bringing in the look of city lights and stage sets and raising the curtain on a dazzling "theater" where people and their movements are integral to the design.

"The clients were very specific about their wishes," says architect David Rockwell, reflecting on the genesis of Twenty/Twenty restaurant in New York's trendy Flatiron District. With his partner Jay Haverson, Rockwell took what could have become a cavernous barn and broke it up into a graceful series of levels that modulate the space in an inventive and pleasing manner.

Pedestrians who used to peer through the glass at an automobile showroom now see white tablecloths, candlelit tables, and black-and-tan wicker chairs. Through the tall glass doors and glass vestibule, patrons enter as if on center stage.

Several steps below—like the orchestra pit of a theater—is the main restaurant area, a substantial 100 feet across and 92 feet front-to-back. Ascending from entry level is a 2,500-square-foot mezzanine that provides see-and-be-seen "box seats" overlooking all the fun. From their favorite round table in the front row mezzanine, within touching distance of a massive copper-painted Corinthian capital, Twenty/Twenty's owners can look out over the entire "stage" and most of the rest of the "theater" as well. In all, the multilevel dining room can seat 240.

"In the daytime, most of the space is front-lit," explains Rockwell. Light streams through floor-to-ceiling windows on the street.

"We selected colors that would appear light and cheery in the daytime. The restaurant's colors are most vivid when the setting of the lights is at its brightest, reflecting off the walls. In the evening, the mood changes. The light becomes more transparent, the colors more muted. The restaurant takes on the glow of the New York skyline," explains Rockwell.

"Defining the walls of the room are vignettes created for atmosphere and visual interest," notes Haverson. Windows, gates, and fire escapes have been constructed in a minimalist style and artfully arranged like simple stage sets in shallow wall recesses. "They give a recognizable element, something to relate to." Here, too, lighting plays an important part.

"We didn't want track lighting," says Rockwell. "We wanted the illumination to be understated. There is no apparent light source here; the light just glows. To achieve this we concealed the main lighting system in the newly built coffered ceiling," Haverson explains. Line-voltage fixtures with pale pink gels are used for general dining illumination, while low-voltage fixtures (with clear bulbs or pale blue gels) are used for architectural accents. In addition, the architects specified special decorative lighting effects: White neon is used as a concealed source to continuously outline and float the five dining tiers; red and orange neon is used as a color wash on the wall vignettes.

The entire complex lighting system—a signature element of Haverson/Rockwell projects—is controlled by four scene-dimming panels broken into twelve channels, allowing for adjustments throughout the day and night and for variations in illumination throughout the different dining areas. Since there are twelve types of light bulbs in the system, the architects couldn't leave bulb-changing to just anyone; a maintenance check is made every two weeks.

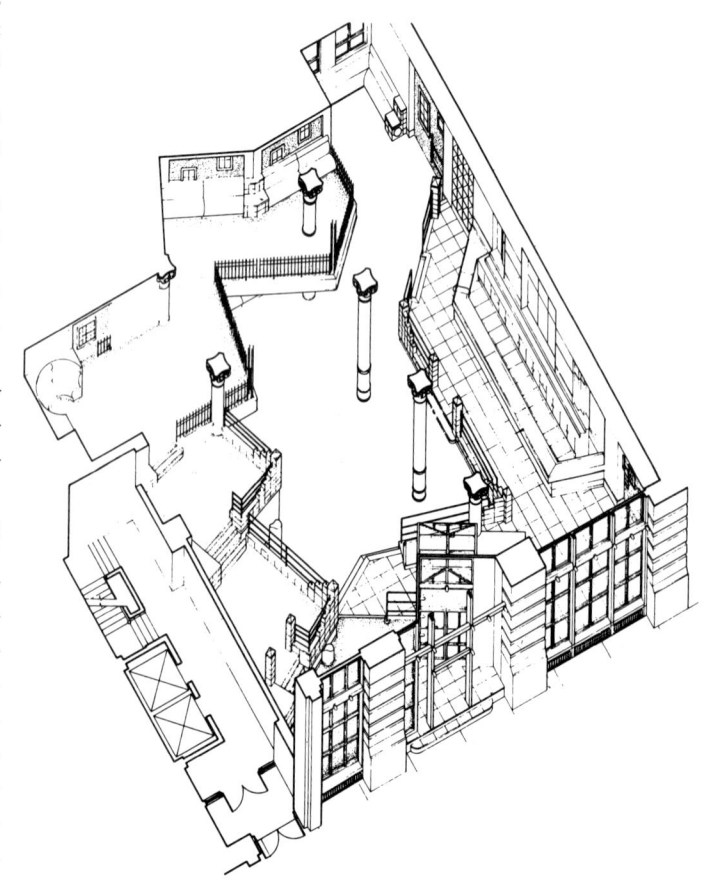

TWENTY/TWENTY	*New York City*
Owners:	*Nick Ashford, Val Simpson, Bobby Ochs, Caroline Ochs*
Architect:	*Haverson/Rockwell Architects, P. C.* *(David S. Rockwell, Jay M. Raverson, project designers;* *Christopher Smith, Hans Paehler, Mike Marshand, design assistants)*
Contractor:	*G. P. Winter Associates*
Kitchen Consultant:	*Jack Freeman*
Lighting:	*Haverson/Rockwell Architects, P. C.*
Graphics:	*Haverson/Rockwell Architects, P. C.*
Project Director:	*Carolyn Weinberg-Haverson*
Budget:	*$2 million*
Seating:	*240*
Time:	*8 months*
Photography:	*© Timothy Hurlsly*

Patrons enter the theatrical atmosphere of Twenty/Twenty through a dazzle of light and glass. Architects Haverson/Rockwell designed everything, from the complex lighting system to the menus. The multilevel dining area (above) seats 240 and provides a variety of views. The architects, not wanting the distraction of track lighting, heating, and air conditioning ducts, have inserted lights in the ceiling and other mechanical elements in walls, ceiling, and floors. An axonometric floorplan is shown opposite.

STRIVE FOR WARMTH AND INTIMACY
WOOD FLOORS, SOFT LIGHT, AND PAINTINGS LEND A HOMEY QUALITY

IN AN ERA when large spaces and loud noise are the norm, young restaurateur Daniel Meyer told his architect, Larry Bogdanow, that he wanted to create an atmosphere that would encourage conversation. Meyer wanted something warmer than usual, something comfortable, something intimate.

Though it bucks the popular *grand cafe* trend, Union Square Cafe is nevertheless fashionable; it serves simple grilled dishes and salads and offers a bar area for dining as well as drinking. Clean, perky, cream-colored walls suffused with a blush of light—the contribution of lighting consultant Celeste Gainey—rise above olive-painted wainscoting. Cherrywood floors give the dining rooms a homey warmth, while earth-toned tiles add texture and interest to the bar. Corbeled mahogany moldings make the high ceiling in the bar area seem lower and more intimate. Toward the rear, a skylight—uncovered during renovation—allows natural light to flood the space, illuminating Judy Rifka's wall painting of *zaftig* female nudes and fruit.

The 4,000-square-foot restaurant joins a host of others that have sprung up near Union Square in a rapidly gentrifying neighborhood that was a longtime center for labor union activity and is home to trendy design, publishing, and photo firms that are migrating from high-rent midtown locations. The Union Square Cafe occupies parts of two buildings: The bar area was once Brownie's, a fifty-year-old health food restaurant and local landmark, while the dining room is sited in the building next door, former home to Brownie's health food store. "We built a connection between the buildings by changing elevation," Bogdanow notes.

The stepped-down main dining area, entered from the bar, seats 65; it is softly illuminated by a bank of windows facing the street. This is a cozy space with a low, white-painted ceiling. Its main decorative feature is a collection of paintings ranging from neoimpressionist to naive (most are still life pictures of food) that adds to the relaxed, almost gentle, residential quality of the space.

The bar itself is divided into three areas: a vestibulelike cocktail/waiting area furnished with comfortable rattan chairs, an oyster bar, and an area offering full-service dining, where people can feel comfortable "dining alone or popping

Ceilings 20 feet high in the Garden Dining Room allow space for a 14-seat balcony and for the mural-like paintings by Judy Rifka. The paintings by Rifka that appear to float on the walls, as well as work by other artists, add to the warmth and sophistication that the owner desired.

UNION SQUARE CAFE	*New York City*
Owner:	*Daniel Meyer*
Architecture:	*I. Bogdanow & Associates, New York City (Larry Bogdanow, Warren Ashworth)*
Lighting Consultant:	*Celeste Gainey*
General Contractor:	*David Elliott Construction*
HVAC:	*Kayback*
Graphic Artist:	*Andrea DaRiff*
Budget:	*approximately $400,000*
Size: *4,000 square feet*	**Seating**: *124*
Art:	*Judy Rifka, Susan Walp, Jim Gingerich*
Photography:	© *Daniel Eifert*

47

The transition from the bar area where patrons can stop by for an informal bite is made by a short staircase that descends into the more intimate main dining area, where low ceilings and warm cherrywood floors lend a homey warmth. The floorplan below shows the variety of eating areas that have been created at Union Square Cafe: entrance (1); bar (2); main dining (3); garden dining (4); balcony (5); kitchen (6).

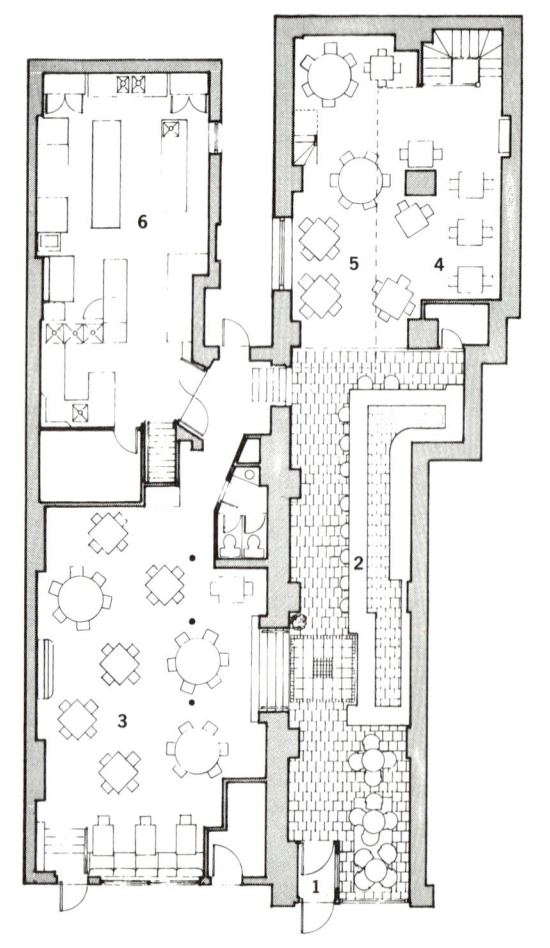

in for a light supper," as Bogdanow puts it. The bar's ceiling height changes correspondingly, rising toward the back of the restaurant, while the bar itself widens and draws the diner in. Both Meyer and Bogdanow are particularly proud of the flat-topped, railless mahogany bar itself, which they describe as "less something to hang onto than something to relax near."

To the rear of the restaurant, beyond the bar, is the Garden Dining Room, a 45-seat area named for the small tree-and-flower-planted outdoor corridor that can be glimpsed beyond the windows there. The dramatic 20-foot ceilings in this part of the restaurant allow for a 14-seat balcony that overlooks the main dining space.

"Dividing the restaurant into various zones—the two dining rooms, the bar areas, and the balcony—allows for quiet intimacy," says Bogdanow. "But those who want to people-watch can get a sense of activity if they sit at certain tables near the bar."

BRING IN A CITY GARDEN
LOW DIVIDING WALLS, A GARDEN HOUSE, AND FLOWERS COMBINE WITH HARD SURFACES AND SOFT FABRICS

The parachute-like light diffusers shown above the bar and dining tables add romance and fantasy to a design that uses hard lines in the moldings and hard surfaces in cast-cement panels and dividers. The same fabric is repeated in floor-to-ceiling drapes. The hard/soft combination has an elegant effect.

HOURGLASS-SHAPED URNS, cement railings topped with cast-stone balls and pyramids, green stenciled floors, a garden house, and floral upholstery are some of the elements used by the architects at Paul Segal Associates for New York's Gotham Bar and Grill.

By selecting an urban garden theme, the architects were able to capture owner Jerome Kretchmer's dictum—"restaurants are the theaters of the eighties"—and to gracefully manipulate the old factory space in Manhattan's East Village into areas both spacious and intimate—ingredients they felt appropriate to contemporary dining.

The 3,700-square-foot space is divided by massive cement railings, creating fluid segments highlighted by cast-stone balls and pyramids. Green squares are stenciled on the floor and urns are filled with fresh flowers.

Most gardenlike and suggestive of going inside to go "outside" is the entrance: a large *l'orangerie*, or garden house. Tall and colorful, this structure features panes of glass trimmed with a geometric latticework of slate-blue–colored wood set into a solid cement frame that is painted brick red with white flecks. This structure ascends three-quarters of the way up into the room and is surmounted with green molding and a pyramid-shaped cap. The total effect establishes scale and a clear point of reference for the other decorative elements in the room.

All the shifts in railing height, molding levels, materials, and color emphasize a strong sense of horizontal layering. As Segal says, this system permits a greater sense of "vertical versatility," enabling the designers to offer both space and intimacy with apparently accidental nooks and crannies.

But to underscore the theatrical aspect of the space, the architects have elevated the bar and have set the central dining area at a slight angle, slanted off the main axis and moving up the center of the space. This slanting, according to project architect James Biber, breaks up the space in an unexpected way and helps to create more intimate sections at both ends while also allowing for interesting views across and down the room.

The rear portion of the restaurant features an elegantly curved wall created alternately of smooth pink sections, segments of cement, and panels of floor-to-ceiling cream-colored

GOTHAM BAR AND GRILL *New York City*

Owners: *Jerome Kretchmer, Jeff Bliss, Richard Rathe, Robert Rathe*

Architecture: *Paul Segal Associates (Paul Segal, James Biber, John Henle, Martin Dermady)*

Lighting Consultants: *Marantz Design (Jules Fisher-Paul); Jerry Kugler Associates*

Graphic Design: *Donovan and Green*

Foodservice Consultant: *Barbara Kafka Associates*

Budget: *$750,000*

Seating: *175*   **Size:** *3,700 square feet*

Photography: *© Norman McGrath*

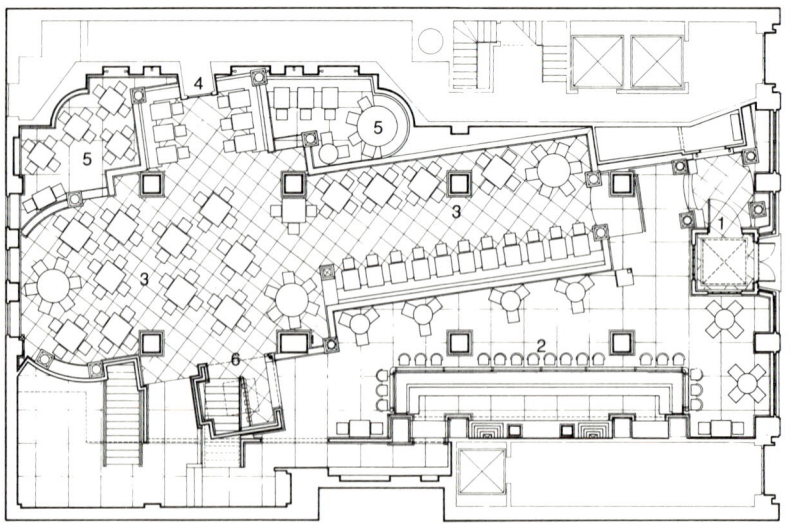

The entrance to the Gotham Bar and Grill (opposite) takes the form of a garden greenhouse and sets the style for the rest of the space. The bar, to the left of the entrance (and shown above) is slightly raised and is formally surrounded by a solid ashwood rail that appears detached. The horizontal shifts of color and texture are particularly evident here. The floorplan shows how the architects have set the design at an angle to the main axis of the room: entrance (1); raised bar (2); dining (3); rear exit (4); raised dining area (5); stairway to bathrooms and kitchen (6) (see picture, bottom).

diaphanous drapes. The effect is formal.

The romantic, diaphanous feeling of the drapery is repeated in the lighting of the restaurant, which is soft and intimate. Parachute-like fabric covers the overhead lights and acts as a diffuser. The gentle, billowing fabric also provides a pleasant contrast to the hard lines and surfaces. In fact, notes Segal, the lighting is meant to be "romantic and evocative and to contribute a softer look to the space."

The choice of such contrasting materials adds interest and permits the elements to retain their own individual values. The interplay of these materials within the urban gardenlike design offers unexpected nuances of light, changes in perspective, and creates a definite shift in mood from the harsh bustle of the city outside.

SCULPT A SPACE WITH STUCCO AND STEEL
ROUGH MATERIALS YIELD SENSUOUS EFFECTS IN A CELEBRITY RESTAURANT

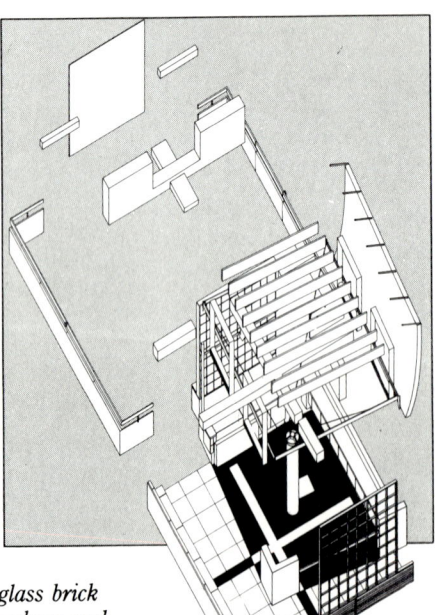

The 10-foot-square glass brick room divider shown above and in the axonometric scheme echoes an artwork created from mirrors hanging at one end of the restaurant, and a window at the other.

LOCATED IN VENICE, California, on a street just half a block from the crowded ocean boardwalk is 72 Market—a restaurant that seems an entire world apart with its surreal juxtaposition of a stark interior and a sidewalk arcade that survives from a failed early-1900s attempt to replicate the ambience of Venice, Italy. Here, the architects have used rough materials to achieve sensuous results, while also creating sculptural complexity out of a straightforward, unadorned structure.

72 Market is located across the street from the residence of its owner, actor-producer Tony Bill. Both client and architects appreciated the street's gritty urban character, as well as the associations of the address—a skylit structure that once served as studio space for designer Frank Gehry and artist Robert Irwin and as an adventurous art gallery. The architects and Bill decided to preserve the rawness and simplicity and to create a bar/restaurant that would be attractive to people who could afford the best but who would respond to the atmosphere of a casual hangout.

The existing building had to be reinforced to meet stringent Los Angeles codes. Usually, old structures are buttressed or extensively rebuilt to protect them from earthquake damage. Morphosis, the architects for this project, tied the exterior walls to an interior tension ring that was braced by tie rods to an asymmetrically placed column. The ring is wrapped in a suspended box of unpainted stucco, which creates an illusion of greater space and a dramatic interplay of solid and void. And the column, covered with etched figures by sculptor Robert Graham, echoes the cast iron columns of the street arcade.

The front dining area, adjoining the bar, can be opened to the street by folding back shutters. The sidewalk, unfortunately, is too narrow to accommodate tables. This space and the larger dining room beyond a glass brick divider are flooded with natural light from above. The austere unpainted stucco walls, slate and stone floor, and exposed steel are complemented by wood paneling and rattan chairs.

As befits a former artist's studio, the art is large-scale and distinguished. On the rear wall is a mirrored construction by DeWain Valentien, commissioned for a 10-foot-square space that balances the room divider and the front window. It is as though an invisible box were limned through the restaurant, counterpointing the box suspended over the bar area. Paintings by Richard Schaeffer and Sandra Rubin are also on display at 72 Market.

72 MARKET	*Venice, California*

Owner: *Tony Bill*
Architecture: *Morphosis (Thom Mayne, Michael Rotondi, principals; Kiyokazu Arai, project architect)*
Lighting/Electrical Consultant: *Saul Goldin*
Structural Consultant: *Gordon Polon*
Mechanical Consultant: *Jerry Sullivan*
Kitchen Consultant: *Tony Singus & Associates*
Photography: *© Tim Street-Porter*

Inside 72 Market, walls are tied to an interior tension ring braced by the tie rods to an interior column, thus meeting stringent Los Angeles earthquake codes. Blonde wood paneling, rattan chairs, and sun from the skylight complement an otherwise austere aesthetic vocabulary.

TEMPER A BRASSERIE WITH JAPANESE REFINEMENT
A BAMBOO GROVE BRINGS SERENITY TO A LARGE OPEN SPACE

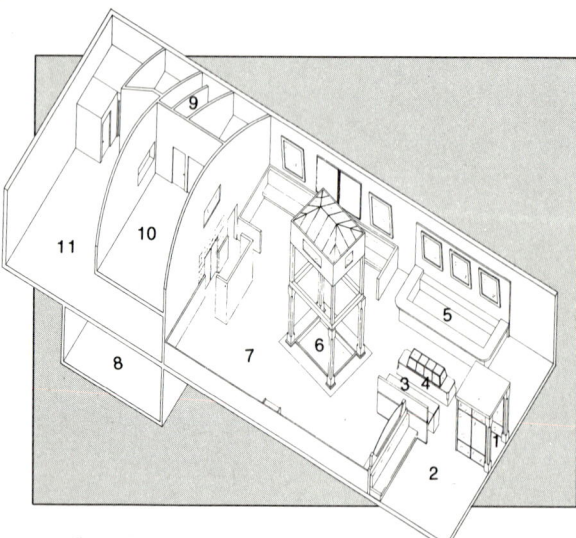

The Chaya Brasserie in West Hollywood combines the casual friendliness and openness of the European brasserie with a Japanese sensibility in menu and decor. The owners—founders of La Petite Chaya in Los Angeles—are related to a Japanese family who have operated restaurants for more than three hundred years. They sought out architects who shared their affection for the legendary La Coupole in Paris in order to duplicate its noisy barnlike atmosphere that attracts all kinds of people, day and night.

The architects, Elyse Grinstein and Jeff Daniels, took a 4,000-square-foot warehouse, originally a 1940s auto showroom, and cleverly exploited various levels of the existing structure to yield a 600-square-foot wine cellar and a 400-square-foot upstairs dining room that seats 20. On the main (ground) level, they divided the space between a dining room seating 130 and a compact 900-square-foot kitchen. The original bow-string trusses supporting the wooden ceiling were sandblasted, and skylights were added to illuminate both dining space and kitchen. For the walls, the architects selected the same faded pink used for the exterior, adding a wainscot of dark-stained wood and big, wood-framed mirrors tilted down to reflect the room's bustle. For flooring, Grinstein and Daniels specified integrally colored black concrete.

These utilitarian materials serve as context for the focal point of the room—a pine-framed, skylit atrium containing a grove of bamboo trees. Visually, it is a reference to Japan as well as to Southern California, as are the Mariano Fortuny–inspired inverted parasol lampshades and the wall paintings by Kenidi Ajoika. For the upstairs dining room, which overlooks the main space, the architects specified prints by contemporary artist Jasper Johns.

Japanese refinement of detail is evident in pine columns that frame the atrium. The columns are chamfered to suggest a temple rather than a rustic enclosure. Likewise, the cast-concrete bar—transformed to elegance by its highly polished surface and smooth, rounded edge—feels Japanese. Paneling the facade and discreetly accenting the restaurant's interior are touches of raw steel, blued like the barrel of a gun.

The restaurant's kitchen, tightly and inventively arranged, was designed by George Tanaka, who worked closely with chef Hidemasa Yamamoto. Tanaka's kitchen combines Japanese economy of space with an awareness of requirements for Western cuisine. It efficiently houses sixteen workstations and a pick-up area for servers.

Seating at Chaya Brasserie is arranged around an atriumlike structure, planted with bamboo (opposite).. The bar (top) is fabricated of integrally colored black concrete. Axonometric plan: entry (1); lounge (2); cashier (3); fish display (4); bar (5); bamboo atrium (6); main dining area (7); basement/wine cellar (8); stairs (9); private dining (10); kitchen (11).

CHAYA BRASSERIE	West Hollywood, California
Owners:	Yuji Tsunoda, Riku Suzuki
Interior Architecture:	Grinstein/Daniels, Inc. (Elyse Grinstein, Jeffrey Daniels)
Kitchen Consultant:	Abrams & Tanaka Associates (George Tanaka)
Contractor:	Kajima International
Total Budget:	$800,000
Photography:	© Tim Street-Porter

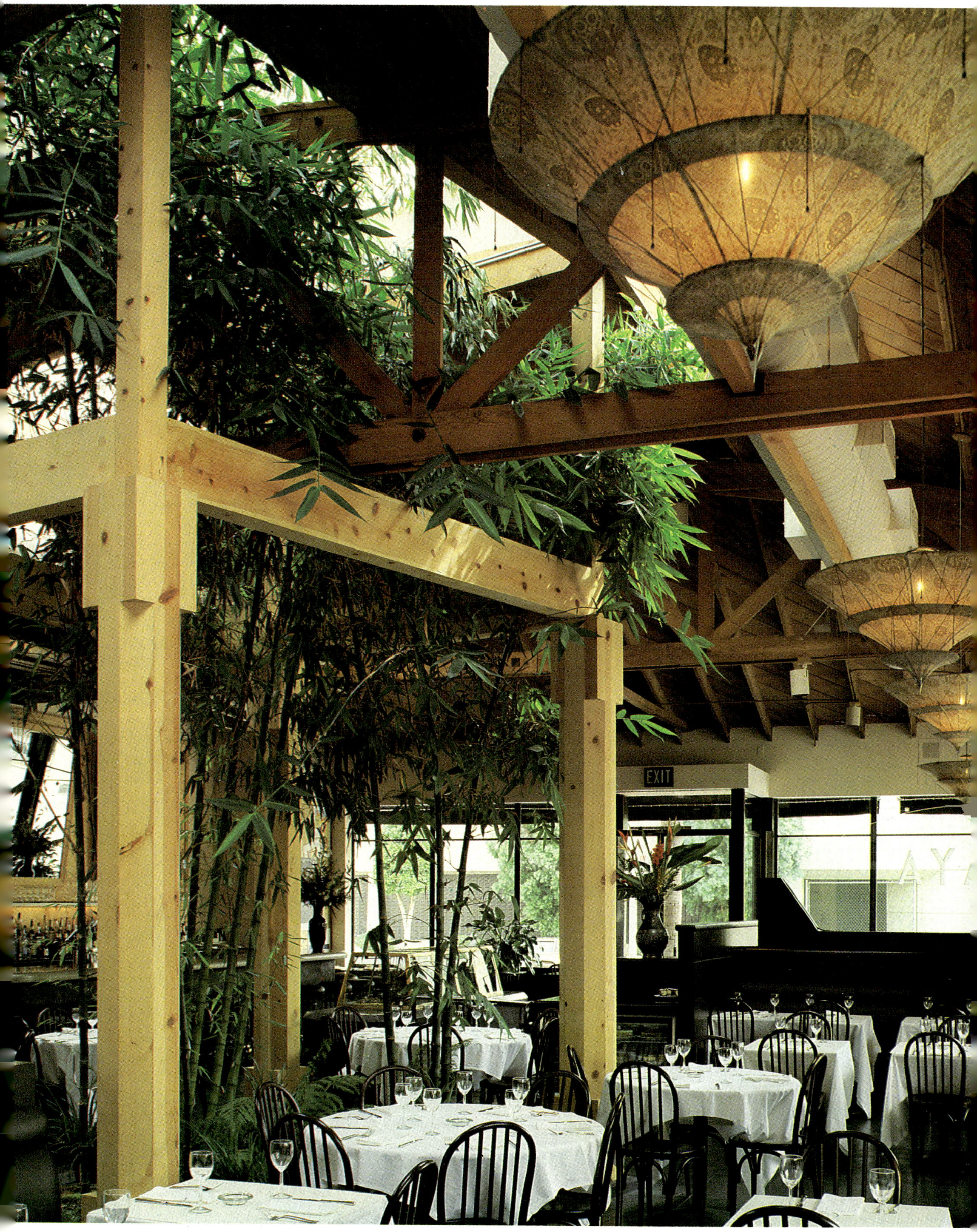
EXIT

TRANSFORM A NEIGHBORHOOD RESTAURANT IN SIX WEEKS
A PROMENADE OF COLUMNS ORDERS THE DESIGN

Four rather whimsically classical columns (above and opposite) define a promenade through the center of Winnetka Grill and also contribute to its postmodern design vocabulary. The painted floor's diamond motif is an elaboration on the design of the column bases.

DESPITE A SIX-WEEK time frame and a modest budget, designer John Cannon of Canon/Davis Interiors in Chicago was able to create an elegant, postmodern-style interior by meticulously tending to detail. He used familiar forms, textures, and materials and rendered them into an abstract classical fantasy.

The mainstay of the design centers on three elements that serve to divide the room—columns, floor treatment, and fabric panels. Four columns spatially define a promenade through the restaurant, setting the pace of the well-ordered design. At the center of this encolumned space is a painted floor medallion that mimics the inlaid *pietra dura* of Renaissance Italy. Its design—an elaboration of the diamond motif found at the column bases—and its *trompe l'oeil* execution, however, have been updated. Adding to the elegance and the intimacy of the space are the graceful fabric panels that descend from the ceiling to the top of each banquette.

Located in a two-story building in the affluent Chicago suburb of Winnetka, the Grill's predecessor was a Greek restaurant of no particular distinction, replete with marbelized laminate, copper hoods, and yellow plastic light fixtures. Only the kitchen was recycled, with a mesquite grill added. After demolition of the remaining space, the designer was left with a 25- by 50-foot area (including service corridor).

Cannon envisioned a gardenlike setting with two separate dining areas. Needing a strong visual element to bisect the space, he designed a dropped ceiling canopy which stretches from the main entrance to the back wall. This canopy hides the ventilating system, audio speakers, and recessed light fixtures. The imaginative columns appear as supports and further carry out the delineation of the space.

A bleached wood floor reiterates the idea of the entry promenade and effectively divides the carpeted dining areas. In the image of a gazebo, the four columns flank a pair of garden benches finished in teak.

Although the original interior was an eyesore, the exterior of the two-story building was inspired. The Grill's entire pastel color scheme is derived from the building's faded brick facade, patined copper guttering, and the blue slate mansard roof.

Cannon's unique wall treatment wraps the entire room in a cloud-filled sky that enhances the subtle garden motif and suggests an Olympian feast taking place high above the realm of mere mortals. Muralist Elise Kapnick painted the bright

WINNETKA GRILL	*Winnetka, Illinois*
Owners:	*John Stoltzman, Henry Markwood*
Designer:	*Cannon/Davis Interiors (John Cannon)*
Time:	*6 weeks*
Graphics:	*Gary Salle*
Photography:	*© David Clifton*

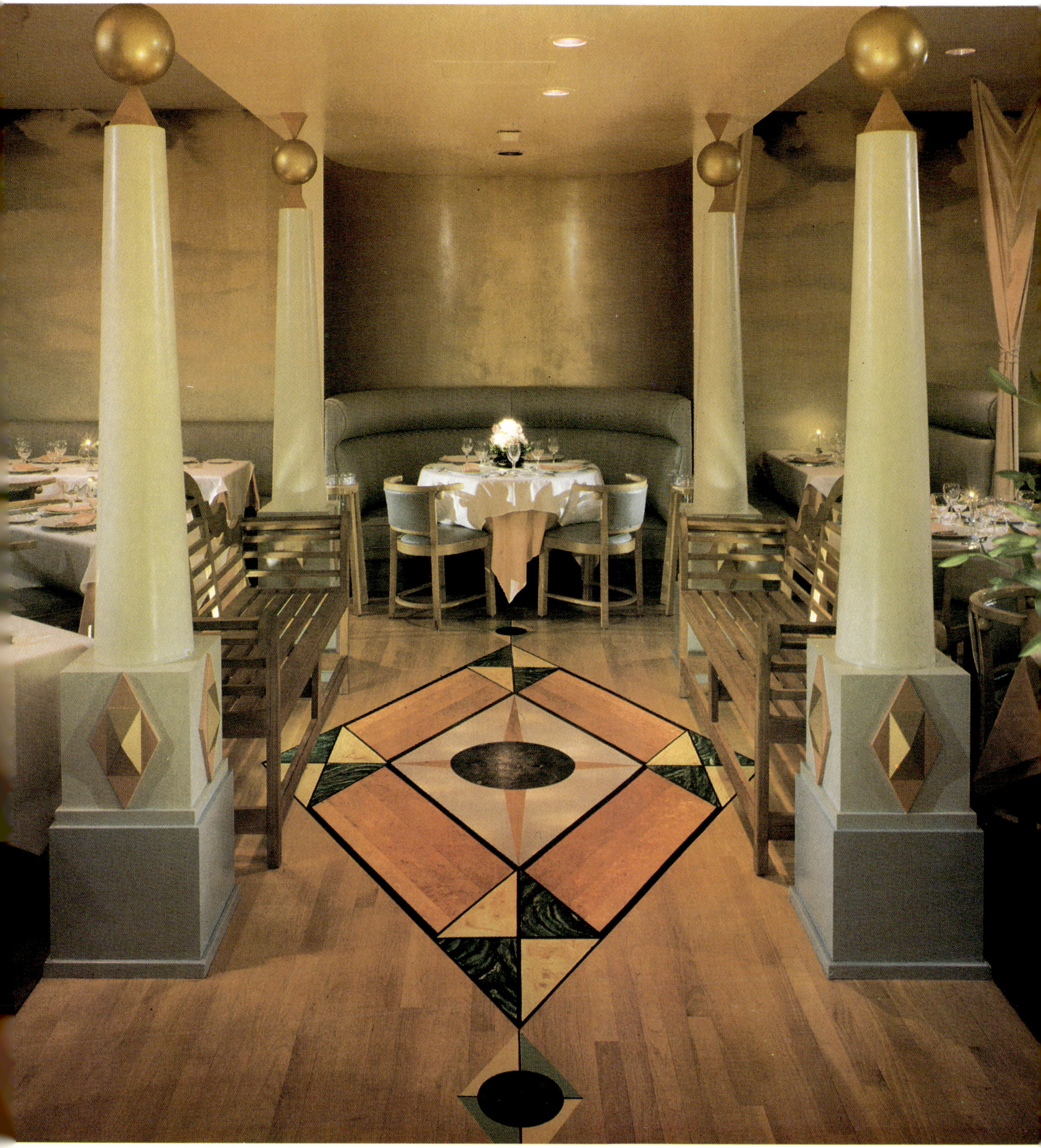

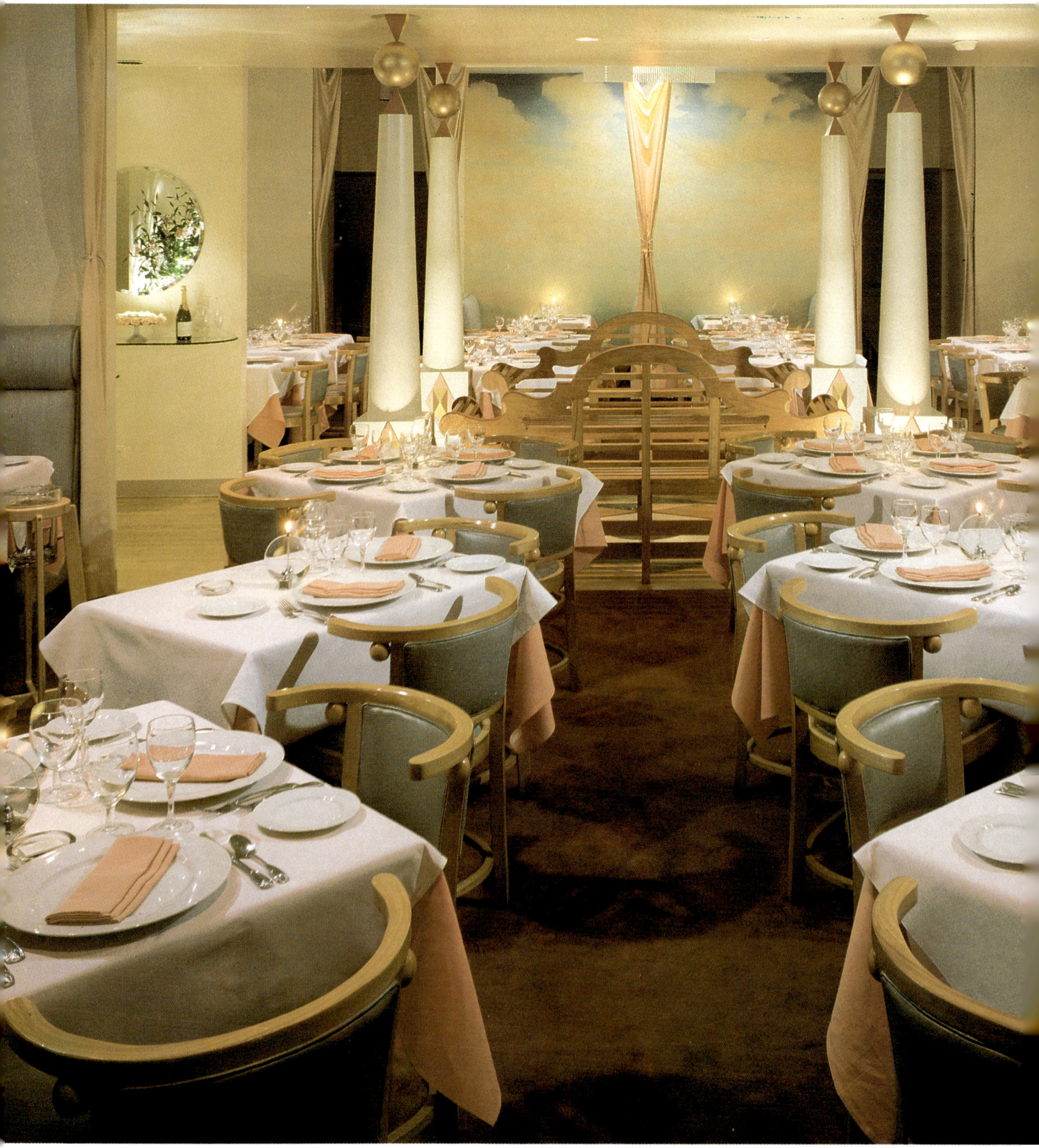

Located in a two-story building, the Winnetka Grill (above and opposite) is successor to a neighborhood Greek restaurant. A complete interior demolition preceded installation of the fanciful postmodern-style scheme. A canopy above the four columns, dividing two dining areas, cleverly encloses the ventilation system, audio speakers, and recessed light fixtures.

blue sky on the uppermost portion of the walls. It gradually diminishes to a range of sunset mauves and pinks at the bottom.

Cannon's lighting system reinforces the mood. Sculptor Joyce Culkin created companion light fixtures of stamped, bent, and welded metal, electroplated ivory on the outside and aqua on the inside. These emit a romantic light that combines with the illumination from other low-voltage fixtures—ceiling-mounted pink gel floodlights and spots that highlight the floral arrangements. Candlelight remains a major source of illumination at the evening dinner hour.

Another detail that has been thoughtfully tended to is the design of the winestands. A collaborative effort by Cannon and owner John Stoltzman, each beechwood stand subtly repeats the angle of the columns while remaining sympathetic to the Josef Hoffmann–style chairs.

In this restaurant, ornamentation is integral to the design itself.

BE ORIENTAL WITHOUT CLICHES
A MINIMALIST APPROACH UTILIZES VIEWS AND THE COLOR RED

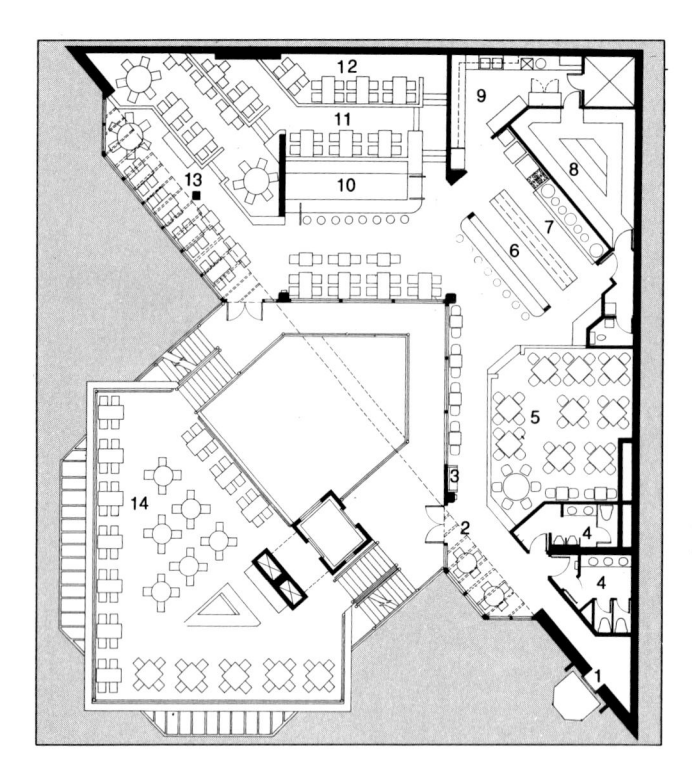

Walls of concrete and glass complement a linear interior scheme at Red's (opposite). Trapezoidal spaces are a logical answer to the unusual angles of the building shell shown in the floorplan: entry (1); entry (2); maitre d' station (3); restrooms (4); elevated dining (5); counter (6); open kitchen (7); pantry (8); workspace (9); bar (10); elevated dining (11); elevated dining (12); dining (13); roof deck (14).

CHINESE RESTAURANTS are legion in San Francisco. If Red's was to rise above the rest, Doug Wong, along with partners Walt and Frank Lembi, knew they had to present a fresh concept. They wanted something different, something spectacular. To do the job in high style, Wong commissioned interior designer Ron Nunn of Tiburon, California, who devised a spatial and visual solution that can best be described as "high-tech minimalism" and which takes great advantage of the spectacular views and the color red.

The site for the restaurant is impressive—the top floor of a relatively new concrete-and-glass building (owned by the Lembis) on the corner of California and Polk Streets overlooking the Nob Hill district. The building's top floor had never been leased, so Nunn had 7,000 square feet to work with, including 16-foot ceilings. Walls of glass and concrete provide excellent views and perfectly complement the lean, linear interior. The angles of the building's shell also inspired Nunn's floorplan, which consists of a series of trapezoidal spaces for the bar, lounge, and dining rooms.

"The space lent itself to grandstand seating," said Nunn, who created tiered platforms to rise behind the bar, located

RED'S	*San Francisco, California*
Owners:	*Doug Wong, Walter Lembi, Frank Lembi*
Interior Design:	*Ron Nunn Associates, Inc. (Ron Nunn, principal; David Berman, architect)*
Graphics:	*Warren Welter*
Seating:	*150*
Photography:	*© Russell Abraham*

immediately to the right of the main entrance. So that guests in the bar/lounge can see into the grandstand and to allow grandstand patrons to have a bird's-eye view of the bar, Nunn specified clear glass behind the bar. He wanted the place to be transparent and to have a lot of sparkle.

As guests enter the restaurant, their backs are to the view that commands attention from every seating area and enhances the sense of transparency Nunn sought. To the left of the entrance are more tables and chairs, plus a grand piano and a bar where guests can sit and watch the art of Chinese cookery performed in an open, 900-square-foot kitchen.

The path through the restaurant's angular spaces is defined by 4- by 4-inch gray ceramic tiles. The raised platforms and other flooring areas are covered in black vinyl. A mirrored ceiling sparkles above the walkway, the lounge, and the maitre d' station. For sound absorption, the remainder of the ceiling is acoustical tile.

Complementing these sleek surfaces are high-tech furnishings, including chrome-framed chairs and barstools, upholstered in red fabric, and chrome-based tables with red lacquered tops. Red means good luck in Chinese, according to Doug Wong; Red is also his father's middle name. The logotype is emblazoned in neon above the stainless steel counter by the kitchen.

Besides the neon, the only wall decorations are a few carefully selected paintings Nunn encouraged the owners to rent from the San Francisco Museum of Art's art-lending service. "These are great walls for art," Nunn said, referring to the concrete surfaces he retained and the few drywall partitions—painted beige and pink—he specified.

61

MAKE FREEWAY ARCHITECTURE THE BACKDROP
PATTERN AND COLOR INTEGRATE THE DESIGN OF A LOS ANGELES CAFE

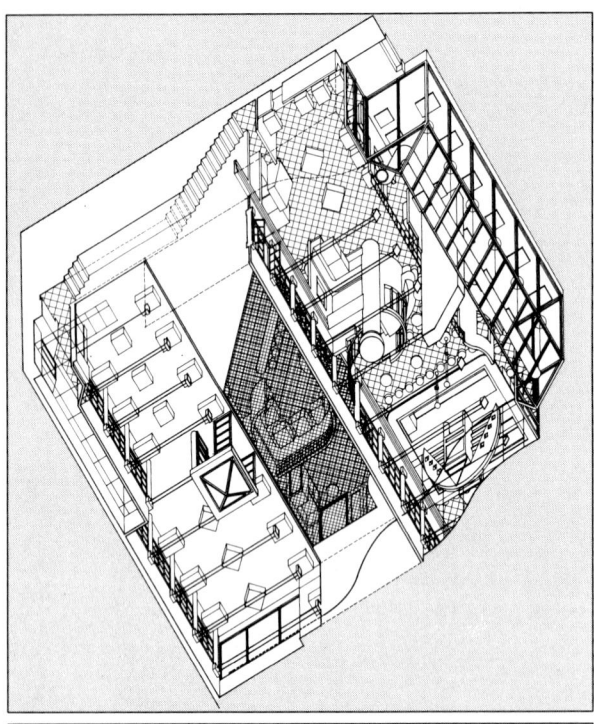

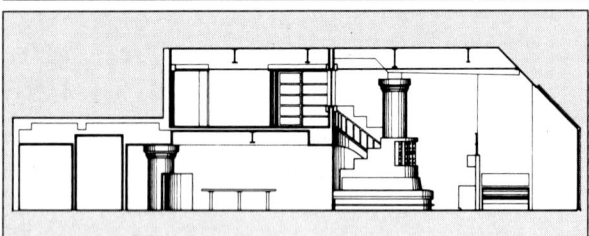

"GIVE ME A BRAND-NEW interpretation of the traditional French bistro, with a lively social atmosphere and a variety of spaces," French entrepreneur André Ramillion told his architect, Johannes Van Tilburg. For $650,000, Van Tilburg completed L'Express in Universal City. Its playful postmodern spirit is enhanced by some of the visual trickery that is the moviemaker's stock-in-trade.

L'Express, Ramillion's fourth restaurant, is located in The Centrum, a speculative six-story office block across the Hollywood Freeway from Universal Studios. The Centrum is an example of freeway architecture—an inverted wedge of mirrored glass thrust into a red brick podium—designed to be "read" at high speed. L'Express occupies 5,000 square feet on the ground and mezzanine levels, and a glass-enclosed terrace that thrusts forward over the sidewalk.

Little has been added to the basic structure, but the surfaces have been transformed by a layering of color and shape, texture and pattern. On the ground floor, three distinct areas define the restaurant: patio, lounge, and a semienclosed area for casual eating, beyond which is a cooking area open to public view.

Downstairs, L'Express seats 100, with another 100 seats on the mezzanine. Throughout, there is a sense of airiness and intimacy; tables are widely spaced and the lighting well balanced. The patio is simple and functional with cutaway or mirrored dividers creating visual lines with the spaces beyond.

The lounge serves as a crossroads, an ideal place in which to see and be seen. There is a cluster of high stools and tables and a blacked-out ceiling accented by white tie rods and undulating cold-cathode tubes. The bar is treated as pop sculpture.

At the center of the room, a structural column has been greatly enlarged, and beside it a staircase has been turned into a theatrical set piece—a vantage point from which to survey, a stage for the entertainment of those below. A skylit atrium, treated in mock ceremonial style, leads from the stairs to two interconnected dining rooms, which can be separated for small parties. Casement windows open onto the lively scene below. The pitched glass roof for the patio offers a final twist. Partly mirrored, it allows views up and down, giving diners tantalizing glimpses of each other.

With its witty use of mundane materials and its sense of rooms within rooms, each enclosure of L'Express serves to enlarge as well as contain space. Leading the potential customer into the restaurant is the neon logo on the facade, designed to be read at top speed; a strip of this neon logo extends into the space as shown along the ceiling of the bar/lounge area (opposite). Designer Van Tilburg calls this area the crossroads for the 5,000-square-foot restaurant. A supersized structural column (partially shown at far left of picture opposite), serves as a space delineator as well as a decorative element. The axonometric and section drawings (above) illustrate the plan and show how the large column anchors the stairway.

L'EXPRESS	Los Angeles, California
Owner:	Ramillion Restaurants
Architecture:	Johannes Van Tilburg & Partners (Johannes Van Tilburg, Gregory Nelson, Alan Boivin)
Electrical Engineer:	G&W Engineering
Mechanical Engineer:	Harold Kushner & Associates
Structural Engineer:	Svend Sorenson
Kitchen Consultant:	R. W. Designers
Seating:	200
Budget:	$650,000
Photography:	© Toshi Yoshimi

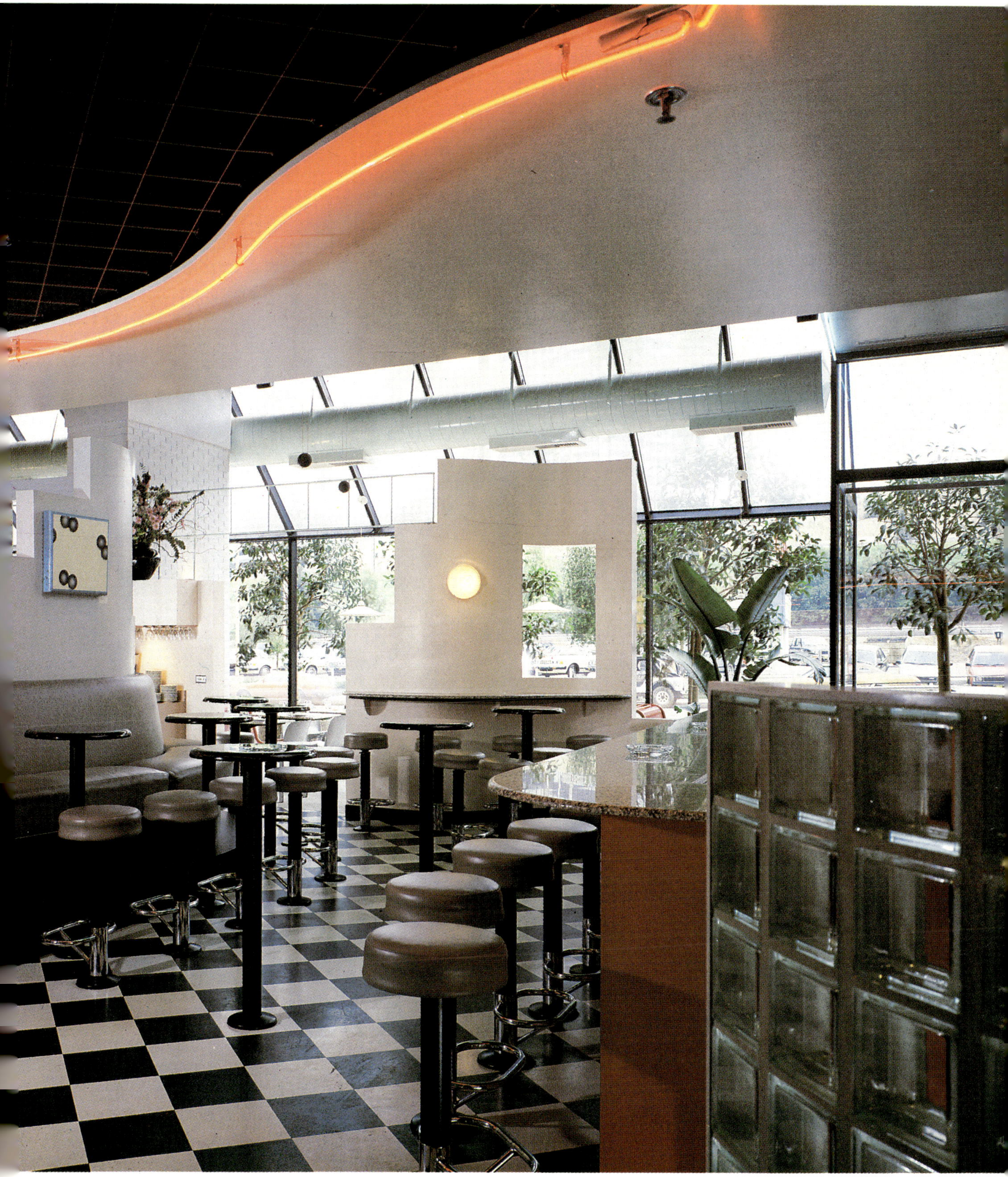

3. FAST FOOD

ESTABLISHMENTS

Many assume that fast food establishments and chain restaurants are one and the same. This is not always so. A quick-service restaurant is not necessarily part of a chain, nor does a chain restaurant necessarily serve fast food.

The fast food tradition harks back to the hot dog stand or lunch wagon, usually owned by a single proprietor. Then came the diner. Most early diners were out-of-service streetcars converted to quick-service eateries.

The menu at quick-service restaurants is the key; like the design, it is geared to encourage quick turnover. The traffic flow, comfort factor, and arrangement of seats are important in hustling customers in and out. Furnishings must be selected for easy maintenance and durability.

Burgers and fries have been the usual fare at such establishments. But a whole new fast food phenomenon developed in the 1980s that has given fast food restaurants—like the ones in this chapter—a whole new approach that affects both menu and design.

The assumption is that upwardly mobile young professionals don't want greasy fries and burgers. They want salad and pasta and fresh fruits and vegetables.

Take, for example, Mama Mia! Pasta, shown opposite. David Houle and Dorothy DeCarlo hired the Chicago-based firm of Banks/Eakin to design this upscale fast food/pasta restaurant. It is slick and lively, with an open kitchen and clean finishes that Houle says are inherent to the design. A lavish use of laminates and tile makes maintenance quick and easy. Other restaurants that illustrate the trend toward more healthful and tasteful fast food dining include Dine-O-Mat in New York City, which capitalized on the look of the old-style diner and brought its new-style offerings out on a conveyor belt; and City Spirit in Denver, which utilizes existing mechanical and architectural elements—a huge boiler, aged brick—in its whimsical, colorful design.

In the quick-service or fast food dining category, no look is too classic or too far out. As in other types of restaurants, the overriding factor is good-quality design that utilizes durable materials.

MAKE AN URBAN EATERY STAND OUT
STRONG IMAGERY DISTINGUISHES A SHOPPING CENTER RESTAURANT

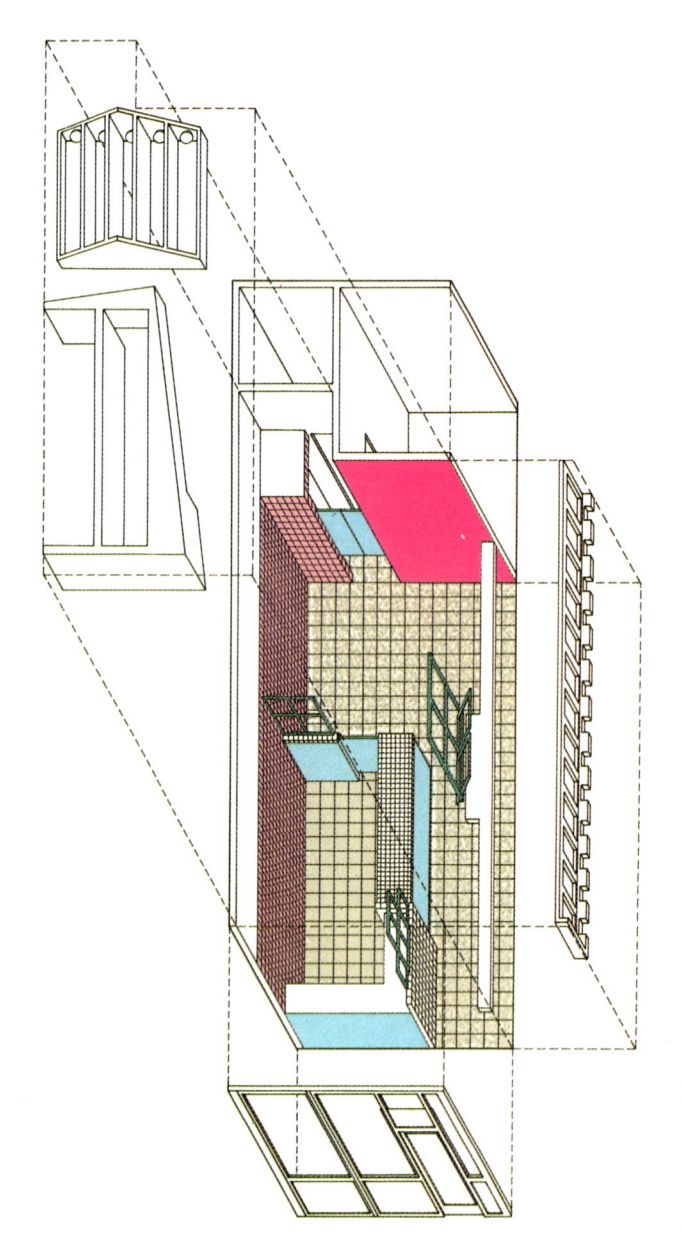

IT'S HARD FOR a modest establishment to stand out from the crowd, especially in one of those corner shopping centers that are replacing gas stations all over Los Angeles, as architects Darrell Rockefeller and Michael Hricak concede. "We intended this restaurant to catch the eye of the driver whizzing by at fifty-five miles per hour. But still, we saw a need to make a 'place' in the midst of chrome and asphalt. The name Mrs. Garcia's implies not only such a place, but the home of a person known for her cooking."

"With this scenario in mind, we designed an abstract 'house' using architectural elements to create a metaphorical landscape, within which there is a progression from the street through the house (the cooking area) to the courtyard (the seating area). To reinforce these images, we designed the lighting and the ceiling to recall the strong role of the sun in everyday Mexican life."

The interior design cleverly manipulates light, color, and angular elements to create a lively, intimate space that still sparkles after months of hard use. An angled hood over the open kitchen conceals the extraction fans and animates the confined space.

The eating area is enlarged and enlivened by a pitched vault with vertical baffles and hemispheric lights, while a strip of yellow neon runs down one side of the room behind a cutout frame.

Cool white stucco contrasts with splashes of intense color. A dramatic fuchsia-colored end wall is echoed in a dado of glazed tiles. Skeletal frames enclose the serving counter and accent the salsa bar. These are painted turquoise, a color that is picked up on the doors and, more softly, on the ceiling.

The vibrant colors and angles suggest a tropical version of De Stijl: Rietveld in Guadalajara. But the brown quarry tile floor and light oak wood furniture give Mrs. Garcia's a homey air. In short, a lot has been done with a little.

Patrons progress through the kitchen area (above) to the dining space beyond. Diners are to feel, metaphorically, that they are entering Mrs. Garcia's home. Natural light, artificial light, and bright, dramatic colors bring a tropical mood to the space and highlight the simple architectural details as well. The axonometric sketch (opposite) shows configuration and spatial progression from the entrance through the restaurant.

MRS. GARCIA'S	Los Angeles, California
Owners:	Mrs. Garcia's Ltd. (Tom Paniz, Michael Sannes, Julian Warner)
Architecture:	Rockefeller/Hricak Architects (Darrell Rockefeller, Michael Hricak)
Kitchen Consultant:	Surfas, Inc.
Electrical Engineer:	Mirahmadi & Associates, Inc.
Mechanical Engineer:	Dehbibi & Associates
Contractor:	Bob Hernandez Construction Company
Graphic Design:	Rockefeller/Hricak Architects
Photography:	© Christopher Dow

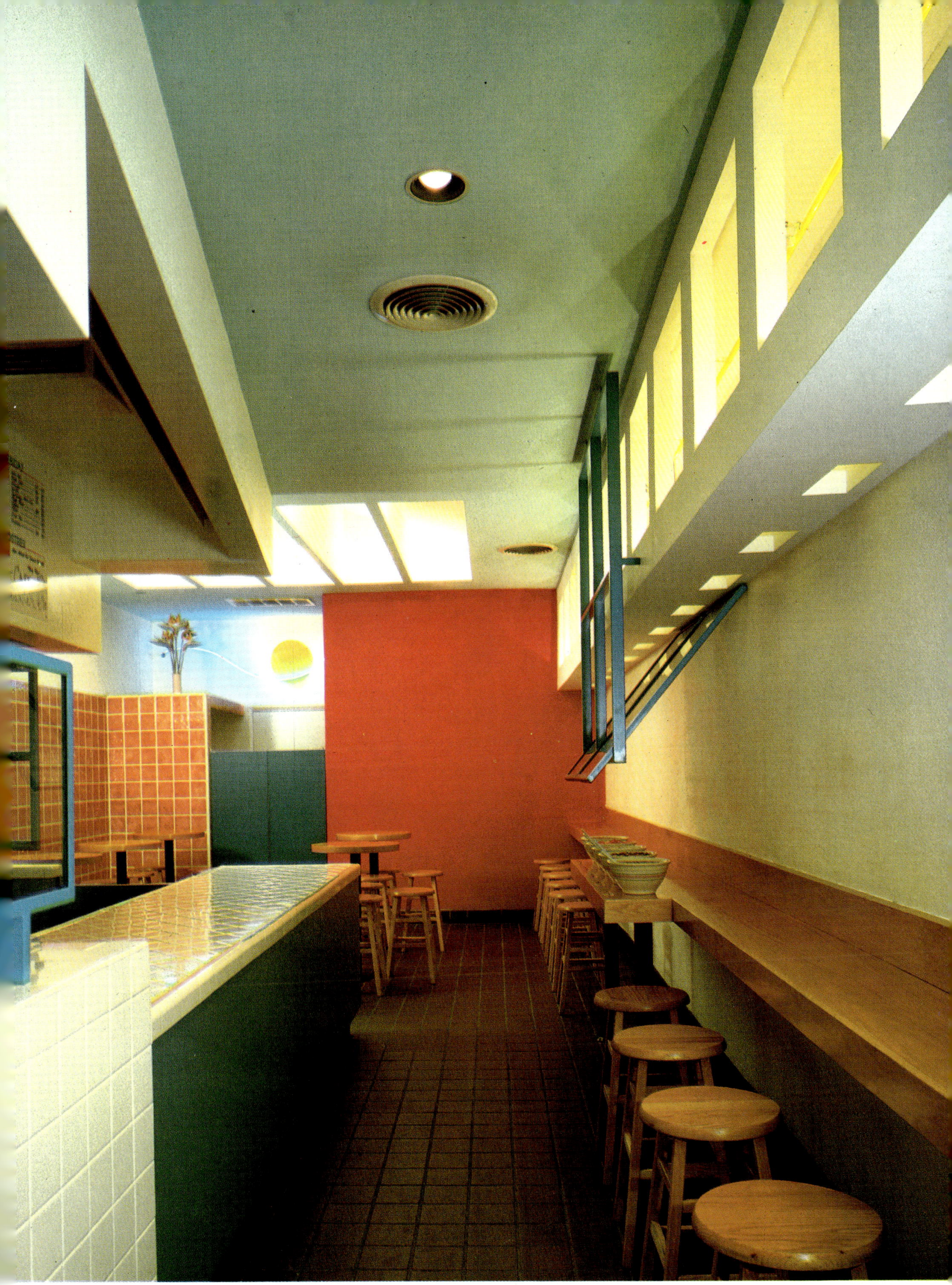

STRETCH THE BUDGET WITH COLOR AND PATTERN
A DENVER BOOKSHOP/CAFE IS ALIVE WITH BRIGHT DETAIL

Floorplan indicates spatial divisions. Within this long, narrow space the artist/interior designer has used patterns and vivid colors inventively to draw patrons into and through the space. Notable are the broken tile floors and murals across from the deli (left) and the painterly use of colors in the booths and bookcases (opposite).

THE PREREQUISITES: to have the design focus on surfaces, to use a lot of color, and especially, to create a fun place on a strict $100,000 budget. The project: a café addition to an art and design bookstore in downtown Denver.

Artist/designer Susan Wick let intuition be her guide in pulling together the dynamic and slightly madcap City Spirit Cafe. The café rides the crest of a new wave of renovation in lower downtown Denver. Because it was conceived as a neighborhood place, the café's designers paid homage to the building's past by integrating some historic architectural details without allowing them to dominate the design. For example, the large boiler between the bookstore and café levels—now painted with clouds and sky—used to provide steam for the entire city block that surrounds the building. The boiler works to unify the different levels, notes owner/developer Mickey Zeppelin.

With Wick, Zeppelin and architect Robert Poeschl worked to make the space inviting and to draw patrons further into the facility. "Color and movement are really the coordinating themes," says Wick. She used bright permanent paints and small pieces of broken ceramic tile to create images, words, and patterns throughout the restaurant. Tile used in wall murals was collected from local dumps and California beaches near abandoned ceramic factories. But for safety and durability, surplus Italian tile was used in the floor mosaics.

The original glass block and skylights at the rear of the building—a former sausage factory—were left to provide ample natural light. Part of a brick wall was also kept, together with the original tin ceilings. A new drywall includes ziggurat-shaped windows and glass shelving with mirrored backing to display books and related objects. Fixtures and kitchen equipment were recycled to help limit costs, while booths and table bases were obtained from an 1880s establishment. The health-oriented menu includes easily prepared items that do not require a grill.

CITY SPIRIT CAFE	*Denver, Colorado*
Owner/Developer:	*Mickey Zeppelin*
Architecture:	*Robert Poeschl*
Interior Design/Art:	*Susan Wick*
Project Manager:	*Benett Bolek*
General Contractor:	*John Francis*
Electrical Engineer:	*Verlin Torgeson*
Lighting Consultant:	*Creative Lighting*
Seating:	*75*
Budget:	*$100,000*
Photography:	*© David Naylor*

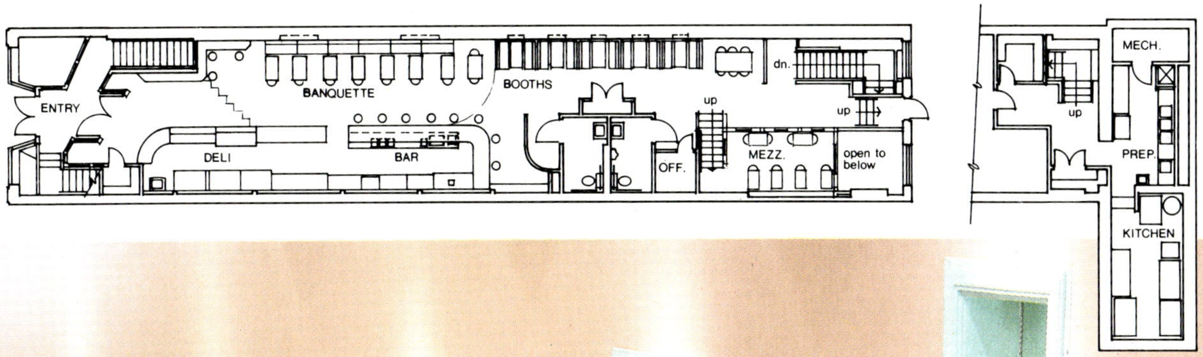
ENTRY
BANQUETTE
BOOTHS
DELI
BAR
dn.
up
up
OFF.
MEZZ.
open to
below
MECH.
up
PREP.
KITCHEN

I GOTTA GO
URBAN
DESIGN
PROCESS

FIND A LOOK FOR A POTATO-SKIN THEME
QUIRKY MENU ANIMATES GRAPHICS

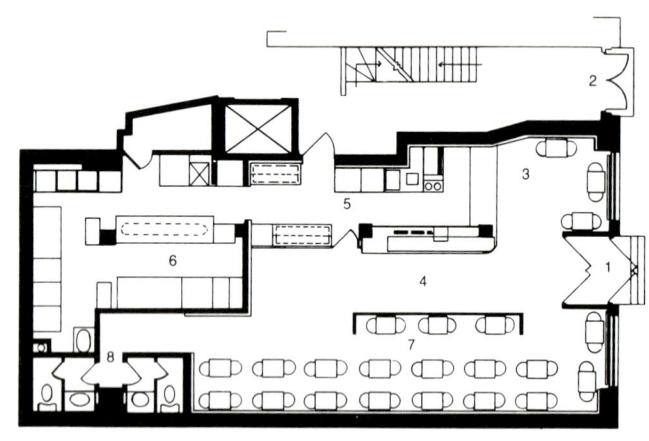

BY STICKING TO a rather eccentric idea and following through with bold, simple graphics, architects Arlen/Fox of New York created a simple fast food spot with a clean, efficient, and lively image.

The idea of sitting inside a "baked potato skin" housed in a building that "has had its roof ripped off by a tornado" seems improbable at best. But Frederick Fox Jr., partner in Arlen/Fox Architects, envisioned the scheme based on the stuffed potato skins (the British call them "jackets") that dominate the menu of client Mary Kahler. A graduate of the New York Restaurant School, Kahler had nurtured and perfected plans for her spud-themed restaurant for about ten years.

In executing the design for Jackets, Fox wanted people to be the conceptual "filling" for his baked potato base—consisting of rust-toned laminate walls decorated with the restaurant's logo. Just above the classic arches of this base, the walls end in an uneven crumble. Though many patrons think this is part of the potato, notes the architect, it's intended to resemble a tornado-sheared wall, with the roof gone and sky showing. A few structural members—in black grid form—remain. "It doesn't matter that nobody gets it," says Fox.

The creative interior scheme has in no way compromised functional requirements. Conversely, the "crumbling" walls are highly compatible with an erratically edged tile application in the service area. They also form a baffle for uplighting that enhances the ceiling height and visually enlarges the small space. The black lighting grid and transparent Plexiglas menu boards over the service counter and take-out area provide an unobstructed view of the restaurant's "sky."

Reiterating the grid used overhead are black tables and chairs—all in settings for two to give maximum flexibility. (Tables for four with only two customers can cost 50 percent of business, notes Fox.) The restaurant and its kitchen occupy 1,400 square feet on the main level; a prep area, storage, lockers, and offices in the basement cover an additional 1,600 square feet of space.

Only a small divider separates dining tables from take-out and eat-in order counters (top). This open plan seems to visually expand Jackets. Design elements, such as neon window signage and the overhead lighting grid (opposite), were also intentionally nonobstructive. Floorplan: entrance (1); service entrance (2); take-out order counter (3); eat-in order counter (4); service area (5); kitchen (6); dining area (7); restrooms (8).

JACKETS   New York City
Owners: Mary Kahler, Cynthia Kipness, Helen Berkowitz
Architecture: Arlen/Fox Architects
   (Samuel S. Arlen, Frederick B. Fox Jr.)
General Contractor: Wellbilt Equipment Corporation
Size: 1,400 square feet
Photography: © Jim D'Addio

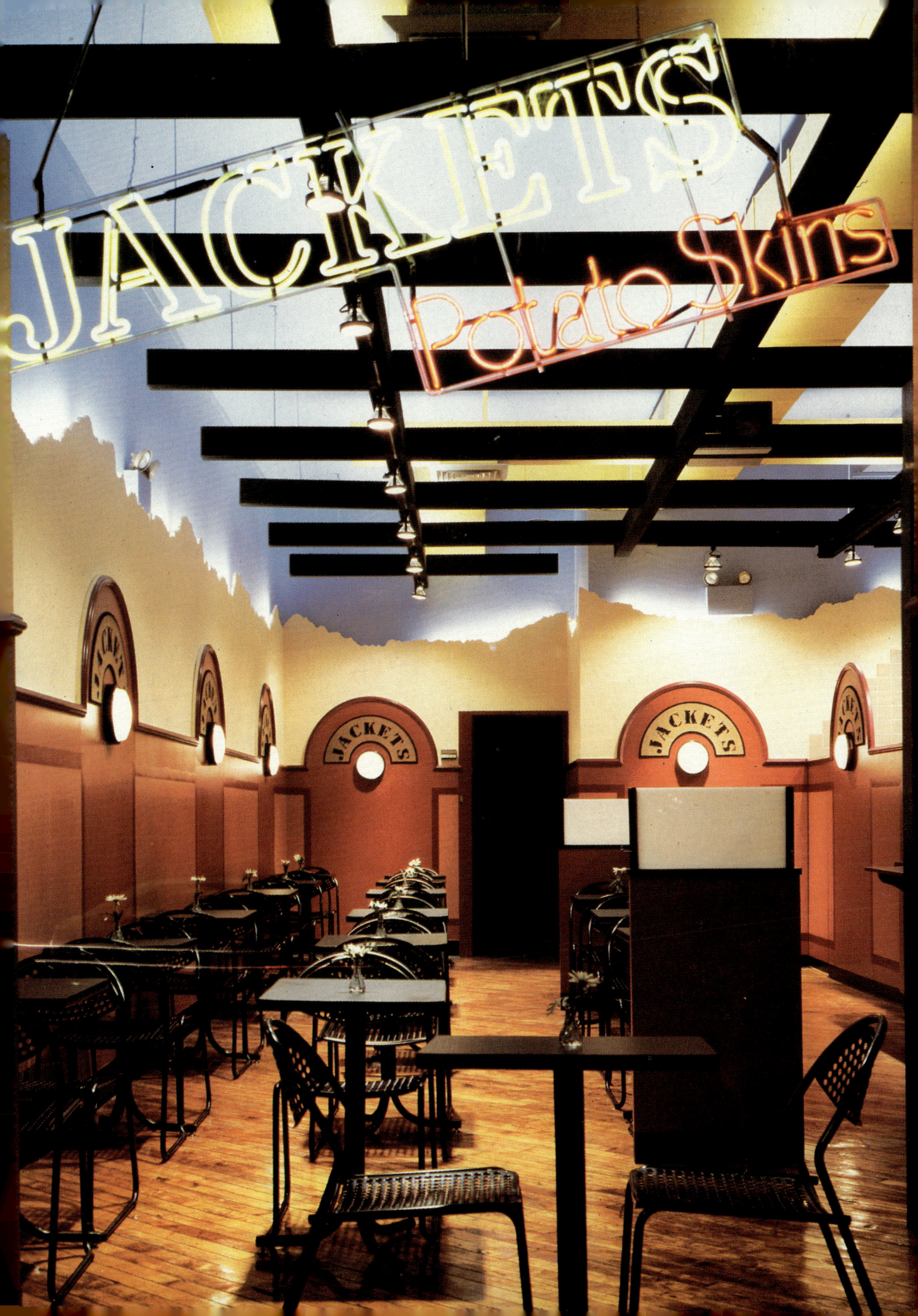
JACKETS
Potato Skins
JACKETS
JACKETS

TAKE A CUE FROM BAROQUE CHURCHES
CHAPEL METAPHORS ABOUND IN THIS CEREBRAL PIZZA PARLOR

THE LOS ANGELES architectural firm of Morphosis wanted to create a standout (but low-budget) café/pizzeria within an 850-square-foot storefront on Melrose Avenue, a street rife with attention-getting facades and boutiques. To do it, they produced a witty pastiche of architectural metaphors that call to mind a baroque chapel.

Angeli's facade suggests both a ruined temple and a broken pediment. Its sculptural look is created by a fragmented frame of rusted steel, pierced by a wooden beam, fronting a plain, two-story stucco box. Below this sculpture is a fully glazed front with doors set at an angle to a panel of glass bricks. Within, the beam counterpoints a projecting service duct; the side walls have sculptured niches lit by stylized candelabra. Niches house baked-dough saints and in place of an altar, there is an impressive pizza oven.

Angeli seats 32 at tables and another four at the bar; it also offers take-out and a catering service. The volume of business is largely determined by the size of the pizza oven. The kitchen is as tight as a ship's galley. Wine is stored in overhead bins at the rear of the dining room.

What makes this tiny space so impressive is the care that has been lavished on the plan and the details. Much of the construction was undertaken by co-owner John Strobel, formerly manager of the Seventh Street Bistro, and by project architect Michele Saie. The total building cost, exclusive of kitchen and fittings, was only $60,000; the steelwork on the facade cost a mere $6,000. But nothing looks skimpy. The space has been cleverly manipulated to make it seem larger than it is—a ploy that is most notable in the recessed entryway and in the geometrically aligned elements overhead.

Co-owner Evan Kleiman says, "The entire space was so small it forced us to be well organized. As it turned out, Angeli is much more elegant—and functional—than any of us expected."

ANGELI	Los Angeles, California
Owners:	Evan Kleiman, John Strobel
Architecture:	Morphosis (Thom Mayne, Michael Rotundi, principals; Michele Saie, project designer)
Lighting/Electrical Consultant:	Saul Goldin
Structural Consultant:	Gordon Polon
Mechanical Consultant:	Jerry Sullivan
Kitchen Consultant:	Tony Singus & Associates
Photography:	© Tim Street-Porter

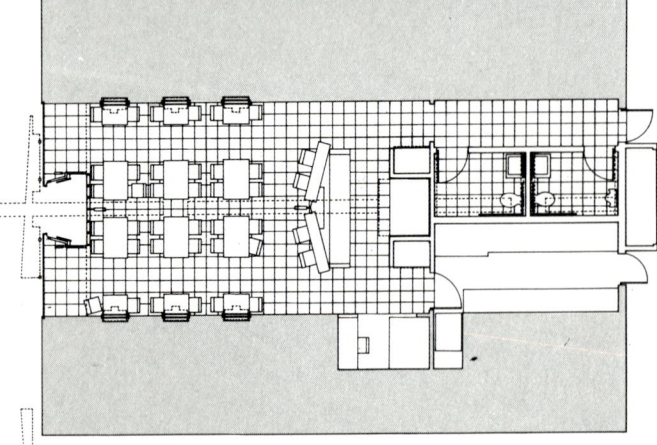

A wood beam pierces the Angeli facade of rusted steel set above a glass brick wall. It counterpoints a projecting service duct in the 850-square-foot interior (top). The restaurant's linear plan (above) resembles the layout of a church and maximizes the efficient use of space.

Inside Angeli, the pizza oven holds the place of pride: the "altar" in the churchlike scheme. Note the stylized light fixtures that resemble candles and the niche containing a baked-dough figure of a saint.

TO FAST FOOD DINING ADD MILANESE STYLE
WITH TYPICAL ELEGANCE, AN ITALIAN RESTAURANT "GOES AMERICAN"

RISTORANTE REPLAY is Italy's answer to the American fast food restaurant—a concept that has gained popularity throughout Italy. The overall design embodies a new approach to the relaxed but elegant Italian way of dining.

Pupa and Giorgio Zerbi, Milan architects who specialize in restaurant renovation and design, were asked to adapt a long and narrow space to create an elegant as well as functional, inexpensive restaurant with 100 seats. The L-shaped space presented a double challenge: to create the illusion of a wider room and to focus the eye on the food offerings in the center of the restaurant.

By using low-ceiling paneling to hide the air conditioning and electrical fixtures, and by carefully choosing colors and materials, the architects made the rooms seem wider.

To draw diners' attention to the center of the narrow restaurant, the Zerbis created several function-related stations, including a self-service bar with prepared dishes to speed up service. "We installed mirror paneling to give the illusion of separate areas," says Pupa Zerbi. The mirrored wall breaks up the length of the room and at the same time enhances the display grill so that people are quickly directed toward the pizza and other featured foods. Nearby is a glass-enclosed wine and beer room and an elegant bar that also serves as an elaborate dessert and salad station.

"The custom-designed flooring was carried out according to *seminato veneziano* tradition—that is, large, different-colored pieces of marble joined with cement and polished on site. From a modern point of view, the flooring reminds patrons of a carpet with stylized flowers," notes Giorgio Zerbi.

For the walls, the designers achieved an elegant contrast using three shades of polished, glazed plaster above a hand-etched cement dado. A halogen lamp system with directional lighting over the tables gives a soft, yet clear, illumination.

Anchoring the restaurant's design is a fountain that serves as an unusual hors d'oeuvre station at the widest point of the room. The fountain has a circular basin of coral-dressed steel. Water springing from ninety-five nozzles splashes against a tall Plexiglas dome that is well illuminated by natural light. The sight and sound of falling water contributes to a pleasant sense of relaxation throughout the restaurant. It also adds to an elegant ambience where privacy is assured, service is quick, and patrons can eat pizza—or more elaborate fare—at reasonable prices.

A fountain (above) in the restaurant's center—its widest area—serves as a focal point. The fountain's circular basin is coral-dressed steel. A mirrored wall (opposite) faces dining tables and brings an illusion of width to the long, narrow space.

RISTORANTE REPLAY	*Milan, Italy*
Architecture:	*Pupa and Georgio Zerbi*
Seating:	*100*
Photography:	*© Francesco Bellesia*

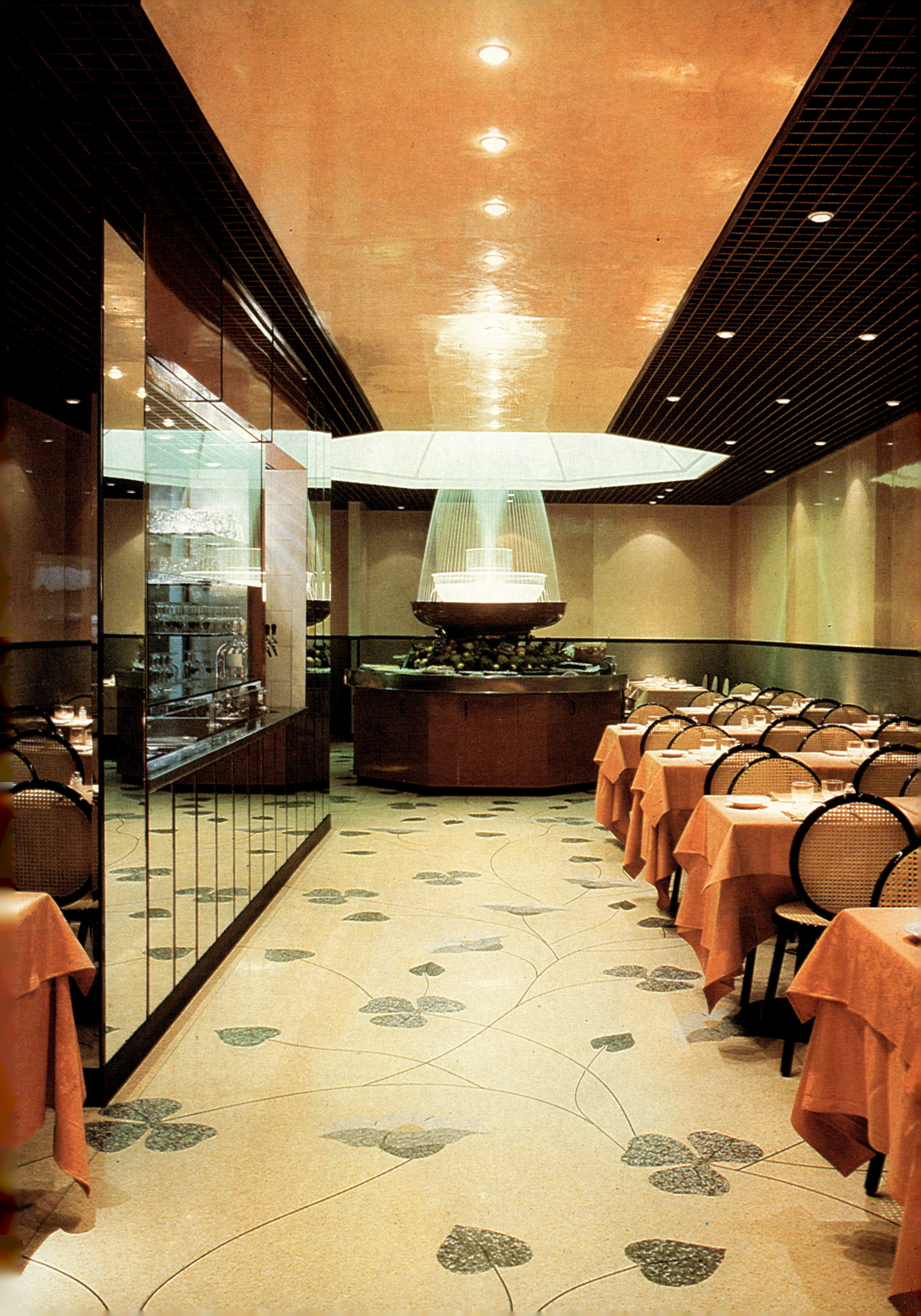

MAKE THE INTERIOR INTERACT WITH THE STREET
SPRITELY PLANT SCULPTURES AND GRAPHICS ATTRACT PASSERSBY

Whimsical pizza-tree sculptures greet patrons at Pizzapiazza (above) in New York City's Greenwich Village. Fresh pastels and the restaurant's tabletop settings (opposite), designed by Lois Bloom of Barbara Kafka Associates, play important roles in the overall design. Tables sport checked cotton picnic tablecloths under glass, dish-towel napkins, and custom-colored chinaware.

THE "PIZZA TREES" GROW right through the roof, because the owners wanted the Pizzapiazza interior to *interact* with the environment. And they wanted greenery. But Danny Bloom and Myron Siegel didn't care for hanging plants that look good at first, then droop forlornly. They requested striking design elements that could be duplicated; they wanted an upscale pizzeria that could become a prototype.

So designer Milton Glaser set a witty graphics program in motion. The marine-plywood-and-steel trees are the work of sculptor Jordan Steckel. Warm, yellow lighting animates the trees and the signage from the outside to attract passersby.

New York architect Charles Boxenbaum of Boxenbaum Associates took the project further, creating a cafélike atmosphere that would express the upscale dimension of this essentially quick-service establishment, which features various kinds of deep-dish pizza.

Boxenbaum's approach is not a decorative one; he relies instead on architectural elements to provide a distinctive look and to give the illusion of limitless light and space above and around the dining area. Along one wall of the restaurant, he has suspended a series of frosted glass "windows" with painted wood frames. They are illuminated from behind with bare lightbulbs screwed into recessed wall sockets.

The ceiling, too, uses architectural illusion to achieve effects of space and light. Its tentlike coves glow with light that emanates from fluorescent bulbs installed above Teflon-coated fiberglass baffles. Boxenbaum credits consultant Bill Leek of B.L.I. (Stamford, Connecticut) for devising the restaurant's entire ceiling coffer system.

As the owners wished, the coffered ceiling, simulated windows, and distinctive "cutout" booth profiles are what Boxenbaum calls "transferable design elements." He has deliberately repeated these elements to "create a series of patterns that can easily be adapted to different spaces."

Pizzapiazza's fresh color scheme incorporates pink walls, gray/green laminated booths and wainscoting, and pale yellow ceiling covers. The wood floor and stone tabletops and bar are a natural beige; checkered cotton tablecloths add verve. Bloom estimates the F/FE expenditure for this potential prototype at $550,000.

PIZZAPIAZZA	*New York City*
Owners:	*Danny Bloom, Myron Siegel*
Architecture:	*Charles Boxenbaum*
Graphic Design Consultant:	*Milton Glaser*
Tabletop Consultant:	*Barbara Kafka Associates*
Seating:	*120, plus bar*
Budget:	*F/FE $550,000*
Photography:	*© Norman McGrath*

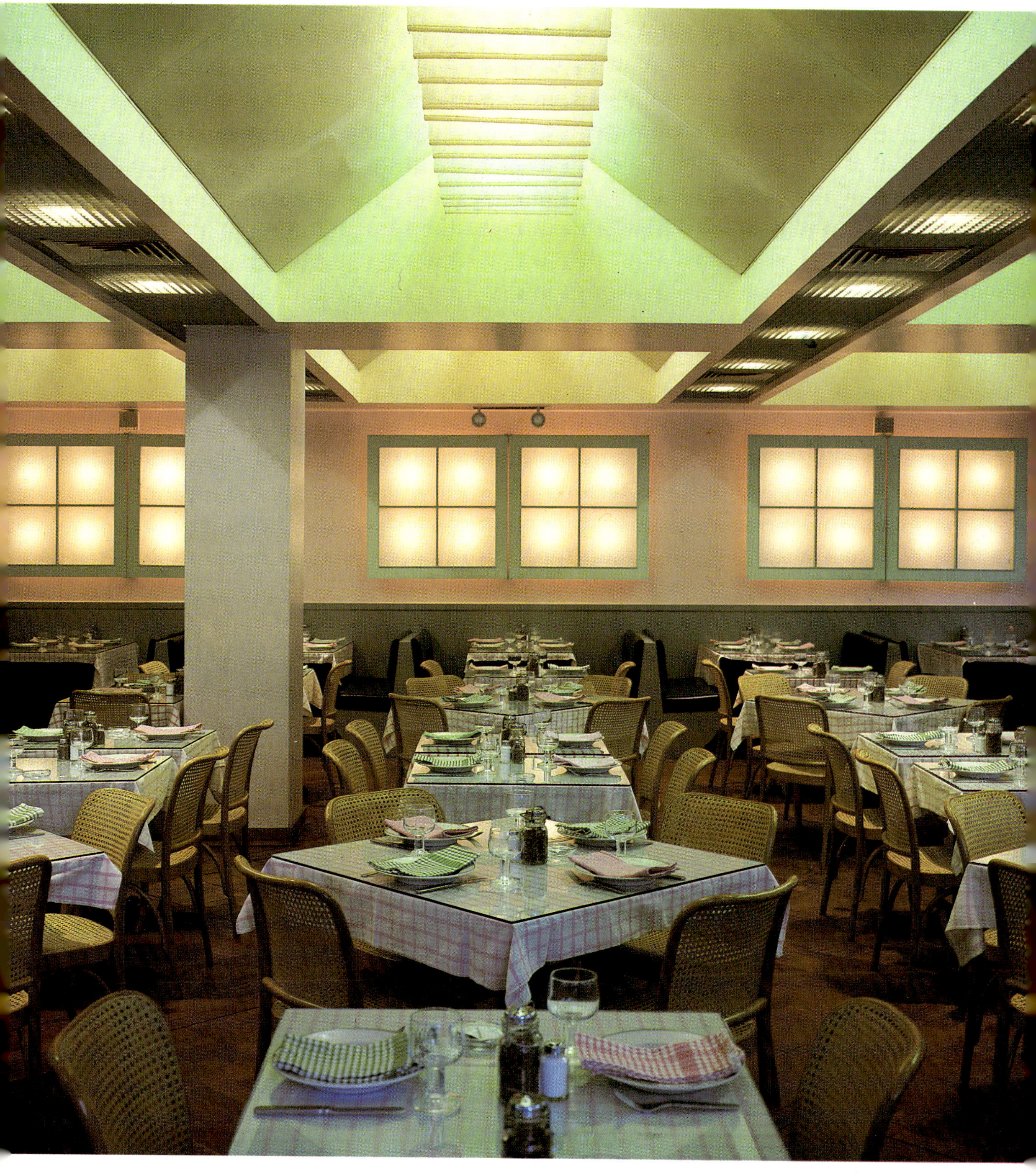

CAPTURE CURVES FOR CLEAN STYLING
A PASTA RESTAURANT TAKES ITS DESIGN CUE FROM THE NEARBY RIVER

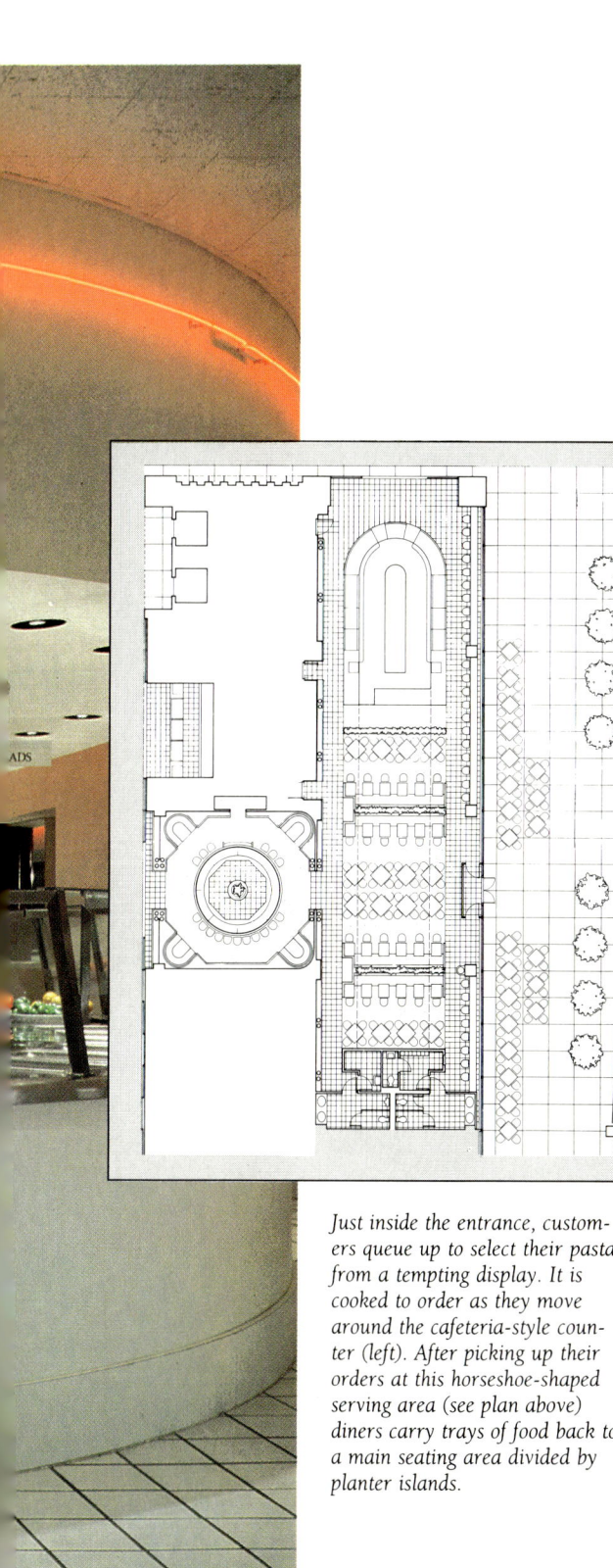

MAMA MIA! PASTA in Chicago's Mercantile Exchange Center steps beyond the traditional. Designed by the Chicago architectural firm of Banks/Eakin, the restaurant avoids cliché in concept as well as appearance. It is slick, lively, and in a location that attracts an equally smart, lively clientele.

Architects Garret Eakin and John Banks steered away from an obvious Italian theme for the restaurant's interior. "We started working with the idea of Italian cuisine," says Eakin, "but then the river gave us the idea of movement, and we wanted to incorporate that." Interpreting the river's motion, the architects developed a softly undulating dining room ceiling that provides a gentle counterpoint to the orderly seating below.

With an earlier Mama Mia! Pasta unit already up and running, owners David Houle and Dorothy DeCarlo opened this expanded version, taking some liberties with the prototype they had already established. Since this larger, 5,700-square-foot "Merc" store permitted some elaboration, the architects designed three distinct spaces: a bar, a self-service area, and a take-out station.

At the front is a large, crisp self-service area with open kitchen and counter seating. A long, narrow dining room stretches out behind, opening into a 44-seat bar that has a separate concourse entrance. The kitchen is adjacent to the bar, but also services the main seating area and a take-out station. A riverfront patio provides additional seating.

Certain key ingredients—the red, white, and green color scheme, as well as mirrors and white tile—were adapted from the original Mama Mia! unit. White tile delineates circulation patterns throughout the restaurant and covers the entire floor of the self-service area. Green is seen in the carpet that covers seating areas and bar, and in the wool wall coverings. The red laminated columns supply visual punch without harping on the Italian scheme.

A system of reflected lighting augments Mama Mia!'s bright, clean look without overpowering the interior. Downlights illuminate circulation areas, and a low-voltage system over the food core places "a hot, focused" light on the pasta, sauces, and salads. In the dining room, cove lights along the "great wave" of the ceiling add soft illumination to ambient daylight from the riverfront window wall. Neon is hardly new to fast food, but the architects have used it here with commendable understatement: A single line of red defines the curve of the self-service area's food core and continues back in the dining room along the outer edge of the soffit, repeating the ceiling's undulation. This neon strip has become a marketing tool: Visible through restaurant windows, it attracts patrons from office buildings across the river.

Quips satisfied owner Houle, "It's an attractive place, and attractive people feel good here."

Just inside the entrance, customers queue up to select their pasta from a tempting display. It is cooked to order as they move around the cafeteria-style counter (left). After picking up their orders at this horseshoe-shaped serving area (see plan above) diners carry trays of food back to a main seating area divided by planter islands.

MAMA MIA! PASTA   Chicago, Illinois

Owners: Dorothy DeCarlo, David Houle

Interior Architecture: (Garret Eakin, John Banks, Sui-Sheng Chang) Banks/Eakin Architects
in association with Lawrence Berkley & Associates Inc.

Exterior Architecture: Fujikawa Johnson and Associates, Inc.

Kitchen Facilities: Lawrence Berkley & Associates Inc.

Contractor: Capitol Construction

Budget: $1.25 million

Seating: 160

Photography: © Orlando Cabanban

PUT THE MECHANICS AT CENTER STAGE
A CONVEYOR BELT JOINS KITCHEN AND COUNTER IN THIS URBAN DINER

Dine-O-Mat's bright and shiny facade (above) showcases the curvaceous end of a classic diner counter. Here, a conveyor belt loaded with food on color-coded plates—rather than a short order cook—takes center stage. (The different colored plates signify different prices.) Inside (opposite), a rear wall of glass block separates the restaurant's kitchen from its 52-seat counter, where diners are tempted by the non-stop parade of freshly prepared food.

INSTEAD OF THE short-order cook flipping burgers and frying eggs behind the counter, owner Bill Liederman wanted a conveyor belt stretching all the way from the kitchen to the diners, offering nothing but high-quality fast food. He envisioned an American interior that would put good food before an impulse-buying public.

He wanted to create the quintessential diner—columns of red-tinted glass block framing a large plate-glass window, through which can be seen an old-fashioned, curving counter attended by the short round barstools so familiar to generations of Americans. He also envisioned a crisp neon logo proclaiming Dine-O-Mat, complete with a bright yellow clock implanted in the center.

After locating a Japanese company capable of fabricating a conveyor belt system to specifications, New York architect Ira Grandberg mapped out a two-fold design scheme. The sleek and shiny result combines an abstraction and updating of the classic American diner with a notion of the restaurant as feeding machine. The conveyor belt—not the cook—provides the theater.

The Dine-O-Mat conveyor belt moves along the rear portion of the 52-seat laminate and stainless steel counter occupying the long, narrow restaurant's entire south wall. Making the most of the diner association, the rear wall behind the counter is faced with molded stainless steel panels, the end piers of which frame beverage machines, beer keg taps, a liquor bar, and menus proclaiming daily specials.

Within the remainder of the 1,400-square-foot space, Grandberg installed a black and gray quarry tile floor, walls paneled in black-enameled stainless steel, and a mirrored panel ceiling. A raised ceiling soffit over the traffic corridor is painted white, a soft foil for banks of uplights. Booths and tables, which are opposite the counter in the rear section of the room (and require waiter service), are sheathed in various shades of pale aqua below a mirrored wall section.

The rear wall which separates the kitchen from the rest of the diner is formed of transparent glass block, allowing a sense of kitchen bustle to flicker through.

DINE-O-MAT	*New York City*
Owner:	*Bill Liederman*
Architecture:	*Grandesign Architects, P. C. (Ira Grandberg)*
Graphic Design Consultant:	*Kenneth Knitel*
Foodservice Consultant:	*Skolodz Associates*
Mechanical Engineer:	*Kim Associates*
Size:	*1,400 square feet*
Photography:	*© Jan Staller*

81

REMODEL A BURGER JOINT ON A SHOESTRING BUDGET

A STOREFRONT RESTAURANT IS BUILT USING PLANES AND CABLES

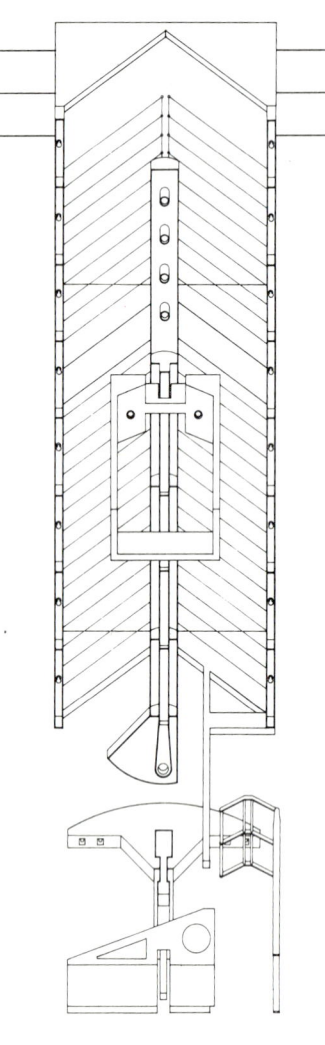

A system of cables defines the steeply pitched restaurant ceiling, as illustrated in the drawing (above). The cables actually suspend the central light trough and are anchored on either side of the narrow room by the wall light troughs, which are formed from sheet metal boxes. The horizontally placed pie case (framed in pale magenta) provides a focus for the front of the room, while the bar and glass rack stretch out perpendicularly behind the case, reinforcing the architectural motif of penetrating planes.

FACED WITH a dismal burger joint/soda fountain—made all the worse by its dimensions, a shoebox 11½ feet wide and 60 feet long, with 12-foot ceilings—architect Rebecca L. Binder of El Segundo, California, began by gutting the space. For only $95,000, she completed a total remodeling of facade, interior, bathrooms, and kitchen, plus stairway and basement office/storage.

Binder's scheme utilizes shadows and forms that are inventively angled and juxtaposed, creating a progression into the space. Most of the adjoining stores use two building modules, each of which is defined by an angled storefront. For Eats, Binder had only one module. To focus the facade she created a logo and a sculptural arc reminiscent of an inverted anchor.

A series of cables defines the steeply pitched interior ceiling, angling up from the side lighting troughs to the center, where they then suspend the central lighting trough. Fabricated of sheet metal, these light boxes substitute for a more expensive system of downlights. Binder estimates that the central trough cost around $2,000, while the two side troughs were built for about $300 apiece.

"Once I came up with the cables, the interior design began to fall into place," Binder says. The second major element became the pie case, which she centered and around which she created a frame. She then designed a glass rack above the bar, which stretches out perpendicularly behind the case.

Interior materials are simple and inexpensive: the black and white tile floor, enamel paint, plastic-clad metal cables, steel and sheet metal light boxes, and laminated cabinetry. Binder also used the same exterior stucco on interior walls to a height of 7 feet.

Binder creates interest and emphasizes her architectural scheme with her use of colors: a soft palette of gray, tangerine, and cream, and a bold stripe of magenta neon suspended below the central light trough. Exterior colors of gray, purple, and yellow give the facade a distinctive appeal and here, again, emphasize and help to resolve the graphic architectural plan.

EATS	*El Segundo, California*
Owners:	*Diane Thomson, George Mkitarian*
Architecture:	*Rebecca L. Binder, James G. Stafford*
Structural Engineer:	*Gordon Polon*
Kitchen Consultant:	*Laschober/Sovich*
Budget:	$95,000
Seating:	30
Photography:	© *Marvin Rand*

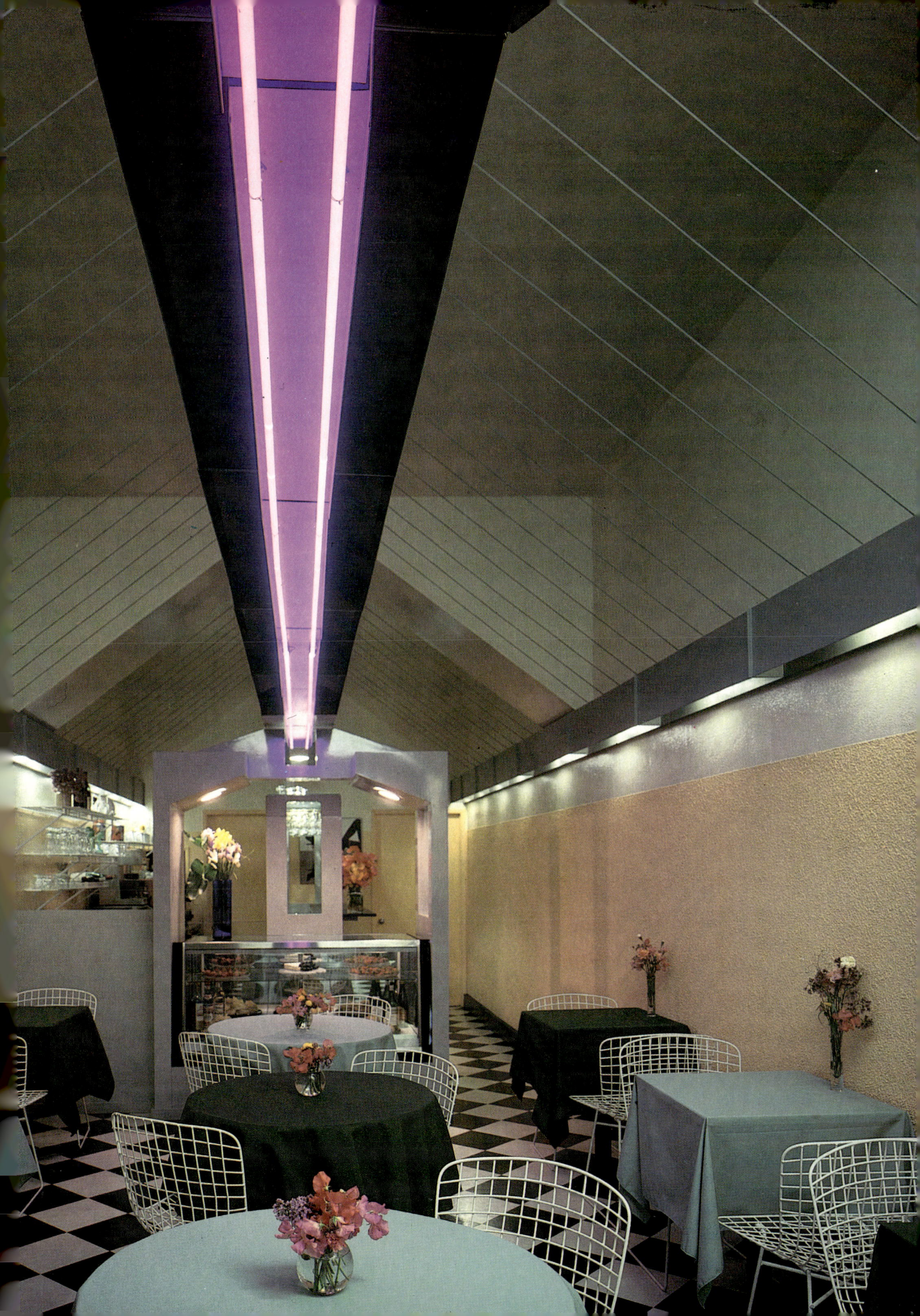

4. CHAIN

RESTAURANTS

Since the 1880s, when the first Fred Harvey Restaurant opened its doors at the Atchison, Topeka & Santa Fe Depot in Topeka, Kansas, chain restaurants have responded to a popular demand for economy and convenience, plus a measure of reliability in the menu and service. And since their inception, chain restaurants have consistently embodied the spirit of their times.

For families, chain restaurants are bastions of dependability, providing affordable opportunities for dining out. Not all of them are quick and cheap. Because the average customer has become more sophisticated and more sensitive to nutrition and ambience, and because chain restaurant owners are always looking for more economical and efficient ways to run their operations, the look of chain restaurants is constantly in flux.

At an innovative McDonald's in Raleigh, North Carolina, (opposite) James Dean and Fats Domino replace Ronald McDonald on the walls. This unique McDonald's opened in commemoration of the chain's thirtieth anniversary. Rehabbing an old theater, Perry & Plummer Design Associates put the kitchen and food counter at the level of the raked floor, where the movie screen had been. Now food is the show. But old movies are also projected on screens above platform dining areas.

When it came time for a facelift at Charley O's, a New York City chain, designer Susan Orsini looked to urban neighborhoods for inspiration. In the theater district, Broadway became the theme, but at another installation on Madison Avenue, the look is more conservative, more corporate.

Out West, in Washington state, the designers for Casa Lupita—a Mexican restaurant chain—devised an introspective scheme that would save the chain money on initial building costs as well as upkeep. In Florida, New York architects Jay Haverson and David Rockwell worked on developing a seafood prototype restaurant for Benihana National Corporation. Fish literally swim at The Big Splash and tanks that are the focal point of the display area in the 280-seat restaurant.

DEVELOP A SEAFOOD PROTOTYPE
FISH TANKS DRAMATIZE DISPLAY ISLAND IN RESTAURANT'S PIAZZA

Sails billow from the grid ceiling that spans the 10,000-square-foot dining area and piazza (right). In the center of the restaurant is a large food display where diners can choose their appetizers or sushi and watch fish swimming about in the two glowing tanks at the prow of the island. Note how the grid ceiling corresponds to the tile floor. Everywhere, lighting is used to dramatic effect; for example, neon slashes across the entrance (left) like a lightning bolt.

WHEN HAVERSON/ROCKWELL ARCHITECTS, a New York City–based design firm, took on the project, their charge was to develop a 14,000-square-foot corner site in North Miami Beach as a prototype for Benihana's seafood chain restaurant concept. It was important, of course, to create a strong identity, an image that could be repeated but which included details that could be altered to suit a variety of locations.

With this in mind, the architects worked out a plan with a central piazza, fountains, an amphitheater for seating (as originally conceived, these would have been on graduated platforms), and fish tanks that suggest a ship's bow for the lavish seafood display island that is placed at the center of the piazza. From first sketch to finish, the project took a year and two months and cost $1.7 million.

From the outside—a dazzling display of pink walls, red grid-motif doors, spotlights, and flashing neon lightning bolts—the architects intentionally manipulated the design to recall a theater marquee, a pier building, a fish market, and an amusement park. Guests enter a huge space flanked by fountains that separate the central piazza and seafood display from the 280-seat dining area. Overhead, architects Haverson and Rockwell created an artificial sky made from rippling

THE BIG SPLASH	*North Miami Beach, Florida*
Owner:	*Benihana National Corporation*
Architecture/Interior Design:	*Haverson/Rockwell Architects, P. C. (Jay M. Haverson, David S. Rockwell, Hans J. Baehler, Richard Granoff, John Paul Dunn)*
Contractor:	*Deland Construction Company*
Kitchen Consultant:	*Walter Hunter (Imperial Kitchen Equipment)*
Structural Engineer:	*Jim Wiesenfeld (Wiesenfeld and Associates)*
Mechanical Engineer:	*Bruce Connors (Robins Engineering Inc.)*
Budget: *$1.7 million* **Time:** *14 months* **Seating:** *280* **Photography:** *© Mark Ross*	

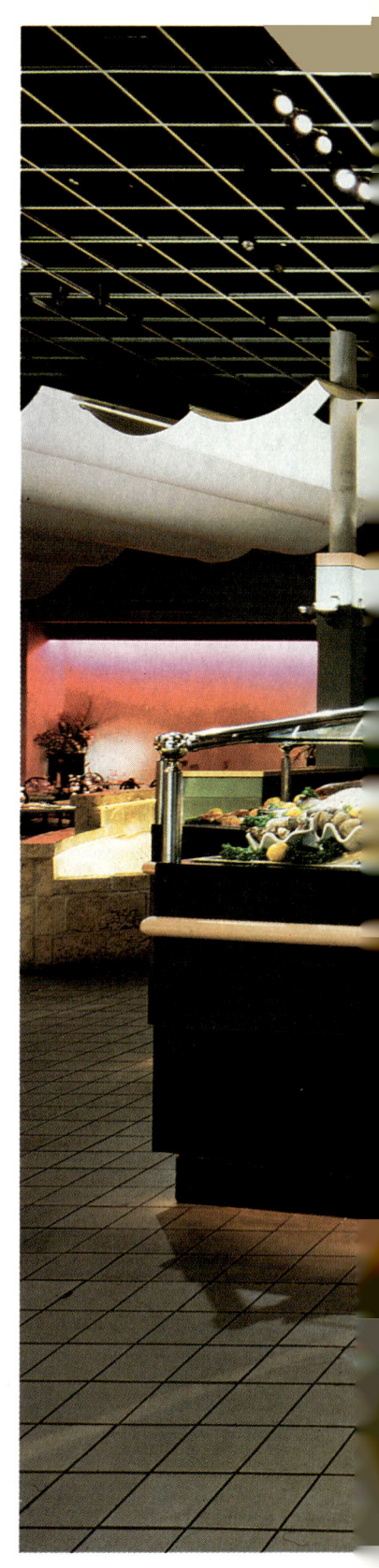

87

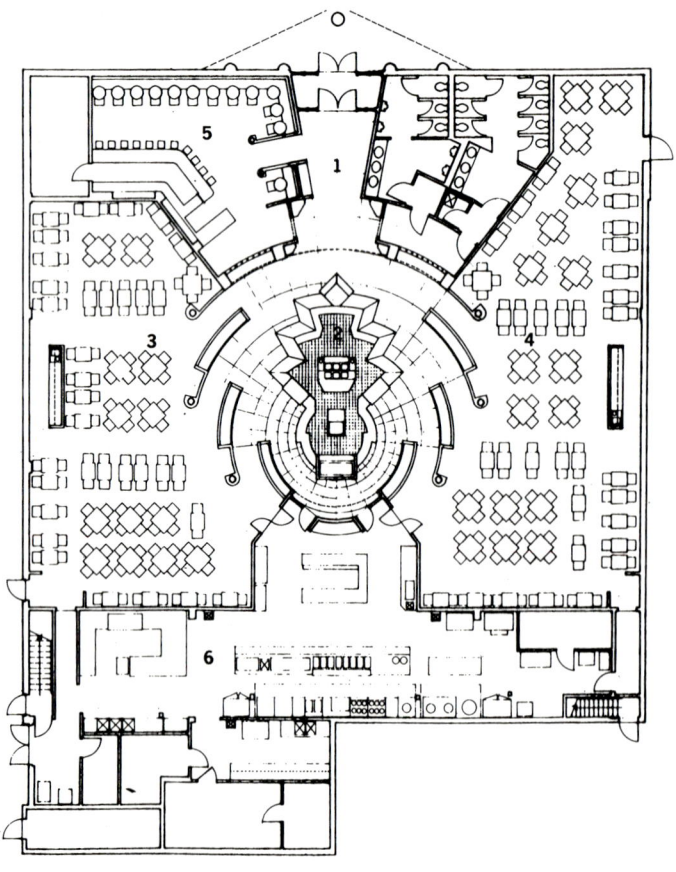

sails that seem to scud like clouds across the firmament. "The ceiling suggests mystery," says Rockwell. "We wanted a strong horizon in such a large space," noting the series of important horizontal references that claim attention: red neon that rings the seating area, the uplights on all columns, the sails, and a pale blue ceiling grid.

Above the grid, composed of 2-foot by 2-foot sections, are all the mechanical systems and the track lighting, painted black. Haverson/Rockwell use a device in all their projects that works as this grid does and above which all mechanical systems are placed.

Lighting is a vital element in the design scheme at The Big Splash. Light falls from the track lights and rises from the wall sconces; it glows from the neon and glistens through the water. Some of the lights used on this project include track lighting with extremely narrow, 25-watt spots, 250-watt spots, and 150-watt floods on a four-circuit track. There are also 300-watt uplights around the columns, 250-watt quartz spotlights in the fountains, red neon lights, and low-voltage miniature tube lights under the display.

"The whole design for The Big Splash really fell together like a jigsaw puzzle," says Haverson, after it was decided that the kitchen—originally planned to attach to the central food display area—was made separate. This allowed the island to float, and it became the central focal point from which other elements radiate. The fountains at the edge of the piazza surrounding the island effectively divide the room and create entryways into the dining areas. The sails suspended overhead also define the seating spaces.

"When designing a room for people, it is crucial to make them look good," Rockwell stresses. "In a large space, it is a particular challenge to do this, because you need elements that give human scale." At The Big Splash, the fountains create the needed scale, rising 3½ feet from the floor. The sails help by lowering the ceiling over the dining area. Indirect lighting is also important.

Guests emerge into a room that glints with color and light. They can stroll around the piazza, select cold appetizers, salads, and fish from the sushi bar, and then move past the fountains to the tables. This is an efficient yet provocative dining environment.

The innovative lighting scheme plays an important role in the overall design (top). Track lighting—spots and floods—are set above the ceiling grid; a band of red neon glows below it. Quartz spots shine through the fountains that separate the piazza from the dining area. Floorplan: entrance (1); food display (2); north dining area (3); south dining area (4); lounge/bar (5); kitchen (6). Drawing by Richard Granoff and Jean Campbell.

REVAMP A PUB'S IMAGE
NEON AND CORPORATE COLORS GIVE A RESTAURANT NEW IDENTITY

"WE WANTED TO MOVE a step away from the dark, masculine bar with beer mugs slamming alongside that pound of roast beef that's thrown between two slices of bread," says Gary Trimarchi, chief operating officer of the Riese Organization, parent to the Charley O's restaurant chain. Trimarchi asked Susan Francesca Orsini of Orsini Design Associates to revamp the image of a New York City restaurant chain known for its murky, publike atmosphere into something fresh and new.

As part of Charley O's chain-wide facelift, Orsini planned each restaurant around a theme unique to its special city neighborhood. For example, a Charley O's in the theater district was given a "Broadway" theme with actors' photographs and other memorabilia. For the restaurant pictured here—a former coffee shop frequented by advertising and banking types who work on nearby Madison Avenue—Orsini selected all-American colors, translating patriotic red, white, and blue into corporate hues of blue/gray, charcoal, parchment, and ivory. Red neon trims the Chippendale-style bar front, the last remaining vestige of the former facility.

Because this particular Charley O's is tucked away on two levels up a flight of stairs from an off-street plaza, Orsini knew she needed to use attention-grabbing color and lighting effects. "Although there is no street frontage, we had to punch out an identity," she explains, "to have catchy translucent signage—especially at night. In this case, the white ceiling and the red neon really glows through the windows, attracting the attention of passersby below."

Orsini distinguished this particular Charley O's with a crisp, visually stimulating ambience, achieved through the sophisticated juxtaposition of colors for maximum energy and contrast. Ivory-, parchment-, and cream-colored Zolatone covers walls above the wood bar and chair rails; charcoal Zolatone with a blue cast is used below, for the effect of a Victorian dado. Natural woods impart an airy freshness. All the woods are maple, Orsini says, including the molding, furniture, and floors: "I like its tight grain and yellow tint."

Still other elements impart sparkle and shine. Bright brass railings define the space; mirrors expand it. To encourage a play of light, glass sconces are mounted on the mirrors. Throughout the restaurant, Orsini placed large photographs of food-related subjects. The pictures are the work of photographer Michael Geiger, well known among advertising professionals in the neighborhood.

Charley O's renovation was completed in 1986 at a cost approaching $300,000, including the mechanical fixtures. Trimarchi is happy with the result. "Restaurants are like theaters," he says. "It's the show that changes, not the theater."

With a red neon trim and a glowing white ceiling, the interior becomes the restaurant's billboard, as seen from the sidewalk below. Mirrors and brass add sparkle.

CHARLEY O'S *New York City*

Interior Design: *Orsini Design Associates (Susan Francesca Orsini, Jane Schwedfeger)*

Operator: *Riese Organization*

Budget: *$300,000*

Photographer: *© Elliot Fine*

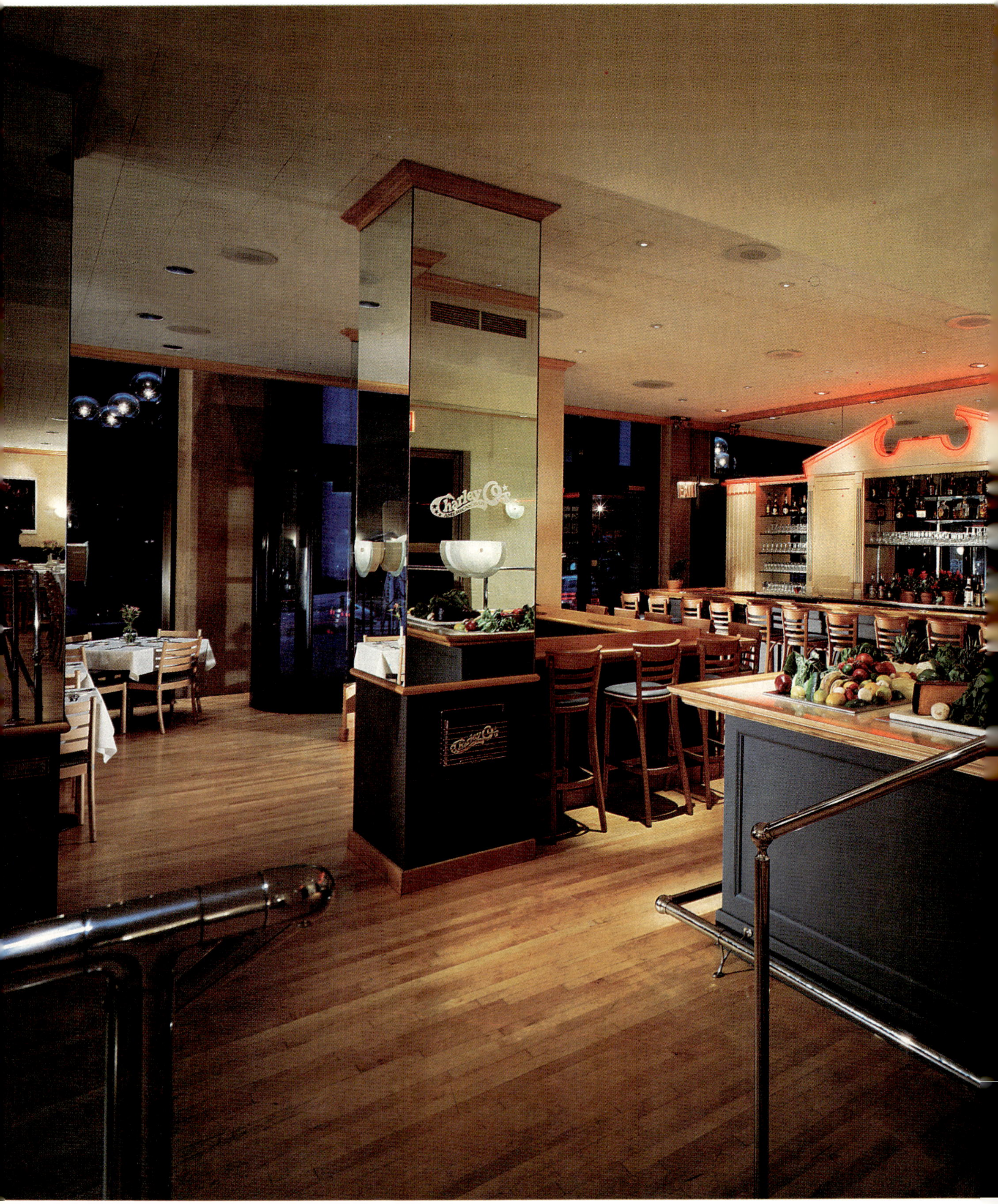

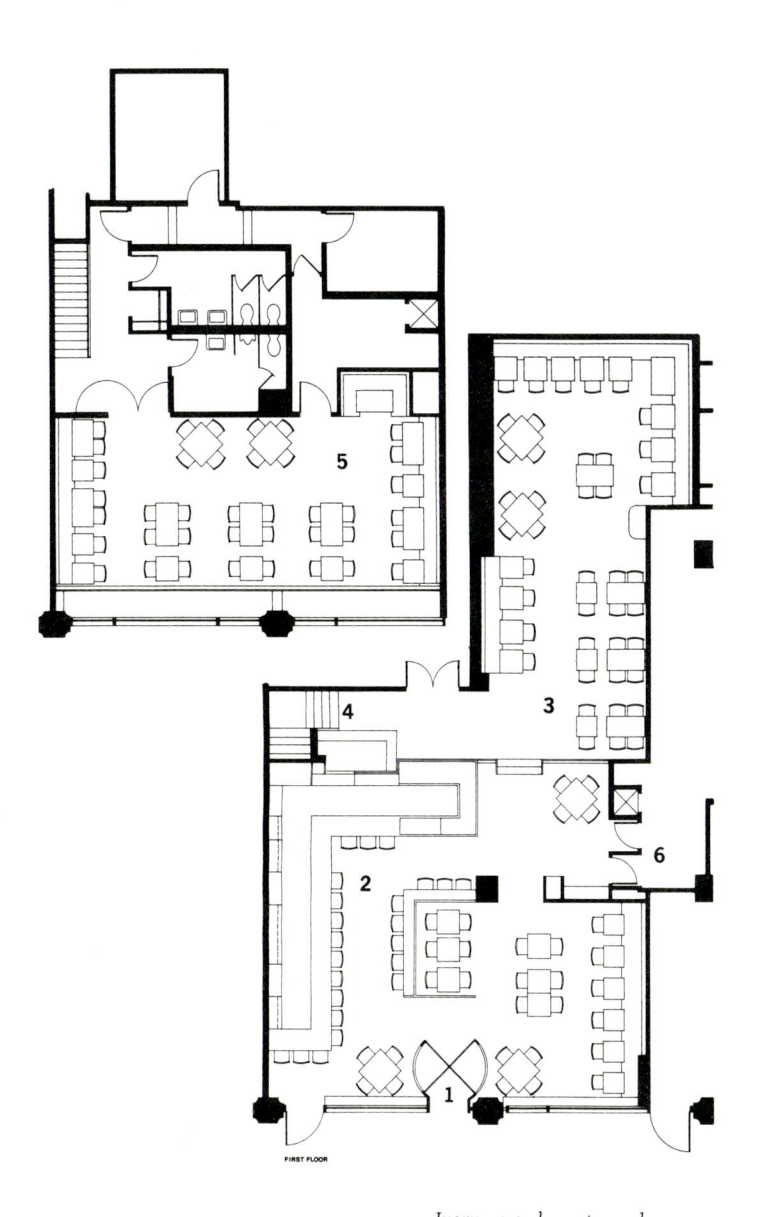

Ivory-, parchment-, and cream-colored Zolatone covers the walls above the banquettes and chair rails; charcoal Zolatone with a blue cast is used below for the effect of a Victorian dado. Floorplan: entrance (1); bar (2); platform dining area (3); stairs (4); upper level dining area (5); kitchen entrance (6).

SIMPLIFY WITH CLERESTORY WINDOWS
INTROSPECTIVE SCHEME KEEPS COST DOWN IN A MEXICAN DINNER HOUSE

CLERESTORY WINDOWS most often bring to mind the hushed interior of a Gothic cathedral, illuminated in its lofty reaches by shafts of light. But for Casa Lupita—a nationwide chain of Mexican restaurants like the one shown here in Totem Lake, Washington—the clerestory is part of a new "introspective design scheme," a prototype that saves the chain money on initial building costs as well as upkeep.

"The plan is very economical," says Gary Dethlefs, president of Louis Owen Inc. in Seattle. Dethlefs explains that his architectural and interior design firm was brought in to rework a basically successful idea, that of the Mexican dinner house. Keeping in mind that the design would be built on many sites, they moved the focus inward and shifted from expensive architectural features to less expensive decorative elements. Indeed, the key to the plan is its architectural simplicity of the interior dining court and its clerestory.

"Basically, the plan consists of a rectangular box with another box around it," says Dethlefs. "It is very straightforward. The only windows are those above the interior court where the ceiling is higher. From these windows, light floods the space, illuminating just about every seat.

"What was challenging about the project," continues Dethlefs, "was coming up with a design vocabulary that had a lot of visual appeal, while keeping costs to a bare minimum. We were looking for a simple shell that could be built anywhere. The earlier Casa Lupita design relied heavily on architectural devices that were costly to construct. There were many skylights, for example. The clerestory solution, which also provides light from above, is not only more economical, it is more in keeping with traditional Mexican architecture."

This design—combined with the use of tiles, stenciling, ficus trees, Mexican pots and other genuine art objects, brightly colored fabrics, paper flowers and ribbons, and a fountain that splashes at the center of the court—gives the restaurant its festive air.

"The ribbon wreaths in the bar and the garlands of paper we invented ourselves, using Mexican paper flowers and belts, and ribbons. It has the feeling of a piñata party," says Dethlefs. "Our overall design concept—together with the interior court arrangement—allows for quick, efficient service. Food pickup has double access and delivery flows around the perimeter or into the court."

The emphasis is on comfort, on getting away. Furnishings that would be flexible were selected. To accommodate a mix of parties large and small, Dethlefs specified banquette seating at the perimeter of the space, which fixed seating and is also easy to maintain. Additionally, fixed cantilever table bases were used wherever possible to provide for easier cleaning and less damage.

In addition to the Totem Lake, Washington, restaurant shown here, there are eleven Casa Lupitas that employ Louis Owen's functional and economical design. At least sixteen more restaurants are in the works. The Totem Lake Casa Lupita restaurant was built for a total of $986,000.

CASA LUPITA	*Totem Lake, Washington*
Owners:	*CLR Development and Casa Lupita*
Architecture/Interior Design:	*Louis Owen Inc.*
	(Gary Dethlefs, George Hanson, Craig Anderson, Cindi Kato)
Decor Installations Supervisor:	*Julie Stailey*
Contractor:	*Construction Associates*
Purchaser/Kitchen Consultant:	*The Wasserstrom Company*
Budget:	*$986,000*

The festive look at Casa Lupita relies heavily on the use of art and artifacts, bright colors, and a simple structure around an interior court. Decor installation supervisor Julie Stailey created the bunting on the far wall (picture opposite) with Mexican paper flowers and ribbons.

CUE A THEME WITH 1940s ARTIFACTS
AUTHENTIC DETAILS INSPIRE A HAMBURGER HANGOUT

WHEN KNOWLWOOD'S—a Southern California chain of gourmet hamburger restaurants—opened its facility in Santa Ana, patrons found themselves suddenly and not so subtly transported back in time to the postwar forties.

The 260-seat restaurant—coproduced by Beckham/Eisenman Commercial Design and Furnishings (Irvine, California) and Thirtieth Street Architects (Newport Beach)—is a stage-set rendition of a late forties roadside rest stop. Patrons enter a simulated gas station service bay, continue on to a counter area inspired by old-time outdoor food stands, and finally decide to eat at one of two main dining areas, the "Bungalow Court" or the "Enlisted Man's Canteen."

"This is something of a Disneyland approach; it was all done from scratch," says architect John Loomis of Thirtieth Street Architects. Instead, Loomis, the owners, and the interior designers began their work with only the dilapidated remains of a long-vacant structure. The clients requested additional interior space, outdoor dining areas (a Knowlwood's signature), and a design scheme that would become synonymous with Knowlwood's good-time family menu of burgers and ribs.

Inside and out, authentic details and the well-conceived design script combine to place this venture beyond the usual nostalgia/theme effort. In the canteen, for example, bunting hangs in corners, and an authentic Wurlitzer jukebox plays late-forties tunes.

KNOWLWOOD'S	*Santa Ana, California*
Owner:	*Knowl-Wood Enterprises*
Interior Design:	*Beckham/Eisenman*
Architecture:	*Thirtieth Street Architects*
Seating:	260
Budget:	$585,000
Size:	7,000 square feet
Photography:	© Milroy/McAleer

Knowlwood's counter area, where customers place and pick up orders (above), mimics a roadside stand complete with 1940s billboards, telephone poles, and a cast iron manhole cover. In the canteen (opposite), the bunting and the jukebox are augmented with period signage and photographs and even sergeants' uniform jackets hanging from coat hooks (not shown).

WELCOME SERVICEMEN
Keep'em Flying!
SANTA ANA ARMY
AIR FIELD
is listening
He wants to know
what you know
KEEP IT TO YOURSELF

INVENT A UNIQUE McDONALD'S
AN UPGRADED MOVIE THEATER SETS FIFTIES DINER THEME

Outside, the original theater marquee advertises the show: McDonald's. The McDonald's arches have been cleverly worked in at the prow of the display. Entry to seating areas is near the service counter (opposite). Overhead, an undulating pattern of neon leads customers through the space.

To commemorate McDonald's thirtieth anniversary, regional managers were asked to select one property in their respective areas that would be shaped into a one-of-a-kind design. Bruce Wunner, the chain's southeast regional manager, chose a newly acquired site in Raleigh: a circa 1920 building last used as a movie theater and located on busy Hillsborough Street, a long artery that fronts North Carolina State University.

The fact that the interior of the building was laid out like a theater, and the fact that McDonald's was founded in 1955, gave Perry & Plummer Design Associates (Wilmington and Raleigh, North Carolina) the inspiration for the design theme. The stage was set for a fifties diner articulated within the shell of the old theater.

But first, the old building needed upgrading. Architect Fred Tolson Associates of Raleigh oversaw all structural changes. The interior was gutted, new plumbing, HVAC, and electrical systems were installed, a special kitchen designed by McDonald's was fitted into the rear of the space, and skylights were punched into the roof. The Hillsborough Street facade was also repaired and stuccoed and a rear entrance was added.

Working with his project manager, Rodney D. Carman, D. Gordon Plummer positioned the kitchen and food counter at the bottom of the old theater's raked floor where the movie screen had been. "The food is the show," he says. Curvilinear partition walls flanking the central aisle enhance that effect and disguise raised seating platforms on either side of the deep space. Overhead, swirls of neon lead customers down the aisle to the counter.

Once they have their food, customers may step up to a table or counter in one of the raised areas or proceed to the back of the space beyond the food counter. There, fifties-style booths, complete with chrome record-selection boxes that are wired to a vintage jukebox, offer additional seating. Besides the fifties tunes that fill the jukebox, vintage movies and cartoons play on screens overhead.

Lighting also plays a leading role in this design. An automatic dimming system brightens or diminishes the light from exposed bulbs that rim the skylights. Lights over the raised platforms—the "theater areas," as Plummer calls them—are also automatically dimmed when the old movies are about to begin.

Although the budget was pretty open-ended, Plummer kept prices down by showing restraint in his application of surface finishes and ornament and by relying on slick, high-end materials, such as black ceramic tile for the walls, and architectural solutions to give the space all the flash and drama it needed.

Total size, excluding the kitchen, is 2,450 square feet. The restaurant seats 126.

McDONALD'S	Raleigh, North Carolina
Owner:	McDonald's Corporation
Architecture:	Fred Tolson Associates (William Friend)
Interior Design:	Perry & Plummer Design Associates (D. Gordon Plummer, Rodney D. Carman)
General Contractor:	Ratley Construction Company
Audio and Project Systems:	Stage & Studio Construction Services
Neon Lighting Consultant:	Howard System
Lighting Control System:	Prescolite Corporation
Photography:	© Rick Alexander & Associates, Inc.

97

DON'T USE A COOKIE CUTTER
REPEATABLE ELEMENTS ARE PERSONALIZED FOR EACH LOCATION

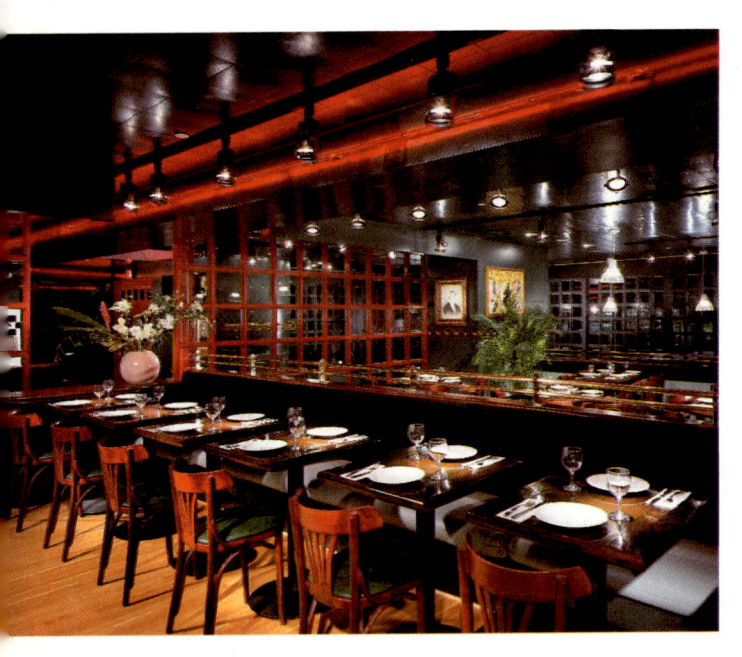

In the Secaucus Pizzeria Uno, designer Charles Morris Mount generated excitement with a vermilion and green color scheme and a ceiling treatment of acoustical tile, track lighting, and mirrors. Neon ceiling strips repeat circulation patterns below.

FORTY YEARS AGO, a Chicagoan named Ike Sewell developed a unique recipe for pizza and called it "deep dish." Imitators of his thick, flaky-crusted pie have since introduced "Chicago-style" pizza to the rest of the country. But until five years ago, Sewell's authentic product was only available at Pizzeria Uno, his own world-famous joint on Wabash Street, and at an annex across the street, dubbed Pizzeria Due.

An entrepreneur named Aaron Spencer, president of Boston-based International Food Service Inc., changed that. In 1979 he consummated a deal with Sewell to take the Pizzeria Uno concept—and its top-secret recipe—national.

Already there are about thirty Pizzeria Unos across the country. The installations in New York City and suburban New Jersey bear lively witness to the growing group's design approach.

While each new facility serves the same special pizza as the original Uno, it could never offer the same atmosphere. Spencer had to replace the uniqueness of the original environment with an expanded menu and emphatically interesting spaces in order to match the pulling power of the Chicago flagship.

Thus, the Pizzeria Uno master plan includes varied and healthful menu alternatives, a full-service bar, a real restaurant atmosphere with well-trained wait staff, and prices that remind customers that this is still, after all, a pizza shop.

From the start, Spencer wanted each Pizzeria Uno to be "comfortable and warm, but not intimidating." He wanted a consistent design philosophy, but not a cookie-cutter formula. "Every place we open, we try to make a neighborhood restaurant. We've got to be able to change things to fit in, and not feel like a fast food operation," he explains.

The two facilities shown here, both designed by Charles Morris Mount of New York City, illustrate how the concept works. Seen together, similarities between the installations are instantly recognizable. But there are remarkable differences as well, showing how the elements can be adjusted to blend in with a neighborhood and attract different clientele. The environmental and social differences between the two locations are quite pronounced: One of the facilities sits in a newly-opened shopping mall in suburban New Jersey, the other in the heart of New York City's Greenwich Village.

Both use black and white tile for all floors and for some wall surfaces. The checkerboard tile concept—now a trademark—was initiated in an earlier unit, now open in Boston, designed by Morris Nathanson of Providence, Rhode Island. (Spencer credits Nathanson for developing much of the Pizzeria Uno design philosophy.)

PIZZERIA UNO   Secaucus, New Jersey; New York City

Owners: Tom Viola (Secaucus),
   International Food Service (New York City)

Interior Design: Charles Morris Mount, principal;
   Tony Chi, project designer

Graphics: Ted Panagopoulos

Photography: © H. Durston Saylor

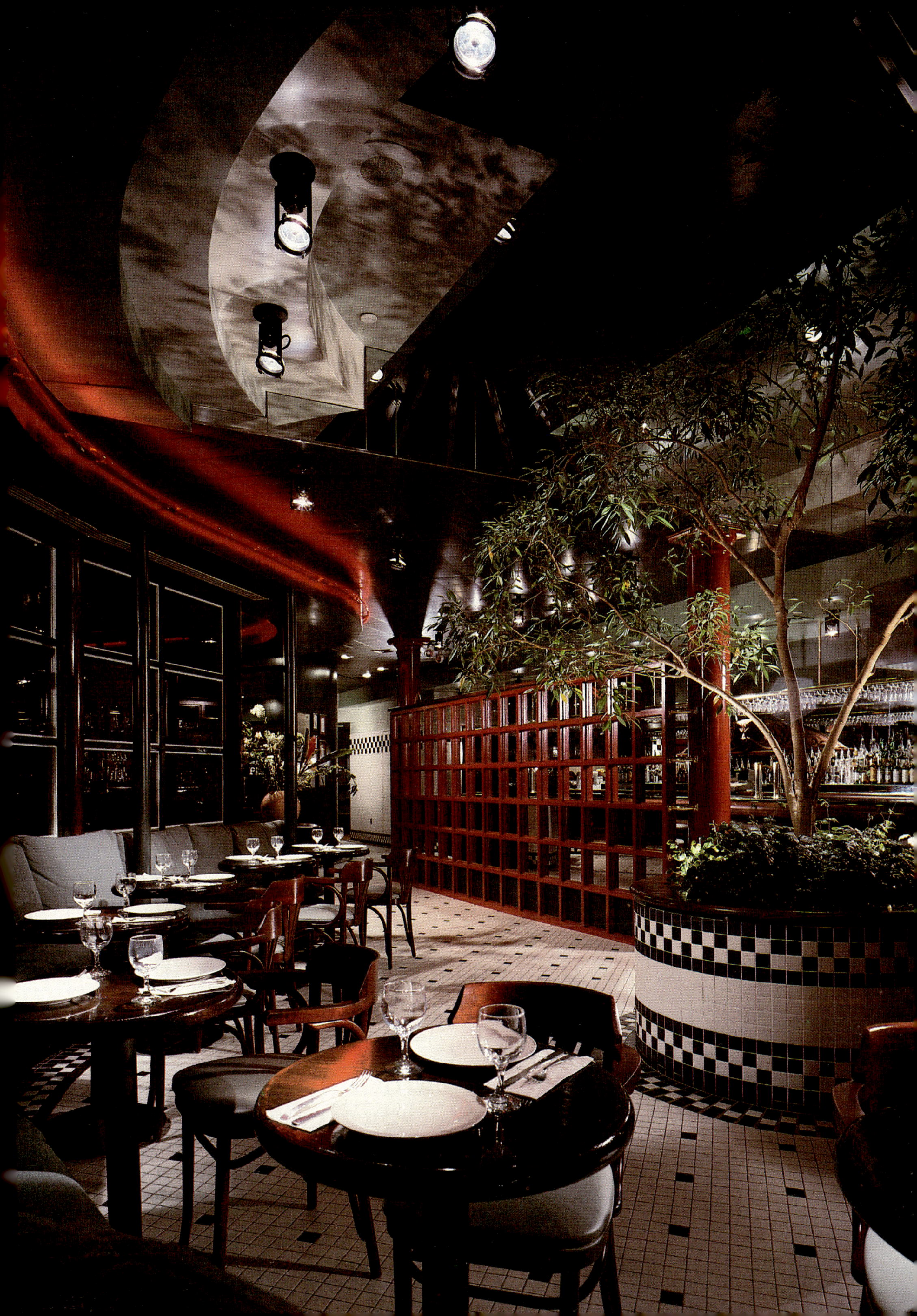

Mirrors, painted wood, and brass, also used in the Boston prototype, complete the surfaces in both of Mount's installations. The two new restaurants also use the same mahogany-stained furnishings. Most importantly, both restaurants are clearly divided into a distinct cocktail lounge and small dining areas, creating a private feeling.

In the 176-seat New Jersey location, the restaurant's market is young and casual. Because the shopping mall's design is indistinct, the restaurant had to add all of its own excitement: Brilliant vermilion and several shades of green brighten the atmosphere and, says Mount, subliminally refer to the colors of the Italian flag. The dining areas are a series of levels, anchored by a circular lounge that feels like a greenhouse.

In New York City, another set of influences are at work. Greenwich Village's Sixth Avenue, visible from nearly every seat, provides all the excitement and drama a diner could want. So Mount and project designer Tony Chi concentrated on creating warmth and intimacy. At the same time, the historic character of the area demanded a more conservative approach, both inside and for the renovated facade.

By using a traditional spiral-patterned floor tile, pendant glass fixtures, and tongue-and-groove wall paneling, New York's Pizzeria Uno recalls the speakeasies and old-time restaurants of the city in the twenties.

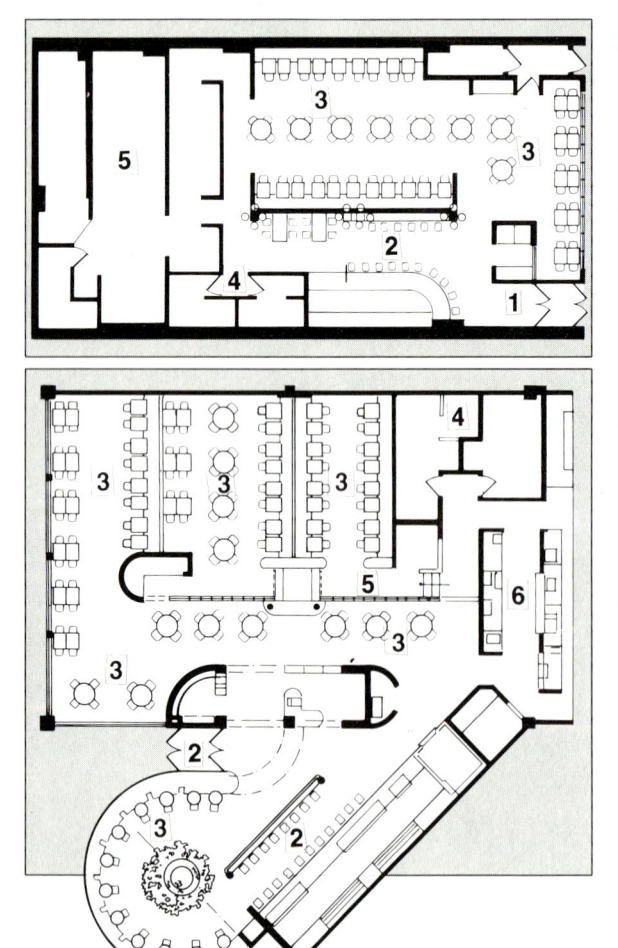

For the New York Pizzeria Uno (above), Mount emphasized the old-time feeling of twenties restaurants with pendant glass fixtures and tongue-and-groove paneling. The checkerboard motif, repeated here, has become a trademark for all the installations. Floorplans: New York (top): entry (1); bar (2); dining area (3); restrooms (4); kitchen (5). Secaucus: (bottom) entry (1); bar (2); dining area (3); restrooms (4); wait station (5); kitchen (6).

CREATE A PROTOTYPE FOR A RESTAURANT CHAIN
DESIGNERS' VIEWPOINTS: PROBLEMS AND REWARDS OF PROTOTYPE DESIGN

For the A&W installation (left) in a Short Hills, New Jersey, mall, architect Charles Boxenbaum created versatile design elements that can be easily adapted to other sites. An example is this service kiosk, which also serves to attract mall shoppers for a quick snack. Photography: © Norman McGrath.

ANY FLEDGLING DESIGNER, or seasoned pro for that matter, would be reluctant to pass up an opportunity to design a restaurant that might be replicated nationwide, or even citywide.

Webster's calls a prototype "a first full-scale and usually functional form of a new type of design of a construction." To some designers, a project is considered a "prototype" even if it is a one-time installation with only a speculative chance of being replicated elsewhere—The Big Splash (shown earlier in this chapter) designed by Haverson/Rockwell Architects for the Benihana Corporation in Fort Lauderdale, Florida, being an example of such a one. At the time of this writing, The Big Splash Restaurant had appeared on television in several "Miami Vice" episodes, but it is still uncertain whether the restaurant, designed as a prototype, will be built on other sites.

To conservative architects like veteran chain-restaurant designer Bill Babcock of Babcock & Schmid Associates, Bath, Ohio, a design is not really a prototype until it has been thoroughly market-tested and rated ready for rollout. "Only when it has proven itself on the bottom line does an installation become a true prototype," Babcock says. "Before that, it's really just a pilot project." Babcock speaks with authority:

Since its launch in the late 1960s, Babcock & Schmid has created successful prototype designs for some of the biggest names in the fast food business—Burger King, Kentucky Fried Chicken, Ponderosa, and Straw Hat, among others.

The difference between pilot and prototype isn't just a matter of semantics, though. Not every designer who is capable of creating an excellent pilot design is willing to make the aesthetic compromises that go along with adapting a pilot for multisite rollout. But most large design firms take this in stride. "With chain prototypes, a designer does not always have control over what a franchisee will put into the unit," Babcock says. "That is why once our pilot projects have been tested by the corporations that commission them—sometimes for as long as two years—we try to offer alternatives for carpet, furniture, fixtures, and so on when we specify the prototype design."

Despite the difficulty of maintaining aesthetic control over installations by different franchisees in scattered geographic areas, it can be easier to work with a large chain than with an independent entrepreneur, says Babcock. "Corporate enterprises have ongoing marketing studies of what does and does not succeed, based on bottom line sales. This is good for the design firm, because there's less ego involvement on manage-

At an Arby's prototype (above) designed to attract a more upscale market, Associated Space Design of Atlanta worked out this sleek, stylish interior with high ceilings, large windows, and aluminum blinds. Photography: © Arby's.

The entrance arch and rusticated facade of Coffee Works (opposite) in Morristown, New Jersey, endow the small store with a look of permanence. Architect Martin Dorf of New York City used warm-toned woods for an upscale, inviting look. Photography: © Marty Dorf.

ment's side—and fewer costly mind-changes—than when the proprietor is an independent." Jerry Voith of FABRAP Architects in Atlanta, which completed a pilot project in Louisville, Kentucky, for Arby's, concurs: "Doing a pilot for market-testing before rollout is a challenge—it is always an experiment. You get to be creative, but you have so many judges you have to take the heat if it goes badly."

The number of people that get involved in such a situation can be a headache for the designer. For example, says Voith, projects undertaken for large corporations often require input from marketing, packaging, construction, and operations personnel. Arby's two years' of market studies showed that customers wanted more menu variety, better service, and a more attractive dining atmosphere, so they invited five architectural firms, including FABRAP, to compete for the pilot project. FABRAP translated Arby's program into a structure that departs radically from the standard "segmented rectangle" layout of a typical fast food restaurant. The new Arby's 3,700-square-foot building is defined by two rectangles set apart at an angle, joined and buffered by a triangular entry and product display space. The service area/kitchen is housed in one of the rectilinear compartments, while the dining pavilion is situated in the other. On the exterior, a curving wall extends beyond the superstructure to shield patio diners from the bustle of passing traffic.

After the Louisville project underwent six months of testing, another pilot installation opened in Atlanta to shake out the problems. After two years of testing the two pilots are refined, and a single prototype has emerged.

FABRAP does not expect to retain control of a design once it is off the firm's drawing board. "This business is too complicated for that," Voith acknowledges. "Even in the Louisville store, we had to put the exit signs where we didn't want them because of the fire laws." The firm does, however, charge a fee for the reuse of its prototype designs. "We will sell the drawings to the franchisee, but for site adaptation they will often go to a local firm," Voith points out.

There is no consensus among operators about whether a prototype design can be successfully rolled out nationwide or if it is better to have variations by geographic market area. For the larger restaurant chains, prototype designs are often replicated in just a few market areas at a time, thus minimizing risks. Just as often, different prototypes are commissioned for different geographic areas or markets.

The issue of payment for replication of a prototype design is also a controversial one, tangled in the thickets of copyright law and rooted in the question, "Who owns the design?" The larger design firms tend to charge a one-time fee for the design, whether it spawns ten replications or a few hundred. Babcock & Schmid, for example, work purely on a fee basis to develop the design concept. Says Bill Babcock, "If we do a site adaptation for subsequent installations, we are paid for that, of course, but not for replication itself."

New York architect Charles Boxenbaum believes the designer ought to retain both ownership of the design and control over the rollout, but he concedes that that is not usually the case. "Although the design really does belong to its creator, payment or royalty for replication can only be assured if specified in the initial contract," Boxenbaum notes. "And that is something you can insist upon if, and only if, you have sufficient leverage. If you own the design, you can control the quality of additional installations and also make money from it. But everybody, the proprietor as much as the architect, wants to own the design."

Boxenbaum does not, in fact, "own" the spirited elements he designed for a new A&W installation in a Short Hills, New Jersey, mall. "A&W had already started construction when they decided the design for this space was not right. They hired us to come up with something that would look good— something that would upgrade the chain's image and be adaptable to different spaces in malls around the country. We created a series of elements: a service kiosk, a group of freestanding product display panels we call 'foodstones,' and some window panels with supergraphics that reference A&W's history. These elements can be used in any mall space."

Cost, as noted earlier, is an important consideration in designing an installation intended as a prototype. Marty Dorf (Dorf Associates, New York City) points out the pitfall of having a more generous budget for the pilot (especially when an independent entrepreneur is involved) than for the rollout, which must be "financeable."

"When you plan a prototype for a new concept, such as the coffee-by-the-pound-or-cup facility we just completed in Morristown, New Jersey," says Dorf, "the owner is very concerned with attracting the interest of investors and mall developers. However, it is not cheap to do the kind of exciting store that will attract franchisees or mall managers. You must spend money to make it exciting, but if it does take off, the developers may be handicapped by having to replicate it at cost."

Dorf's prototype project, Coffee Works, is a 720-square-foot store that cost $130,000 to build and equip with fixtures, according to owner Paul Kastl. Dorf and Kastl worked closely together from the start of the Coffee Works project on all aspects of implementation, including marketing the concept to prospective developers. They hope to bring the cost of replication down to $105,000 while expanding the square footage by 15 percent for future installations in other New Jersey malls.

Prototypes are not commissioned only for brand-new projects. Marketplace repositioning of a restaurant, vis-à-vis menu or customer base, often compels large chains to commission prototype designs that will reflect a change and consolidate a new image. For example, when the York's chain decided to move away from its familiar Tudor-style steakhouse position toward restaurants with the wider menu of Choices—which purveys fresh foods and take-out items—they hired Babcock & Schmid to create a pilot store in a Troy, Michigan, mall. The resulting restaurant is cheery and warm, with an open facade to attract mall customers and to encourage the sale of a wide variety of retail foods at a frontal counter.

According to firm principal and project designer Jurig Schmid, "The York's people did a lot of strategic planning ahead of time, but we had a free hand in expressing the concept. We wanted a warm and comfortable environment, not so high-style as to be intimidating."

The increasingly sophisticated marketplace has called for the repositioning of many familiar chains, especially those in big cities like New York.

Repositioning can be a touchy issue, because owners don't want to put off the tried-and-true customers who have come to count on a certain menu and look they find reliable. At the same time, a thoughtful revamp can mean holding onto customers and attracting new ones. To update a Wendy's in New York City, for example, New York architect Lew Dolin took on this challenge. The owner didn't want "a slick and cold redo"; he wanted something old-fashioned and authentic. At the time Dolin was given the job, the standard Wendy's design package tended toward thin veneer, plastic-face Tiffany-style lamps, and plastic tin ceilings.

Dolin responded by using Wendy's theme colors (black, red, yellow, and white) in a more sophisticated way. He had entire sections of the restaurant painted, including walls, chairs, table edges, and plant holders, in these bright, primary colors. The fields of primary color evoke a more dynamic, sophisticated look. In addition, Dolin installed real tin ceilings and hung lamps with real glass shades, rather than the Tiffany look-alikes. Live plants and black paint over some of the simulated wood further upgraded the installation. Dolin even left an old brick wall bare.

In another example, California architect Mike Douglas worked out an "evolving" restaurant image. From two existing Sgt. Pepperoni's restaurants located in southern California, he produced a third, which combined elements of both into a new prototype. The first Sgt. Pepperoni's was infused with what Douglas described as "posthippie warmth," while the second Sgt. Pepperoni's adopted a high-tech graphic image.

What Douglas and owner Dave Patterson arrived at was a reuse of the redwood lath from the first Sgt. Pepperoni's—combined with other woods and sculpted into geometric forms recalling the high-tech style of the second, but warmed by rheostat-controlled hanging incandescent lights and fluorescent strip fixtures. The cartoon graphics, including a large yellow submarine dangling from the ceiling, are present but never overwhelming as they were in the second Sgt. Pepperoni's. The resulting amalgam pleased the owner; it was a successful attempt to reposition without destroying the original feeling and idea, to which customers were loyal.

While the current trend in developing or repositioning

York's Choices (right), in the Oakland Mall, Troy, Michigan, is Babcock & Schmid's prototype for a series of restaurants that will offer a wide menu of fresh foods as well as retail goods available at the kiosk. Photography: © Maquire Photographics.

For an update of a tried-and-true Wendy's prototype (above) architect Lew Dolin of New York chose natural materials, combined with the chain's signature primary colors. He used authentic tin ceilings and let the brick walls show. Photography: © H. Durston Saylor.

Built into the shell of a would-be savings and loan building, the third Sgt. Pepperoni's, in Irvine, California (above), features redwood lath strips sculpted into geometric forms. Other elements include suspended lighting and cartoon graphics, features from previous facilities that are combined here to create a new look. Photography: © Milroy/McAleer.

For Franks for the Memory (opposite), a prototype in Vancouver, B.C., that is located within a restored structure used as a rapid-transit terminal, the design theme is a simple one: a hot dog with everything. Photography: © Gary Otte.

FRANKS FOR THE MEMORY

prototypes for large chains relies heavily on market research, prototypes can be developed in a number of other ways.

Although it usually does not happen, it is possible for a marketable prototype concept to evolve fortuitously from a one-shot design project. That was the outcome when Canadian designer Shelly Mirich of Mirich Developments was hired to design a hot dog stand inside a restored landmark being used as a rapid-transit terminal.

Mirich rejected a costly idea to continue the architectural detailing of the building into the area of the stand. Instead, he tried blending the stand with the building using similar colors for a more radical and marketable fantasy. The designer used every kind of event associated with the consumption of the classic hot dog and accompanying malts, popcorn, and soda pop and called it "Franks for the Memory."

Every inch of the resulting restaurant carries with it some association with a sporting event, fair, or carnival. The floor is covered with synthetic turf, with a mannequin near the entrance dressed as a vendor. Crowd control barriers convert to a stand-up eating bar flanked with chain link fence. Restaurant equipment is hidden behind a bay of gym lockers. Menus are designed to look like scoreboards. With so many easy-to-repeat elements that have no stringent space requirements, the concept for Franks for the Memory became an excellent one for a prototype, ready for the road.

5. THEMATIC

DESIGNS

There was a time when a "designed" restaurant *was* a theme restaurant. The province of family dining, the traditional theme restaurant had a formula as predictable as sunrise. For example, a seafood establishment required several yards of fishnet, clusters of glass floats, and perhaps a life ring. Just as ubiquitous (and hackneyed) was the "nostalgia" theme restaurant decorated with vintage photos, roughhewn boards, and Victorian knick-knacks.

Today, the trend is toward more sophisticated theme establishments. Their "authentic" ambience, achieved by serious research into a specific time, place, or idea, is intended to steep patrons in a special mood or to create a three-dimensional fantasy. Over the past few years, theme restaurants like Ruby's (opposite) in Balboa, California, have emerged. In the case of Ruby's, the time is World War II and the forties atmosphere is resonant, created by such carefully selected details as a vintage cigarette machine and red vinyl booths.

In today's theme restaurant, decorations have become integral to the design; they are not simply hung on walls. At Liberty Cafe (designed by MGS Architects in New York City) the idea of freedom is conveyed by wheeling gulls, expansive views, and a map mural of the United States that covers an entire long wall and part of the floor. Terrazzo "rivers" even flow down the stairs. At Extra! Extra!, designed by Sam Lopata in the New York Daily News Building, the newspaper is the key element.

No detail is extraneous. Everything serves the central idea; the layering of detail enriches the experience. Special effects can be quite elaborate. In Bubbles—a vintage Miami Beach deco nightclub re-created in Newport Beach, California—a brightly lit, larger-than-life plexiglas column of "champagne" bubbles from floor to ceiling, where still more bubbles gently waft from air vents.

Pretty is not a requisite for today's theme restaurant, but authenticity is. On the next page, Pirelli tile floors and a car's front-end parts take on new meaning. In this world of make-believe, everything is possible.

CHOOSE AN AUTOMOTIVE THEME
A 1930s "GARAGE" UTILIZES EASY-CARE MATERIALS THAT LOOK INDUSTRIAL

TENLY ENTERPRISES had the name, the menu, a 50- by 100-foot cement block shell, and the idea for a theme restaurant centered on automotive artifacts and memorabilia when they approached designers Banik-Cumby of Swarthmore, Pennsylvania, to pull it together.

It took the design team six weeks to refine the concept. At the library they researched old garages and settled on a look from the 1930s that could be created with old-style materials such as brick, shingles, beaded board, wrought-iron hardware and plank floors—and with contemporary industrial supplies that would be durable and functional yet evocative of another time and place.

Pirelli tile floors, glass block, carpeting, top-of-the-line office furniture, authentic car seats, metal deck roofing, exposed ducts, and sprinkler system, mag wheel tables and Mercedes Benz seats, old license plates, and bins of nuts and bolts were installed to evoke the atmosphere of an automobile repair shop.

"One of the main considerations when designing this restaurant," explains Jane Banik, "was to give returning customers a sense of variety by providing several separate dining areas in addition to the bar and lounge. We accomplished this by installing a 'pit' dining area and a mezzanine, as well as two raised platform areas."

Creating the old-time atmosphere was a challenge that the designers accomplished in straightforward and unusual ways. The designers took inspiration from old photographs and antique cars. They haunted flea markets and antique shops. They created sculpture from old auto parts and booths from carriage seats. Even the carpeting, in a particularly tight weave, was selected because it resembled the type used in old cars.

Originally, Tenly Enterprises had expected to attract young adults, aged twenty-one to thirty-five, to their theme restaurant. But they discovered that the nostalgic atmosphere appeals not just to the young, but to car buffs of all ages.

CURLY'S GARAGE *Salisbury, Maryland*

Owner: *Tenly Enterprises Inc. (now a wholly owned subsidiary of Sizzler Restaurants International)*

Architecture/Interior Design: *Banik-Cumby, Swarthmore, Pennsylvania*

Budget: *$2.5 million*

Time: *9 months*

Completion: *1985*

Seating: *228*

Photography: *© Barry Halkin*

A 1930s Ford radiator, bumper, and headlights is the graphic symbol for Curly's restaurant, where auto memorabilia is the order of the day. The photomural on the far wall of the mezzanine shows just one day's production at Detroit's Ford plant in the early thirties. Along with materials such as exposed pipe, beaded board, rubber tile, and top-of-the-line office furniture, such artifacts help set the automotive theme.

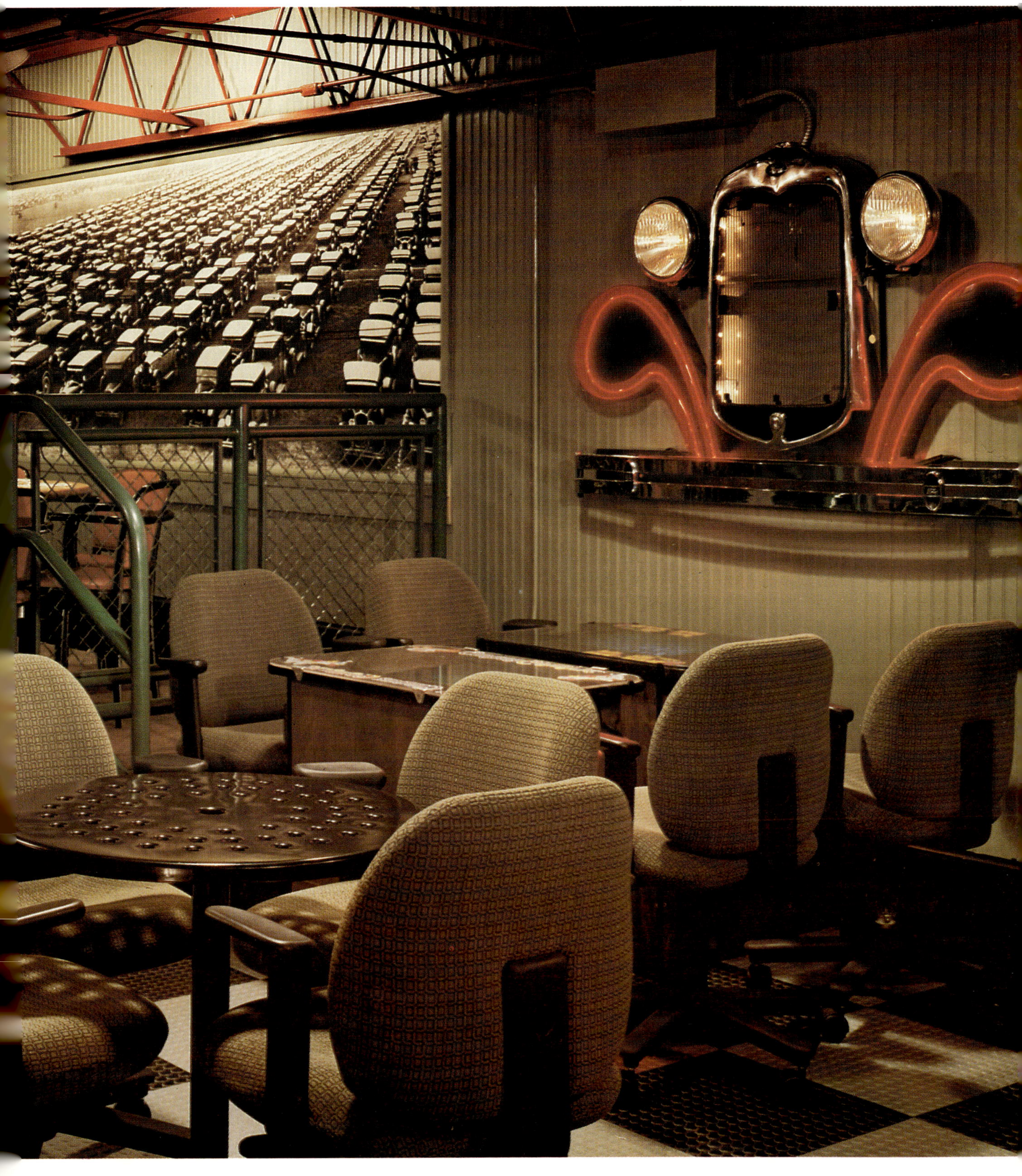

IMPLY FREEDOM WITH IMAGERY
WHEELING GULLS AND A MAP OF WIDE OPEN SPACES SUGGEST LIBERTY

Tiered seating (left) assures every diner a grandstand view at Liberty Cafe. The platform is covered with lightweight epoxy terrazzo in sunny colors that pick up wall mural details (right).

LIBERTY CAFE'S CONCEPT arose from a brainstorming session among owners Bob Stetcher and Gerard Renny and the MGS Architects. Subliminally, some things may have been suggested by the space—6,000 square feet perched atop South Street Seaport's Pier 17—but the owners and architects say not.

The choice of decorative details was unusual: a map mural, sculptured seagulls, and a miniature train that chugs around the bar on a recessed track. "These are all symbols of freedom," says Bill Soloway. "The name Liberty, when it came up, seemed to fit right in." That the restaurant commands a panoramic view of the East River with the Statue of Liberty as centerpiece was fortuitous.

"When we were negotiating with the Rouse Company—South Street Seaport's developers—we knew only that we wanted a unique restaurant in a unique place," says Stetcher. "We hadn't yet settled on the name or the theme; it just had to have terrific food, and it had to be fun. Our target customers,

LIBERTY CAFE	*New York City*
Owner:	*Razamataz Inc.*
Architecture:	*MGS Architects (E. McClintock, A. Grammenopoulous, W. Soloway, with S. Rose, R. Laufer)*
Lighting Consultant:	*Consolidated Edification*
Mechanical Engineer:	*Abraham Joselow*
Electrical Engineer:	*Chester Schiff*
Kitchen Consultant:	*Basic Leasing*
Contractor:	*George Hoffman & Sons Inc.*
Budget:	*$1.1 million*
Size:	*6,000 square feet*
Photography:	*© Mark Darley*

New Yorkers aged twenty-five to forty, don't want to be serious when they go out to eat. They want to relax and enjoy themselves."

Enjoyment is the very *raison d'etre* of Pier 17, a promenade-encircled complex of trendy shops and restaurants that is part of the South Street Seaport Landmark District. The space Stetcher and Renny acquired early in 1985—a 30- by 180-foot strip on the pier's third level—is enclosed by a south-facing greenhouse that opens onto a dining deck. There's a breathtaking view of the Seaport's restored ships, the lower Manhattan skyline, the East River, and the harbor beyond.

To make the most of their special site, Stetcher and Renny interviewed many designers before tracking down MGS Architects (New York City), creators of the successful Ernie's café. The low-profile young threesome—Libby McClintock, Anthony Grammenopoulos, and Bill Soloway—were just finishing America, another soon-to-be New York City hit restaurant.

Liberty's two entrances—one on Pier 17's escalator atrium, the other on its eastern promenade—initiate a spatial progression from opposite ends of the restaurant toward a central tiered seating platform that Soloway calls "the main physical event in the space." Rows of circular columns and glass-globed torchieres, plus exposed ductwork hung with a flock of plaster gulls, penetrate Liberty's long axis, drawing the eye inward and defining the traffic flow from entrance to entrance.

Guests arriving from the atrium side pass a small, railed-off cappuccino bar on an elevated platform to the right; to the left is a colorful food display counter, fronting an open kitchen where the cooking is finished. "The lively kitchen activity is intended to draw passersby from the escalator area," McClintock explains. The less-sightly prep kitchen—a long, sliver-like space—is hidden behind the mural wall. To accommodate heavy cocktail-hour business from nearby Wall Street, Liberty's bar is situated near the east entrance, where the view is best and standees can spill out onto the adjoining promenade deck.

"We kept the interior plan simple because the view is the main attraction," McClintock notes. Liberty's primary decorative detail, the large mid-America map mural, was painted on 6-foot muslin strips at EverGreene Studios (New York City) while other construction proceeded. Seams were overpainted after mounting. The mural's blue rivers flow right down into the epoxy terrazzo dado and flooring of the platform. "Epoxy terrazzo comes in great synthetic colors," says Soloway, "and it doesn't need special structural support, because it's so lightweight." A bright tile floor, pale oak chairs, and white napery contribute to Liberty's sunny ambience. In the evening, strategic downlights give the mural a soft glow; tables are spotlighted, and the row of torchieres becomes a dramatic accent.

Liberty accommodates 263 diners indoors and 130 on the deck, which the owners hope eventually to enclose. The bar seats 42 and stands 18 indoors, 30 outdoors. Stetcher says cost overruns "due to trade unions" nearly doubled the café's original $1.1 million budget.

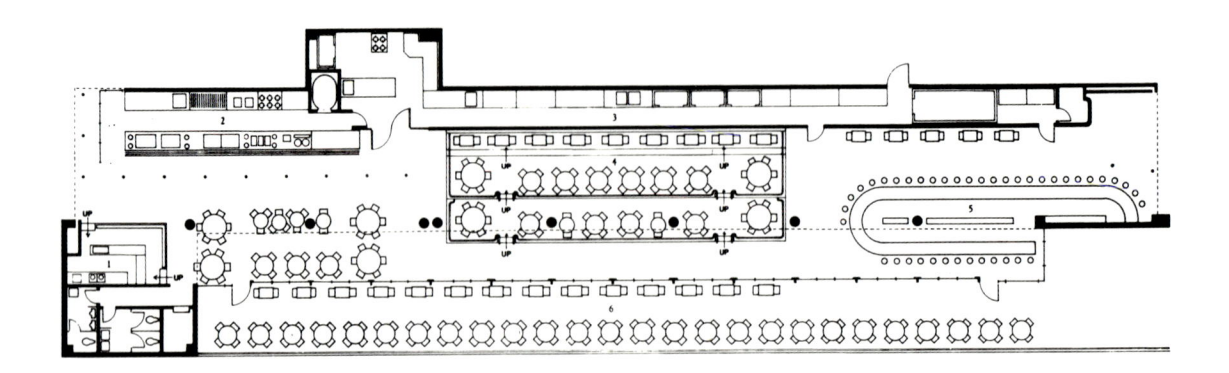

Bar (opposite) is enlivened by an electric train (not shown). A seagull overhead has 6-foot wingspread. Glass awnings on a track enclose indoor dining area (left); additional seating on promenade deck overlooks restored ship, Wavertree.

The floorplan shows dual entrances on east/west ends of Liberty Cafe. Placement of kitchen facilities was dictated by existing ductwork; the woodburning pizza oven with specially sprinklered and filtered chimney required a fireplace permit. Tight layout affords little storage for foodstuffs, so marketing is done daily.

REFINE A TEA ROOM WITH ART NOUVEAU
GRACEFUL CARVED SHAPES, ANTIQUE FURNITURE, AND IRON FRETWORK SET THE MOOD

The 4,800-square-foot Willow Tea Room features a meandering entrance corridor (opposite) linking dining areas. In the salon, right of the entrance, peacock-patterned linen upholstery lends a richness to seating. The main dining area (left) is defined with curling iron fretwork that is carried through from the entrance.

COLLABORATING WITH DESIGNER Michelle Pheasant-Angelo of Michelle Pheasant Design, Inc., Monterey, California, Joan and Don Miller chose refined Parisian Art Nouveau styles for their Willow Tea Room restaurant. "We didn't want to frighten people with Art Nouveau," says Don Miller. "So often it can be overdone: too elaborate, too decorative. We live in a comparatively stark period so we decided to go with examples of the pure French style. It's a little cleaner in its overall look."

The Millers' desire to embrace an Art Nouveau theme was no passing whim. Fifteen years ago, when Joan and Don Miller saw some Art Nouveau dining furniture at an antique show, something clicked. Their "discovery" generated such enthusiasm—now an obsession, they say—the Millers went on to found shops for Art Nouveau antiques, books, posters, and gifts. They subsequently taught a course in Art Nouveau at the University of California at Irvine, and finally opened the Willow Tea Room, centered around Art Nouveau furnishings, crafts, and styles.

Don Miller's studio and Pheasant's design firm aimed for a real sense of authenticity. Miller admits taking designs from others to achieve an effective result. "I believe in stealing. I don't believe the modern designer can create Art Nouveau. I don't believe you can escape your period. The only way to recreate is to refine existing designs," he says.

In keeping with the principles of the Art Nouveau movement, the Willow Tea Room is fully integrated aesthetically. Graceful shapes, serpentine ceiling coving, Art Nouveau fabric motifs, and coordinated tabletop furnishings create a cohesive look. An elaborate carved wood door opens to a meandering entry corridor that connects a private dining room, the salon, and the main dining room. Iron fretwork separates spaces and relates to gently curved, highly detailed fixtures—while also helping unify the interior.

According to Pheasant-Angelo, "The Millers gave us resource material to study; in essence we were educated about Art Nouveau by the Millers. This enabled us to direct the project and give an overall serpentine effect to the space. It was an unusual case, but the Millers were part of the design team and follow-through. We assisted in the detailing and execution."

Including custom work and handcarved furniture, the Willow Tea Room cost about $500,000.

WILLOW TEA ROOM	Carmel, California

Owners: WTR Studio

Interior Design: WTR Studio (Joan and Don Miller); Michelle Pheasant Design, Inc. (Michelle Pheasant-Angelo, principal; Linda Lamb; G. D. Case)

Budget: $500,000

Size: 4,800 square feet

Photography: © Russell Abraham

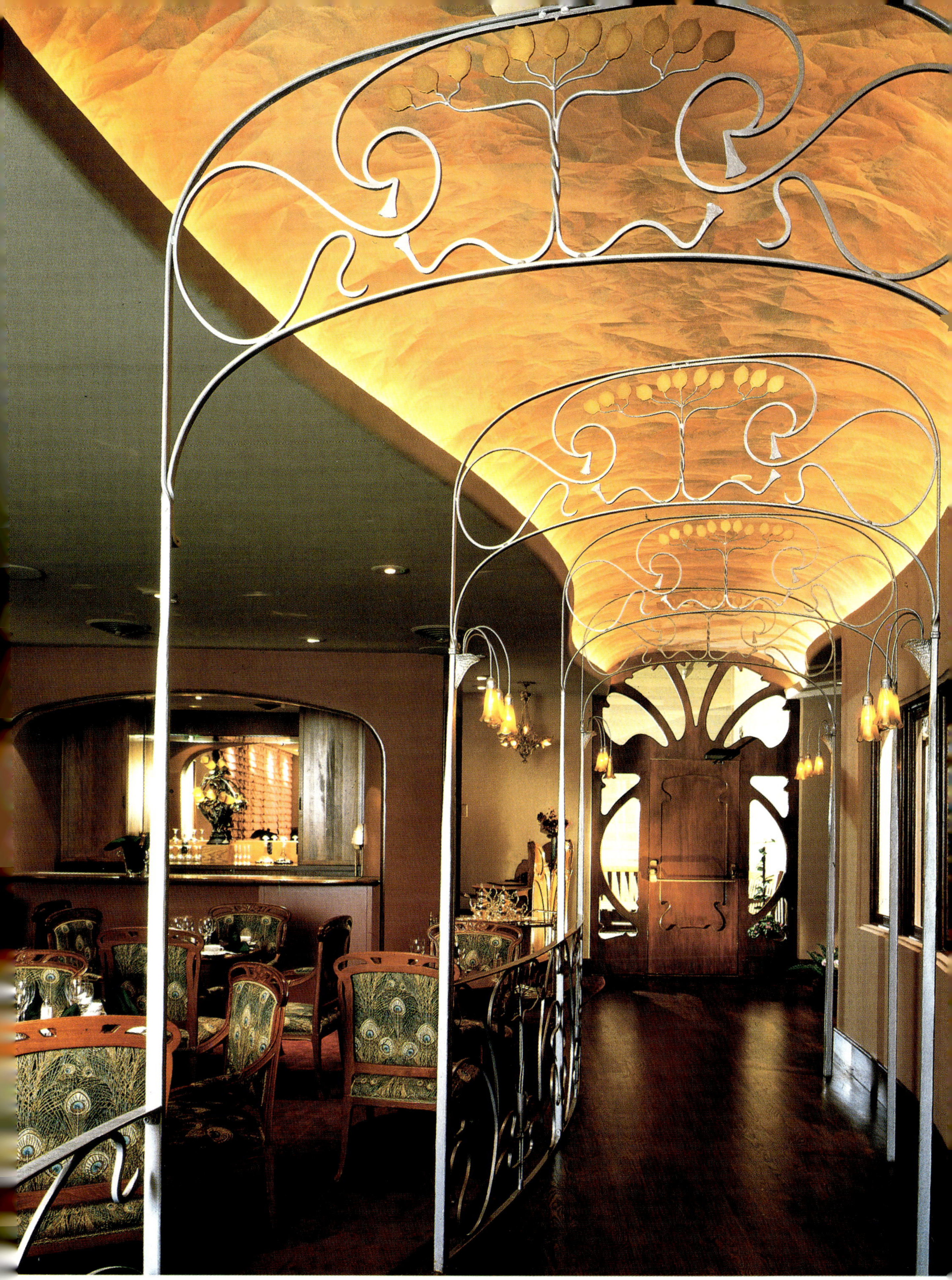

RECALL THE MOOD OF THE FORTIES
THE ESSENCE OF AN OLD DINER IS RECREATED AT THE END OF A PIER

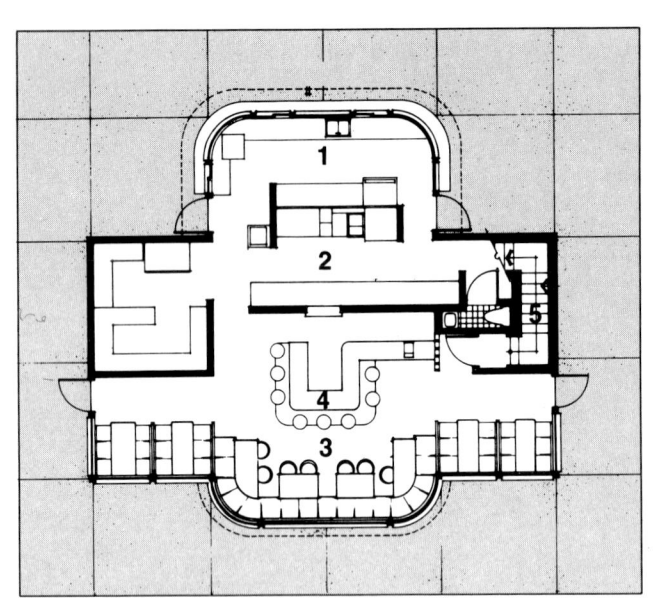

A vintage cigarette machine and original soft drink posters—used just as they might have been in the 1940s—contribute to an authentic period atmosphere (opposite). Floorplan: take-out area (1); kitchen (2); dining area (3); counter (4); stairs to roof (5).

RUBY'S IS A THRIVING re-creation of the spirit of American life in the period during and after World War II. Built as a bait shop in 1940, but vacant and rotting since about 1977, the symmetrical, boxlike structure that has become Ruby's featured rounded corners and lots of paned windows encased by simple frame construction. Doug Cavanaugh, a Balboa resident, and Ralph Kosmides were inspired by it.

"I admired its innate Art Deco design, streamlined corners and all," says Cavanaugh. The idea of a casual, diner-style restaurant seemed right for Balboa. The locals tend to be young and affluent, and the area's beaches attract visitors year-round. The subsequent commitment to rehabilitate the building to be consistent with its original period followed naturally. Cavanaugh is quick to note that the 1940s were the Balboa area's heyday, and that "despite the war, it seems like people had a lot of fun."

Before making a formal proposal to the city of Newport Beach, which owned the structure and the pier, Cavanaugh and Kosmides did their homework. They researched diners in general, and those of southern California in the 1940s in particular. Then they hired Thirtieth Street Architects of Newport Beach to draw up rehabilitation plans necessary for a formal proposal to the city.

In the end, the structure's exterior was kept intact, save for minor additions to the two flat sides (including building a stair for access to the building's rail-crowned flat roof). The interior was gutted. In its place a simple layout was wrought that provides for 50 diners at booths (placed along windows overlooking the water) and an old-fashioned counter.

Brown's and Cavanaugh's extensive research into the essence of forties diners paid off inside. The interior is a bright burst of sunny, white walls, a counter trimmed in stainless steel banding, unadorned windows, and accents of red vinyl on booths and counter stool tops. The floor is mottled black and white vinyl sheeting. Round, nautical windows, set into doors, and glass block wall extensions continue an architectural theme Brown terms "steamship moderne."

From the vintage (and completely rebuilt) cigarette machine and cash register to the mounted soda ads, the owners and Brown stuck to one thing that remains key to their successful, clean design: authenticity.

RUBY'S BALBOA DINER	*Balboa, California*
Owners:	*Doug Cavanaugh, Ralph Kosmides*
Interior Design:	*J. S. Brown Design (Scott Brown)*
Architecture:	*Thirtieth Street Architects*
Photography:	*© Milroy/McAleer (Mark Milroy)*

Yes
Coca-Cola
INSERT MONEY BELOW
THANK YOU FOR YOUR PATRONAGE
Cigarettes

START WITH A DEPRESSION DINER SCHEME
A 1920s RAILROAD DINING CAR SETS THE SCENE FOR NOSTALGIA

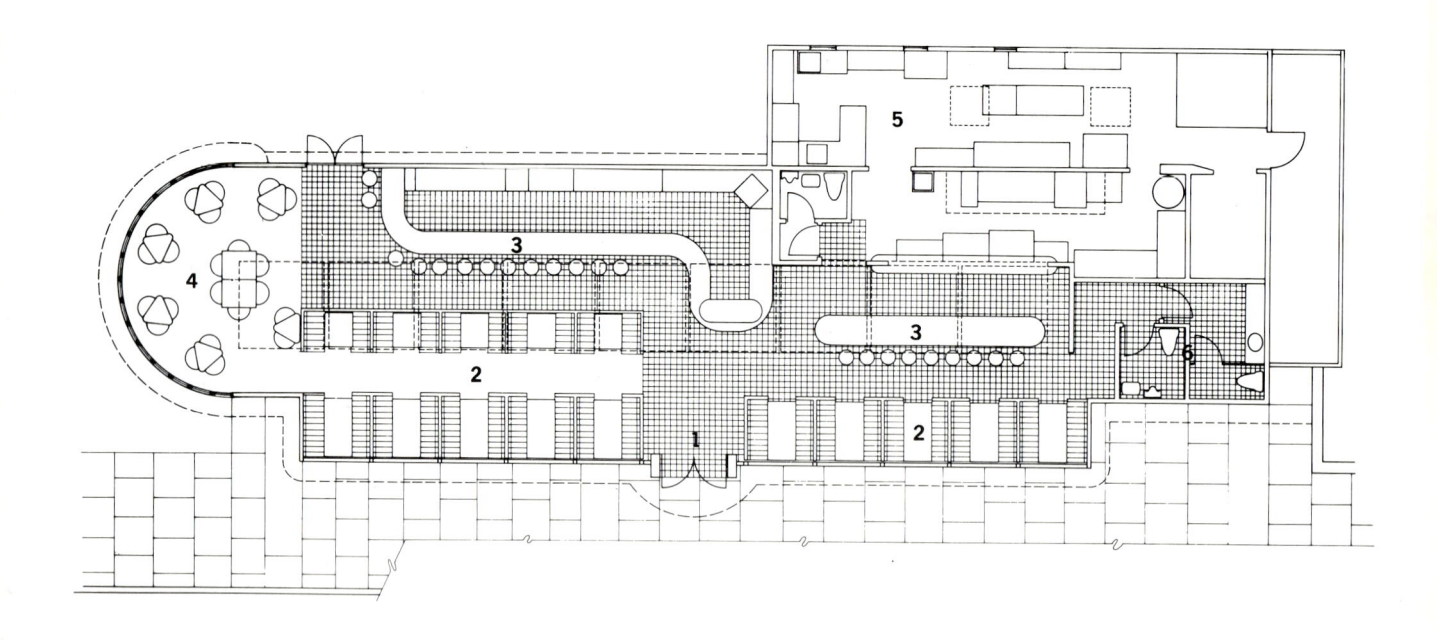

BACK IN THE DEPRESSION, diners offered hamburgers, apple pie, and coffee in a setting as starkly unadorned as that of an Edward Hopper painting. As the original diners succumbed to changing tastes, they were replaced by prettified pastiches with pricey menus and deco trim.

But for the Fog City Diner, architect/designer Patrick E. Kuleto took his cue not from the highway, but from the railroad tracks and the waterfront situated at the back of his site. The stainless steel and neon exterior has the familiar streamlined diner look. But the interior, with its brass fittings and polished woods, was inspired by 1920s railroad dining cars and the 1930s San Francisco–Oakland ferry.

The diner occupies the site of a World War II army garage, a decrepit shack that offered one advantage: Rebuilding within the same envelope required fewer permits than building on open ground, although the cost was higher. The site yielded 3,400 square feet, seating 112 in generously proportioned booths and accommodating 40 at the bar, with standing room for more. Big windows provide lots of natural light. At lunchtime, they can be lowered like those in an old-fashioned railroad car.

Many of the furnishings are custom-made. The overhead lamps are of handcrafted brass and hand-blown glass. The bar is topped with translucent Mexican onyx, with neon backlighting. Booth ends and rails are of mahogany, ebony, and walnut, repeatedly polished for a vintage feeling, and subtly curved to suggest an Art Deco fan. Checkerboard tiles (which also trim the facade) border booths and bar and are reflected in the mirror-finish stainless steel doors. A 50-seat extension, resembling the observation car on a 1940s train, will be added behind the bar, if planning approval can be secured.

Pat Kuleto has specialized in restaurant design for nearly twenty years; Fog City was his one hundred tenth project. It was built for owners Bill Higgins, Cindy Pawcyn, and Bill Upson at a cost of about $500,000, including furnishings and fittings.

Despite gracious craftsmanship, Fog City has more of the character of a hip brasserie than that of a traditional chophouse. It's an informal place where you can eat very well or very simply, and where the wine list rivals those of more pretentious restaurants.

FOG CITY DINER *San Francisco, California*
Owner: *Real Restaurants*
Interior Design: *Patrick E. Kuleto*
General Contractor: *Kuleto Consulting & Design*
Budget: *$500,000*
Size: *3,400 square feet*
Seating: *112*
Photography: *© Rob Buelteman*

Behind Fog City Diner's streamlined exterior is an interior inspired by 1920s railroad dining cars and the 1930s San Francisco–Oakland ferry. The floor-plan (opposite) harks back to the traditional Depression diner format: entrance (1); booth (2); bar seating area (3); table dining area (4); kitchen (5); restrooms (6).

MAKE A SPECIAL FOOD THE THEME
SPANISH PROPS, LIVELY COLORS CREATE ENERGY IN A TAPAS RESTAURANT

To step into Chicago's Cafe Ba-Ba-Reeba is to step into another world, to enter an atmosphere popping with color and a festive Spanish feeling. The concept emerged from pop restaurateur Rich Melman's Lettuce Entertain You Enterprises think tank. It follows the successful Ed Debevic's and Shaw's Crab House restaurants. Driving the theme was Melman's wish to introduce tapas—those delectable "little dishes" from Spain—to the Chicago palate in a setting that would be part fifties and part Madrid.

Toreador jackets hang from the ceiling. Imported olive oil bottles and pottery take their places on marble counters. Salt cod and hams, copper pots, garlands of garlic, basil, and dried red peppers hang from chrome railings along the ceiling. Paella and roasts are baked in a traditional wood-burning oven, imported from Spain and set into the wall under a brick arch.

"We asked ourselves what would define this restaurant as Spanish rather than Mexican," says Bill Aumiller, project team manager and partner of Aumiller/Youngquist P. C. (Mt. Prospect, Illinois). "The interpretation we came up with is expressed through color and materials."

One can imagine that young Ernest Hemingway would have felt at home in a place like this: a comfortable Spanish restaurant with worn floors, chairs of every style, bright peasant colors—a hearty place filled with cooking aromas. Despite its Spanish references, the space has a distinctly American flavor with subtle allusions to the imagery of the 1950s.

Wide curving chrome moldings, mahogany glass-front coolers, and plump, square red or turquoise bar seats are

CAFE BA-BA-REEBA *Chicago, Illinois*

Owner: *Lettuce Entertain You Enterprises*
  (Richard Melman, Marv Magid, Gabino Sotelino)

Architecture/Interior Design: *Aumiller/Youngquist P. C.*
  (Bill Aumiller, Jeff Everett, Maureen McFarlane,
  Mary Timm, Charles Bennett, Richard Melman)

Contractor: *Capitol Construction*

Mechanical Consultant: *G&C Consulting Engineers*

Photography: © *Mark Ballogg (Steinkamp/Ballogg)*

design elements that reach into the recent American past. The new wood floor, like the cabinetry, was made to look old. Patches were torn out of the floor and replaced with mismatched woods. "This was intended to create a certain comfort level in the restaurant," explains Aumiller.

Bright colors, architectural detailing, collage effects, and three open cooking areas generate energy and achieve the architects' wishes: "We wanted something that was very kinetic, not sedate," says Aumiller.

Turquoise, pinks, deep reds, blacks, and touches of gold and green are the colors most frequently used. They are strikingly combined in the artfully mismatched tile on the counter facings. Some areas of tile resemble Sonya Delaunay's patchwork quilts, while others chart countries on a map.

"We went to a tile supplier and asked to see his back lots," recalls Aumiller. "We let our imagination go and did what felt right. Eventually we carried it to the point where the design became irreverent, funky, even a little trashy."

The design team invited three artists, as well, to push their imaginations to the limit. They were commissioned to paint wall murals with Spanish, Chicago, and fun-loving party references. One mural has been dubbed "Picasso's Chicago Guernica" while another might be described as a cross between the work of Roy Lichtenstein and an animated music video. These murals add to the visual energy of the space and draw people through one room into the next.

Open cooking areas fulfill a similar function: They stimulate the senses and encourage patrons to move into and through the restaurant. The front counter area tempts diners with cold tapas; another section offers hot ones. Still other sections display hot entrees and desserts. "I hate to use this word," confesses Aumiller, "but we wanted to encourage 'grazing.' We wanted people to move around, to sample different foods. This kind of varied activity assures that each time a person returns to the restaurant, the experience will seem fresh and new."

The 215-seat Cafe Ba-Ba-Reeba cost $950,000 and covers 11,000 square feet. Excluding kitchen and support areas, 7,600 square feet are "actual, usable public space, laid out in sections to vary the mood," says Aumiller. "Above all, we wanted to keep things lively, colorful, moving."

Brightly colored toreador jackets hang from ceiling-height chrome rails above one of the tapas bars. Nearby, paella and roasts are baked in a traditional wood-burning oven imported from Spain.

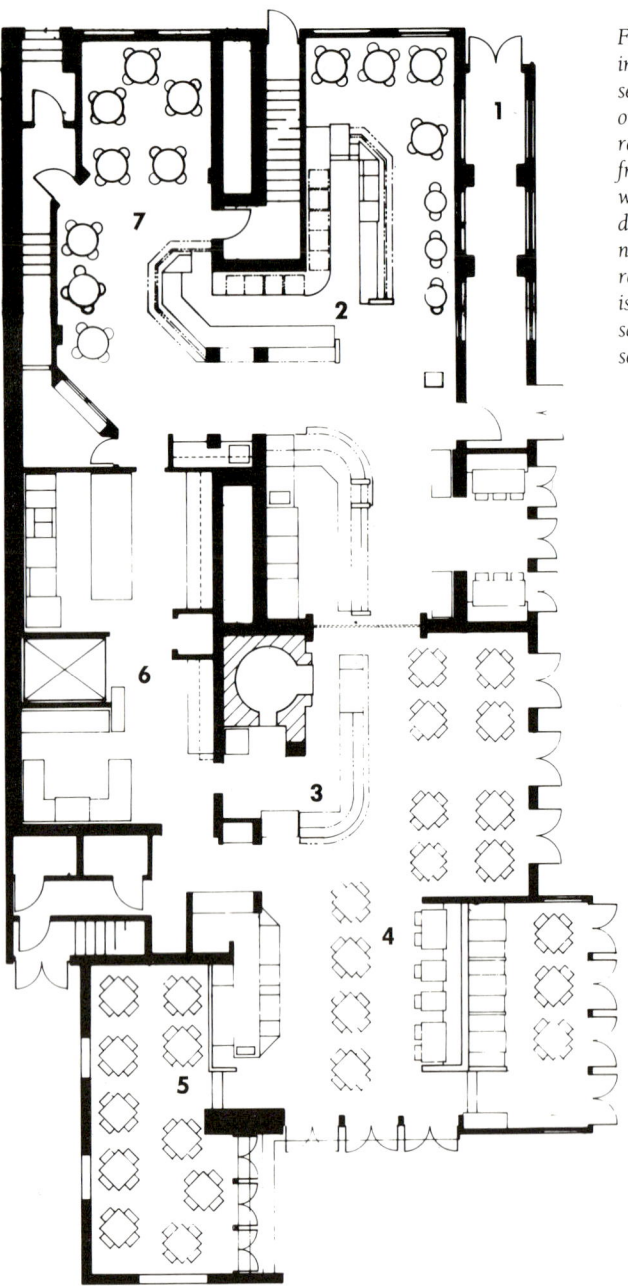

Floorplan: entrance (1); bar serving hot and cold tapas (2); hot serving area featuring Spanish oven (3); main dining area (4); rear dining area (5); kitchen (6); front dining area (7). Iron grillwork and a mural—playfully dubbed "Picasso's Chicago Guernica"—give Cafe Ba-Ba-Reeba's rear dining room (right) a Spanish atmosphere while plump square red and turquoise bar seats recreate a 1950s look.

125

REDO A RESTAURANT WITH LIVELY GRAPHICS
OLD-TIME FUNNIES, "INK," AND CROSSWORD PUZZLES ANIMATE A REHAB

WHAT'S BLACK AND WHITE and "read" all over? If you remember that old riddle, you'll relate right away to this work of designer Sam Lopata's restaurant whimsy. It's a perky overhaul of Extra!Extra!, a nearly new eatery on the ground level of New York City's landmark Daily News Building.

Walking in the door, one is surrounded by lifesize cutout characters from the old-time funnies—Wimpy, Dagwood, the Katzenjammer Kids, Mutt N' Jeff. The walls are alive with newsprint: A giant crossword puzzle runs up one wall; oversize personals provide an apt background for lunchtime gossip. Shiny splotches of "printer's ink" on the tile floor, carefully avoided by first-time customers, suggest a real, working news shop (in a sense, given the noon-hour business crowd, it is).

The theme simply cannot be ignored. It shouts. Lopata's gutsy remake is worlds away from the unassertive minimalism of the original Extra!Extra!, which opened to a ho-hum reception early in 1986. At first, says owner Jeff Spiegel, he was satisfied with lunchtime business, but soon he realized that a livelier ambience was needed to attract the after work and neighborhood dinner crowd. Lopata agreed with Spiegel that "the place had an identity problem. Nobody could see there was a restaurant in the building. We had to catch the eye of the passerby." Since the building's landmark status did not allow for changes to the facade, Lopata concentrated on making the interior graphics so compelling they would project right through the sidewalk-to-ceiling windows. He had a budget of $150,000 and a two-week time frame for construction and installation, following a three-month planning period.

"Before we could get to the fun stuff," Lopata says, "we had to deal with a layout problem. The restaurant is basically an open space on three levels, but it was functioning as three separate rooms, without a lot of customer interaction. We took out the little, formal mahogany bar and installed a big snake of a bar that curves around a corner, unifying the space. We also opened up the closed-in wait stations. After all, the servers' stations are part of the show."

Lopata kept the original tile flooring, splashing it with those disconcerting puddles of acrylic "ink." With lighting consultant Ken Billington, he worked out a plan that utilized the original lighting system, fixtures, and outlets, adding old-

Life-size cartoon figures (opposite and above) populate Extra!Extra!, setting the stage for lively informal dining. Throughout, the feeling is "open, to encourage mingling and moving around," says designer Sam Lopata.

EXTRA!EXTRA!	New York City
Owners:	Don Lubin, Jeff Spiegel, Tom Roline
Interior Design:	Sam Lopata, Inc.
Lighting Consultant:	Ken Billington, Inc.
General Contractor:	Wave Dancer, Ltd.
Electrical Contractor:	Albin Gustasson Company
Plumbing Contractor:	M. Krauss
Budget:	$150,000
Time:	14 weeks
Seating:	152
Photography:	© Milroy/McAleer

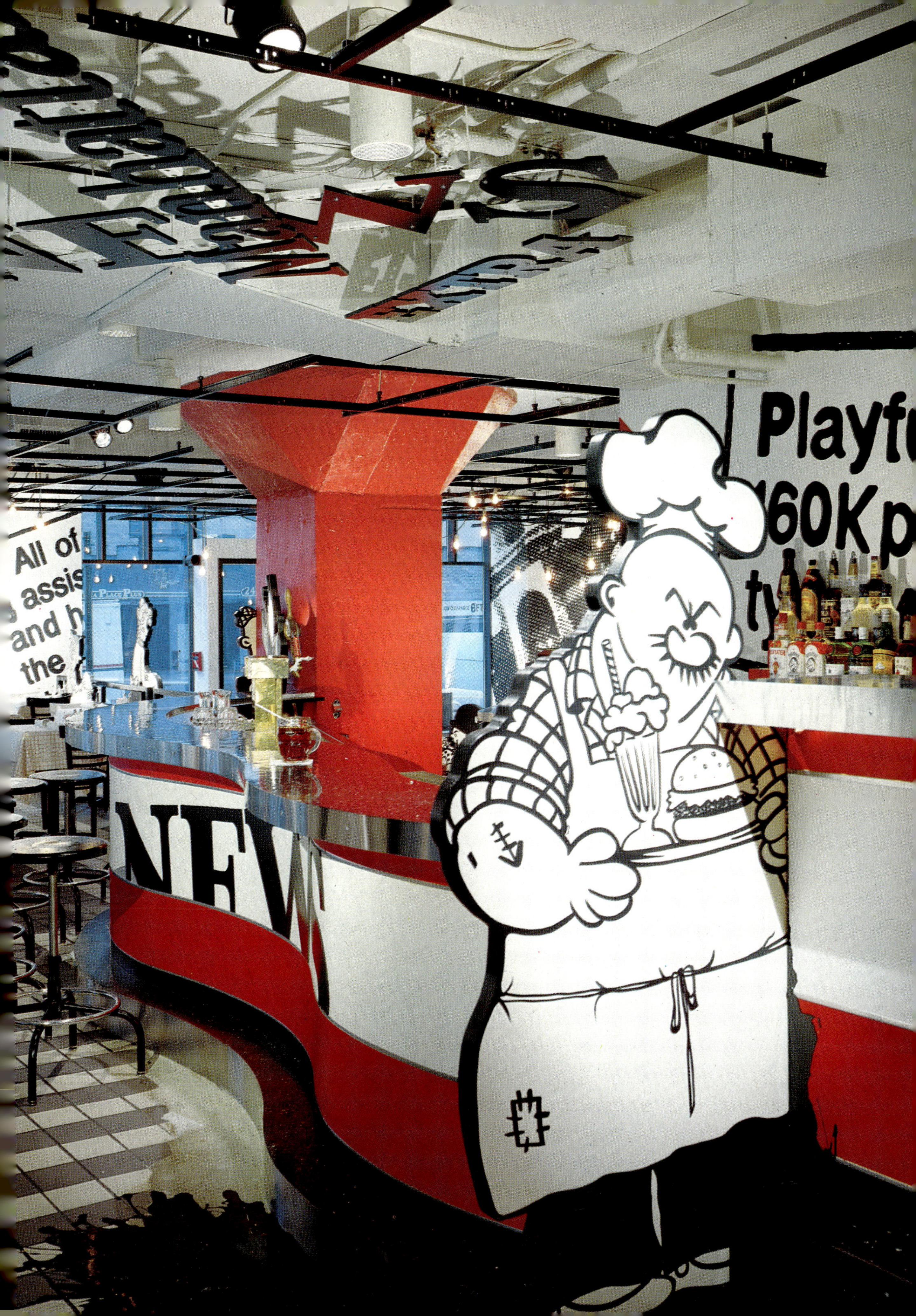
Playfu
160K p
All of
assis
and h
the
NEW

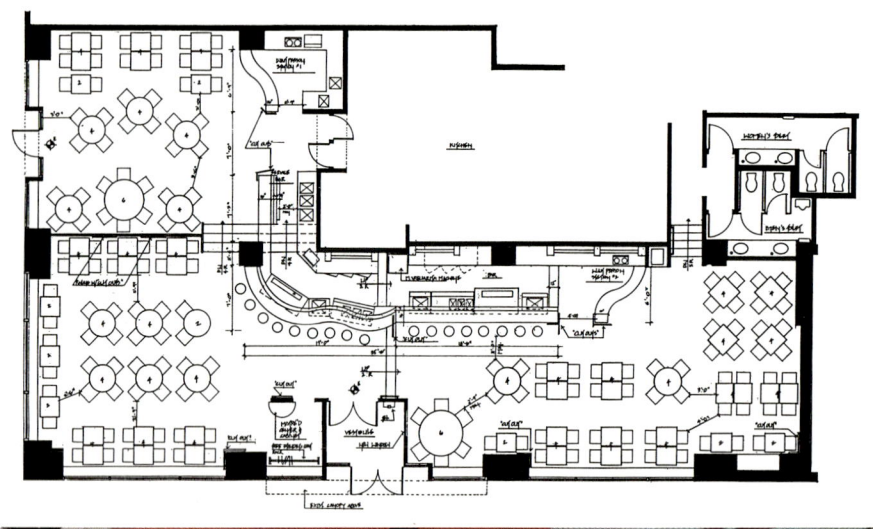

fashioned open-filament bulbs strung on wires from a grid. To cut costs, he also reused the original tables and chairs.

For the painted surfaces that give Extra!Extra! its zip, Lopata engaged Serpentine Studios (New York City), a team he often works with. "We did full elevations and planned the general idea and the cartoon characters," Lopata says. "Then Serpentine came in and painted. For the cartoon figures, we had to use a professional cartoonist; he was the only one who could understand how to blow them up to the size we needed. Even then, we had to be choosy. Dagwood worked, but Betty Boop and Dick Tracy just didn't make it in Big."

Today, the "new" Extra!Extra! seats 152 diners, with room for 18 at the bar. "It's fun to watch how people react when they enter the restaurant," Lopata says. "They come in, they smile, they relax. There's a lot of movement from table to table."

Since the landmark New York Daily News Building is sited on a corner, ground-level Extra!Extra! is flooded with daylight from large windows on two streets (see floorplan). The L-shaped space is laid out on three gently stepped levels to accommodate the grade. The lowest level (above) seats 42 diners and opens directly onto the kitchen.

In the bar area (right), Lopata suspended restaurant signage from an open ceiling grid.

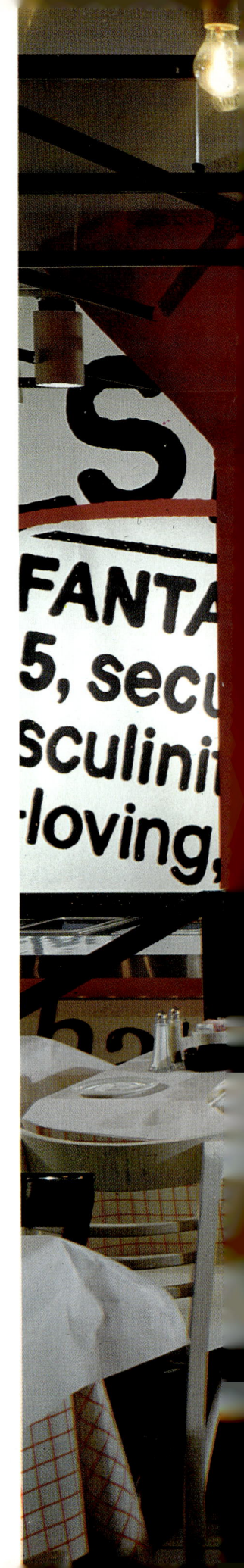

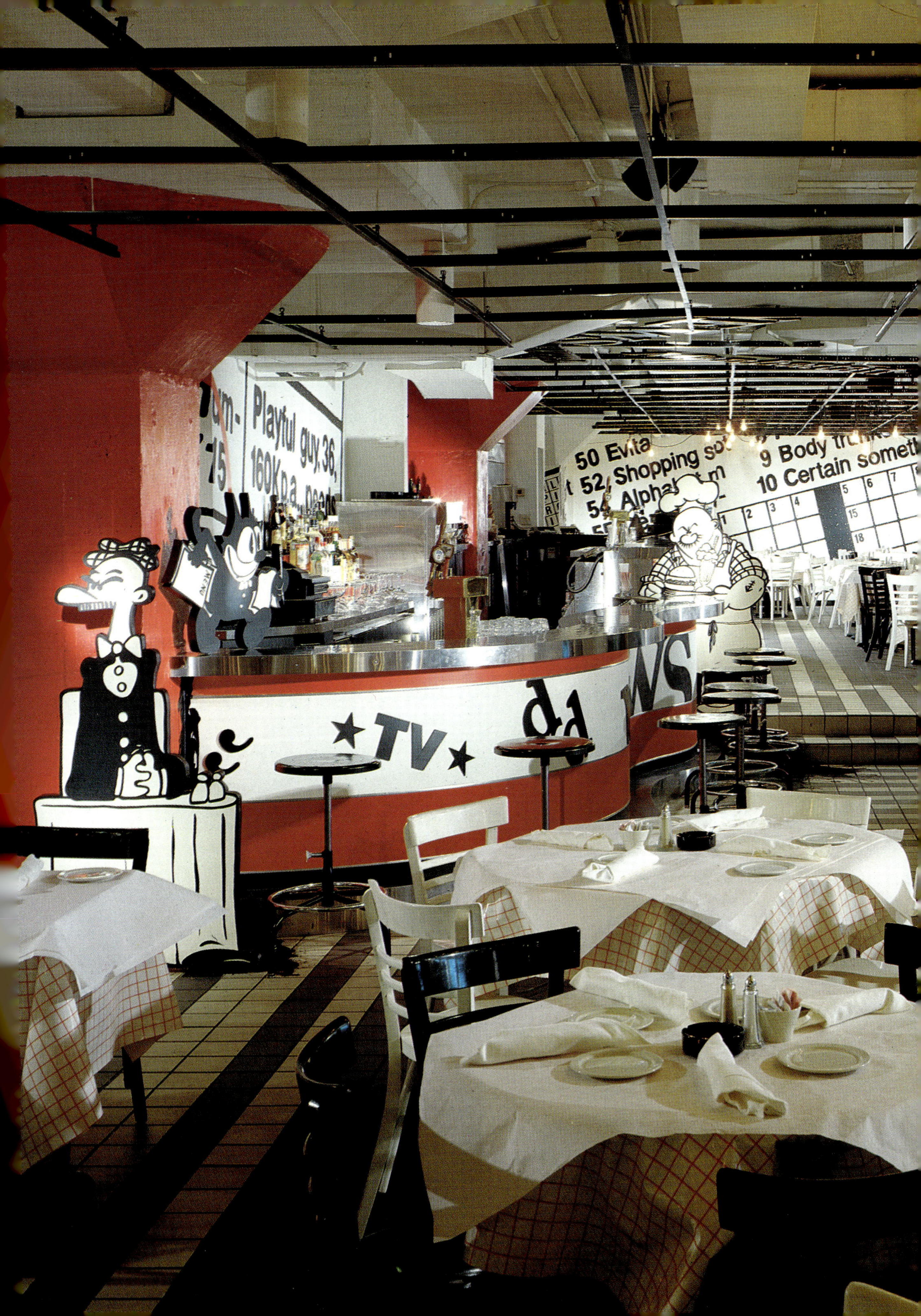
Playful guy,36,
50 Evita
TV

STREAMLINE A SPACE WITH WHIMSY
MIAMI BEACH ART DECO IS INFUSED WITH CALIFORNIA BUBBLES

A mirror etched with bubbles backs the curvilinear bar (above); the bubble motif also appears in the carpeting. Sleek banquettes (opposite) provide maximum seating.

BUBBLES, A RESTAURANT-LOUNGE on the Balboa peninsula in Newport Beach, is a loving recreation of thirties high style so convincing that although Fred Astaire and Ginger Rogers won't be seen drinking champagne cocktails at the bar or gliding across the dance floor, it is easy to imagine that they made a movie here.

Streamlined moderne was a distinctively American response to European Art Deco and to the hard times of the Depression. Buildings and consumer goods were styled in the manner of trains, planes, and oceanliners to evoke the excitement of speed and the exhilaration of technological progress. Streamlined styling boosted sales and raised spirits; Hollywood musicals and the New York World's Fair conjured up a more prosperous future.

The revival of the thirties streamlined look combines nostalgia for the aesthetic of sweeping lines and subtle curves, chrome flashes and glass brick walls, with wistful appreciation of a time when people still looked hopefully ahead. Bubbles is a time machine, and an affluent young crowd comes along for the ride.

Bubbles was classed as a renovation, to meet requirements of the Coastal Commission and other planning authorities. In fact, only the back wall from the previous building was retained. The newly built exterior, with its black-tiled base and curvilinear stucco moldings in pale green and salmon pink, its rounded windows, portholes, and stepped prow, might have sailed in from Miami Beach. It is an exuberant pastiche of tropical Art Deco. Neon is used with period pizzazz for the sign.

Inside, neon cove lighting casts an intense pink on the salmon walls. Upholstery and ceramic flower vases introduce a note of green. Shiny black stools, chairs, and tables, accented with stainless steel, give the bar the sophistication of a chic thirties nightclub. Dominating the dining room is a brightly lighted acrylic cylinder that resembles a giant highball glass of champagne. When the waiters break into a close-harmony chorus of "Happy Birthday," which seems to happen every fifteen minutes, iridescent soap bubbles pour out of ceiling apertures and float through the room.

The Hill Partnership of Newport Beach designed the restaurant in association with co-owners Doug Cavanaugh and Ralph Kosmides—who had previously restored Ruby's, a streamlined café at the end of Balboa Pier, a short distance

BUBBLES   Balboa, California
Owners: *Doug Cavanaugh, Ralph Kosmides*
Architecture: *The Hill Partnership (Larry Frapwell, principal-in-charge; Ron Van Pelt, project architect; John Morris, interior designer)*
Electrical/Mechanical/Lighting Engineer: *William R. Ishii & Associates*
Structural Engineer: *Harold Larson*
General Contractor: *Cavanaugh Development Corporation*
Foodservice Equipment: *R. W. Smith & Company*
Photography: *© Milroy/McAleer*

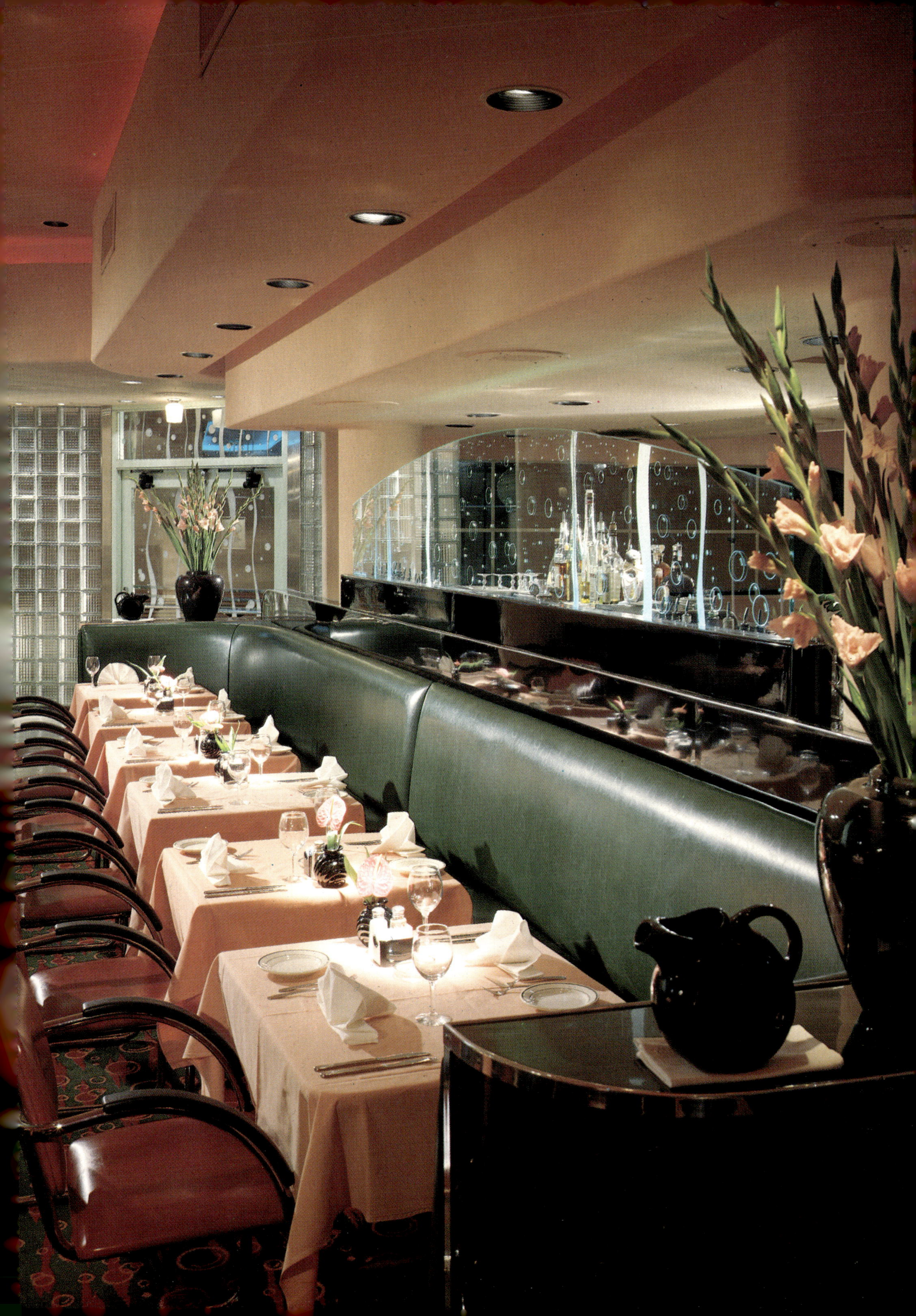

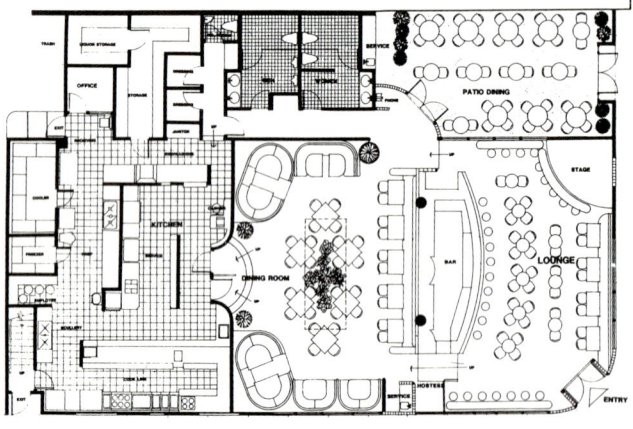

Stainless steel–trimmed furnishings create a sophisticated, streamlined elegance in the dining room (opposite). At the center of the space, a "champagne"-filled acrylic column creates a fascinating focal point. Outdoor dining (top) takes on a light and airy look. Floorplan (above) indicates spatial configuration.

away (see pages 118 and 119). The owners did extensive research, absorbing the spirit and detail of the period, taking "hundreds of photos" of Art Deco elements in Miami Beach and purchasing original artifacts. The Hill Partnership, meanwhile, had moved beyond its sober corporate clients in Orange County to design fantasy interiors, notably for Las Vegas casinos.

At Bubbles, they gave special attention to the details. Furniture has been designed to replicate original examples. Wall light fittings are shaped like martini glasses. The mirror behind the bar is etched with bubbles, a motif that also appears in the carpeting. Ice buckets are shaped like top hats. The cigarette machine is vintage 1930s, as are the paintings of women named after popular cocktails. Even the restrooms have shiny black and silver walls and authentically styled fixtures, mirrors, and lighting. "Our goal," says Larry Frapwell, principal of the Hill Partnership, "was to erase fifty years of history for anyone who steps into the restaurant."

A resident musical group, the Inkspots, sustains the period flavor; however, the menu is definitely 1980s California. The dining room and bar each seat 80, and there is seating for another 40 patrons in the enclosed patio. Offices and restrooms are located on the upper floor.

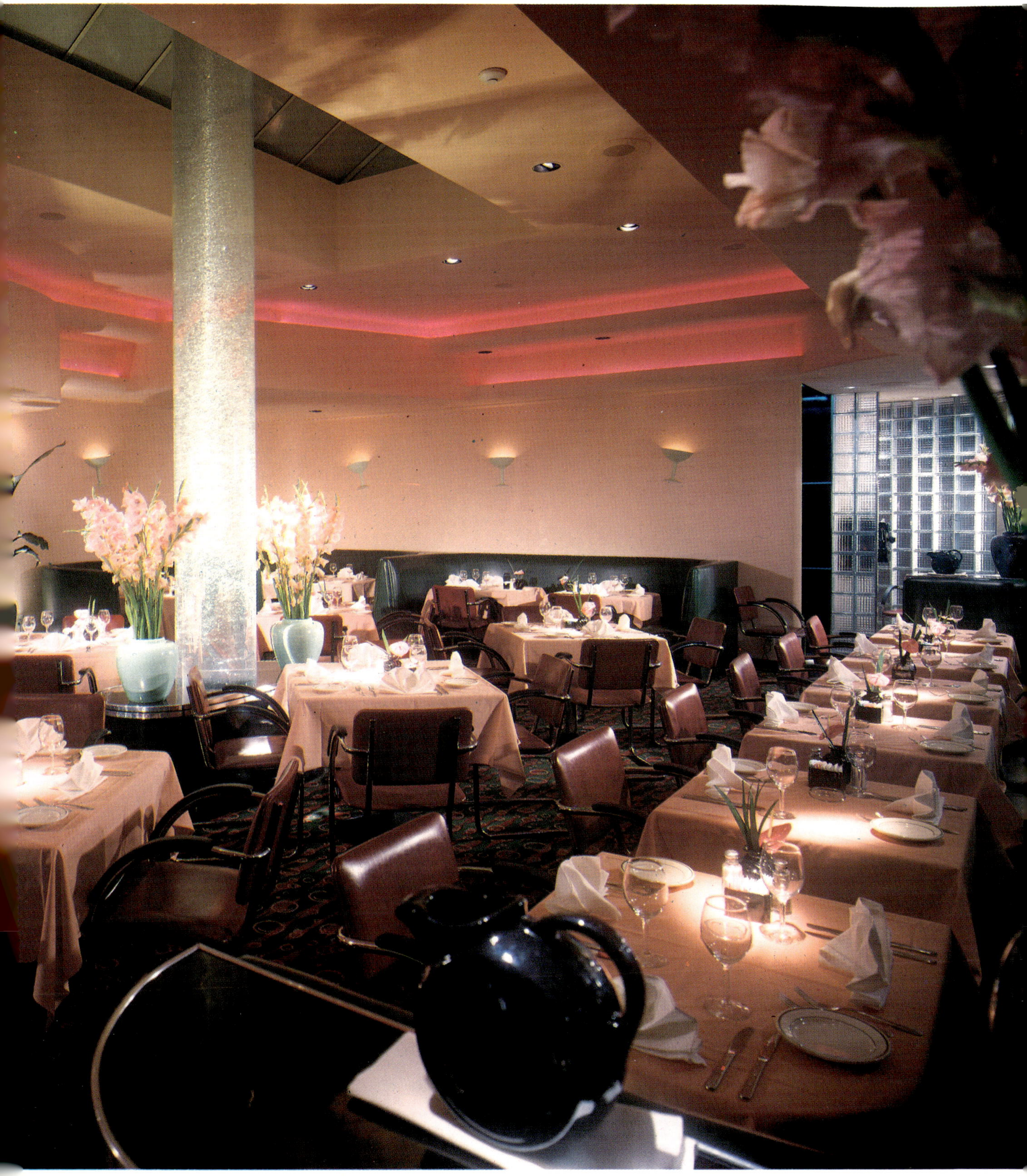

6. ETHNIC

RESTAURANTS

Ethnic restaurants no longer fit stereotyped images. Gone are the red temple doors and golden dragons, Chianti wine bottles and checked tablecloths, and sari-bedecked banquettes. Designers have moved beyond visual clichés and past traditional expectations to create imaginative and surprisingly understated expressions of ethnicity.

The message is often subliminally delivered. At Indian Oven in New York City (opposite), Peterson Littenberg Architects used the concept of the Indian mogul garden as inspiration for their clean, modern scheme that copes gracefully with a long, narrow, and difficult space. In a spirit of subtlety, it suggests, rather than proclaims, an Indian theme. Moving away from merely "decorated" space is a trend that is well supported by those who commission designers. For example, the owners of Indian Oven restaurant wanted "a modern space for eating." The designers were, in fact, a little apologetic when they presented plans derived from an Indian architectural motif.

In the case of Kiiriohana in San Francisco, architect H. Lynn Harrison abstracted his memories of Japan, applying his own graphic style to a scheme that emulates the spare subtlety of Japanese design. In still other ethnic restaurants, the expected "decoration" is missing entirely; such a place is Tuileries in New York City, where a spare moderne aesthetic belies the classic French menu.

However, there are still those ethnic restaurants that strive for an "authentic" ambience—the feeling of being transported to a distant land. In Shilla, Chicago, architect Norman DeHaan has recreated the mood of a traditional Korean gentleman's dining room, planned around a courtyard. DeHaan paid careful attention to authentic architectural detail, even hiring Korean craftspeople to work on certain aspects of the design. Such meticulous attention to detail is not unusual in today's ethnic restaurants. Ethnic dining today is infused with a purity of spirit and a dignified sense of history that the design does much to create.

BORROW FROM THE ARCHITECTURE OF SOUTHERN FRANCE

SIX INTIMATE DINING AREAS DEVELOP THE AMBIENCE OF A COUNTRY HOME

Etched mirrors and extensive millwork surround the bar in the Bistro Lounge (left)—one of six dining areas in the restaurant. The large hearth (opposite) serves as a focal point and helps create the mood in the Country Kitchen section. It is based on an original built in France in 1768.

WHEN THREE of the world's most famous French chefs plan to open a restaurant one might expect them to do it in Paris, New York, or perhaps Los Angeles. But Paul Bocuse, Gaston LeNotre, and Roger Verge picked Orlando, Florida, for their Cuisine Des Chefs. Despite—or because of—this unlikely location, they wanted the restaurant to look like a home in the south of France.

These longtime friends of Walt Disney were already familiar with the Florida territory; each of them has a stake in the French restaurant at Epcot Center. Cuisine Des Chefs marks their first private U.S. venture.

The trio brings architectural and gastronomical traditions of southern France—and a combined eleven Michelin stars—to central Florida. Bocuse, a Chevalier of the French Legion of Honor, owns a restaurant in Lyons, France, that is one of the world's finest. LeNotre, a noted pastry chef, owns Precatelan Restaurant in Bois de Boulogne, France; Verge runs two restaurants, including Le Moulin de Mougins, in the south of France.

To design the perfect country French setting in Florida, Bocuse, LeNotre, and Verge hired Raleigh & Associates, an Orlando firm specializing in hospitality design. The site—a Mediterranean-style marketplace—and interior concept had already been selected by the owners. According to principal and project director Christopher Raleigh, "The client's direction was to create an interior that would reflect the traditional architecture of the south of France. This fits in well with the style of the shopping center, as well as complementing the chefs' regional culinary skills."

Notes Raleigh, "We wanted a concept that would create a feeling of Provençal intimacy rather than spacious grandeur. This was attained by creating six separate dining environments, each intimate in scale. To further the sense of a country home, each area evokes a different mood."

Dining areas in the 7,800-square-foot restaurant include wine cellar, country kitchen, formal dining room, patio dining area, and bistro lounge. A foyer provides access to a

CUISINE DES CHEFS	*Orlando, Florida*
Owners: *Paul Bocuse, Roger Verge, Gaston LeNotre*	
Interior Design: *Raleigh & Associates (Christopher P. Raleigh, principal in charge; Lynda E. Chesser, project designer)*	
Architecture: *McCree Inc.*	
Budget: *$795,000*	
Seating: 238 **Size**: *7,800 square feet*	
Photography: *© Dan Forer*	

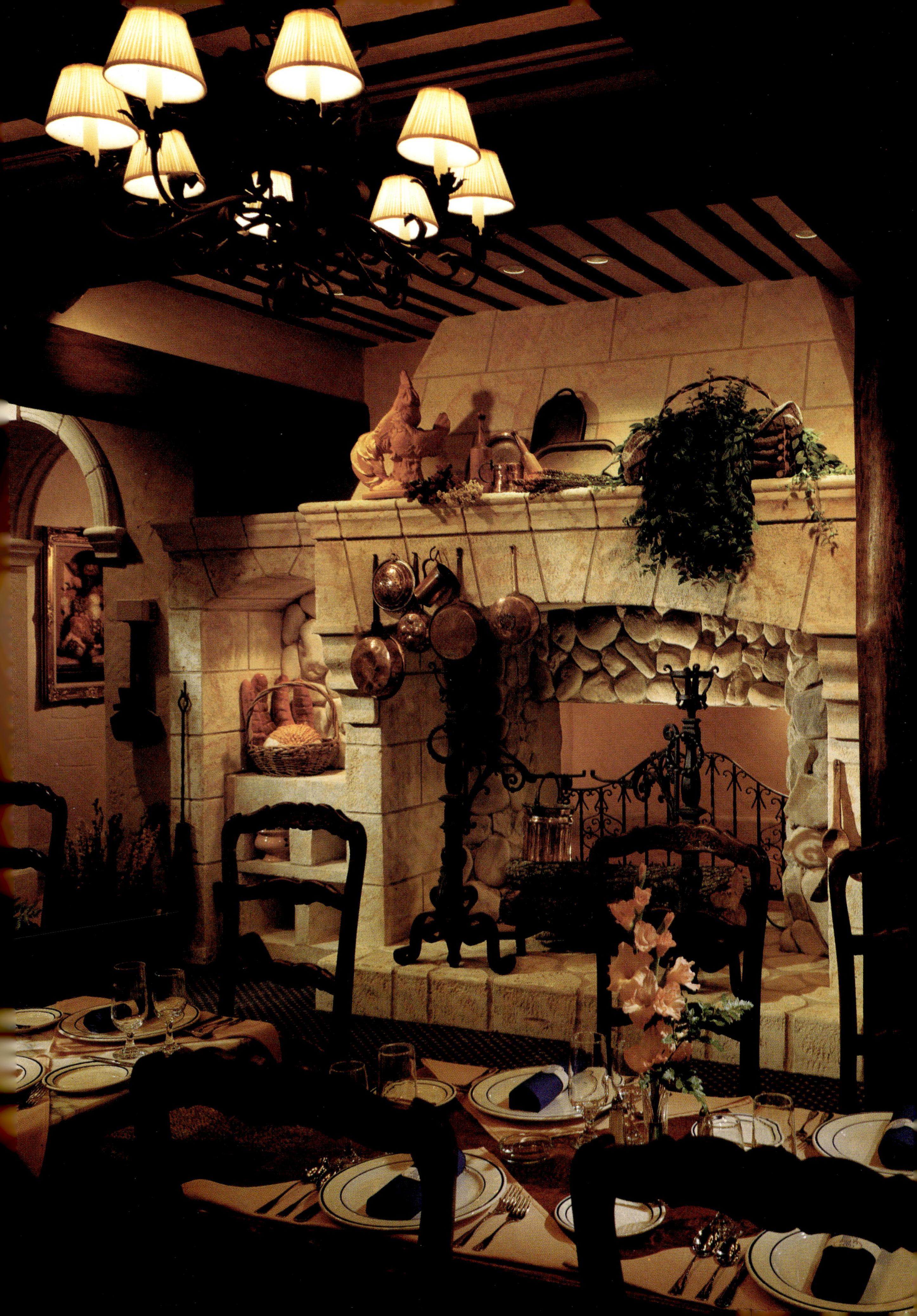

The Dining Room (right) offers a more formal setting, but still retains the homey feeling with the wooden ladderback, rush-seat chairs and with intimate lighting. The wine storage areas on the far wall repeat the shape of the arched ceiling.

gourmet shop, the cocktail lounge at right, and a corridor that leads into the dining areas at left. The cocktail lounge, a departure from traditional Provençal interiors, features Art Nouveau styling. A 30-foot mahogany bar with Alphonse Mucha–inspired Sarah Bernhardt figures in etched glass dominates the space. Raleigh specified pale rose and green marble-topped bistro tables, inlaid tiles, and pastel carpeting to "evoke a turn-of-the-century French bistro."

Interior dining spaces and the sidewalk café follow a U-shaped plan that surrounds a waiting area and lavatories. Though not cramped, the space is effectively used: Even corridors allow seating in small niches.

Patrons entering the dining rooms first encounter the wine cellar with its textured walls, barrel-vaulted ceilings, and recessed wine niches. Paisley cushions pad wood banquettes opposite ladderback chairs; sisal mats cover the floor. In the next room, an immense limestone fireplace evokes a French country kitchen. The fireplace, flanked by log bins and bread oven, is based on an original built in 1768 at La Balugue in the Camargue. Describing the room, the designer notes, "True to the period, the massive post-and-beam structure was fashioned from tree trunks and reworked salvaged lumber. The slatted ceiling is an artful simulation of the narrow *rondins* [crossbeams] and intervening light stripes of plaster used in eighteenth-century Provençal houses to support the second story." Raleigh also specified wrought-iron chandeliers, Provençal cotton draperies, and intricately carved armoires. Sponge-painted walls create a time-worn effect.

In the formal dining room, Louis XV fireplaces of carved limestone, Louis XV chairs, and floral Axminster carpeting create a more elegant environment. Lace curtains cover small-paned windows that face the sidewalk café. The café itself is surrounded by wrought-iron railings and terra cotta pedestals that support geranium-filled urns.

This 238-seat restaurant was completed for $795,000 including F/F&E and all construction.

UPDATE A DESIGN WITHOUT CHANGING THE MOOD

GOOD LIGHT, STRONG COLORS, AND A SENSE OF THEATER BRING A CHINESE RESTAURANT INTO THE 1980s

FRANK FAT OPENED his first restaurant in Sacramento in 1939, offering thirty-five-cent lunches and free gardenias for the ladies on Fridays. The food was basic Chinese-American, and the location was excellent—two blocks from the State Capitol. It soon became the after-hours resort for legislators and lobbyists. "Some of the best laws in the state of California were born, nurtured, lobbied, and actually passed right here in this restaurant," declares U.S. District Judge Thomas MacBride. But by the 1980s, the restaurant needed a facelift.

Frank Fat, with his son Wing, who now manages the restaurant, hired Hollywood-based designer Anthony Machado. Earlier, Machado had designed Fat City restaurant in San Diego for Frank's grandson. Their brief to Machado was simple: "Stick to the familiar plan and ambience and keep the regulars happy."

Machado transformed a claustrophobic space into a brilliantly articulated sequence of light, bright dining areas, using strong colors accented with brass rails, neon, and gilded antiques. But he heeded Fat's warning, and the regulars are as delighted as the tourists.

Machado's flamboyant sense of theater is here allied to an extraordinary sense of customer psychology. What made Frank Fat's so successful (it continues to draw everyone from the Governor on down) is that there is space for everyone and every occasion. Those who want to see and be seen are seated on a 40-foot bench inside the entrance and across from the bar; the traffic is channeled conveniently between these two viewing galleries. In the rear is the power table—a large open booth. Beyond, what was formerly the ladies' dining room has been transformed into an intimate, elegant, and above all sociable eating area. The back room, with its eight enclosed booths, has the air of a private club.

The entrance, a stylized arch, makes a statement with commendable restraint. A low passage leads to a lofty dining room. Structure contributes to decor; the middle dining room has a tinted skylight. A Plexiglas chandelier, black lacquered chairs, and museum-quality antiques—including a nineteenth-century gold-embroidered Mongolian warrior's robe and golden relief panels—complete the effect. A private dining room above the entrance has a similar refinement, achieved through pink neon soffit lighting, polished surfaces, and circular etched glass windows at either end.

By contrast, the front and back rooms have a bolder character derived from coordinated magenta, purple, turquoise, and midnight-blue upholstery, deep rose-pink walls, gold-papered ceilings, and black granite tabletops. The effect is rich but not gaudy and is everywhere enhanced by Machado's sense of theater and detail. Blue-tinted mirrors create dramatic vistas and give the narrow space an illusion of depth. A sawtooth Art Deco plaster frame sets off a century-old tapestry above the bar. A golden Buddha has been carried over from the previous restaurant, and the Chinese character for "Fat" is stylized and used as a motif for a succession of etched glass lunettes. Lighting is varied: pinspots shining onto the tables, pink-tinted concealed lighting, Italian cone-shaped wall sconces, and hanging lights. The intensity of illumination can be varied according to the time of day and the brightness outdoors.

To achieve this spatial drama and to successfully negotiate so extreme a shift from the mundane to the opulent—from polished brass to silk brocade—bespeaks the shared goals of client and architect. Machado reiterates the need to respect Frank Fat's distinctive style and conservative following: to be both tasteful and consistent, while avoiding trendy gestures.

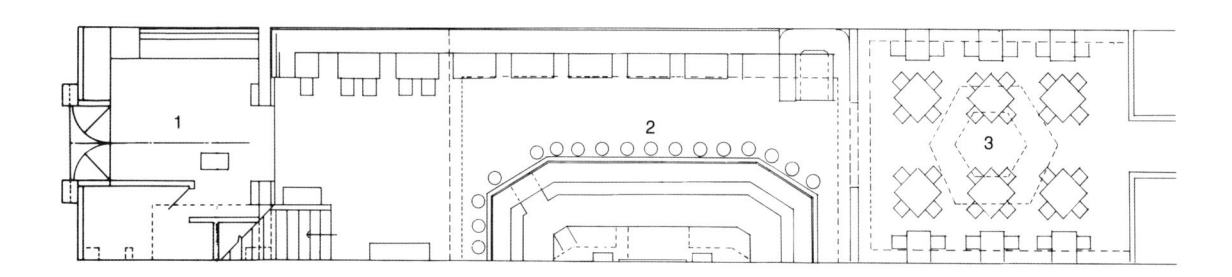

FRANK FAT'S   *Sacramento, California*
Owner: *Frank Fat*
Interior Design: *Anthony Machado*
Photography: © *Steve Simmons*

Anthony Machado retained the basic floorplan of the original Frank Fat's, with a spacious bar for all the local customers to see and be seen. There is a private dining area beyond. Even more intimate is the rear dining room consisting of eight enclosed booths (not shown in floorplan): entrance (1); bar (2); middle dining room (3).

139

Patrons enter the bar area (shown in the background of the picture opposite) where they can socialize. From there, they move back into the first dining room where brilliant colors, a tinted skylight with Plexiglas chandelier, black lacquered chairs, granite-topped tables, and museum-quality antiques create an elegant setting. The private dining room (above) offers a striking array of banquette upholstery in its eight enclosed booths, giving the room a clubby air. Blue-tinted mirrors create depth.

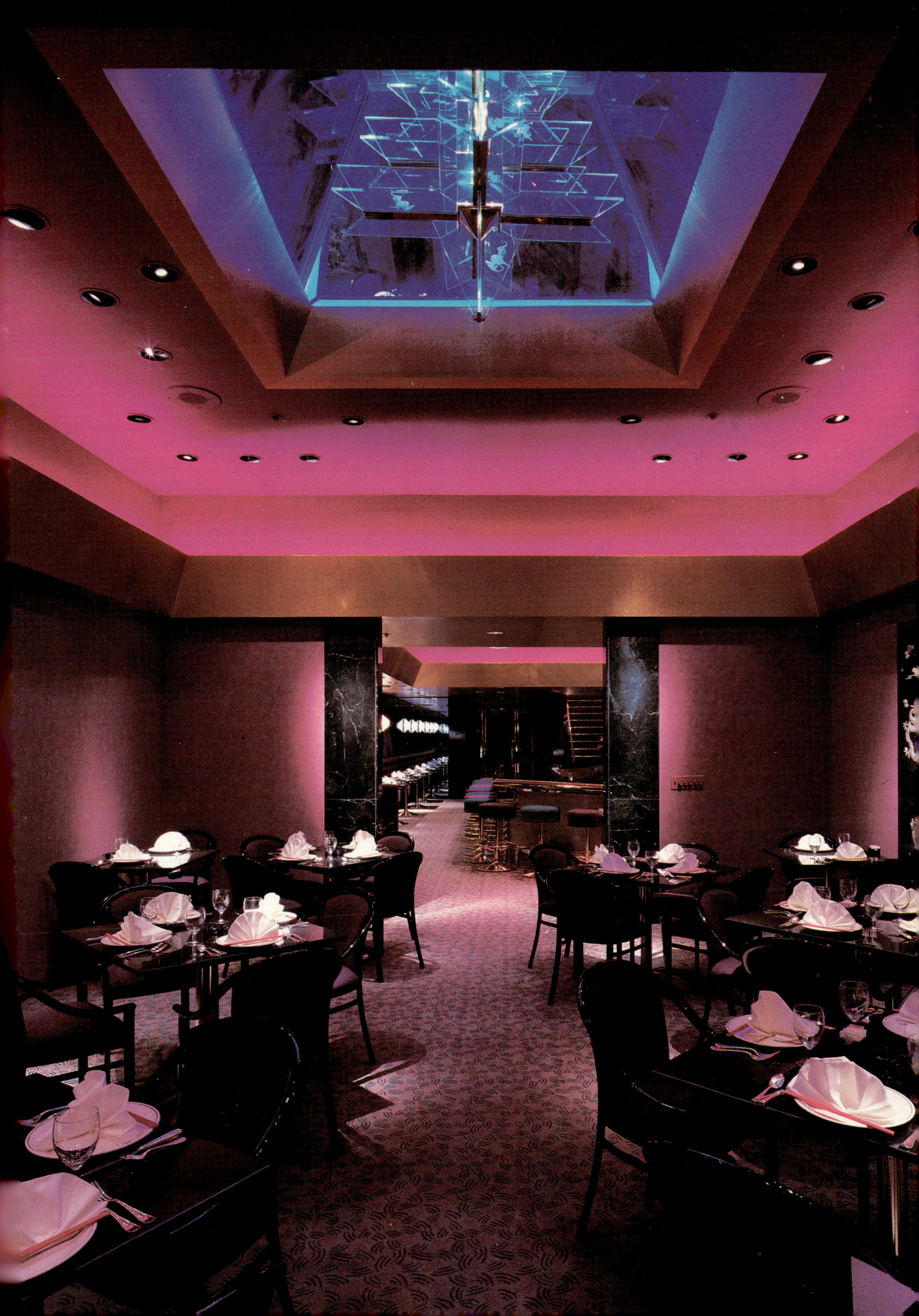

EVOKE JAPAN WITH SUBTLETY AND ILLUSION
GEOMETRY AND COLOR LURE PASSERSBY INTO A SUSHI RESTAURANT

Kiiroihana's exterior geometrics (left) anticipate its interior theme. Inside (opposite) crisp tile patterns are interrupted by sections of carpet. Note how the ceiling suggests an expansive, mysterious sky. The natural wood tones below, in the furnishings and along the walls, provide a warm contrast.

THE JAPANESE RESTAURANT Kiiroihana in San Francisco was designed by an American architect, H. Lynn Harrison, drawing on the memories of his travels in Japan and his expertise in graphic design. Working with a tight schedule, a budget of $125,000, and two adjoining turn-of-the-century storefronts with just 1,500 square feet of floor space, Harrison has created an airy restaurant and sushi bar that seats up to 70 guests. Like the best Japanese buildings, its apparent simplicity conceals a private world of subtlety and illusion.

North Beach is a San Francisco neighborhood best celebrated for its old-world Italian restaurants, topless bars, and literary bookstores. Carol Doda and a fading memory of the beat poets draw the tourists. It's an unlikely location for the city's most unusual Japanese restaurant, which faces the spires of St. Peter and St. Paul, a block from the honky-tonk of Broadway.

The facade of Kiiroihana offers tantalizing glimpses of the room beyond. A vermilion grid over the transom above the picture window reveals the neon frieze on the back wall. At night the effect is dramatic, but even by day it attracts the passerby with its varied geometry.

KIIROIHANA	*San Francisco, California*
Owner:	*Pacific Restaurant Corporation*
Architecture:	*Amick Harrison Architects*
General Contractor:	*Schendel Construction*
Specialized Wall Finishes:	*Jeff Work*
Budget:	*$125,000*
Size: *1,500 square feet*	**Seating**: *70*
Photography:	*© Christopher Irion*

Inside, a strong central axis, defined by a pair of load-bearing columns and two checkerboards of floor tiles, bisects the room from the projecting entrance canopy to the sushi bar. Tables are arranged symmetrically on both sides of this axis. The symmetry and repetitive geometry of the decor are cleverly modified by the use of color and texture: light and natural below, colorful and mysterious above. Diners feel that they are drifting along in a graceful open ship beneath an expansive sky.

Kiiroihana is the Japanese word for yellow flower, and the neon frieze on the back wall includes intense yellow flower shapes floating amid a streamlined cobalt blue version of the traditional Japanese graphic for water or clouds. This design recedes to infinity through the mirrors on the upper side walls. The ceiling is also painted cobalt blue.

The back wall, below the neon, is painted a soft pink that is graduated in intensity to suggest a woodblock print and is overlaid with a pattern of traditional graphic emblems in vermilion. The lower side walls and central columns are animated with a horizontal pattern of wood half-rounds over gypsum board that are painted in light ochre and hand-stippled with a tricolor overlay of blue-gray, vermilion, and cadmium yellow. A peach-stained *torii* (Shinto temple arch) frames the corridor that leads back to the kitchen and restrooms.

The custom-designed lighting includes ceiling pendants and fluorescent uplights concealed in curved-profile continuous sconces along the side walls, with shorter lengths on the paired center columns. The parallel rows of low-wattage, exposed-filament lights hang by a zigzag of white cords from ceiling tracks. They sparkle like stars against the intense blue of the sky above.

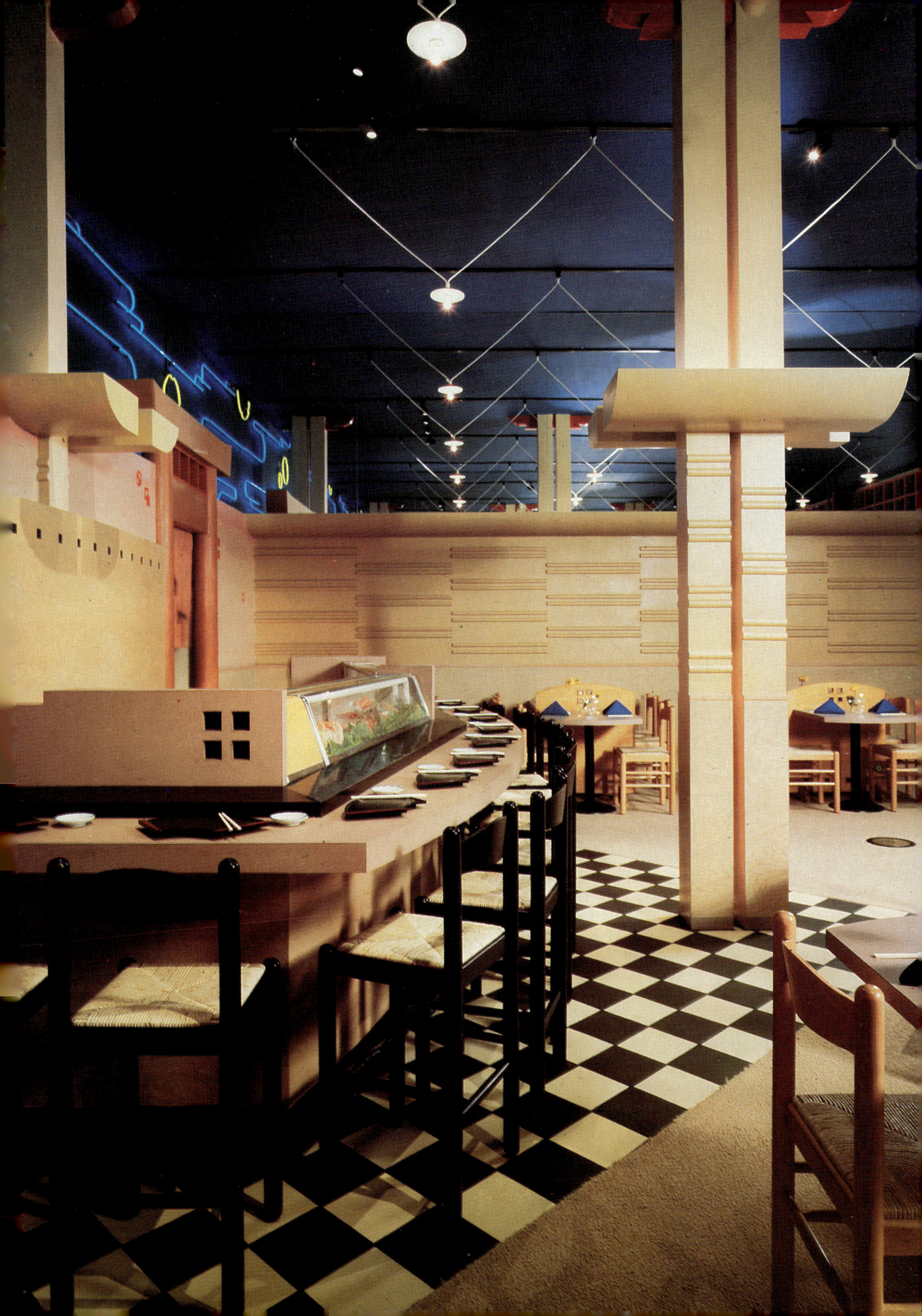

144

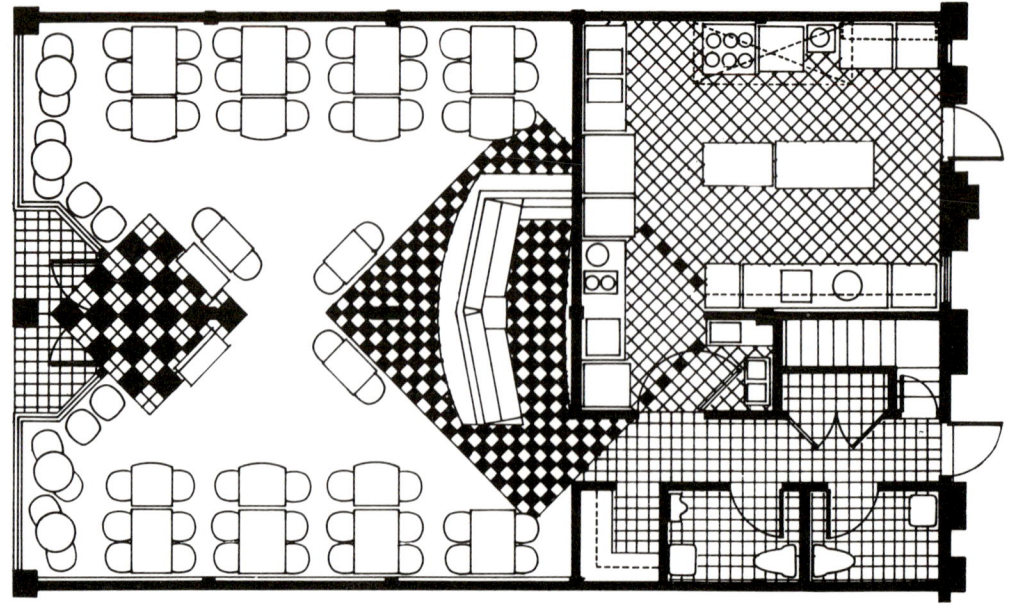

Tables symmetrically line the perimeter of Kiiroihana's main dining space (opposite, top), where the focal point is the sushi bar. The floorplan (left) shows inventive use of the geometric flooring. Neon forms in vivid colors tie the meaning of Kiiroihana—yellow flower—to the interior scheme (above).

The custom furniture is covered with plastic laminates and a Japanese bow silhouette is employed in the curves of the sushi bar, the wood screen behind, the smaller tables, and the *tsuitate* wood screens that separate adjoining tables. Harrison has played similar variations on a four-square pattern that was inspired by the original cast-iron sidewalk vents. The pattern is stenciled on the rear wall and is employed as a decorative cutout on the sushi bar and a functional handhold on the *tsuitate* screens. And, in place of a curtain, a pattern of translucent squares has been sandblasted on the window glass.

Kiiroihana is a marvelously inventive and exotic fusion of Eastern and Western idioms, plus traditional and new wave styles, that appeals to Westerners and Japanese alike.

DESIGN A MODERN, ARCHITECTURAL SPACE
NO DECORATIVE CLICHÉS CLUTTER THIS INDIAN RESTAURANT

Looking in from outside (left), it is easy to see that the architects' distinctive use of trim harmoniously unites interior (opposite) and exterior elements of a design based on classic Indian architecture.

INSTEAD OF A decorated establishment, the owners of an Indian Restaurant in New York's fashionable Flatiron District wanted "a modern space." Thus, explains architect Steven K. Peterson, "We set out to make an architecturally good environment for eating, rather than a restaurant with interior decoration. We believe that a good restaurant can be made out of a good room." Peterson, with his partner Barbara Littenberg (Peterson, Littenberg Architects, New York) conceptualized the project as a metaphoric garden with linked arcades.

"The space suggests design elements basic to Islamic architecture," Littenberg says. "We were sheepish about presenting our clients with a design that relied heavily on the gateways and thresholds of Indian mogul gardens, but we believed it was a perfect way to order the difficult 100-foot-long, 12-foot-wide space inside a nineteenth-century structure. We were careful to point out to our clients the difference between classic Indian architecture and a pastiche of Indian objects."

"With the long, narrow space we had a processional problem and a problem of perspective," says Peterson. Their solution included recessing and angling the entrance and partially screening it from the street with geometric trim. This device serves to integrate the modern facade with the cast-iron front of the old building in much the same way an *iwan* masks the raised dome at the entrance to a royal mosque. As Peterson explains, it also initiates the sequence of arches that leads the eye back into the restaurant.

The effect is pristine. The trim that appears on the exterior repeats on a reduced scale throughout the interior and operates as an independent system, providing continuity and animation. Notes Littenberg, "It is also a device by which wall surfaces can be modulated and proportioned, establishing the shaped volumes by connecting walls, ceilings, and floors together."

The architects took an awkward space and effectively created a refined result, for which they used ordinary materials with a keen sense of visual balance; even the emergency lighting fits in well. They have effectively combined classic Indian architectural motifs and clean contemporary design. The cost of transforming the space was $375,000, a modest sum for the 4,000-square-foot facility, which includes a 100-seat dining room and bar, plus prep kitchen, office, and basement party room.

INDIAN OVEN	New York City
Owner:	Indian Oven Restaurants Inc.
Architecture:	Peterson, Littenberg Architects (Steven K. Peterson, Barbara Littenberg)
Contractor:	Mayo Construction Company
Engineers:	Bong Yu, P.C.
Budget:	$375,000
Size: 4,000 square feet	**Seating**: 100
Photography:	© Peter Margonelli

147

The architects developed their plan (below) along the lines of a classic Indian mogul garden. This resolved the long-and-narrow space problem with a procession of arches. They were careful not to create an Indian restaurant that was a decorative cliché.

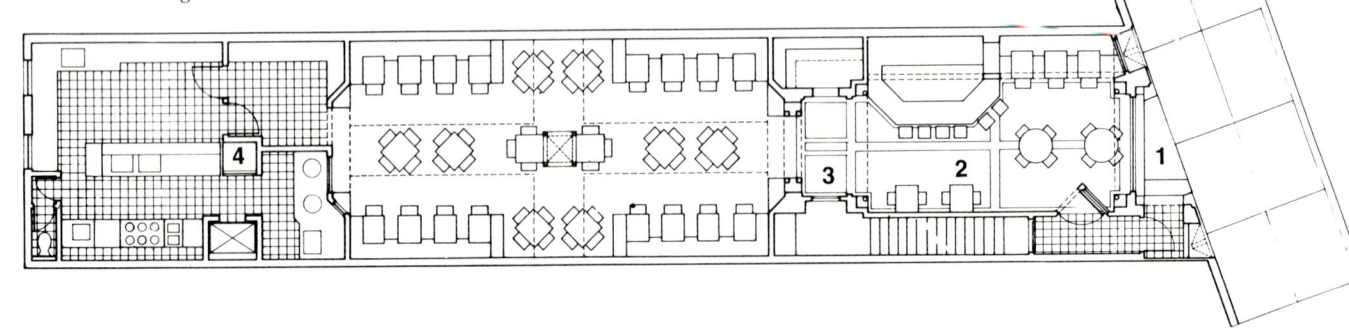

RECREATE A GENTLEMAN'S DINING ROOM

IN A TRADITIONAL KOREAN RESTAURANT,
A CENTRAL COURT IS ADJOINED BY SMALL ROOMS

All of Shilla's dining areas feature traditional swinging, top-hinged panels that open over the porch and fretted sliding panels that separate the rooms.

When they decided to introduce a taste of Korea's Shilla Dynasty to Chicago, Mr. and Mrs. Won Bo Keel hired Norman DeHaan (Norman DeHaan and Associates), a local architect/designer who had lived in Korea for several years. Together they committed themselves to transforming a one-story, 1950s finance corporation office building into a modern-day replica of a Korean gentleman's dining place. Plans were drawn and three months later, Shilla was born.

To create the gourmet operation, DeHaan gutted the large, open space and installed a kitchen to the right of the entryway. The site lent itself to the traditional Korean restaurant layout—always a U- or L-shaped format. Typically, the design calls for an open courtyard encircled on three sides by adjoining rooms.

At Shilla, DeHaan used the main dining room as the "courtyard" and surrounded it with private dining rooms and banquet facilities. To the east, five rooms are treated in customary Korean manner: The floor is raised 18 inches with a wide plank platform (*toit maroo*) and handrails. Customers step onto a radiant-heated *ondol* floor—a seven-hundred-year-old Korean tradition. (The heating systems in the building were revamped to accommodate Shilla's *ondol*.) This element is included in all but two rooms, where tradition gives way to comfort with the installation of leg wells under the tables. All of Shilla's dining areas feature traditional swinging, top-hinged panels (*yo daji moon*) that open over the porch, as well as fretted sliding panels (*mi seo ki*) that separate the rooms. On the southern side of the building are banquet facilities; on the west side are additional Western-style rooms that open to seat up to 40 people at standard-height, formally set tables.

Other details effectively blend the historic with the new. Doors are paneled with heavy, handmade, Korean rice paper; the Shilla Dynasty crown ornaments a fretwork screen in the bar area; and carvings over the service area suggest Korean roof rafter ends. A scarlet-framed collection of rubbings from eighteen-hundred-year-old Shilla Dynasty roof tiles is prominently displayed and all hardware is hand-hammered iron from Korea. The door carvings of floral and animal motifs are the work of Korean craftspeople.

With a $427,000 budget, DeHaan and Mr. and Mrs. Won Bo Keel have succeeded in recreating a genuine Korean upper-class dining experience.

SHILLA	*Chicago, Illinois*
Owners:	Mr. and Mrs. Won Bo Keel
Interior Architecture:	Norman DeHaan Associates, Inc. (Norman DeHaan, Barnett McCulloch)
Kitchen Design:	Edward Don & Company (Jery Don)
Contractor:	Triangle-Grand Contractors, Inc.
Budget:	$427,000
Photography:	© Jay Wolke, Norman DeHaan Associates

From the central dining courtyard around which the entire restaurant is planned, five rooms, all treated in the traditional Korean manner, are seen to the east.

151

USE A FESTIVE TENT FOR FOCUS
PATTERNS, FABRICS, AND TINY MIRRORS EVOKE A SENSE OF INDIA

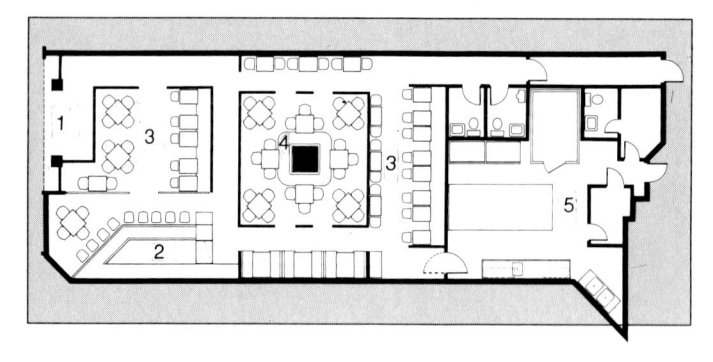

Along the entrance wall the designers placed wooden display shelves filled with miniature children's toys from various regions of India: soldiers in a row, hand puppets, musical instruments, and silk paintings. Their colors, and the colors of the frieze, the upholstery, and the napery are enhanced by the subtle cream-colored stucco walls. Floorplan: entry (1); bar (2); dining area (3); tent dining area (4); kitchen (5).

"SHAMIANA" MEANS festive tent. A huge embroidered tent serves as the focal point in Shamiana's main dining room. There, designers Gordon Micunis and Jay Korbin succeeded in creating "an environment that offers the illusion of India."

The main challenge: transform a long, narrow 2,500-square-foot shopping mall site into an evocative ethnic restaurant. "While the mall offered no architectural detail to work with, we could create anything we wanted," says Micunis. There were restrictions relating to service access, fire entrances, and other code requirements. In addition, most of the construction had to take place after mall business hours.

The result of the designers' efforts is an effective blend of authentic artifacts and contemporary American pieces that suggests the mood of India. A huge, elegant, woven tent draped above a grouping of formal tables and plush banquettes provides the focal point of the room and the design.

Since Shamiana literally translates as festive tent, Micunis and Korbin used the vibrantly colored tent, made from pieces of fabric woven together from Shamiana owner Rashid Munshi's family collection, to reproduce a colonnaded garden. The deep red banquettes surrounding the four sides of a mirrored column (a structural pier that was enlarged to achieve this palatial effect) deliberately mimic garden benches, luxuriously finished with washable suede seats and textured tapestry backs. Within this "square," set off by castellated corner dividers that echo the lines of the Taj Mahal, the designers have created intimate enclaves of seating arrangements, each offering seclusion for private conversation. (The Taj Mahal itself is represented in one of the sepia enlargements of nineteenth-century drawings from the owner's collection that decorate side and entry walls.)

Lining the entry wall are long wooden display shelves filled with authentic miniature children's toys from various regions of India: soldiers in a row, hand puppets, musical instruments, and silk paintings of Indian processions.

Unifying the space is a distinctive frieze that wraps around the room. This reproduction of a Victorian-era Persian print was custom-made for the designers. The rear wall of the space is covered with huge jars of the herbs, spices, and dried legumes that are essential to Indian cuisine.

SHAMIANA   *Stamford, Connecticut*

Owners: *Rashid Munshi, Shamiana Indian Cuisine, Lakhaana Foods, Inc.*

Architecture: *Marmont Design Associates (Richard Montaine)*

Interior Design: *Gordon Micunis Designs (Gordon Micunis, Jay Korbin)*

Kitchen Consultant: *Edward Hirschenfeld*

Contractor: *L. Epstein, Inc.*

Photography: *© Norman McGrath*

153

ABANDON "FRENCH" CLICHES FOR A CLEAN LOOK
1930s INTERNATIONAL STYLE IS USED TO RESOLVE AWKWARD SPACE

The logo became part of the flooring (above) at the entrance to Les Tuileries, crossing over the floor's grid pattern. The grid is echoed in the symmetrical placement of overhead air diffusers. Dining areas with low ceilings (opposite) called for inobtrusive recessed downlighting and spotlights. The hard terrazzo flooring and clean, hard edges of the room's design provide a foil to the plush banquette upholstery. Axonometric: entrance (1); bar (2); cocktail/dining tables (3); dining area (4); restrooms (5); open patio (6).

ALTHOUGH THE PROPERTY commands superb eye-level views of New York's Central Park just across Fifty-Ninth Street, the long-and-narrow configuration of Les Tuileries combined with its low ceilings and awkwardly placed structural/mechanical columns presented Compton Architects with significant challenges in redesigning the classic French restaurant.

"The limitations that the space imposed helped to dictate the way the design was done," explains Christopher Compton. "A lot of the spatial geometry was organized by the columns." From the cocktail area, where windows face the street and park, all the way through to the back, where glass walls embrace a small garden, groupings of tables play off round, square, and rectangular columns, as well as freestanding panels that back banquettes in the restaurant's layout.

In this 3,500-square-foot room (it is just 36 feet wide, with 8-foot ceilings) it was necessary to create the illusion of greater space. To this end, the design team specified staggered and free-floating panels of lacquer, marble, and taffeta, with textures that soften progressively through the space. Cornice-height mirrors and additional mirrored panels "expand the space and reduce the depression and loss of perspective that so often occurs in rooms with low ceilings," says Compton.

The textures and materials—terrazzo, marble, granite, steel—employed in these panels and elsewhere, coupled with a neutral palette of black, gray, and pale beige, add up to a style reminiscent of "1930s International," which is precisely what Compton intended for Tuileries. There is little overt concession to the "Frenchness" of the design. Several randomly placed bright red panels, plus the racy horizontal striping in the marble tile of the bar and maitre d' post, serve as lively accents in the restaurant's otherwise quiet color scheme.

With chandeliers "out of the question," the designers opted for a combination of track spots and recessed downlights to "soften edges." Providing an additional contrast to these hard edges and materials are the plush gray banquettes, after the International Style.

The configuration of the interior at Les Tuileries created additional problems in planning the kitchen. There was simply not enough space on the restaurant floor for a complete kitchen. Thus, a 1,750-square-foot cooking kitchen was sited on the main level, while storage, prep, and dishwashing facilities were put in the basement.

LES TUILERIES *New York City*
Owner: *Jean Buchert*
Architecture: *Compton Architects (Christopher Compton, Diane Lewis, Peter Mickle)*
General Contractor: *Wanco Construction Corporation*
Photography: *© Paul Warchol*

155

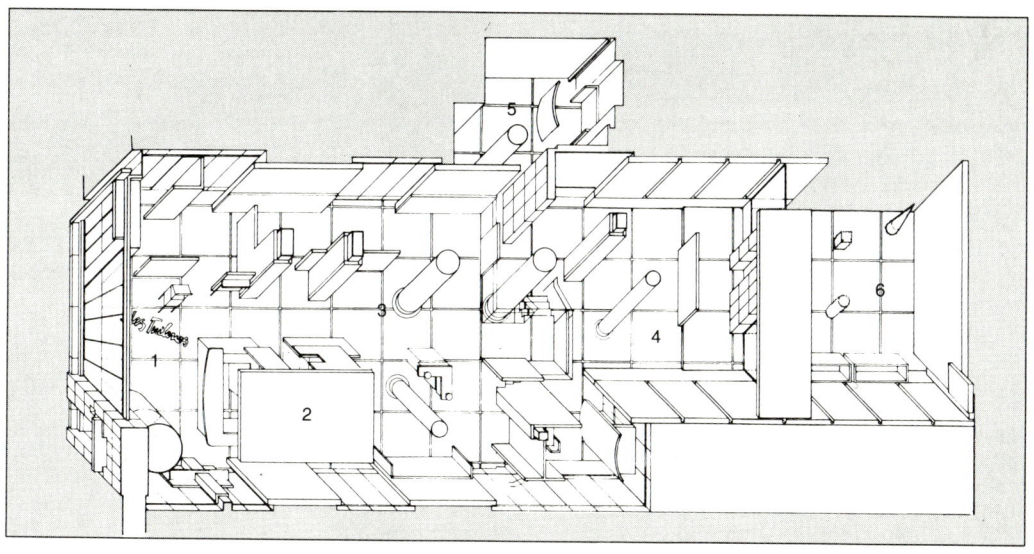

HONOR OLD CRAFTS FOR AN AUTHENTIC MOOD
JAPANESE CARPENTRY BRINGS WARMTH TO A MODERN SUSHI BAR

USING TRADITIONAL Japanese carpentry, architect Kazuyuki Murata satisfied the client's wish for a contemporary sushi bar/Japanese grill where diners could watch their food being prepared. In the long, deep site (20 by 76 feet with 14-foot ceilings), Murata arranged the sushi bar, robata-yaki grill, and seating for 60 patrons, as well as the kitchen, storage area, and restrooms in a well-ordered design.

Clearly visible through good-sized windows that front on a commercial Seattle street, Aoki beckons passersby with interiors of glowing wood. "The entry to the restaurant and the passage along the sushi bar were treated as a semi-exterior space, with a granite tile strip giving a tactile sensation like that of stepping on a cobblestone street," says Murata. To create a cozy feeling, a master carpenter from Japan installed a traditional Japanese gabled roof under the high ceiling over the sushi area. Further back, an illuminated 30-foot shoji screen divided into an "auspicious" number of sections is tilted "to suggest a rooflike overhang above the diners," notes Murata.

Bench-type seating against the wall is covered with plastic laminate in multicolored sections that correspond to divisions of the shoji screen above, and like them, have symbolic significance: "Equal widths of red and white strips represent spring, summer, day, and the rational or predictable; black and white represent night, and the irrational or unpredictable. These divisions also reflect the influence of seasonal variations on Japanese culinary arts," Murata says. Even the cash register cabinet is a finely crafted modification of a traditional Japanese chest, or *tanus*. A small private dining room to the rear, well removed from cooking activities, offers quiet contrast to other areas.

Aoki's project budget included $37,000 for Japanese carpentry and cabinets, plus $104,000 for architecture, equipment, and ducts.

Traditional Japanese cabinetry and architectural elements distinguish Aoki's sushi bar (above) and dining area (opposite). To the rear of the restaurant a private dining area is included. Floorplan: sushi bar (1); cash register (2); grille dining area (3); private room (4); kitchen (5).

AOKI	Seattle, Washington
Owners:	Mr. and Mrs. Takao Aoki
Architecture/Interior Design:	2S2M Architects (Kazuyuki Murata, Christopher Murray, Lee Stubbe)
Carpentry:	Shimoi Construction
Cabinetry:	Van Horn Design
Graphics:	The Wells Design Group
Contractor:	Norcoast Construction
Budget:	$141,000
Photography:	© Tom Collicott

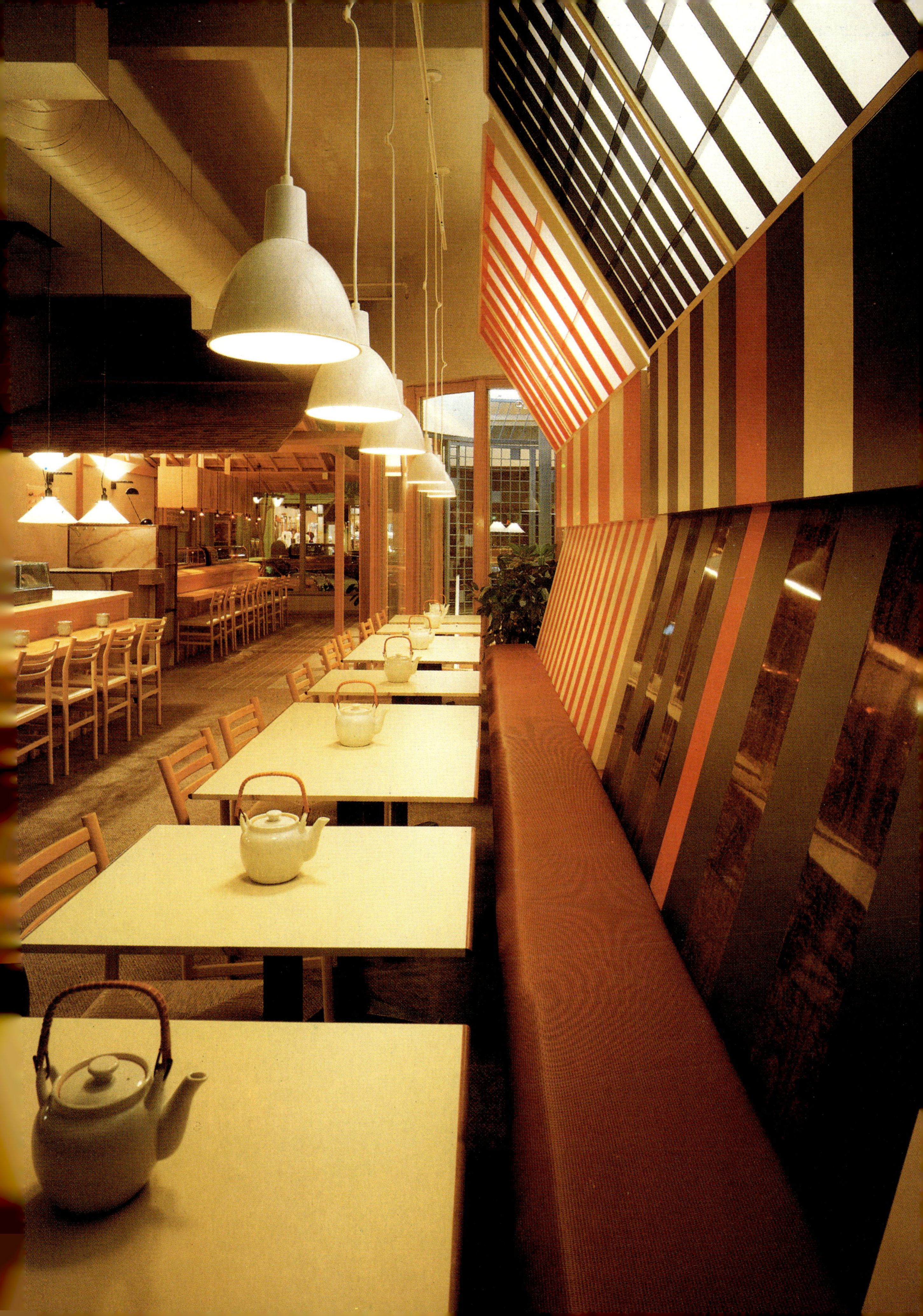

7. EAT-IN/TAKE-OUT

ESTABLISHMENTS

Take-out foods have become big business. And to capitalize on this avenue of trade, restaurant owners are making new demands. Not only must designers accommodate the sit-down trade, they are also accountable for the merchandising of take-out foods under the same roof.

This new brand of retail food establishment caters to on-the-move men and women who are too busy to go home and cook a soufflé or a *boeuf en croute* but who would like to enjoy such delights in the privacy of their homes or offices.

As at Polcari & Sons in Boston's North End (opposite), lavish food displays are becoming the norm in eat-in/take-out establishments. Displays of foodstuffs are created to entice pedestrians off the streets or shopping mall corridors. At Polcari's, special glass-walled refrigeration units replace windows, allowing pedestrians to see the tempting foods stored there, as well as to glimpse the bustle inside. Polcari's also offers a lobster bar to woo the customer into having a quick drink and a lobster claw before heading home. The temptation to buy more food is, of course, the object of this marketing ploy. Piret's in Beverly Hills, California, uses this technique too. In a small space that emphasizes sit-down dining, the designers have created a "food machine" unit that consolidates the wine and food displays and the food prep counter.

Often, the menu for the sit-down diner at places like Polcari's—and Lakeside Deli in Oakland, California—is also available for the take-home shopper. Dining areas are strategically placed, forcing the customer to walk through food display areas in order to reach their table. Lighting and traffic patterns are keys to the design. Although it allows the retailer to pinpoint special offerings and adds to their decorative effect, lighting must be arranged with care so that heat does not accumulate on refrigerated surfaces. Aisles are not straight. Paths often move on a diagonal (as at Tutti's in Montecito, California), allowing shoppers unbroken views of displays and people beyond.

CREATE A FOOD THEATER FOR THE 1980s
TWO RETAIL RESTAURANTS SET LAVISH GOURMET DISPLAYS AGAINST A BACKDROP OF OAK AND BRASS

For the Beverly Hills DDL Foodshow (above and opposite), designer Adam Tihany recreated the design of the original shop (formerly located on Columbus Avenue in New York City) using oak cabinetry, brass, lavish food displays, and dramatic lighting.

WHEN FILM PRODUCER Dino De Laurentiis decided to turn his attention to food, he opened his DDL Foodshow, a 12,000-square-foot extravaganza on Manhattan's trendy Columbus Avenue, then went on to open two more of these deluxe deli-bistros—one in midtown Manhattan's Trump Tower and one in Beverly Hills, California. His brief to the architect: All attention must focus on the food. De Laurentiis wanted to feature quality food, well-dressed shoppers, and the last word in pricey convenience in a stunning, well-crafted setting.

Adam Tihany, principal of Adam D. Tihany International Ltd., New York City, who had sheathed the Columbus Avenue DDL in rich oak cabinetry, shiny brass, and Italian tile, and then installed jazzy theatrical lighting, was asked to impart similar personalities to the new stores. But the spaces at Trump Tower and Beverly Hills had little in common with each other, let alone with the Columbus Avenue original. And, beyond that, the celebrated original DDL, which had captured so much attention on its opening, in fact had never lived up to its advance billing. A series of managers proved unable to make the shop competitive with other, longer-established food stores on the New York's Upper West Side.

Tihany, who was brought in on the original project after much of the planning was complete, subsequently worked with Di Laurentiis on several operation/design changes within the ambitious prototype. In the end, however, the Columbus Avenue operation was sold.

Undaunted, Tihany proceeded to take on the two new sites. The Beverly Hills space was a barnlike former clothing store with a 40-foot ceiling and 11,500 square feet of space. The DDL Trump Tower site, on the other hand, had to be integrated into the 10,000-square-foot atrium level of a public shopping arcade. By sticking with certain of the luxurious materials and furnishings already incorporated into the Columbus Avenue store, and by treating both new spaces with flair, Tihany was able to achieve a continuity of look and, more important, of feel, making each shop say "DDL."

The Beverly Hills store actually gave Tihany more freedom to create the desired dramatic presentation of food, a key element in the DDL equation, than did its Columbus Avenue counterpart. For unlike the labyrinthine Columbus Avenue store, installed on the street level of a then newly renovated cooperative apartment building, here was a rectangular open space, and thus, says Tihany, "the opportunity to design a more cohesive scheme—to make a complete statement."

This statement is immediately apparent, for Tihany makes sure visitors see all of the various areas of merchandise and the restaurant (placed atop a rear balcony) as soon as they

DDL FOODSHOW *Beverly Hills, California; New York City*
Owner: *Dino Di Laurentiis*
Interior Design: *Adam Tihany International (Adam D. Tihany, principal; Deborah Branham, Doug Middleton, project designers [Beverly Hills])*
Photography: © *Yoshi Yoshimi*

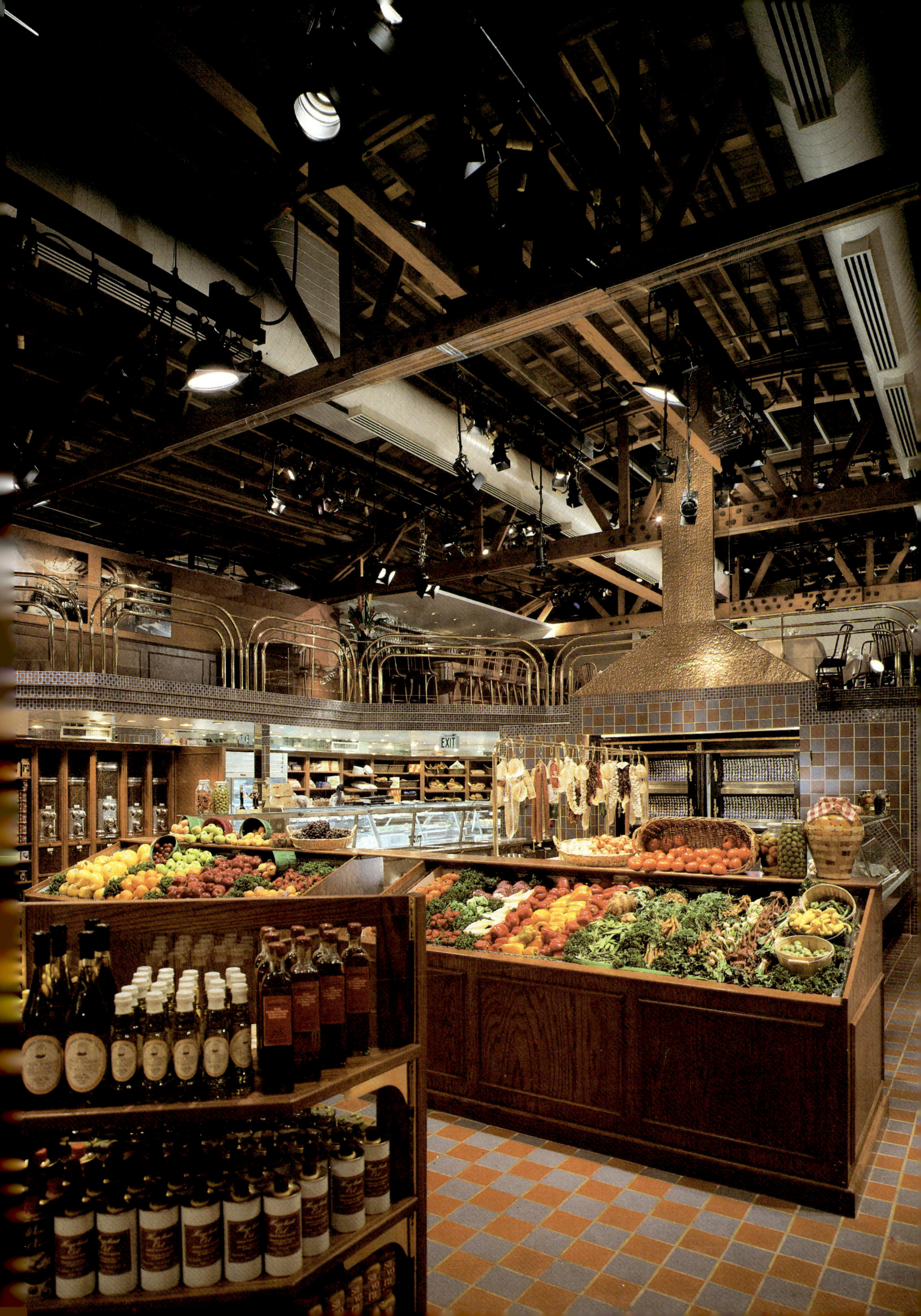
EXIT

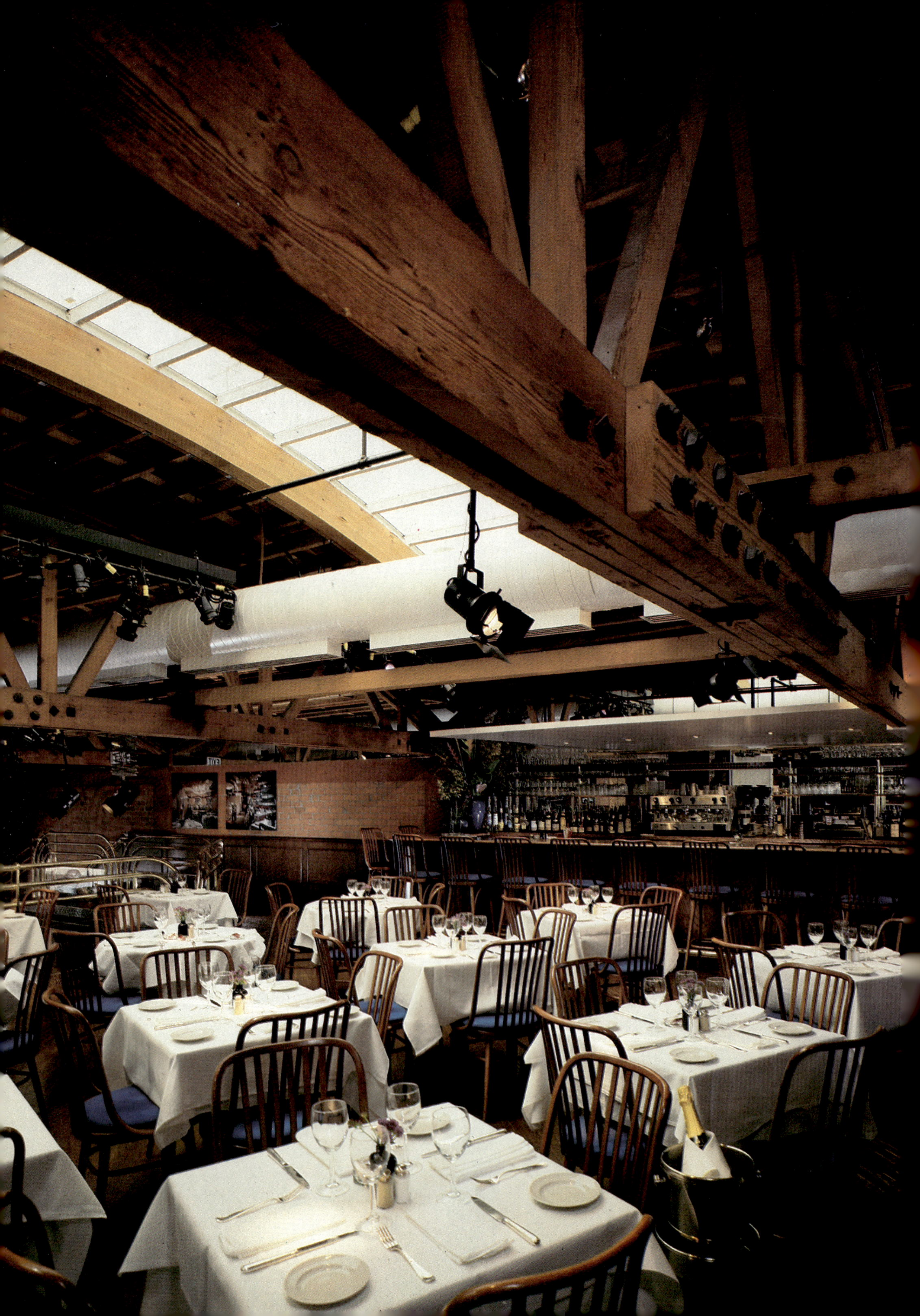

enter the front door. "I wanted a picture of the whole offering in one shot," he says.

What visitors see in this $2 million renovation is very similar to what customers at DDL on Columbus Avenue saw: merchandise displayed in and atop fine oak cabinets, plenty of brass railings, a floor paved in blue and terracotta-colored tiles, exposed brick walls, and—for a real movie touch—big, black boom-mounted lights, which make theater of even the lowliest bag of pasta. Yet there are also some key differences between this and the original DDL. For instance the room's great height opens it up, while exposed wooden ceiling beams (salvaged from the original building) impart a somewhat folksy touch that works to bring the grandeur down to a more human level.

Moreover, the layout is more logical, building from V-shaped display cases of packaged foods, through a fresh produce display, past pastries and pasta/bread, then on to a cold prepared-food display (*gastronomia*) and a hot prepared-food display (*rotisseria*). This final area is dominated by a huge copper-and-gold-mirror smoke shaft rising majestically to the ceiling from the *rotisseria* ovens.

Above this rear area is the balcony, where bistro tables sit waiting for plates of North Italian gourmet food. A skylight has been added to the ceiling above the restaurant. Explains the designer: "This light creates an indoor/outdoor feeling—it's very 'L.A.' Also, it's a problem drawing people all the way back and up to the balcony, and this light helps attract them."

Creating what he calls "a food theater for the eighties" proved more difficult for Tihany at Trump Tower. Here, the lobby/shopping arcade, a six-story open space sheathed entirely in rose-hued marble, already possessed a strong identity of its own—namely, the signature of another strong personality, New York City real estate developer Donald Trump. Tihany also faced severe restrictions in terms of signage and general architectural guidelines.

Given the sensitivity of the undertaking, Tihany tried to integrate the DDL outlet as much as possible into the lobby while holding fast to an identity of its own.

There are four distinct pieces to the DDL at Trump Tower: a glass-enclosed deli (a miniature version of the food sections designed for the other two DDLs); a 1,000-square-foot bar area where customers buy drinks and sandwiches; the main atrium space where the food and drinks are consumed (and separated from the bar by an escalator), and, finally, a 2,000-square-foot formal dining area/bistro, partially blocked from the atrium by plants and railings—the one space in which the designer could create a sense of theater.

The entire dramatic effect was created at Trump Tower on a $700,000 budget. The lighting here is also provided by spots: small gold spots rather than the giant booms found in the other DDLs. The bar chairs and stools are identical to those in the other DDLs, and they help identify each section of the Trump store. For example, the bar chairs and stools are black with red velvet seat covers, while the atrium's chairs are oak with green velvet seat covers, and the bistro's chairs are, again, black with red seats.

Tihany has captured the "DDL Look" without resorting to signage or gimmickry by repeating the spirit of the design of the original store: uncluttered elegance, luxurious materials, and a dramatic stage set for dining and shopping.

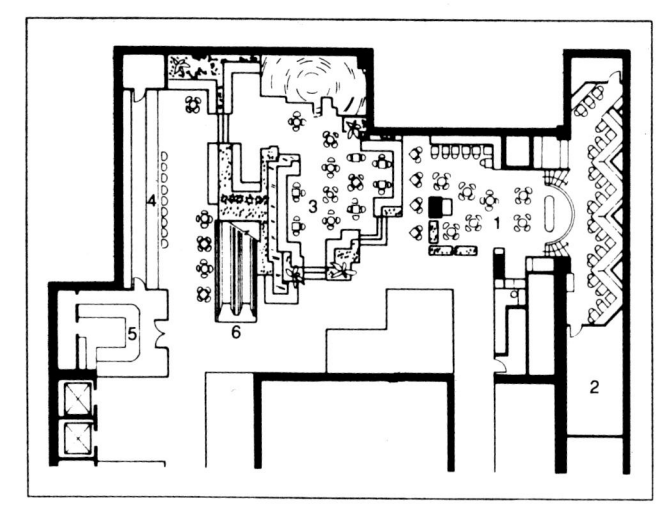

At Trump tower (above), the DDL operation consists of four elements: a small, glass-enclosed deli, a bar for drinks and sandwiches, a formal dining area, and an atrium space. Floorplan: bistro (1); kitchen (2); atrium (3); bar (4); foodshow (5); escalators (6).

A full-service restaurant located on a balconied upper tier at the Beverly Hills location (opposite) serves a wide variety of dishes prepared in the DDL kitchens—and available at retail downstairs. Floorplan showing ground floor and balcony of Beverly Hills DDL (below): entrance (1); catering area (2); cashier (3); groceries (4); chocolates (5); wines (6); coffee/tea (7); hot foods (8); cold foods (9); rotisseria (10); cheese (11); fish/paté (12); pasta/bread (13); stairs (14); dining area (15); restrooms (16); bar (17); buffet (18).

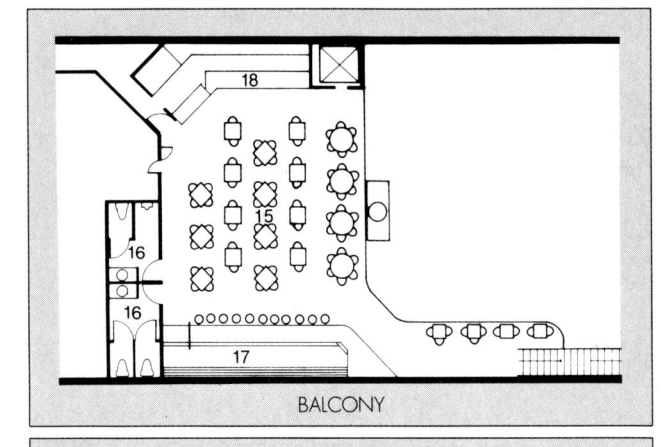

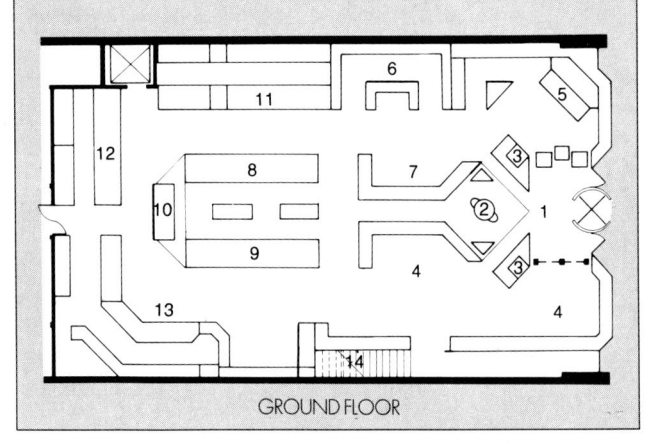

UNEARTH AN ANCIENT THEME
REFERENCES TO CLASSICAL ARCHITECTURE ANIMATE THE RENOVATION OF THIS EAT-IN/TAKE-OUT DELI

The designers of Lakeside Delicatessen pretended they were unearthing and restoring the remains of an ancient structure, obscured by modern construction: to wit, the classic columns, the sea god, and the numerous other classical allusions. Inside the rotunda (left) the designers discovered the sea god Triton inside the terrazzo flooring. An arcade with market stalls (opposite) connects the entrance rotunda with the outdoor garden. The forced perspective arcade can be seen from the second-story dining area.

ON A QUIET shopping street in the Lakeshore district of Oakland, one can enjoy espresso and cannoli in a skylit rotunda, buy pasta and prosciutto in an arcaded market, and sip wine beside an antique grotto. The place is the Lakeside Delicatessen, a neighborhood institution for fifty years, recently transformed by Ace Architects (Oakland).

The Ace partnership—Lucia Howard and David Weingarten—took their inspiration from classical Italian architecture, with a bow to the wit and erudition of that pioneer of postmodernism, Charles Moore. Like Moore, Howard and Weingarten create illusions of space and textural richness with the simplest materials, animating practical, low-cost structures with ornament and color. Moore's vision of a building's potential ("It's only a tiny piece of the real world, yet this place is made to seem like an entire world") is one they apparently share.

The Lakeside Delicatessen is witty and whimsical, scholarly in its architectural allusions, and strikingly dramatic. It is a popular success, holding the loyalty of longtime regulars while luring a new generation of young customers. It cele-

LAKESIDE DELICATESSEN	*Oakland, California*
Owners:	Edward and Mary Curotto
Architecture:	Ace Architects (Lucia Howard, David Weingarten)
Structural Engineer:	Steven Tiping and Associates
Landscape Architecture:	Meacham O'Brien
Kitchen Design:	Cunningham/Kamada
General Contractor:	Michael Muscardi
Seating:	47
Photography:	© Russell Abraham

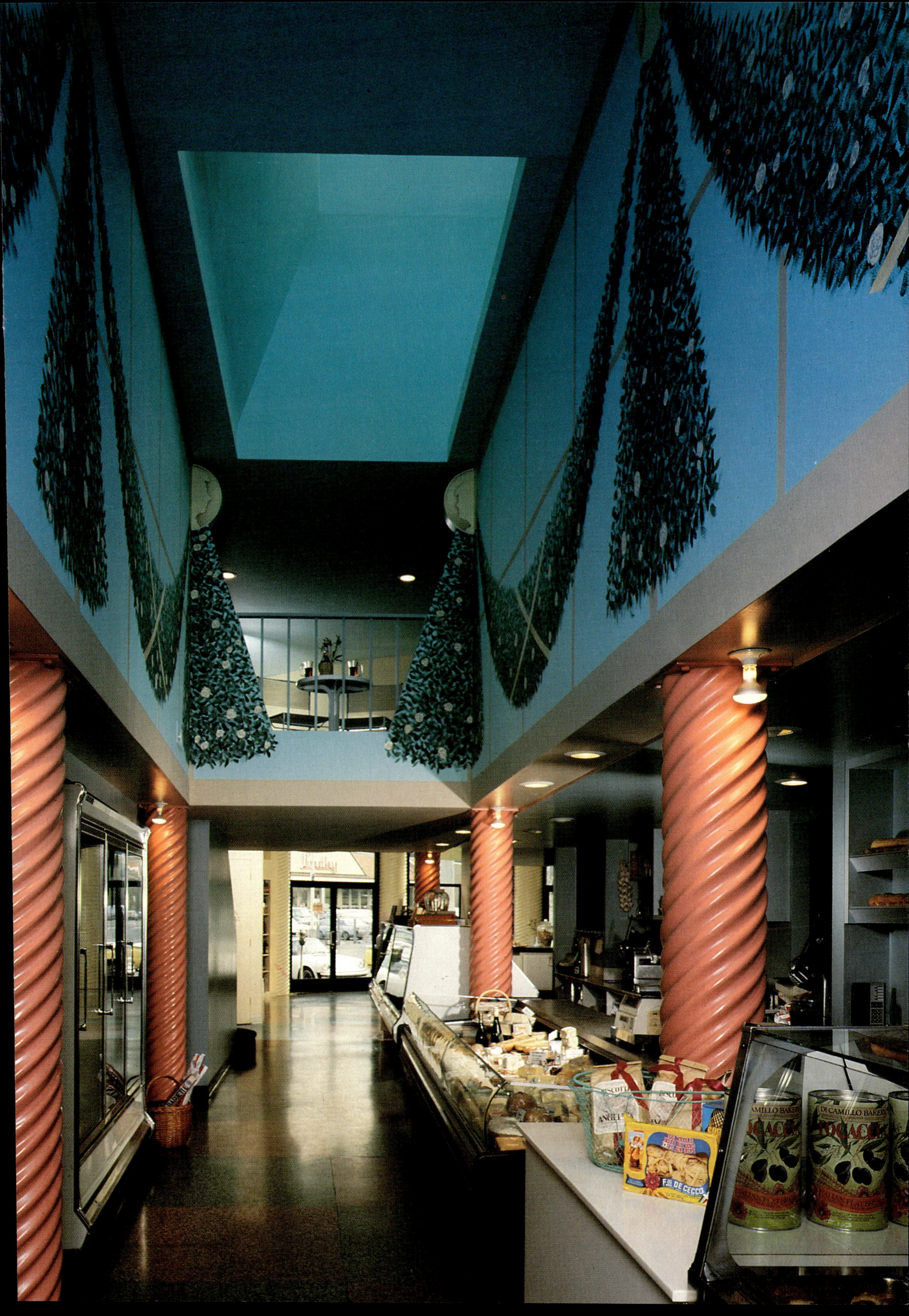

A "Neptune" fountain, an ivy-clad trellis, and columns decorate the café gardens.

brates a shift of ownership from father to son (the present owners are Ed and Mary Curotto) and the continuity of family tradition.

As a spur to invention, Howard and Weingarten pretended they were unearthing and restoring the remains of an ancient structure, obscured by modern construction. The partners "discovered" a pantheonlike rotunda bulging through a thirties tiled facade. Below the layers of the floor was "found" a green terrazzo figure of the sea god Triton, and above, in the dome, an oculus that focuses a beam of sunlight on the desserts at lunchtime. Stripping the walls "revealed" an antique wallpainting dedicated to the pleasures of food and wine. From the rotunda, a *prospettivo*—an arcade in forced perspective—leads back past market stalls of food to a tiny garden. The arcade is framed by columns, with painted trellis and ivy above, and extends outdoors to a grotto with a Neptune fountain and a superstructure of ivy-clad trellis.

These fancies were as much fun for the architects as they were for the owners. But this is no folly. Inventive use has been made of the existing structure, combining restaurant, café, and store without clutter or overcrowding. The sequence of sunlit rotunda, bustling market, and tranquil garden offers dramatic shifts of mood and scale.

The Deli offers seating for 47—the greatest number that local regulations would permit on this site—and lightweight Italian chairs and tables are deftly inserted into the garden, the rotunda, and a tiny mezzanine-level gallery. The snappy facade is created with the simplest of means: a neon pediment, suspended swags, and neobaroque drainage-pipe columns that are used again in the arcade. There is a sense of theater that is as appropriate to an American Main Street as to the Genovese heritage of the Curottos.

REWORK A NEIGHBORHOOD TRADITION
A BELOVED SEAFOOD RESTAURANT GETS TOTAL DESIGN UPDATE

WHEN JOHN POLCARI decided after twenty-five years in the restaurant business that he wanted to change his whole operation, Ristorante Polcari closed down. Scaffolding went up around the landmark Italian restaurant in Boston's North End, and no one was talking. Ten months and $1.3 million later, black and white tiles, glass brick, expansive windows, and canvas awnings replaced the old, austere facade. A grocery-eatery replaced a traditional Italian restaurant.

The spiffy new awning that reads "John B. Polcari & Sons—Since 1922" was John Polcari's tribute to his parents, who started the business as an Italian-American grocery soon after they arrived in the United States. Polcari will show you a picture of the old establishment: His older brother beams from behind a food-laden counter; sausages hang overhead; canned goods fill the shelves behind. In the new restaurant, Polcari wanted to recreate this old-fashioned mood within the context of the eighties experience. He wanted, moreover, to cater to the changing neighborhood, tapping the new market of young professionals in the North End.

POLCARI & SONS	*Boston, Massachusetts*
Owner:	*Polcari Enterprises*
Architecture/Interior Design:	*Robert Flack & Associates, Inc. (Robert Flack, Fran Forman, John Betts, Frederick Kuhn, David Reiss)*
Lighting Consultant:	*Chris Ripman*
Graphic Consultant:	*Robert Flack & Associates*
Structural Consultant:	*Bolton DiMartino*
Mechanical Consultant:	*Atkinson Engineering*
Contractor:	*Lloyd Ripa Construction*
Budget:	*$1.3 million*
Time:	*10 months (construction)*
Photography:	*© David DuBusc*

Polcari's black and white tile facade (above) establishes a spirited theme that carries through the groceria (right), designed to woo passersby and shoppers.

For design team members Robert Flack and Fran Forman (Robert Flack and Associates, Cambridge), that translated into a grocery store with a bar in the middle and a restaurant with an open kitchen. "People grow up in kitchens; they feel comfortable there," says Polcari. "I thought he was crazy," says Flack, "wanting a groceria and a dining room and a bar and an open kitchen. And then later, I suggested he add a café too!"

The entrance to Polcari's was moved 30 feet to allow customers to enter through the groceria past a 500-gallon fish tank. Flack feels this was the single most important innovation, because it made patrons experience the space before coming in to dine. "We've laid out the restaurant so that one literally becomes a part of the atmosphere on the way to the dining room," Flack says. To the left, glass cases display an array of tantalizing delicacies. The expansive windows behind the counter double as glass refrigerator units—their contents on view to both customers and passersby. In the middle of the rooms is a circular produce stand; to the right, a café and bar. Beyond is the wide entrance to the bustling kitchen. Through the white-tiled archway, beyond the busy groceria, is the dining room, tiled in black and white. Mirrors line the wall opposite the windows, reflecting movement on the street and adding life to the room.

Patrons are encouraged to move around and to interact with the staff. "The fact that you can go back into the kitchen and talk to the cooks was very important to Polcari and subsequently to the evolution of the concept," says Flack. "Since we were involved in planning from the start, we were able to integrate the architecture, the interior design, and the graphics, giving all the elements of the design a consistent, strong image. The space is highly functional and it's characterized by honesty."

This is not to say that the function-related design is considered "finished." As the cook or the manager of the groceria discovers more efficient ways of conducting business, aspects

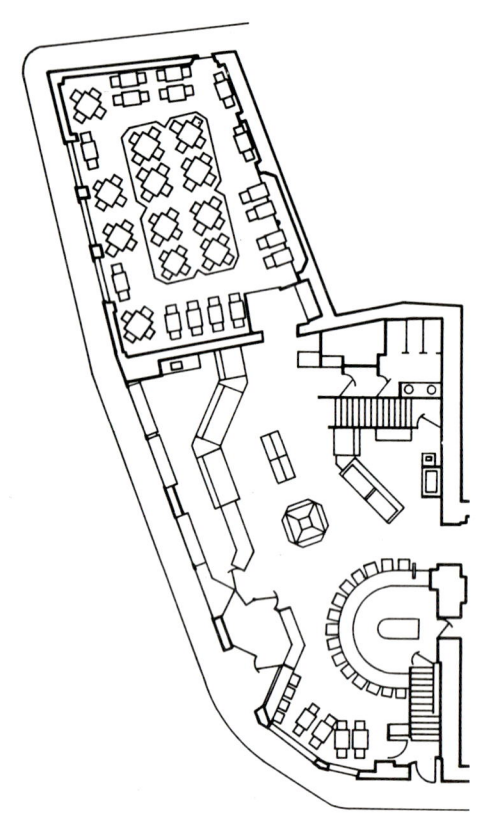

The floorplan (top) shows the entrance that was moved 30 feet to enable customers to shop, stop at the lobster bar (right) for a drink, and then move through the archway to the new dining room (opposite).

of the design will also change. The owners agree: In this type of facility, constant revision is necessary.

According to Flack, while the retail sales function dictated the design aesthetic in the groceria ("It was all aimed at producing sales"), the designers relied on stylish materials such as tile and glass block to key the dining areas, integrating them visually with the groceria and the facade. "The project would have been a lot simpler if we could have torn down the building and started over. As it was, we had to completely redo wiring and plumbing and in some areas work through 3-foot walls. Were it not for that, the openings to the dining room and kitchen would have been much wider, allowing even greater interaction than is possible now," says Flack.

Graphics—everything from the awnings to the labels on the spice containers—play a large part in unifying the experience of Polcari's. Forman explains that labels, aprons, menus, matchboxes, tabletop wares, and signage were all selected to suggest the concept of a grocery store. "Even the paper that the menus are printed on carries the theme—it comes off a roll, crisp white, like wrapping paper. The grid motif is suggested by the tiles on the interior and exterior of awnings and aprons. The black rule in the logo is seen again on the simple white Royal Doulton china. Everything relates to everything else," says Forman.

IN A SMALL SPACE, FOCUS ON A "FOOD MACHINE"
A LAMINATED UNIT COMBINES FOOD PREP AND DISPLAY PLUS RETAIL SALES

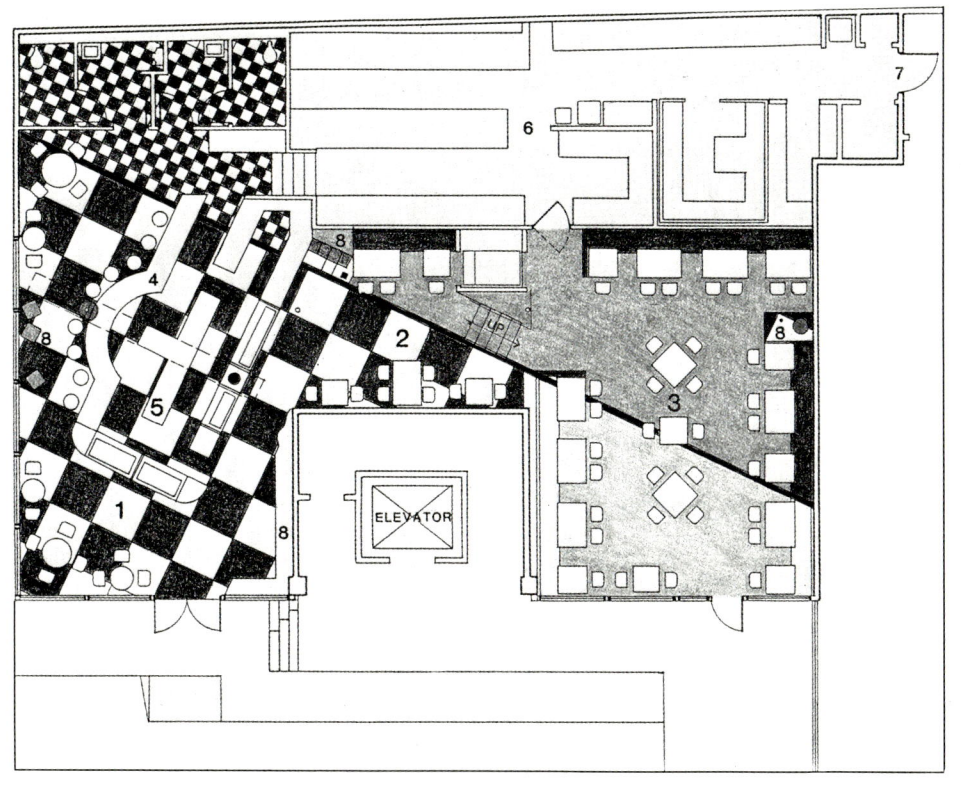

The new Piret's in Beverly Hills includes a retail food operation, a bistro, and a fine dining area. Interior lighting supports outside neon signage to create a unified exterior. In the "swing area," elements of the bistro and dining room interface. Piret's efficient marketing tool is its "food machine," a custom-designed 450-square-foot display unit (above). Floorplan: bistro dining (1); swing area (2); fine dining area (3); cappucino/wine bar (4); food machine (5); kitchen (6); receiving (7); custom display unit (8).

MOST CALIFORNIANS think of Piret's as a gourmet food and cookware store with a cooking school, a wine shop, a dining area, and take-out service. But the six-store chain shifted its emphasis slightly by putting a lot of emphasis on the restaurant portion of its establishment in the new seventh Piret's in Beverly Hills.

Looking to attract the business lunch crowd as well as after-theater diners, Vicorp took a 3,500-square-foot space on the main level of a commercial building and told designers to "maximize seating and de-emphasize retail a bit." The design team had a problem fitting everything in; the new location was just half the size of the other units.

This Piret's, which does not have a cooking school, offers one central retail section to market a variety of products. To consolidate the displays of wine, the food prep counter, and the refrigerator display cases, Vicorp created a "food machine," a 450-square-foot unit clad in white plastic laminate. Kitchen functions are part of the unit. A central island yields more counter space for food preparation. Traffic flows around its perimeter. The unit is angled out (see floor plan) to maximize visibility of the food unit from the street and enhance the marketing efficiency of the store.

In addition to its minimal size, the site had a U shape to allow for the building's elevator core and stairwell and a 2½-foot change in floor levels, front to back.

PIRET'S	*Beverly Hills, California*
Owner:	*Vicorp Specialty Restaurants*
Architecture:	*Colwell Ray Hornacek Okinaka (CRHO) (Robert J. Hornacek, principal-in-charge; Mark A. Spatz, project designer; Eva Sloan, project architect)*
Interior Design:	*CRHO, Inc.*
General Contractor:	*Vicorp Specialty Restaurants*
Seating:	*96*
Photography:	*© Jack Boyd*

DRAMATIZE A DELI WITH ANGLES
EVEN THE KITCHEN IS OPEN TO VIEW IN THIS "GENERIC DELI"

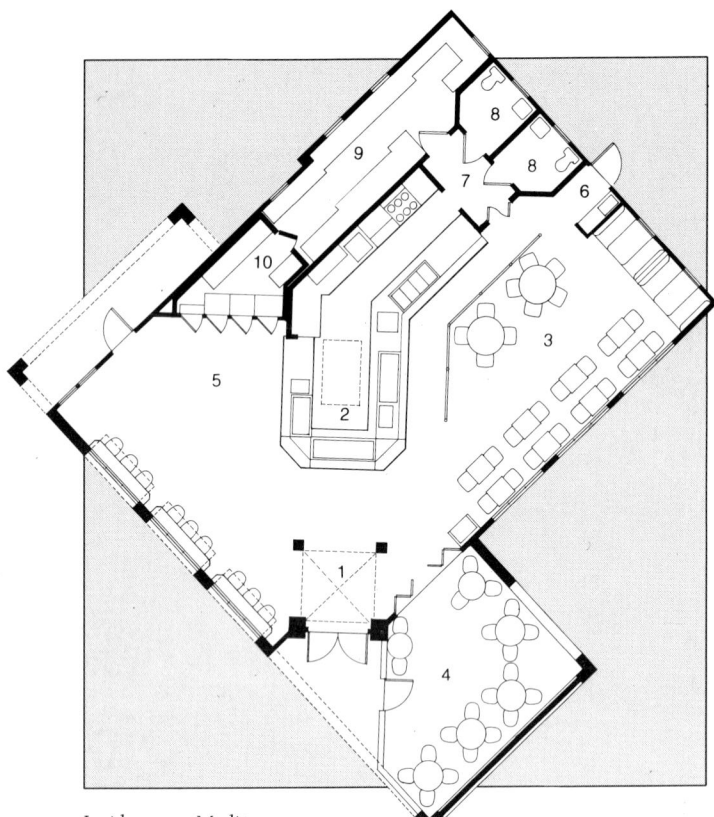

Inside a neo-Mediterranean structure lit by a neon sign that reads "Tutti's," black nylon rails separate an open kitchen and deli counter from the mixed-use operation's main dining room (opposite). Access to take-out and dining areas is to the left and right of the entrance. The interior arrangement is based on a repetition of forty-five-degree angles in the open kitchen and seating areas, as well as in the packaged food department. Floorplan: entry (1); deli display cases (2); dining area (3); outdoor dining area (4); retail service (5); service entry (6); foyer (7); restrooms (8); kitchen (9); cooler (10).

At Tutti's, an eat-in/take-out deli located in Montecito, California, designers John Leggitt, AIA, T. R. Kipelainen, and Brad Emerson, all of the Santa Barbara–based Designworks firm, have integrated influences from different decades and countries into what Leggitt calls a "low-tech generic deli."

With an exposed kitchen, and emphasis on food presentation, "we have created theatrics by having the people interface with the entire cooking operation," says Leggitt. The neo-Mediterranean style of the building's exterior shell, with its plaster finish, tilework, and quasi-Spanish theme tower evolved in response to a Santa Barbara city ordinance mandating Hispanic architecture.

To add warmth and attract passing traffic along the north-facing streetside entrance, plate-glass windows and skylights were installed, and blue neon Tutti's signage and a 20-seat, 310-square-foot exterior dining patio were added.

At the entrance to the 2,000-square-foot interior, the designers placed one spotlighted deli counter just beyond two blue tiled columns and beneath the crowning hot salmon-colored interior of the tower. The packaged food sales area lies to the left, the open kitchen and 60-seat dining area to the right.

What makes it all work is the repeated use of forty-five-degree-angles in the open kitchen and seating areas and in the packaged food department; the angles give impact to the food display and guide people through the space. Customers are immediately aware of the take-out, and they see diners too.

While the forties theme is not instantly apparent, the architects researched old-fashioned Mom and Pop delis to adopt their familiar materials, colors, and finishes. The food display cases, the metal tables, and the terrazzo floors hark back to the 1940s, while the salmon, turquoise, and peach colors were lifted directly from vintage magazines. "The connections are subliminal," Leggitt attests.

A mix of incandescent spots, wall sconces, and soffit-hidden fluorescents light the multipurpose interior. In the open kitchen, low-voltage fluorescents bring out the food colors without overlighting the adjacent dining area. In fact, at night the dining area is lit exclusively by candles, helped along by light spilling in from the kitchen and spotlighted food display counters. There is no need for artwork—the food says it all.

TUTTI'S	*Montecito, California*
Owner:	*O'Hagen and Klein, Inc.*
Design:	*Designworks (John Leggitt, T. L. Kipelainen, Brad Emerson)*
Size: *2,000 square feet*	**Seating**: *80*
Photography:	*© James Chen Studios*

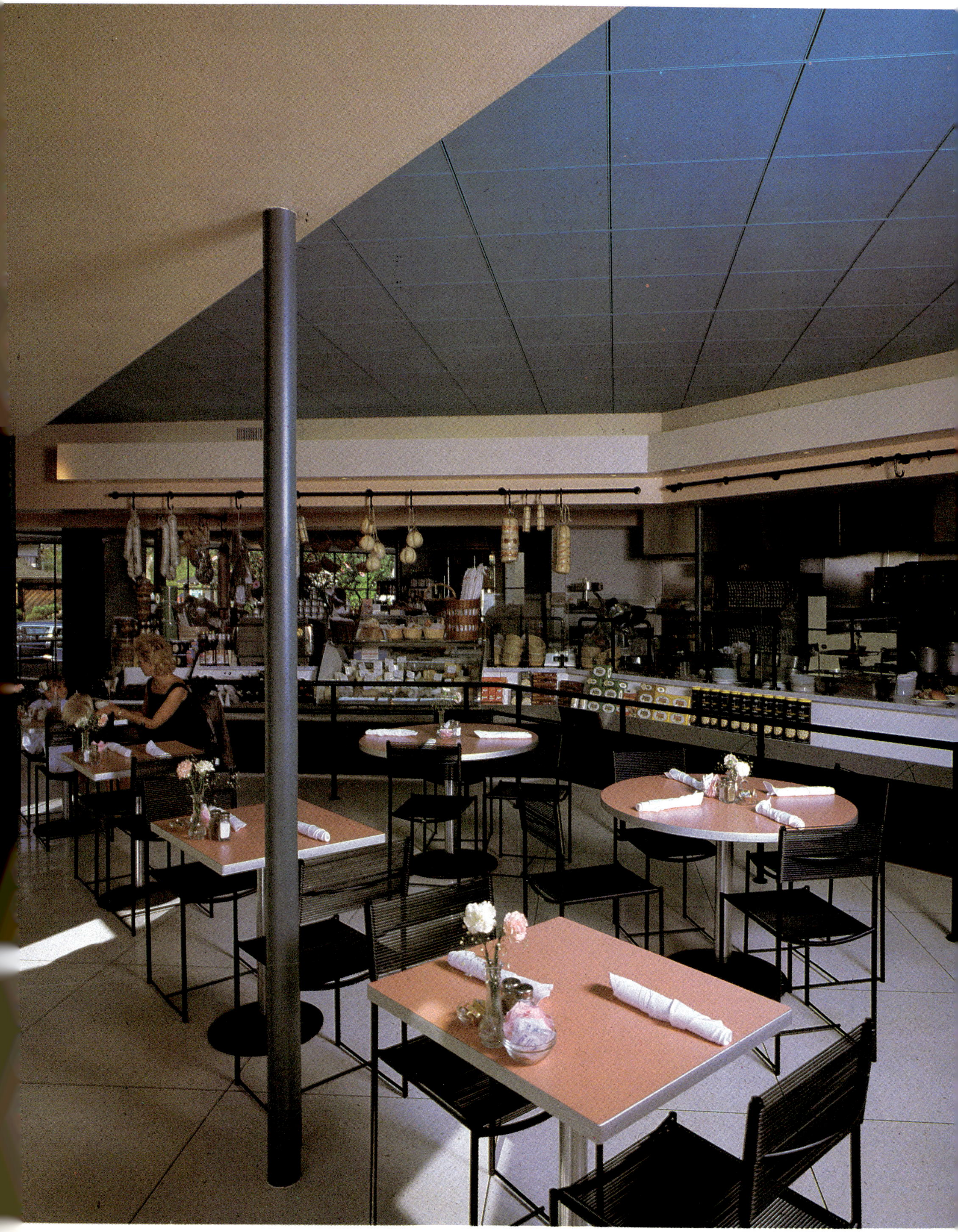

SHOWCASE TAKE-OUT FOOD
TWO RETAIL FOOD FACILITIES DESIGNED TO MAXIMIZE IMPULSE PURCHASES

TAKE-OUT FOOD establishments, which have appeared all over the map, meet different demands. Some, like Duck and Decanter in a Scottsdale, Arizona, shopping mall, feature a gourmet deli café that spills into a courtyard shared by other boutiques. Another, Panache in Fullerton, California, woos vehicular traffic with "glitz."

Duck and Decanter's project architect Bill Larson (Mittelstaedt Kesler Ltd., Phoenix) believes that to develop an eat-in/take-out establishment, it helps to have experience in mainstream retail design. Larson's client, the owner of the Camel View Plaza Mall, had budgeted $450,000 for the gourmet deli and dining court and expected the job to be finished in just eight months. The facility would not only serve shoppers during mall hours, it would also function as a catering hall.

The heart of the project is the 5,000-square-foot retail enclosure, which offers kitchen equipment as well as snack lunches, gourmet foods, and wine. Using shiny white showcases and pristine tile flooring, the designers have created an attractive environment that highlights the merchandise. They intentionally arranged foods to maximize spontaneous purchases, placing candies near the sandwich counter waiting area, for example. Lighting is also arranged for retail impact: There are downlights over pieces of refrigeration equipment and track-mounted flexible can lights for changing displays.

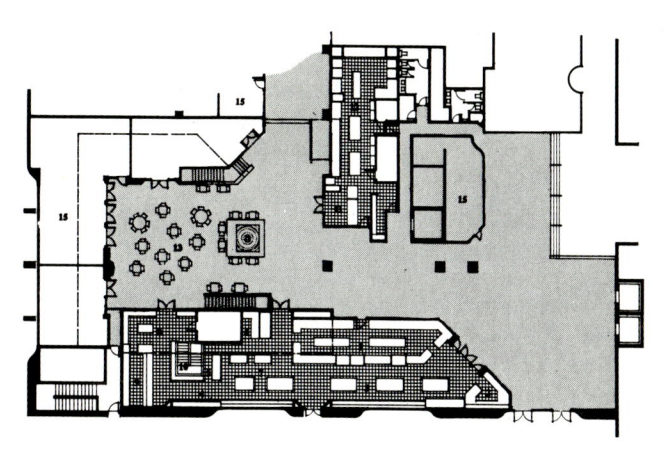

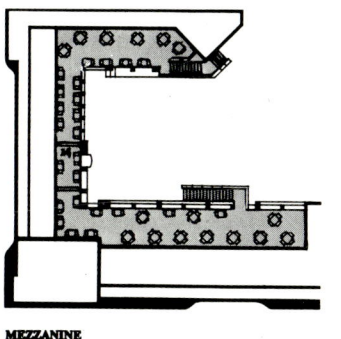

Duck and Decanter's cathedral ceiling (opposite) is reflected in a mirror over the wine bar. The designer used shiny white, easy-to-care-for materials. The white surfaces are accented with equally practical polyurethane-finished light oak trim. Floorplan: Duck and Decanter courtyard, above; mezzanine, left. Photography: © A. F. Payne.

At Panache, located at a busy crossroads in Orange County, California, designer Michael Bolton (Michael Bolton Designs, Carmel, California) used neon graphics that can be seen by cars passing the window walls of the 6,500-square-foot ground-level space. The script signage is in colloquial French to satisfy the client's wish for European ambience.

Low-energy neon takes the load off the incandescent lighting, and low-voltage downlights emphasize the merchandise. Bolton believes "you have to understand the psychology of sales" to plan a successful food-retailing project. To maximize visibility, food-showcase design must not be lower than three feet from the floor.

Bolton set Panache on the diagonal to compensate for the somewhat difficult L-shaped space and to ensure "that you can't turn around without being sold something visually. You get both a distant focus and a point-of-sale focus."

The project came to $1.5 million, including $350,000 worth of refrigeration and display equipment and the black and white checkered marble floors.

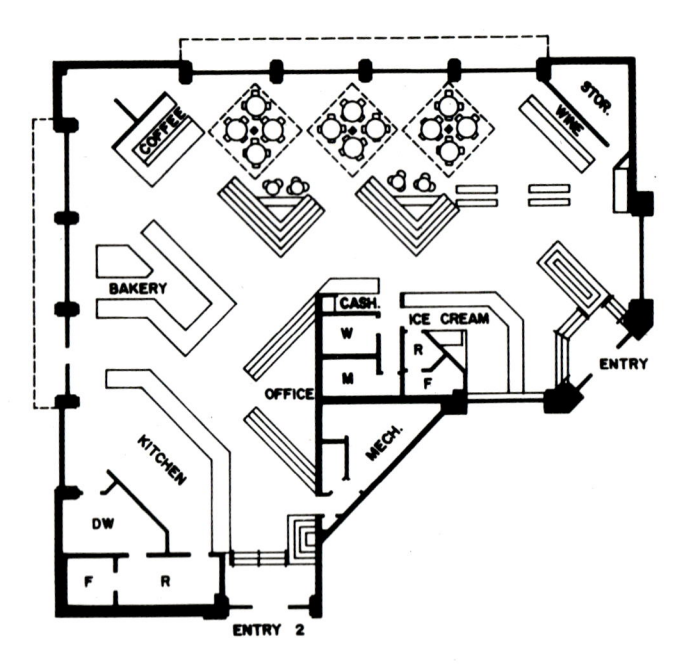

Panache's neon signage delineates retail areas such as the ice cream bar (opposite). L-shaped space is laid out on a diagonal (above). Marble checkered floors were installed at a hefty expense because the designer believes that customers "perceive the floor first, so that's where we put the money, to impart a feeling of substance and quality." Photography: © Lange Photography.

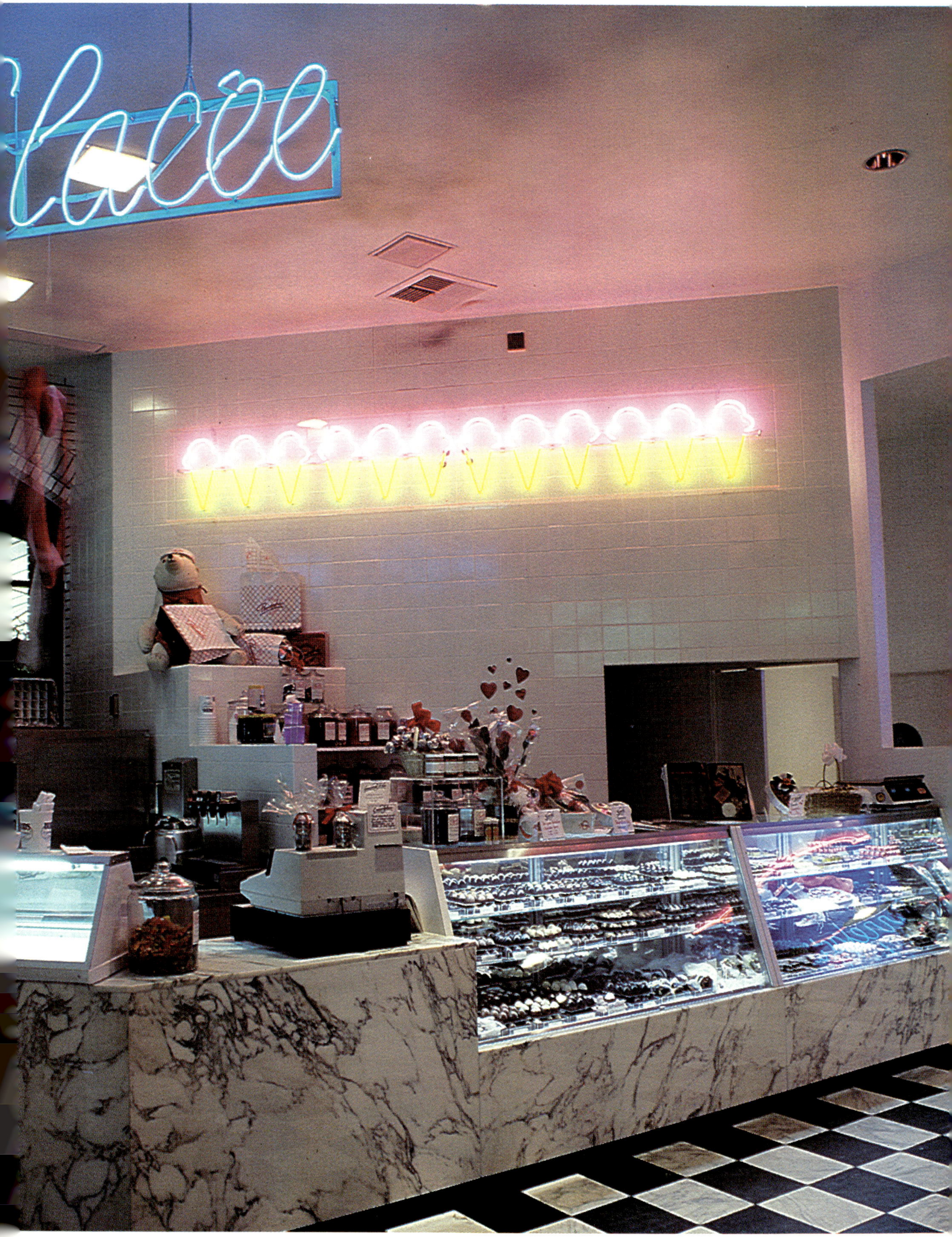

RECALL A WATERSIDE MARKET
AN URBAN REDEVELOPMENT SCHEME BRINGS OLD NEW YORK BACK TO LIFE

Despite the trendy quality of the upscale retail food shops found in nearly every major American city today, the take-out concept originated centuries ago with the traditional European marketplace, where fresh foods were piled up in open-air stalls.

Boston's Quincy Market, restored in the mid-1970s by the Rouse Company, was the first notable recent success of this kind. It sparked enthusiastic response from pedestrians and speculators alike. On its heels came New York's South Street Seaport, also developed by the Rouse Company; here too, an old market building—in this case, the Fulton Street Fish Market—became the centerpiece. Its plan consists of one long, wide corridor studded with "stalls" and pushcarts and punctuated at either end with sit-down restaurants. The two sides of the building that face into the project are predominantly composed of floor-to-ceiling glass with sections that open completely in warm weather, providing extra points of access.

Situated in about seventy 600- to 800-square-foot retail stalls in the market are a florist, several bakeries, a cheese shop, a fish vendor, a pickle vendor, and several "country stores" that sell things other than food.

Key to the designs on both levels of the Market Building is exciting graphics. Graphics work to shape the individual shops and lend direction to design; without strong graphics it would be difficult to determine, in many cases, where one stall begins and another ends. Signs, menus, matchbooks, and logos help determine a strong and memorable identity for each vendor.

Only a few of the many shops are shown here: A & D Mercantile and Merchant's Coffee, Tea, and Spice, both establishments designed by Madeline Speer of New York; Paxton & Whitfield and Provisions, both designed by Judith Stockman. The Fulton Market Building itself was designed by Benjamin Thompson of Boston.

The first floor of the Fulton Market Building mixes period and modern design. Favored materials include woods, stone (slate and marble), brass, and metal. Lighting fixtures and a ceiling grid recreate outdoor market roof structures, contributing to the rugged atmosphere of the new building. Retail space is divided into stalls with 44-inch-high walls, vivid graphics, and overflowing displays. In total, it expresses The Rouse Company's vision of a huge market with bustling stalls that flow into one another. Originally, the concept called for the displays to be changed daily in their entirety, but as it turned out, a portion of each stall remains fixed while the rest can be dismantled. Most designers gave merchandising flexibility top priority and chose movable tables for the display at the stall's front perimeters. Shown above are Merchant's Coffee, Tea, and Spice (top), and A & D Mercantile (above), a food-related store, both designed by Madeline Speer. Photography: © Bill Kontzias.

The massive Fulton Market Building (top, left) recaptures—in a neighborhood of old and new buildings—a seaport oriented community, as an open-air museum of the street. The interior of the market building reflects this atmosphere as well, with its rugged mechanical ambience. Benjamin Thompson and Associates of Boston, designers of the overall project, retained exposed structural elements such as painted columns, red iron stairwells, and steel roof decking. They also used industrial lights and a white ceiling grid. Judith Stockman, who designed the two projects shown here, Provisions—a country store illustrated in two views—and Paxton & Whitfield—an English-style cheesemonger shop (above, left). "The trick," says Stockman, "was to create an individual identity within an overwhelming space of definite character." Allowing for easy traffic flow within the two spaces became key to Stockman's design solutions: At Provisions she used display islands and attractive open shelving, and at Paxton & Whitfield she created a marble-tiled, donut-shaped counter area with built-in refrigeration units. Photography: © Norman McGrath.

8. RESTAURANTS

Photography: © Peter Paige

IN HOTELS

No longer are hotel dining rooms considered automatic money-losers, necessities designed just for hotel guests. Now many of those rooms are planned as destination restaurants to attract local patronage—and to provide an independent profit center for the hotel operation.

Today's hotel restaurants are more distinctively designed and more readily accessible from the outside than were their predecessors. In many establishments, the quality of the hotel restaurant has come to speak for the quality of the entire enterprise. As one hotel owner (Bill Wilkinson of Campton Place Hotel in San Francisco) puts it, "The easiest way to evaluate a hotel today is to eat in its restaurant."

Another fine example of the new breed of restaurants in hotels can be found in the recently opened Westin Hotel in Washington, D.C. (opposite). There, the 140-seat Colonnade restaurant incorporates "a classic Michelangelo idea," according to its designer, Sarah Tomerlin Lee of Tom Lee Limited (New York). Balanced by columns, its focal point is a dome that incorporates a radiant skylight. In it, Lee has created a room that glows both day and night. Its conservatorylike feeling is enhanced by its pink and green palette, flower-patterned fabrics and china, and graceful floral arrangements. Bright with sunlight during the daylight hours, the restaurant takes on a mellow, peachy glow as softly tinted lights reflect off the pink walls in the evening. The international set who are apt to dine here feel at home; the ambience is gracious and continental.

Undeniably, hotel restaurants are putting a new, more important face to the world. They can be found anywhere from Kennebunkport, Maine, where the second-floor dining room of The Schooners inn maximizes panoramic seaside views, to Paris, France, where Le Paris Hotel takes design inspiration from elegant deco oceanliners like the *Normandie*. Other notable hotel restaurants, destinations in themselves, include those of the Plaza Athénée in New York, the Ritz-Carleton in Naples, Florida, and tiny Morrison House in Alexandria, Virginia.

MAKE ELEGANCE THE STANDARD
FINE APPOINTMENTS UNDERSCORE QUALITY IN THIS HOTEL RESTAURANT

A coffered ceiling, subtle lighting, and carefully selected, high-end furnishings help create an atmosphere that speaks for Campton Place's quality. The architects sought a timeless elegance that would be flexible enough to accommodate customers as graciously at breakfast and lunch as it would at dinner. The peach-colored walls complement the gray upholstery and add a glow to the warm wood tones of the ample chairs.

AT THE CAMPTON PLACE HOTEL, a $25.5 million property in San Francisco, president Bill Wilkinson planned the hotel's first-class restaurant, also called Campton Place, to underscore the hotel's quality. "The easiest way to evaluate a hotel," says Wilkinson, "is to eat in the restaurant."

Considering the high-end market (business executives and luxury travelers) Wilkinson aimed for when he opened Campton Place, the restaurant became a cornerstone of the plans. And with only *one* restaurant, the design was even more challenging.

Beginning with a space that had been gutted to its structural steelwork, Wilkinson and James Northcutt, a Hirsch/Bedner affiliate who now owns his own Los Angeles architectural firm, sought to create an overall atmosphere of "well-scrubbed elegance" that also provided flexibility. Breakfast required a bright and cheerful ambience, while lunch and dinner required a more formal setting. Northcutt articulated Wilkinson's strong concepts with a design that isn't "period," yet suits San Francisco's formality. "We wanted a place that looked as though it had always been there," explains Northcutt. Carefully appointed with fine artifacts, artworks, and furnishings, Campton Place achieves precisely that effect.

The dining room's 12-foot ceilings seem almost Palladian, a treatment that carries over from the adjacent lobby ceilings. (There is also a separate street entrance.) Walls are a soft, warm peach tone, providing an attractive background for diners. The darker "high-style" carpeting is an attractive, practical floorcovering that sets off gray velvet upholstered armchairs and banquettes.

Northcutt specified a variety of lighting systems to provide flexibility and to accent the room's refined mood. Cove lighting encircles the space, bathing the room in a warm glow. Wall brackets emit soft light, and low-voltage downlighting brings out tables and artwork.

Tabletops are fitted with hand-blown crystal and retail-quality china. Mahogany table surfaces are sometimes bared for breakfast service but are covered with linens for lunch and dinner. Food comes from the adjacent kitchen. Two private dining rooms of 12 and 16 seats provide additional dining areas on the mezzanine and second levels. The adjacent cocktail lounge also opens to the lobby where beverage service is available.

CAMPTON PLACE	*San Francisco, California*

Owner: *Ayala Inc.*
Architecture: *Hirsch/Bedner & Associates (James Northcutt)*
Graphics: *Arais & Sarraille*
Millwork: *Ice-A-Boxa*
Contractor: *Ralph Larson & Sons*
Photography: *© Jaime Ardiles-Arce*

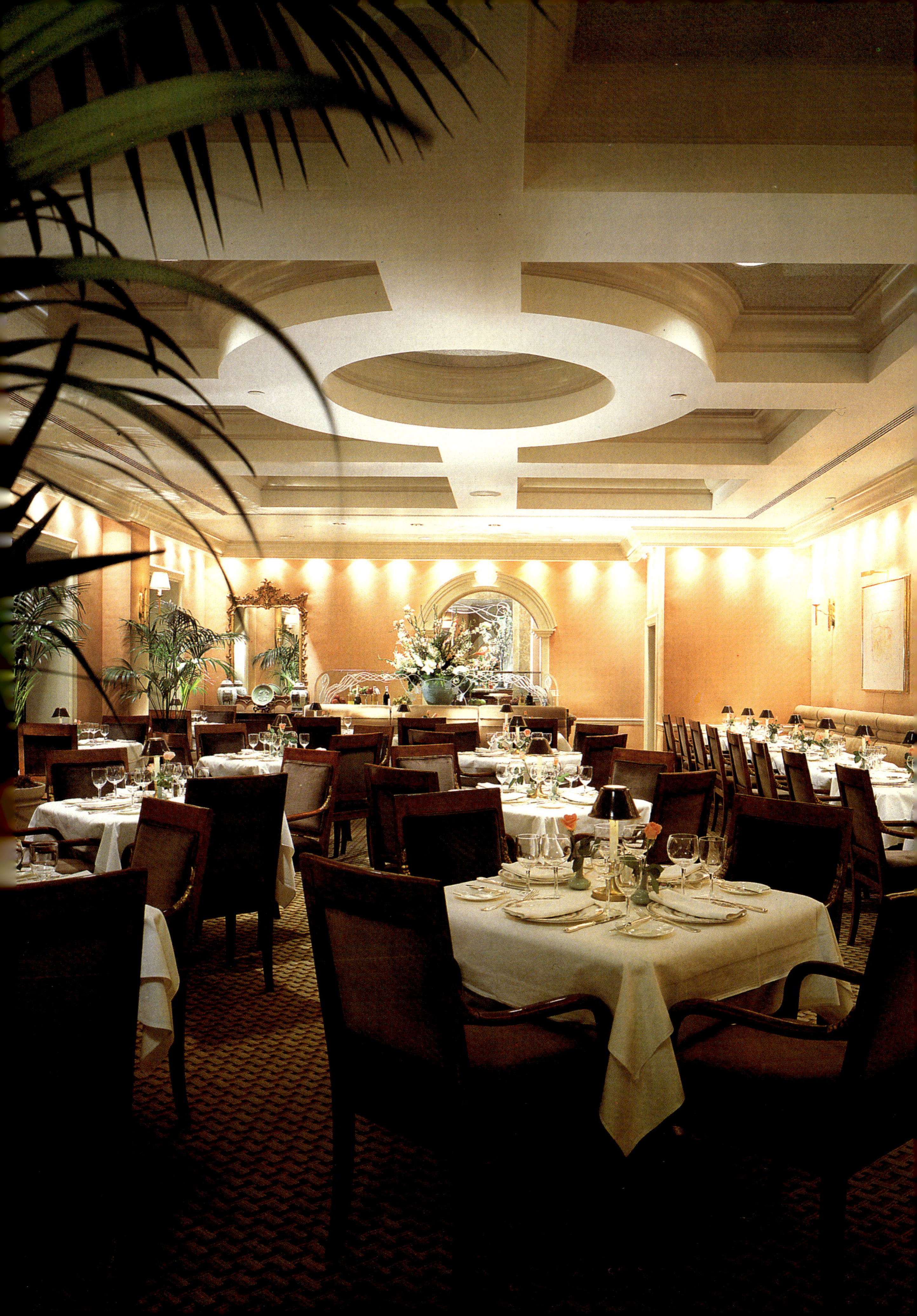

REPRODUCE THE FEDERAL STYLE
THE TRUE-TO-PERIOD DETAILS RECREATE A GRACIOUS ERA

Nineteenth-century American-style architectural details and furnishings in rich but quiet colors give the restaurant (opposite) the elegant ambience of a private home. But beneath the carefully recreated period look is unmistakable twentieth-century comfort and convenience. Each guestroom, like the one shown here, set up for breakfast, relies heavily on shades of peach, lemon, and celadon. Swagged drapes and crystal and brass light fixtures add to the period elegance.

MORRISON HOUSE appears to be the quintessential Early American inn, with a perfectly appointed restaurant to match. Located in Old Town, Alexandria, Virginia, it is housed in a five-story, forty-seven-room, Federal-style building with a facade of red brick laid in Flemish bond. The inn has arched windows throughout and a horseshoe-shaped staircase ascending from an attractive garden to an elliptical portico entrance. On the surface, it seems to be a nonpareil example of early nineteenth-century American architecture. In fact, Morrison House was built in 1985.

Nowhere is the ambience of Morrison House more keenly felt than in the two-room restaurant. Here, simplicity is combined with elegant touches that are true to the period. The restaurant (called Le Chandon d'Or) is located in the perfectly scaled nest of public rooms at the heart of the inn. It seats 50 in two rooms decorated to the taste of the Federal period, with Louis XVI-style armchairs covered in peach silk to match the walls. Swagged drapes, lighting fixtures of crystal and brass, fine napery, a beveled mirror, and nineteenth-century-style flatware, crystal, and silver add to the effect of elegance and the mood the owners and the designer wished to recreate.

The new-old inn is the brainchild of Robert E. Morrison, a Washington, D.C., developer, and his wife, who were influenced by the personal service and elegance of Europe's small hotels. They believed there was room for a similarly gracious restaurant and inn in the Washington area. To create it, they turned to Dan Bairley (Bairley & Maginniss, Alexandria, also architects for the contemporary office building on an adjoining plot of land) and Mary Douglas Drysdale (Drysdale Design Associates, Washington, D.C.), who was responsible for the inn's interior design, including the closely researched architectural detailing.

Keeping in mind that the Morrisons wanted their inn to look like an authentic Federal residence (one, however, that boasts every modern comfort), Drysdale managed to create interiors that evoke a bygone era without the slightest suggestion of kitsch.

MORRISON HOUSE	Alexandria, Virginia
Owners:	*Rosemary and Robert Morrison*
Interior Architecture/Design:	*Drysdale Design Associates (Mary Drysdale)*
Architecture:	*Bairley & Maginniss (Dan Bairley)*
Seating:	*50*
Photography:	*© Anne Gummerson*

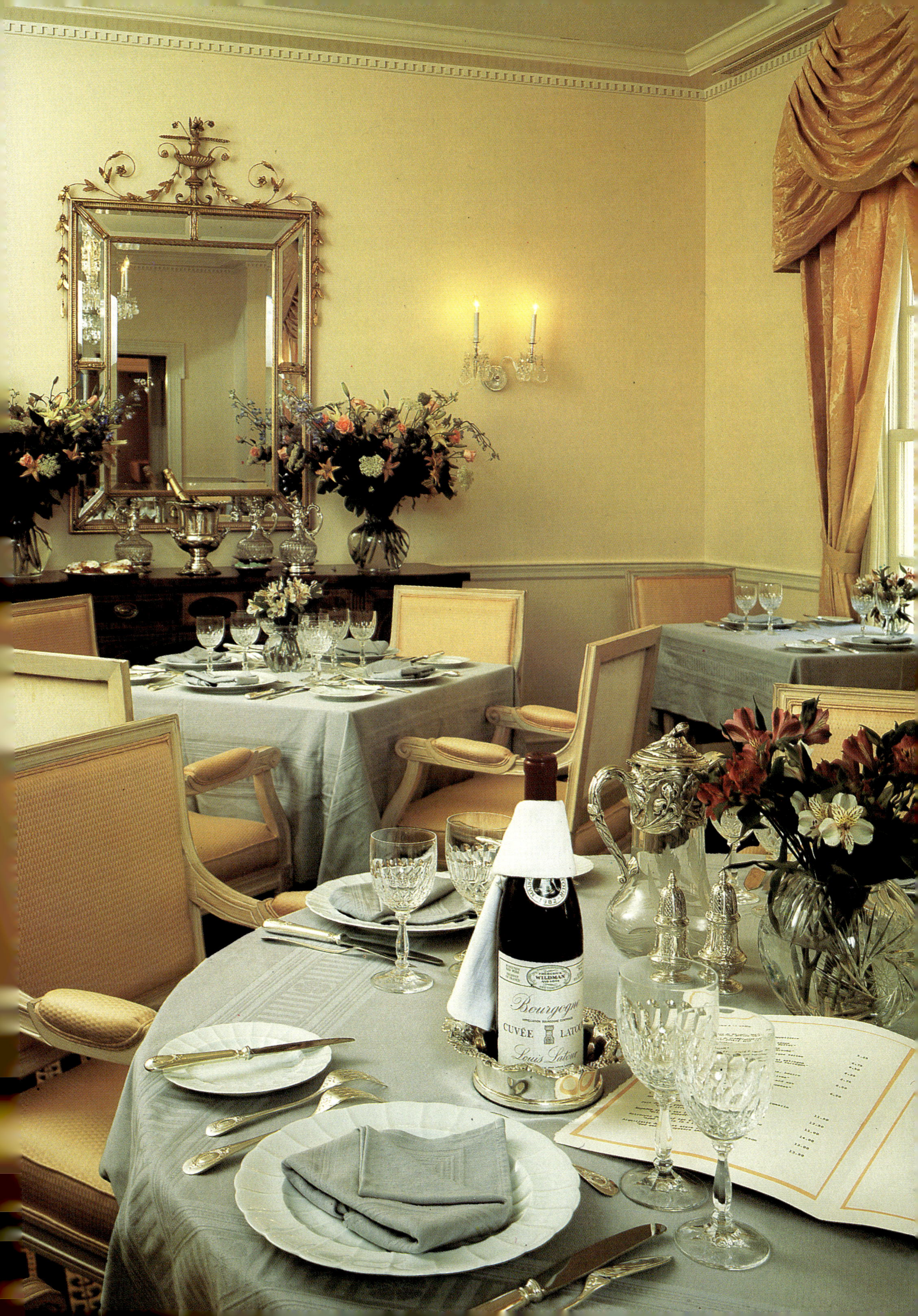
Bourgogne
CUVÉE

STEAL FROM STEAMSHIPS
THE *NORMANDIE* AND THE *FRANCE* PROVIDED INSPIRATION FOR A FINE HOTEL RESTAURANT

Large, geometric chandeliers, custom-designed by Slavik, anchor the main dining room at Le Paris. The scheme evokes the luxurious elegance of transatlantic liners of the 1920s and 1930s.

DESIGNED IN the classic, nostalgic fashion of a great oceanliner, Le Paris restaurant is located near St. Germain des Pres in the Lutetia Hotel—a recently renovated 1910 structure with two hundred and ninety-five bedrooms, twelve private rooms, a brasserie, and a bar.

For the restaurant, hotel management chose to recreate the atmosphere of the vanished luxury liners that once transported a happy and wealthy few across the Atlantic in high style. To carry out the theme, they selected French designers Sonia Rykiel and Slavik, who took classic Art Deco steamships such as the *Normandie* and the *France* for their inspiration.

Slavik has specialized in café and restaurant interiors for some thirty years; Rykiel is best remembered for her introduction of supple textiles, many in violet and black, to fashion and interior design. (She was responsible, among other projects, for the restoration of the Hotel Crillon, a landmark building on the Place de la Concorde.) Between them, Slavik and Rykiel have produced a tastefully understated design filled with elegant woods—lemon, wild cherry, walnut—and aglow with soft light.

The restaurant is entered through a revolving door that opens directly onto the main dining space. On levels separated by just three steps, 14 oval and round tables are deftly arranged. Walls are sheathed with wood paneling inlaid in trompe l'oeil fashion. Mirrors alternate with the luxuriously grained wood to create an illusion of depth and space. Geometric sconces and soft cream-colored ceilings offset the black carpeting and black velvet upholstery that dominate the scheme. A custom-designed geometric chandelier by Slavik is the focal point of the room.

Each table in the 40-seat restaurant is decorated with orchids and furnished with a simple battery-operated candleamp—a relatively new feature in European dining places. The cost of the entire project was slightly more than 2 million francs.

LE PARIS RESTAURANT	Paris, France
Owner: *Lutetia Hotel*	
Interior Design: *Sonia Rykiel, Slavik*	
Budget: *2 million French francs (approximately)*	
Seating: *40*	
Photography: © *Christian Rausch*	

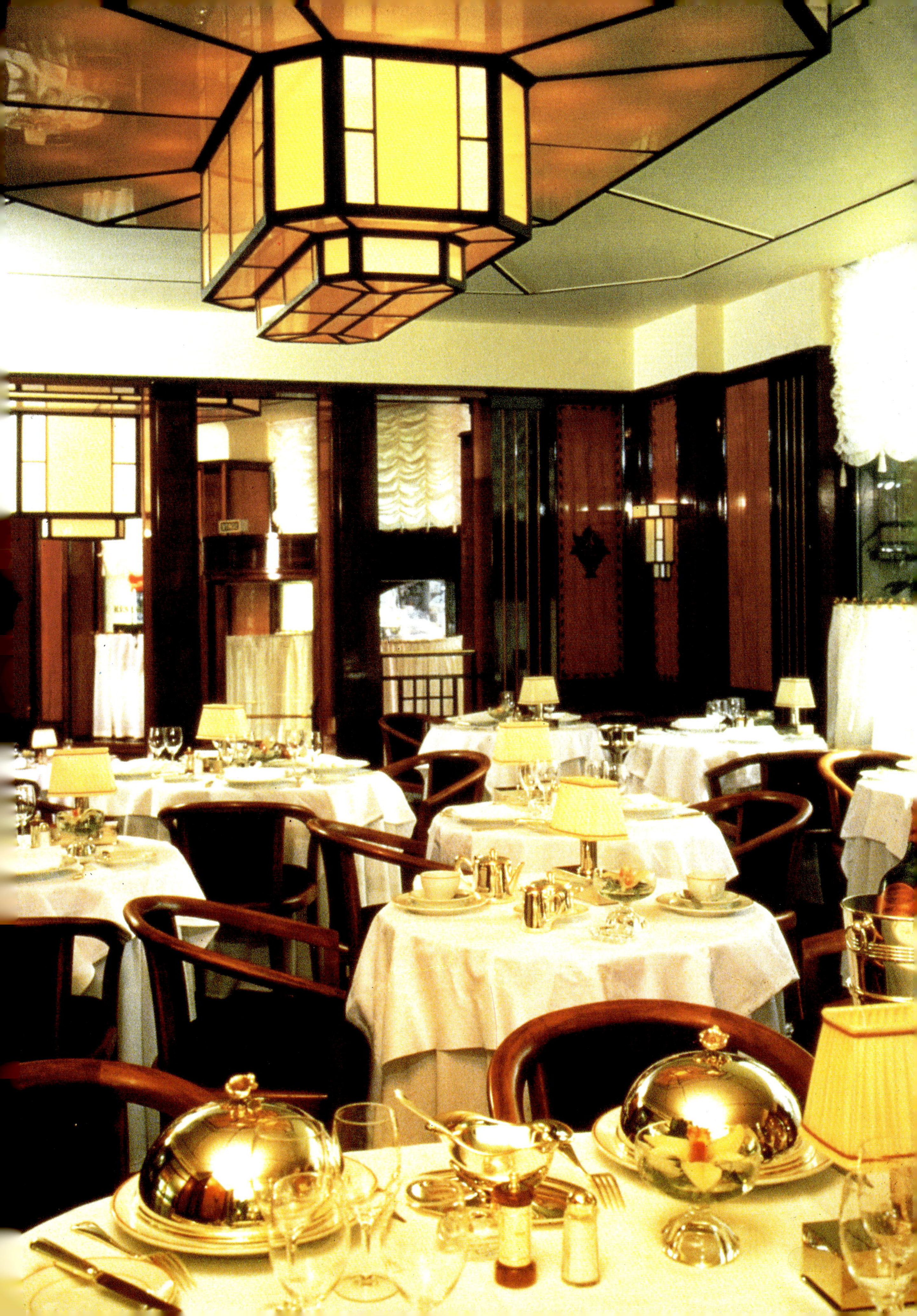

PLAN A PAIR OF DINING ROOMS
THE VICTORIAN ERA INSPIRES TWO SPACES—ONE "LADYLIKE," ONE CLUBBY

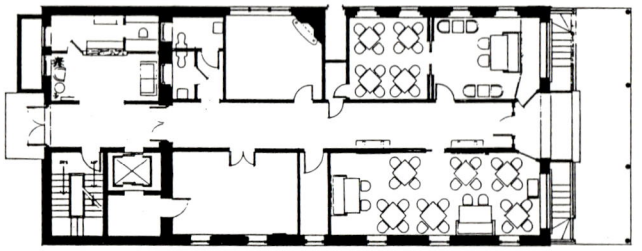

THE IMPERIAL HOTEL has been a familiar sight in Chestertown, on Maryland's Eastern Shore, for more than eighty years. Located in a National Register Historic District, the red brick building with its welcoming front porch was constructed in 1903. Adjacent to the three-story hotel is a rebuilt 1885 carriage house. In its early days, the Imperial served as an unpretentious "traveling salesman's" hotel and provided offices for the local builder who built the Imperial. The hotel's upper floors were later converted into apartments, and in the 1970s the deteriorating structure was partially renovated to house six small, ground-level shops. When the George Deans bought the building in 1984, they decided to turn it into "a real hotel" with an upscale restaurant and an elegance it had never known.

Antique collectors themselves, the Deans favored the look of a mid-Victorian mansion for the interiors. But to qualify for the restoration tax credits that would make the job economically feasible, they had to maintain the integrity of the building's 1903 exterior. They hired a Chestertown firm, Chesapeake Associated Architects Inc., to take charge of the project.

"Timing was critical," recalls Chesapeake principal Marsha Fritz. "We had just eight months to get the hotel restored, open, and working to meet tax-related deadlines." When interior designer Janet Richardson (The H. Chambers Company, Baltimore) came into the project in mid-1984, she had just six months to design, specify, and arrange for the fabrication and installation of all interior finishes and furnishings.

The Imperial Hotel Restaurant was a special challenge for Richardson. It is composed of two distinctly different dining spaces laid out in 32-foot by 12-foot rectangles on either side of the center hall. "The twenty-seat Wilbur Hubbard Room—named for the son of the hotel's original owner, now master of the regional hunt—is masculine and clubby. Its inspiration was Balmoral, Queen Victoria's Scottish hunting retreat, which is decorated in plaids. I used a lot of plaid on the carpeting and draperies and put hunting prints on the walls. This room can be divided with doors for private parties. The dining room across the hall, which seats thirty-six, is planned around rose-colored prints that are cheery at lunch, yet intimate and formal at dinner."

Both rooms bespeak the hotel's style and ambience—a Victorian sense of graciousness and decoration tempered by a touch of contemporary comfort.

THE IMPERIAL HOTEL   Chestertown, Maryland
Owners: Mr. and Mrs. George Dean
Architecture: Chesapeake Associated Architects Inc.
Interior Design: The H. Chambers Company (Janet Richardson)
Photography: © Ron Solomon

When the Imperial Hotel was built in 1903, an office and a shop occupied first-floor spaces that are today lavish and inviting dining rooms that reflect the hotel's essentially Victorian style. One dining room (opposite) seats 36 and uses a floral motif on curtains, upholstery, and carpeting. Across the hall (top), a more clubby atmosphere inspired by Queen Victoria's Balmoral retreat is achieved with plaid carpeting and drapes and dark green walls.

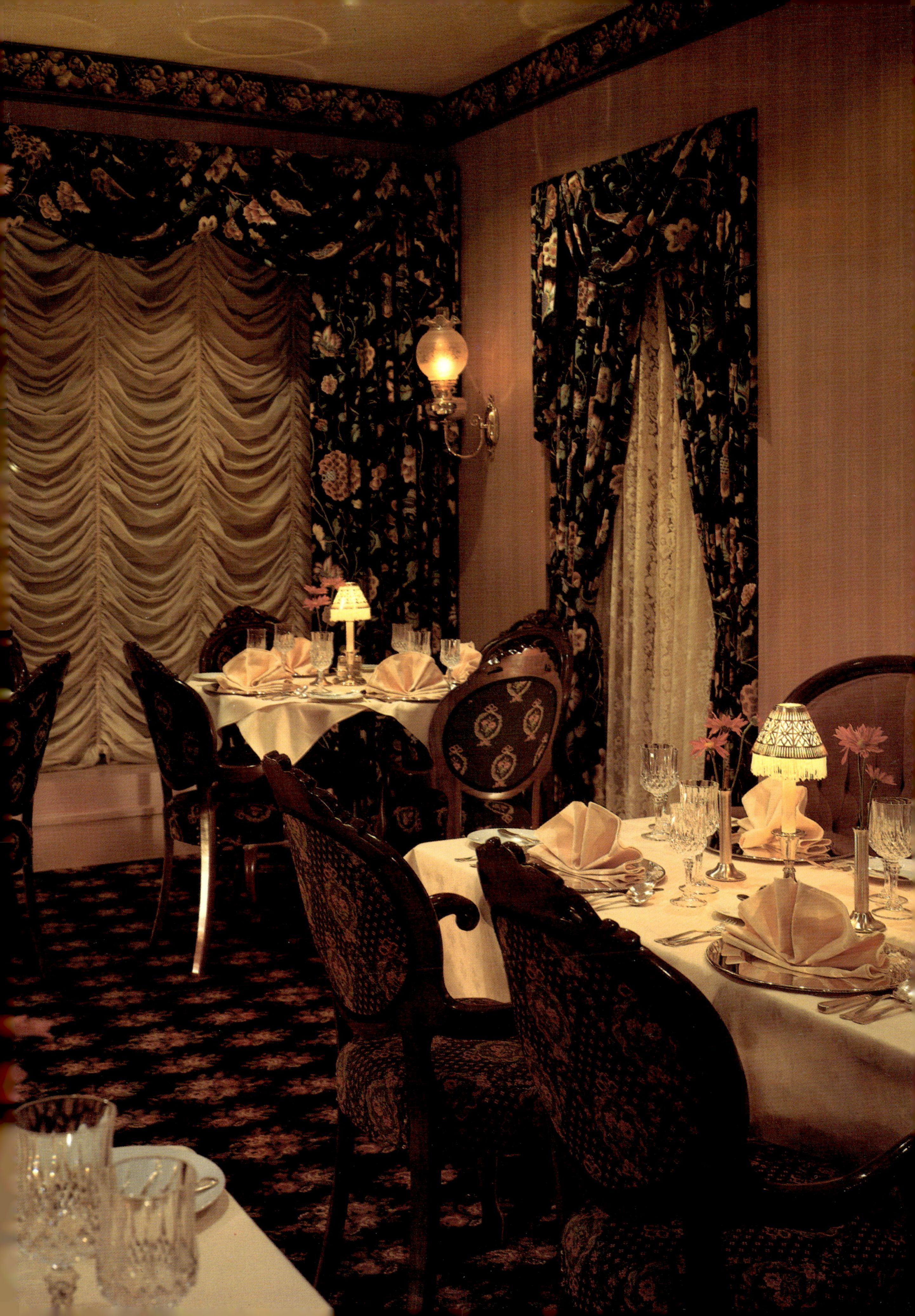

MAXIMIZE THE MINIMAL

A SPARE DINING ROOM ALLOWS THE MAINE COAST TO SHINE THROUGH THE WINDOWS

WITH ITS CLAPBOARD siding, white trim, and gabled roofline, The Schooners—a small inn on the Kennebunk River in Maine—represents New England architecture at its best: unaffected and understated. "The building footprint and general character evolved as a reference to the existing buildings on the site. This response was essential in creating an understated, timeless building," says David Webster, AIA, principal-in-charge for Portland Design Team (Portland, Maine), which designed both building and interior. Named for the whaling schooners that sailed from the village in the 1800s, the three-story, seventeen-room inn features a program and design particular to the region. While the inn's exterior echoes the clean-lined architecture of its coastal surroundings, its spacious interior has a more contemporary finish.

Overscaled columns, fascias, and built-in casework create alcoves of intimacy on the second level, where the octagonal dining room is located. Here the architect has created residential-scaled spaces through the use of a colonnade that parallels the exterior glass walls. Each of three dining room walls that face the sea frame dramatic views of the ocean and river—in sum, a view encompassing 180 degrees. (Railroad-style corridors running on the street side of the inn and centrally located service spaces reserve river views for the first-floor lounge and the guestrooms on all three levels, as well as for the restaurant.)

Built-in cherrywood cabinetry and furniture take advantage of available space and enhance the elegant simplicity of the inn. The subtle appointments also enable the most to be made of spectacular views; the one is allowed to complement the other.

Overlooking the Kennebunk River and, from the second floor, the ocean, The Schooners Restaurant was designed for three-meal-a-day dining and for taking advantage of panoramic views. The exterior (above) reflects the New England style of surrounding buildings. In the center of the rambling structure, three sides of the octagonal dining room jut outward, creating an architectural focal point from the exterior, while maximizing views.

THE SCHOONERS   *Kennebunkport, Maine*
Owners: *SHAPE, Inc. (Anthony and Paul Gelardi)*
Architecture/Interior Design: *Portland Design Team*
Associated Architecture: *Bertaux + Copley and Associates*
Contractor: *Ledgewood, Inc.*
Acoustical Consultant: *Cavanaugh-Tocci*
Photography: © *Brian Vanden Brink; Jon Bonjour*

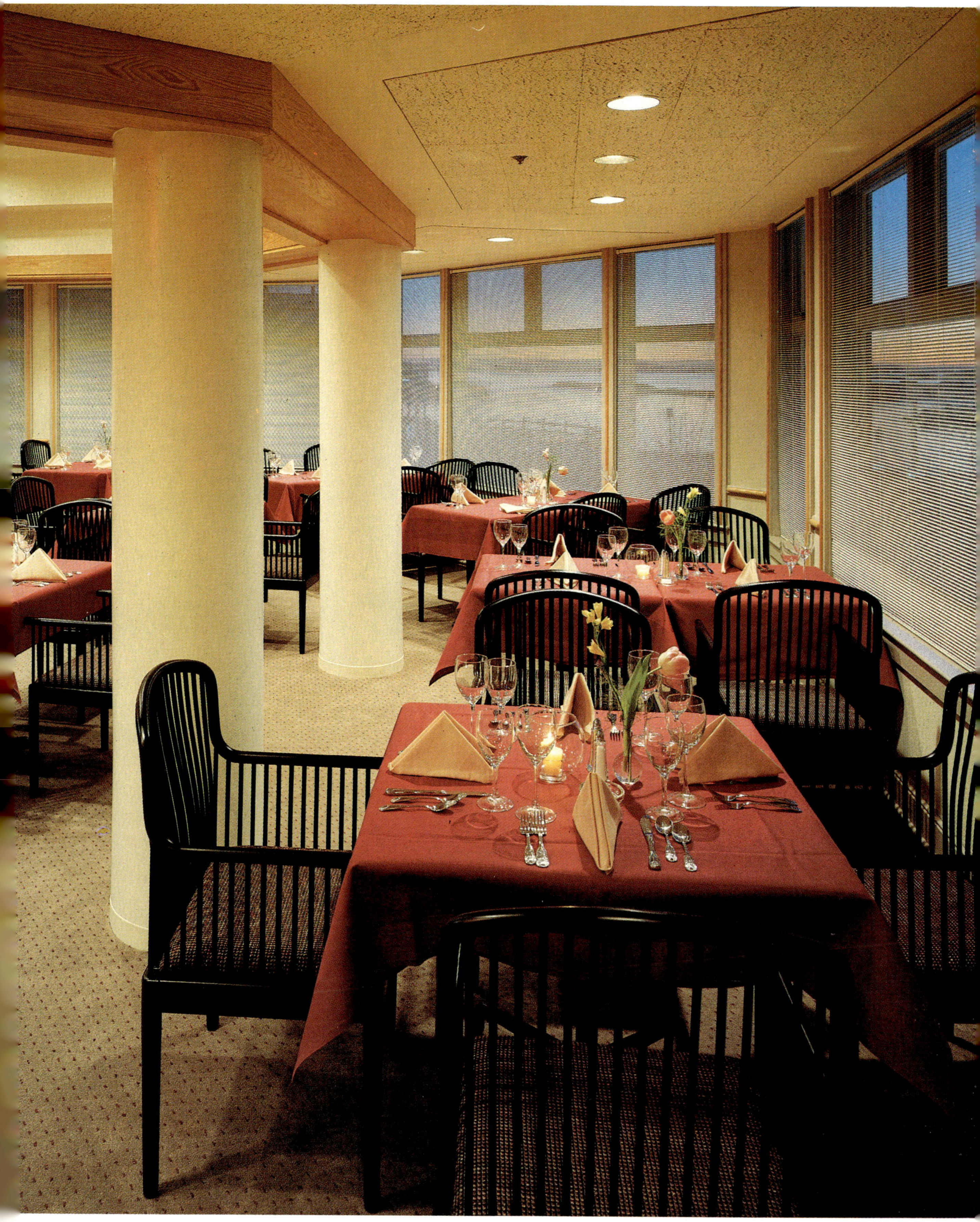

INVOKE TIMELESS CLASSICISM
FINE PAINTINGS AND ANTIQUES WARM A NEW HOTEL DINING ROOM

THROUGHOUT THE NEW Ritz-Carlton Naples Hotel, interior designer Frank Nicholson (Frank Nicholson, Inc., Concord, Massachusetts) strove for the atmosphere of formal, residential elegance that has become the defining characteristic of the upscale Ritz-Carlton chain. "Because timeless classic proportions increase the longevity of an interior design, we began there," explains Nicholson. Each area is arranged living room–style with intimate seating, fine antiques, period decorative arts, and paintings.

Eighteenth- and nineteenth-century British and American paintings have come to express the distinct character of the Ritz, Nicholson says. These and other art objects grace the food and beverage facilities on the hotel's main level, helping to develop the spirit that architect, designer, and owner/developers wished to convey. In The Dining Room, for example, Nicholson uses a pair of portraits of young girls (one from Stair & Company in New York; the other discovered in New Orleans) as focal points. Custom-designed floral silk draperies introduce a subtle Oriental note, picking up the chinoiserie motif of the carpeting, while dining chairs are covered in two fabrics for residential luxe.

Nicholson also relies on art to set a clubby tone in The Grill: nineteenth-century equestrian and animalier bronzes, landscapes, and animal paintings predominate. Despite his adherence to the "Ritz formula" in finishing the Naples hotel, he has also given it a distinctive sense of place—"a little more emphasis on the oceanfront location and a little more color than in the other Ritz locations."

The budget for the hotel included $2.5 million in artworks purchased in London, New Orleans, California, New York, and Boston.

THE RITZ-CARLTON HOTEL Naples, Florida

Owner/Developers: *W. B. Johnson Properties, Inc., The Ritz-Carlton Hotel Company*

Architecture: *Wimberly, Whisenand, Allison, Tong & Goo; Milton Pate & Associates*

Interior Design: *Frank Nicholson, Inc.*

Kitchen Consultant: *Unicorn*

Purchasing: *Ritz-Carlton Development*

Photography: *© Milroy/McAleer*

The Grill (opposite) is filled with animalier art, which—along with antiques and a fireplace—gives a clubby quality to the room. From left: bronze casting of "Huntsman and Hounds," after Pierre Jules Mené; "The Hunt," unsigned eighteenth-century Swiss School painting; "White Horse and Squire" by William Barrand (England, 1810–1850); French eighteenth-century terra rosa marble fireplace surround; reproduction Foo dogs; nineteenth-century terra cotta bust by Paul F. Berthand; and "Horse and Jockey" bronze cast after Isidore Jules Bonheur (France, 1827–1901). The same deep blue crystal is used on the round outdoor dining tables on the terrace (above).

The proximity of the sea and the classic arches that repeat along the ground level of the hotel combine to create a spacious outdoor dining terrace with a classic touch.

In The Dining Room (above) Staffordshire and old ironstone Rothschild plates fill a circa 1780 English secretaire. Some of the paintings that adorn the walls here are, from left, "Portrait of Miss Ellen Smith" by Sir William Beechey (England, 1753–1839), unsigned "Country Road with Two Boys" (nineteenth-century Dutch School), and "The South Dorset Hunt" by Frederick W. N. Whitehead (England, 1853–1938).

SUGGEST A FAMOUS COUNTERPART
A DINING ROOM EVOKES THE ELEGANCE OF ITS PARISIAN PREDECESSOR

THE HUNDRED-AND-SIXTY-ROOM Plaza Athénée on New York's Upper East Side recreates the same spirit of elegance as its elder French sister, thanks to architect John Carl Warnecke and interior designer Valerian Rybar who transformed it from the tired and dingy 1927 Hotel Alrae. The mood of the original Athénée is particularly notable in the exuberant dining room, Le Regence, situated in a space without windows on the first level. Since it is the only foodservice facility in the hotel, its decor had to be suitable for three-meal service. Says Rybar: "We had to make the windowless room seem like a daylit place." With mirrors and adjustable soffit lighting, the room and its cloud-painted ceiling seem awash with natural light. Pale turquoise-painted *boiserie*, highlighted in off-white, is reflected in mirrored seating recesses and in the carved gilt mirrors that hang over elaborate serving consoles. Ample banquettes and oversized *fauteuils* assure comfortable seating.

THE PLAZA ATHÉNÉE *New York City*
Owner: *Trusthouse Forte*
Architecture: *John Carl Warnecke*
Interior Design: *Valerian Rybar & Daigre Design (Valerian Rybar)*
Photography: *© Oberto Gili*

Soffit lighting creates a morning or evening ambience in Le Regence. Because there are no other function rooms in the Athénée, a section of the dining room can be partitioned off for private meetings or parties. Rybar's love of opulent detail is expressed in the bronze-doré-and-crystal chandeliers and wall sconces.

9. NIGHTSPOTS

From Rascals in Honolulu, Hawaii, to Overtures in Birmingham, Alabama, lighting and sound are basic elements of good 1980s nightclub design. Everywhere, the beat throbs, the lights blink. Between the moments of darkness come flashes of red, green, blue, and yellow. The dance floor seems to move, but it is the music and the light that lend a sense of motion and animate the space.

"A disco needs to be a fantasy," says architect Norman Lacayo of Rascals (opposite). And nothing contributes more to an air of fantasy than an innovative system of illumination. Rascals features a wall of light streaming down from a 20-foot height. Power tracks, 12 inches on the center in 8-foot sections, crisscross to form a ceiling grid of spotlights that cast colored beams on the floors, walls, and columns. The illusion of space keeps changing as the light moves with the music.

At Pulsations, in Glen Mills, Pennsylvania, a circular neon "spaceship" descends to the dance floor and spotlights twirl through a mist emitted by four "infinity towers" that rise from a sublevel and spin in sync with the music. A polished aluminum ceiling and mirrored columns double the effect of the light show. At Zakie's in York, Pennsylvania, a three-story neon comet (salvaged from a 1950s Comet Drive-thru and rewired to synchronize with the music) plunges to the dance floor, dramatically unifying the space.

Not all nightspots, however, go to such sensory extremes. At Overtures—one of a new breed of nightclubs for mature revelers—the designers have created relatively quiet areas for conversation. These are intimate spaces with tiered seating and clear views of the action on the dance floor.

With so much importance placed on lighting, special consultants are normally hired for the completion of nightclub projects. These experts are proficient in the coordination of light, sound, and video systems. Common elements now in most nightclubs include disk jockey booths near a dance floor, video screens (showing musicians and the dancers on the floor), tiered levels, and a flexible seating (and lighting) system that encourages interaction of patrons.

BUILD AN EARTHBOUND SPACESHIP
AN IMAGINATIVE NIGHTCLUB MAKES DAZZLING TECHNOLOGY ITS FOCUS

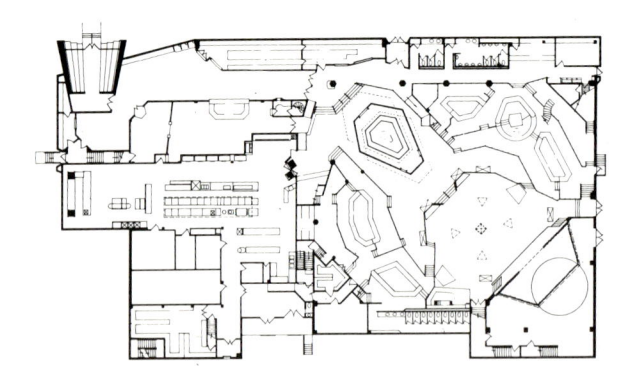

A polished aluminum ceiling, mirrored columns, and metal laminates provide sparkle, which doubles the effect of the light show at Pulsations (left and opposite). "Nothing," according to the designer, "is flat or regular." A large, mirrored entrance echoes the geometrical logo and draws patrons into a truly theatrical experience—a technological tour-de-force.

SHORTLY AFTER MIDNIGHT, the circular neon spaceship begins its journey across a starry "sky" and descends to the dance floor. Spotlights twirl through mist emitted by four triangular "infinity towers" that have sprung up from the floor, their green neon centers spinning in sync with the music. As the spaceship lands, its alien passenger—a dazzling robot named Pulsar—disembarks to dance with guests for the evening.

The spectacle is part of what designers Arthur Altemose and Holly Mazzola of Altemose Architects & Engineers (King of Prussia, Pennsylvania) have created for the continuously changing environment of Pulsations nightclub in Glenn Mills, Pennsylvania.

Other technological feats include speakers and lights on hydraulic lifts and a "floating" bar that moves 30 feet to accommodate crowds of up to 2,200 people. "We conceived the project as an entertainment environment," says project architect Arthur Altemose. "People can return often and see something new each time."

The club is an extensive renovation of an old roadside restaurant. "The structure, which originally seemed reusable, turned out to have deteriorated to the point where we were continuously revamping our plans. To make the project economical, we had to increase its scope," Altemose says. "The flexible space can be used for fashion shows, meetings, conventions, receptions."

"Ideas for the interior grew as the project grew," adds designer Mazzola. "In some places, we cut brightly colored carpet into triangles and arranged them like a stained glass window. We used velvet carpet even in heavily trafficked areas to give the club a plush look."

PULSATIONS	*Glen Mills, Pennsylvania*
Owner:	*Leon Altemose*
Architecture:	*Arthur Altemose*
Interior Design:	*Holly Mazzola*
Acoustical Engineer:	*Acoustilog Inc.*
Lighting Consultant:	*O. J. Productions*
Photography:	© *Lawrence Williams*

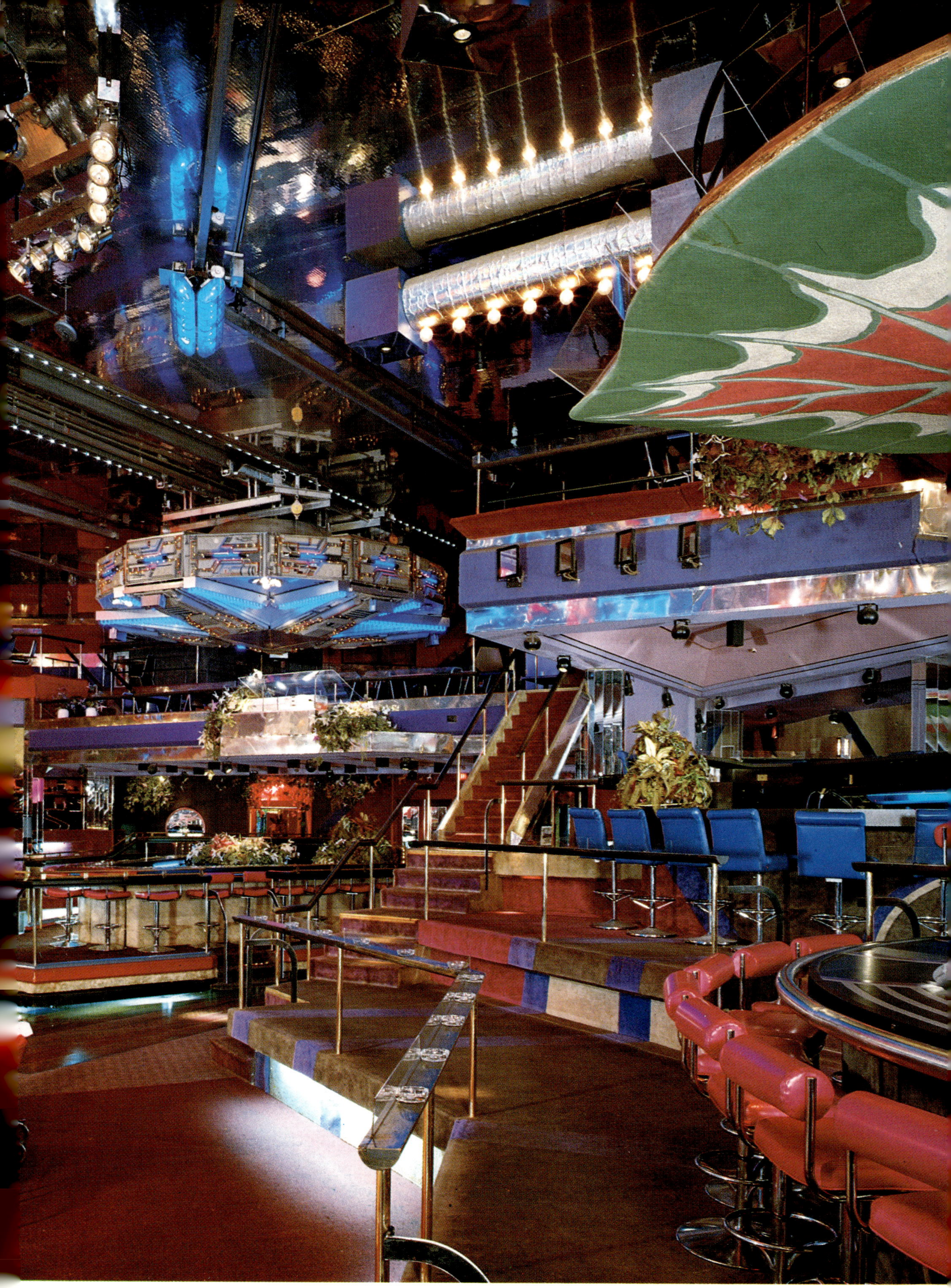

ADAPT A HISTORIC BUILDING FOR NIGHTCLUB USE
SALVAGED NEON UNIFIES THREE LEVELS OF AN OPEN INTERIOR PLAN

A neon comet that rises three stories and theater lighting salvaged from the 1950s flash above the dance floor. The comet has been wired to pulse in sync with the club's sound system.

OWNER DUNCAN SCHMIDT wanted a lively, elegant nightclub unique to south central Pennsylvania. And downtown York's turn-of-the-century Zakie Building—now on the National Register of Historic Places—seemed perfect. But design team Carol Hickey and Elvin Hess (Hickey/Hess Architecture and Design, Lancaster, Pennsylvania) had work to do: The roof was gone and four inches of ice covered the top floor.

To qualify for preservation-related tax credits, Schmidt had to retain most of the original structure, while complying with stringent local safety codes. "It was an especially difficult building because of the various levels and stair systems," Hess explains. "Some stairways had to be enclosed in fireproof glass. We restored the open space above the dance floor, knocking out part of the top two floors between what had been original outside walls. The remaining second- and third-floor areas had a lot of odd rooms and spaces, but these were assets to circulation."

Much of the 9,000-square-foot project's $650,000 budget went into structural work. "We needed to upgrade every single square foot," says Hickey. Elaborate ventilation and sprinkler systems, electrical service, and plumbing were installed. Zakie's exterior was reconstructed from historic photographs. The stucco facade is rusticated to resemble the original stonework, and the awning copies the original. Glass doors replicate old retail display windows.

ZAKIE'S	*York, Pennsylvania*
Owner/Developer:	*Duncan Schmidt*
Architecture:	*Hickey/Hess Architecture & Design*
General Contractor:	*L. R. Poe*
Sound and Lighting Consultant/Contractor:	*Kevin Landis*
Photography:	*© John Herr*

"There was no way to create effective exterior signage with all this glass," says Hess, "but we didn't need it. Passersby can look through the windows to see what's going on inside. It looks like a forties movie theater."

In the club, guests first notice the dazzling three-story neon comet on the wall. Electrical engineer Kevin Landis reconstructed the comet (salvaged from Lancaster's Comet Drive-thru, circa 1950) and rewired it to synchronize with the club's sound system. He also salvaged colored spotlights from York's Strand-Capitol Theater.

A separate entrance to the second floor is used for private parties. Both the second and third floors can be closed on slower nights, keeping the club comfortable for small crowds. These upper levels, says Hess, are "intimate places for patrons to sit, talk, and drink—yet feel part of the activity." Original decorative wood trim is painted white.

"Everybody can find something to relate to in Zakie's," Hickey explains. "It has many old things people recognize, but enough modern elements to indicate that the building has been through a change and now is talking to a contemporary group."

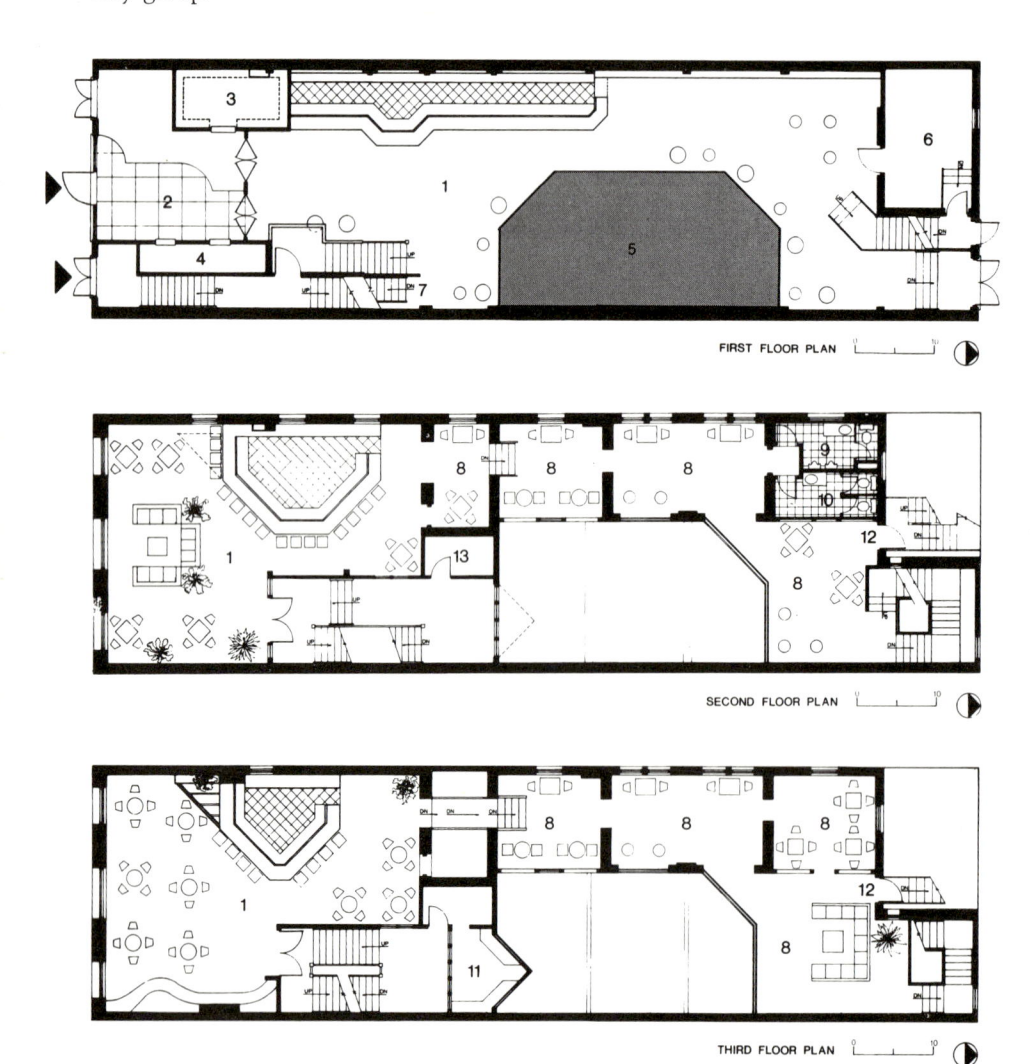

FIRST FLOOR PLAN

SECOND FLOOR PLAN

THIRD FLOOR PLAN

Looking down at the dance floor (opposite), guests can see lights twinkling at various levels. Wood trim adorns windows of what used to be the outside wall and unifies the nightclub's complex spaces. Steel beams added in the 1940s lend color and support. The floorplans show the layout of the three different levels at Zakies.

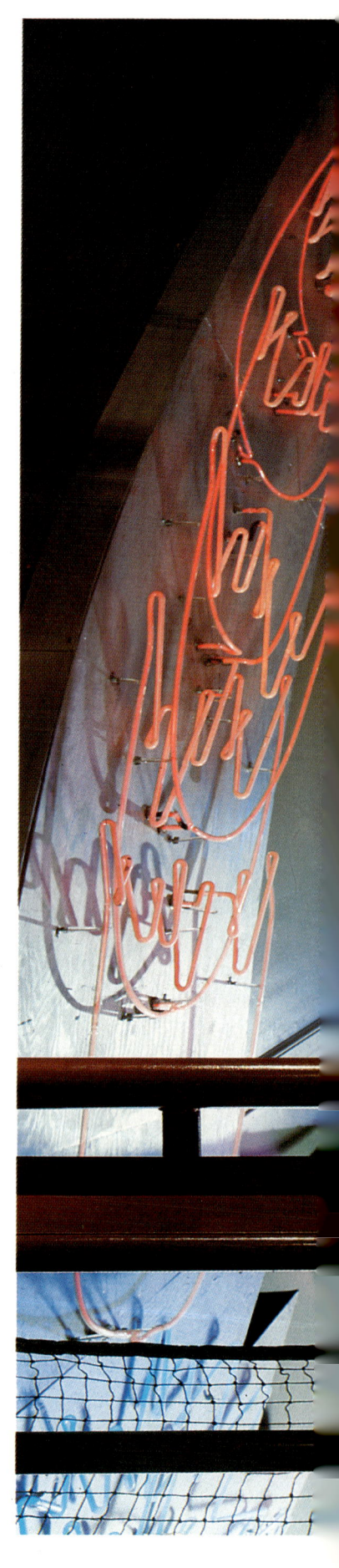

203

INFUSE A CLUB WITH CARIBBEAN COLOR
IRREVERENT MURALS AND NEON TURN A DISCO INTO A VISUAL FANTASY

The outrageous graphics (above) are daring in both content and color treatment. These hot colors are integral to the overall design. Lavish use is made of neon; it bands the walls of the room and outlines the palm fronds on the giant trees that punctuate the space.

SHREWDLY LOCATED on Houston's southwest side in the heart of a vast playground for apartment-dwelling young singles, Fizz nightclub is an unabashedly razzle-dazzle effort that boasts a glittering entryway, lascivious wall murals, video screens that descend from the ceiling on all four sides, a state-of-the-art sound system, and chilly clouds of carbon dioxide.

The show begins outside on the sidewalk with an avant-garde neon marquee that sets the entire building ablaze. The tunnel entry, with one visual fantasy superimposed upon another, finally explodes into an enormous central area awash with splashes of colored light.

The dramatic scale of the club is brought into more comfortable perspective through the use of neon tubing piped around the perimeter of the space. Neon also provides a flattering light that enhances the pink decor and an eclectic ensemble of neon-edged Art Deco palm trees. The space is further animated by changing floor levels, by four separate bars, and by gigantic billboards of voluptuous lips and legs.

"Our goal was to create a visual interpretation of the music in order to accent the rhythms and enhance the mood of the dancers," says Duncan. "The audience is young, fickle, and demanding. Because of that, the audiovisual rhythms at Fizz must stir the blood and move the feet."

Duncan went to New York, Los Angeles, and—more importantly, he believes—to Acapulco and Mexico City for inspiration. The cities in Mexico, says Duncan, are particularly sensitive to currents in international entertainment. He also visited the competing nightspots in the Southwest. The hot Caribbean colors he chose seemed to hit the mark.

Fizz cost $850,000 or about $70 per square foot.

FIZZ	*Houston, Texas*
Owner:	*(Steinmann Interests) Mike Steinmann*
Architecture:	*Duncan Design Associates*
Lighting/Sound Consultant:	*Sound Chamber*
Billboards:	*Bob Avery, Craig Wallace, Duncan Design Associates*
Logo/Graphic Design:	*Waithe Studios*
Budget:	*$850,000*
Photography:	*© Carolyn Brown*

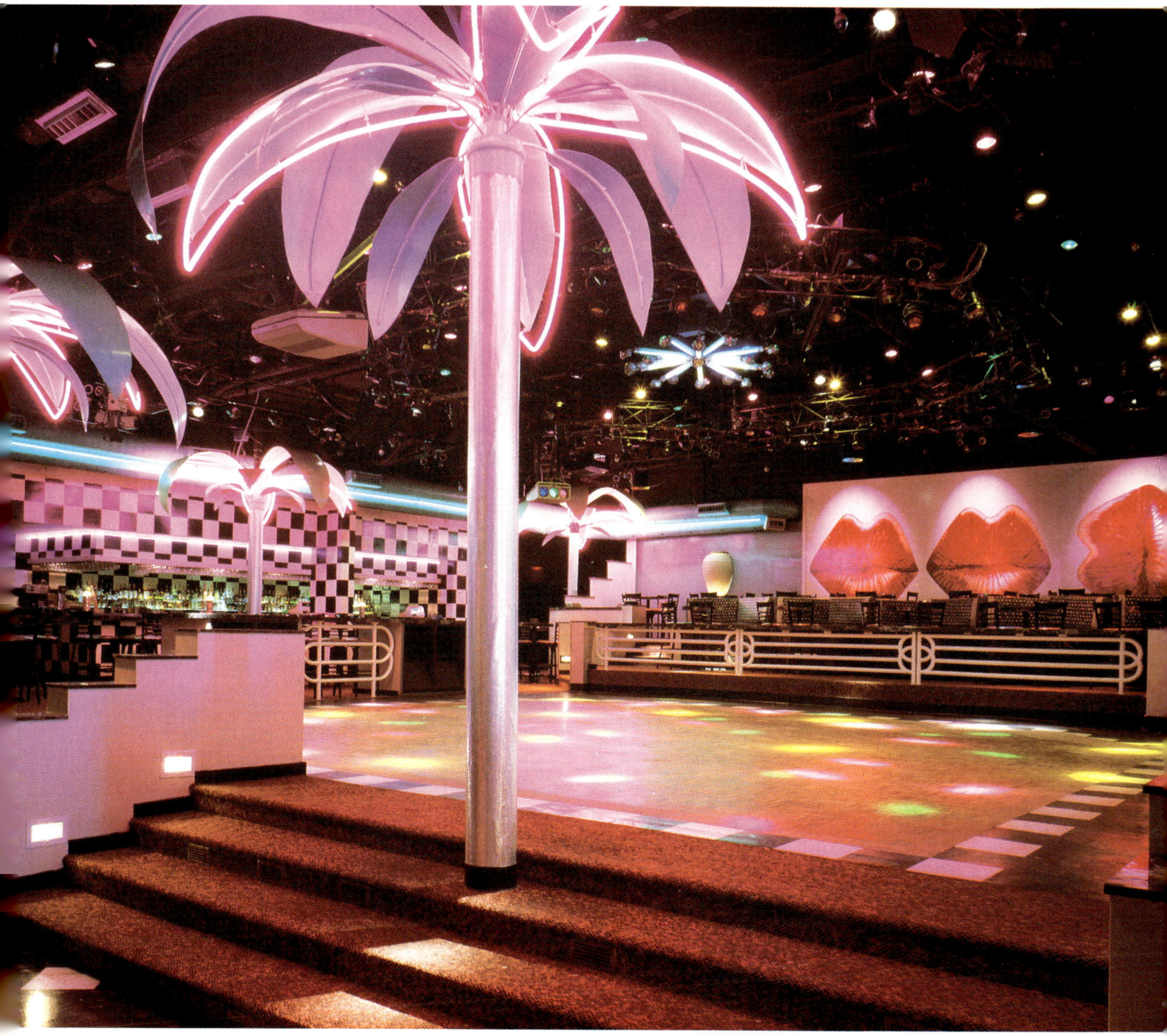

TEMPER NIGHTCLUB HEAT FOR ADULTS
A HOTEL NIGHTSPOT OFFERS DANCING AGAINST A POSTMODERN BACKDROP

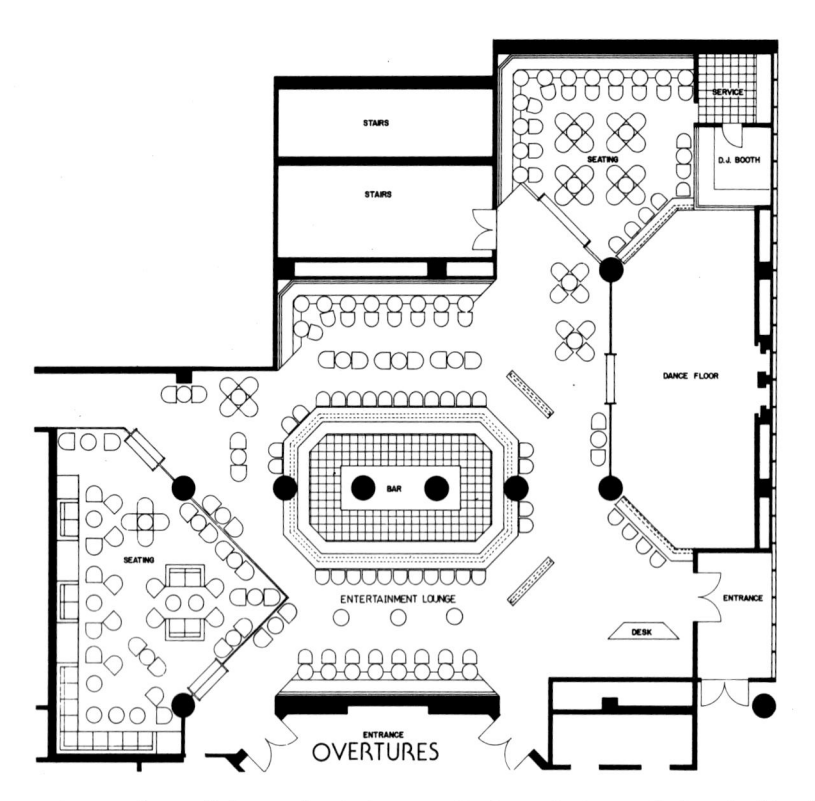

AT THE WYNFREY HOTEL in Birmingham, Alabama, the design team from Joyce K. Wynn, Inc. of Dallas achieved a delicate balance in the design of Overtures Lounge: The nightclub blends with the hotel's formality yet projects enough spark to attract an affluent local crowd.

Explains project coordinator Andrew N. Howell (Joyce K. Wynn, Inc.), "We came up with a lively idea that met practical requirements as well. The space is elegant enough to attract high-end clientele; nothing else in the area competes in terms of nightlife/entertainment for the thirty- to fifty-year-old crowd. An exterior entrance also indicates the club is a destination of its own—apart from the hotel."

OVERTURES LOUNGE Birmingham, Alabama

Developer: *Jim Wilson & Associates*

Operator: *Wynfrey Hotels, Inc.*

Interior Design: *Joyce K. Wynn, Inc. (Joyce K. Wynn, principal; Deborah Lloyd Forrest, project designer; Andrew N. Howell, project coordinator)*

Architectural Consultant: *Burson & Cox (Rodger Burson)*

Building Architect: *Hellmuth, Obata & Kassabaum*

Lighting Design: *Architectural Lighting Design (Craig Roberts)*

Graphic Design: *Savage Design Group (Paula Savage)*

Sound/Disco Specialist: *London Towne Associates*

General Contractor: *Harbert International/McDevitt-Street*

Seating: *193*

Budget: *$350,000*

Photography: *© Robert Miller*

Project designer Deborah Lloyd Forrest relied on a lozenge-shaped, gray marble bar to anchor the space overall, a sculptural postmodern backdrop to define the dance floor, and tinted mirrors to reflect activity and add excitement. "Looking across the bar to the dance floor, patrons can see black-tinted mirrors that line the walls. Everybody views the action without actually looking around. The tint means the mirror is reflective but not bright," Forrest explains.

Just behind the dance floor, Forrest placed a "stylized postmodern shape that gives the area a focal point even when people aren't dancing." The postmodern backdrop is composed of elegant, curving architectural shapes that contain jewel-toned bands of neon. The circular images are picked up in patterned carpeting, which ties together peach, aquamarine, and charcoal colors of upholstery and wallcovering.

"This is primarily a sophisticated entertainment lounge with recorded music; it really wasn't planned for live entertainment," according to Howell. As a result, while the dance floor can be viewed from all areas of the club, it is not the main element. "We created two raised seating areas completely separate from the dance floor to emphasize something besides dancing. The dance floor occupies only about ten percent of the club's total square footage," he says. Strip lighting and unusual neon above the dance floor set it apart from the brighter seating areas.

"We think the lighting is one of the most important elements in the space," notes Forrest, who selected two types of lighting for Overtures Lounge. The "disco" lighting is high-energy and controlled by the disc jockey in sync with the music; general room lighting is not controlled by the DJ, but is preset on automatic controls.

Stylized architectural elements with neon accents provide an energetic backdrop for the dance floor. Seating areas (not shown) got special lighting and acoustical treatments to make conversation possible. Because the lounge nightclub is located in a hotel, the designers used a special sound wall and specified a ceiling treatment to help buffer sound. There are two entrances to Overtures, as the floorplan shows. A vestibule off Wynfrey Hotel's lobby helps contain sound. Outside, signature signage marks the entrance; a small waiting area accommodates crowds.

DIVERSIFY SPACE FOR CHANGE OF MOODS
FOUR DIFFERENT ACTIVITY AREAS MARK THIS HANGOUT

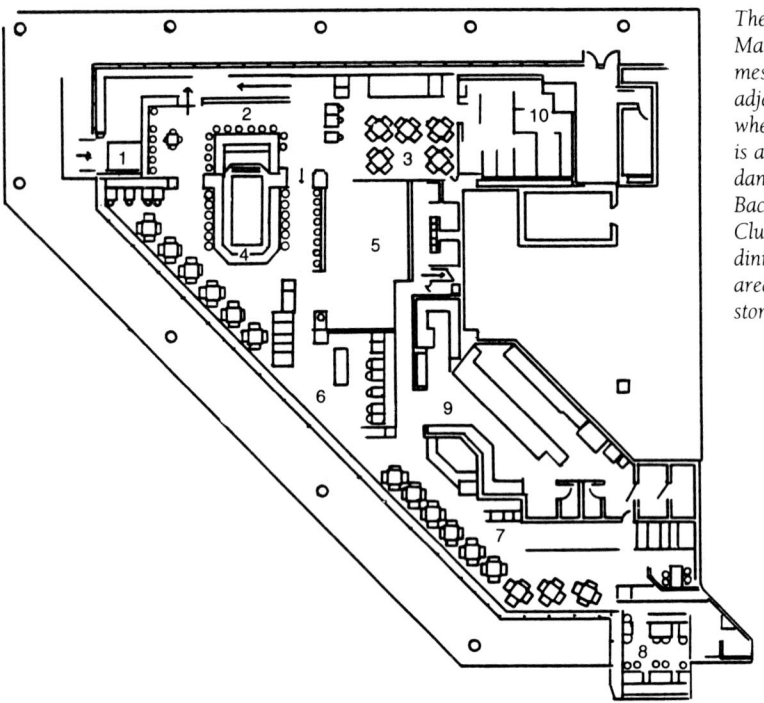

The fifties ambience of Pete & Marty's "Diner" (opposite) meshes well with the look of the adjacent Backstreet Bar. Elsewhere in the nightspot restaurant is a Hot Club and a sunken dance floor. Floorplan: entry (1); Backstreet Bar (2); diner (3); Hot Club (4); dance floor (5); Upper dining area (6); Court dining area (7); Bistro (8); kitchen/storage (9); restrooms (10).

FROM THE EXTERIOR, Pete & Marty's seems modest and unpretentious—a run-of-the-mill restaurant/nightclub with a low-key atmosphere. But as designer Bob DiLeonardo (DiLeonardo International, Warwick, Rhode Island) points out, surprises await on the inside, where patrons can dine or dance in any of several distinctively designed spaces.

Pete & Marty's street-corner location is atop one of Toronto's famous underground malls. Its triangular, 7,200-square-foot structure may be entered at street level or accessed directly from the College Park Mall below. Patrons who enter at street level find themselves in the Backstreet Bar—a straightforward industrial setting with a chain-link fence, ceramic floor tiles, neon signage, and a brick bar face.

Directly behind Backstreet Bar is a café/diner that seats about 40. A jukebox, bomber logo, booths with metal-banded linoleum tabletops, and clothes trees evoke the atmosphere of a 1950s diner.

Extending to the right of the Backstreet Bar and up a short flight of stairs is the Hot Club, which accommodates approximately 60. It's adjoined by a sunken dance floor that can be furnished with seating for the lunchtime crowd. Again, the mystique of the fifties and sixties prevails in a wall display of guitars from popular artists like Jimi Hendrix and Paul McCartney. But the pipework lighting grid and network of video monitors situated above the dance floor give this space a refreshingly contemporary look.

Diners may also be seated in the Upper dining and Court dining areas, located between the Hot Club and the Bistro at Pete & Marty's underground mall entrance. These two spaces, occupying 1,600 square feet, act as a transition between the lively atmosphere of the Hot Club and the more sedate environment of the Bistro. A dropped tin ceiling over the Upper dining and Court dining areas, plus a carpeted floor, frosted bowl lighting, and mahogany accents distinguish these dining areas from the Backstreet Bar and Café, easing into the mood of the 389-square-foot Bistro, located at the mall entrance of the nightclub.

A wide traffic aisle wending through the facility encourages patrons to mingle and, along with the selection of gray, black, pink, and red colors, gives continuity to the space. Budget for the project was $800,000.

PETE & MARTY'S *Toronto, Canada*
Owner: *Marty Soltys*
Interior Design: *DiLeonardo International*
  (Thomas Limone, Nancy Rodrigues, Carol Schauer)
Architecture: *DiLeonardo International*
  (David LaRoche, George Nunes, David Cameron, Kathy Dodge)
Budget: *$800,000*
Photography: *© Warren Jagger*

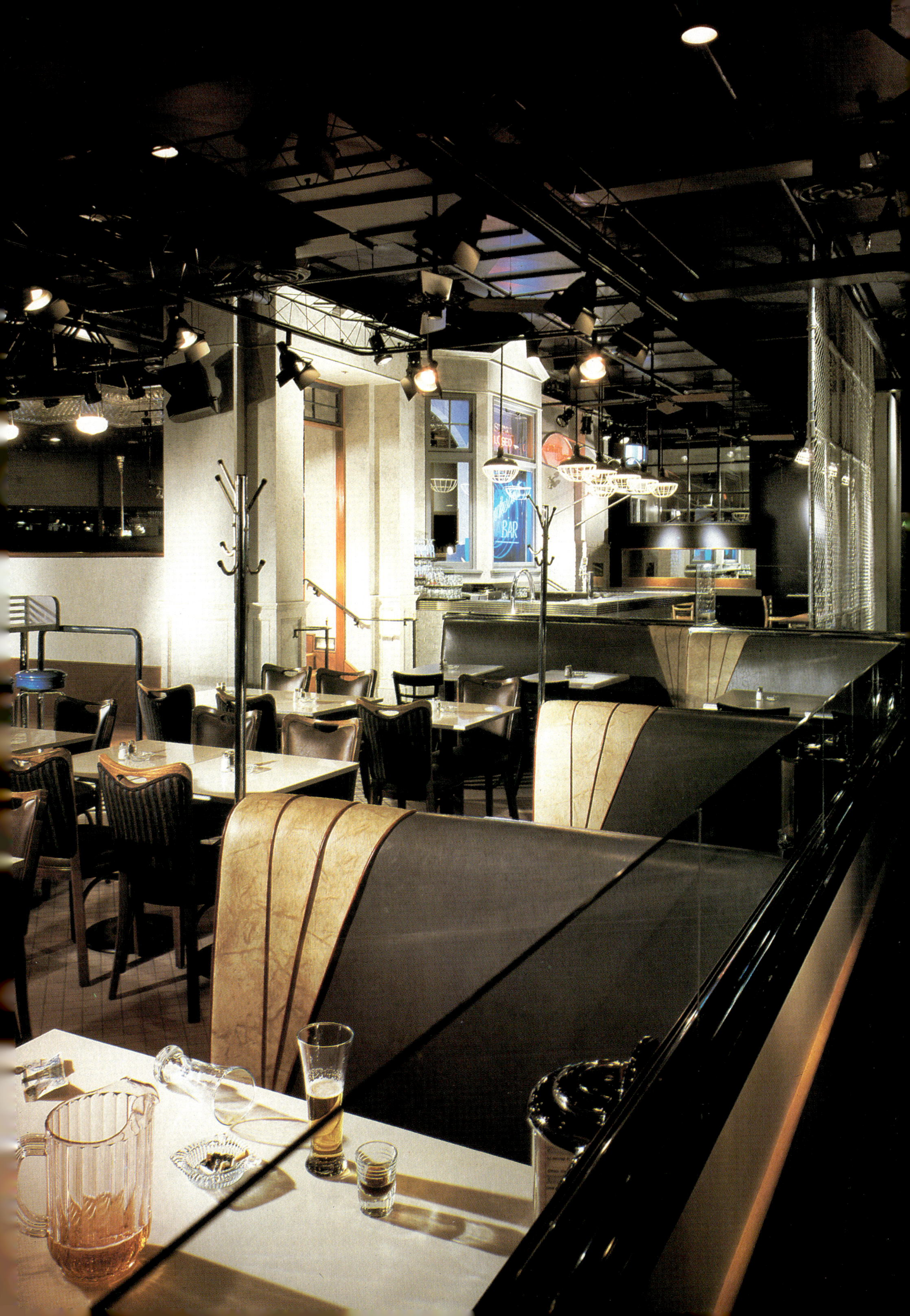
BAR

GUT A PUB TO YIELD A SINGLE GRAND SPACE
WHIMSICAL SCULPTURE DOMINATES THIS WIDE-OPEN SUBURBAN NIGHTCLUB

Sleek divers (above) cascade over a raised dance floor, lined with nautical railings. Other whimsical sculptures suspended from the ceilings and hanging from the walls include wooden sunglasses, flamingos, palm leaves, swordfish, and neon musical instruments. Two elegant oak bars (one is shown opposite) remain from the restaurant that formerly occupied this space, but they have been embellished with tile tops and painted panels.

UNLIKE ITS COZY, publike predecessors, the Snuggery nightclub explodes in color and flashy graphics designed to attract the young singles crowd in the affluent Chicago suburb of Northbrook. Located in a former chalet-style restaurant, Snuggery was born only after small rooms and fireplaces were eliminated from the space. "We wanted total interaction of the whole crowd," explained owner Freddie Hoffman. Gutting the site opened a main floor of 4,000 square feet and made way for a dance floor.

According to project designer Tom Ullo of Skyline Design in Chicago, the place is festive—"like a New Year's Eve celebration every night." Whimsical wood sculptures, video screens, and neon seem at home amidst a daring color scheme: Mauve, teal, turquoise, charcoal, mint, and lavender are mixed with abandon.

Since Skyline Design of Chicago's principal business is wooden wall murals and relief sculpture, the Snuggery project was an ideal outlet for the firm's creativity. Graphic figures, usually made of stained oak and lacquered composition board, as well as plastic and neon, were custom-designed. Decoration of the $1 million nightclub—almost 6,000 square feet—cost about $100,000.

Skyline's decorative objects are as whimsical as the color selection and set the tone for Snuggery. The front half of a full-sized Packard, made of oak, rests on a lavender chair rail. A huge, old-time radio set hangs opposite the dance floor. Suspended from the beam ceiling is a trio of hardboard cutouts of sailfish leaping through neon rings. Large, multicolored flamingos caricature the Miami Beach of the 1930s, while palm leaves cap structural columns and neon musical instruments float overhead.

Client mandates for design, according to Skyline Design's Charles Rizzo, included unbroken sight lines and a bar located close to the entrance. All the decorative sculptures accommodate these demands.

Opposite an elevated seating level, featuring vinyl "lizard skin" wallpaper and campy "neoclassic" sculpture, is the disco area with DJ booth and the largest of the club's numerous video screens. This part of Snuggery is geared for action. Customers seeking a quieter environment can move from the entry bar to an area downstairs, where the space is more subdued. Oak strips and poster art enliven the walls, but there's whimsy here, too: a pair of supersized sunglasses hangs from the ceiling.

SNUGGERY	*Northbrook, Illinois*
Owner:	*Freddie Hoffman*
Interior Design:	*Skyline Design of Chicago (Tom Ullo, Charles Rizzo, Jeff Rutter)*
Contractor:	*Surman Construction*
Budget:	*$1 million*
Size:	*6,000 square feet*
Photographer:	*© Tim Wilson*

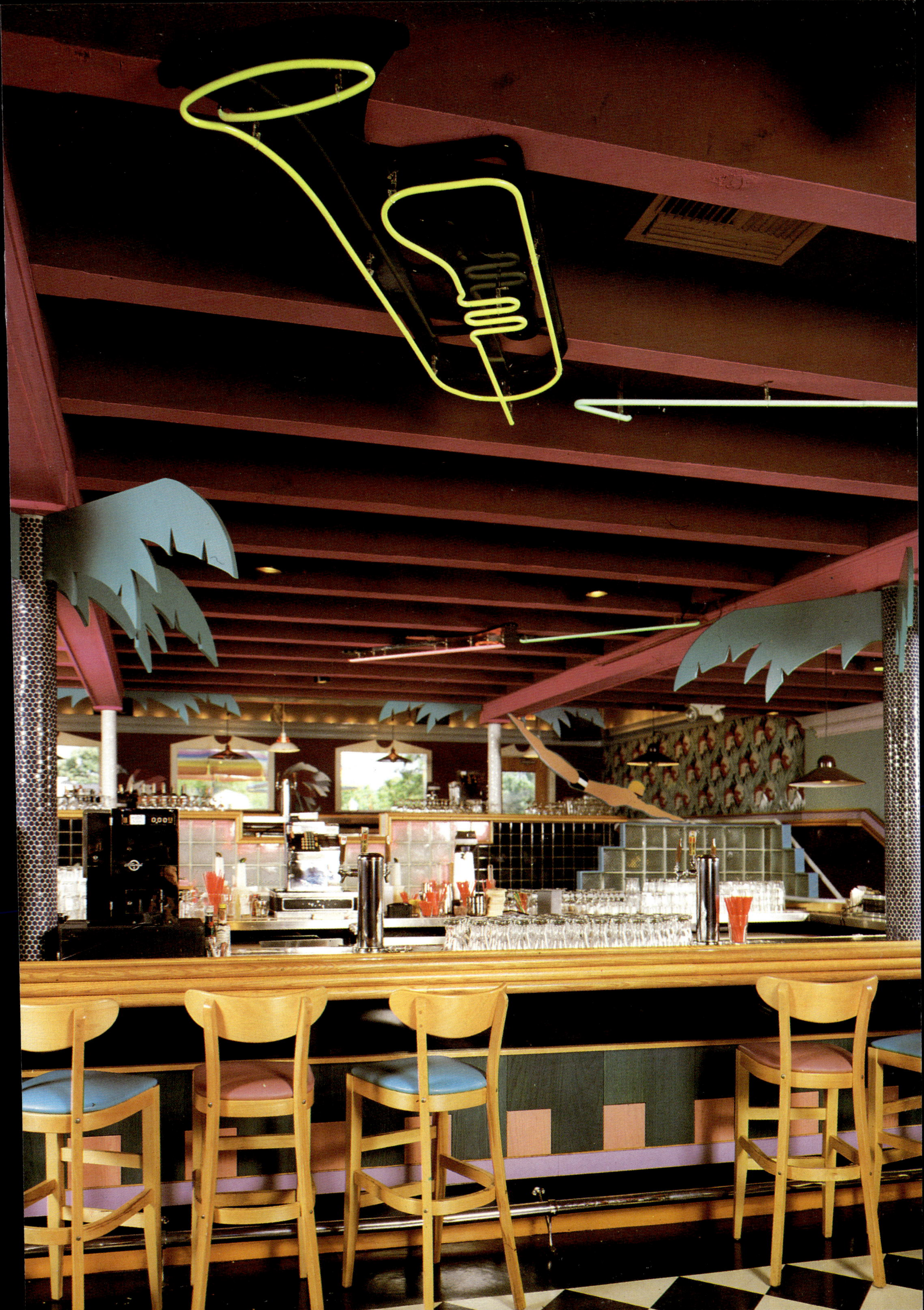

CAPITALIZE ON HIGH CEILINGS
AWKWARD BEAMS AND COLUMNS BECOME DESIGN FEATURES

Curving shapes constitute the primary design vocabulary in Rascals; beams are encased in rounded forms. Midnight blue–painted ceiling gives the impression of a void; an "infinity mirror" behind the main performance pedestal focuses the action.

Rascals' open, many-level layout was made possible by the multi-sloped roof structure, which is 8 feet high on two sides and 26 feet at the center.

EXCEPT FOR potted banana palms stretching upward toward a maze of colored lights in its vaulted ceiling, Rascals—within earshot of Waikiki's pounding surf—betrays no hint of standard Hawaiian kitsch. "It's like nothing else in Honolulu; a combination of *Star Wars* and a Cecil B. DeMille version of *Ben Hur*," quips architect/designer Norman Lacayo of Honolulu.

The nightspot, which offers a full dinner menu in addition to drinks and dancing, is located on the second and third levels of Kuhio Mall, a well-trafficked tourist center near the major Waikiki resort hotels. Rascals owners Paul Bowskill and Mike McCormack wanted to attract an upscale crowd of local couples who would support the dining operation as well as the disco. With that in mind—and on a firm budget of $932,000—Lacayo looked for ways to provide the most excitement for the money in the 6,300-square-foot facility.

"The space we had in Kuhio Mall was barnlike, with a high ceiling, and broken with all sorts of visual obstructions—steel columns wrapped in plaster, horizontal beams at an awkward 12-foot elevation. Fortunately, we were able to turn all that to good advantage."

By encasing the horizontal beams and some mechanical elements in round tubes normally used to form concrete columns, then finishing the tubes with glossy white paint, Lacayo did away with clutter and created a distinctive design feature. He left other mechanical elements exposed against the high black-painted ceiling.

The high ceiling was itself a boon: It permitted a series of activity levels in the space. "Instead of coming straight in," Lacayo says, "you walk up to be seen, make an entry, check the place out. From a midpoint, you drop two intermediate levels to the dance floor. There's also a mezzanine." The main dining area, tucked away behind the bar, is laid out on descending levels. It accommodates 90; additional booths

RASCALS *Honolulu, Hawaii*
Owners/Developers: *Restaurant Investment Partners (Paul Bowskill, Mike McCormack)*
Architecture: *Norman Lacayo, AIA, Inc. (Norman Lacayo, Pam Lacayo)*
Electrical Engineer: *Rick Moss*
Contractor: *Construction Plus*
Budget: *$932,000*
Photography: *© Augie Salbosa*

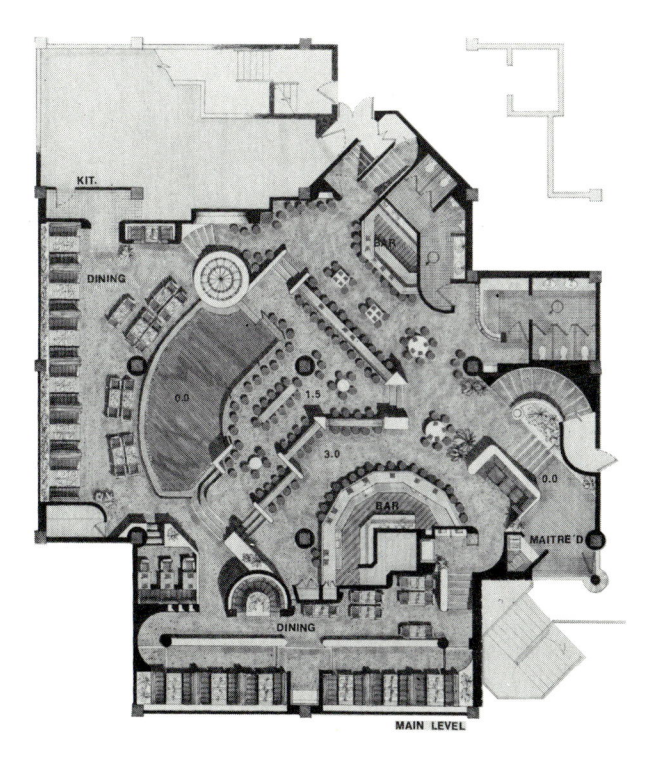

near the dance floor allow spillover dinner service for up to 150 patrons.

To draw attention away from inexpensive finishes like the painted plaster and composition granite, Lacayo relied on dedicated lighting that would brighten focal objects, not whole areas. Lighting elements, as well, are critical components in Rascals' engagingly theatrical atmosphere.

"We used consultants to carry out the technical aspects of the lighting plan," Lacayo says, "but the design—and the dramatic moods it creates—are the work of our firm. For the most theatrical effect, we envisioned a wall of light streaming down from a 15- or 20-foot height. We accomplished it with power tracks, 12 inches on the center, in 8-foot sections that crisscross to form a ceiling grid of spots with colored gels." Sections of the grid can be turned on and off in any sequence, so the illusion of space keeps changing as the "wall of light" moves, casting colored beams on the floors, walls, columns, and tubes.

Strings of low-voltage lights edge stairs that connect the various levels, and they line soffits above the bar, reflecting candlelike off the shiny painted ceiling. They also encircle the mirrored "infinity box" that frames a glowing Rascals logo.

Caressed with colored light, a gilded reproduction of the Hellenistic "Winged Victory" presides over the main dance floor. "Nobody in Hawaii knows who Winged Victory is, but they like it," says Lacayo. "It adds a neat air of fantasy. A disco needs to be a fantasy anyway."

10. CAFETERIAS

Gone are the days when cafeteria dining meant shuffling along an endless counter, facing an unappetizing assortment of overcooked food, and eating amidst a sea of tables. Today, corporations, museums, hospitals, and other institutions are treating cafeterias as public amenities and management tools for boosting employee productivity and morale. Not only do cafeterias prove to be the primary source of social interaction within an organization, they also serve as private places of respite from the workplace.

To ensure coordination between design and construction of dining, serving, kitchen, storage, and food preparation areas, it is generally agreed that foodservice consultants should be involved from the beginning of any cafeteria project. A paramount reason for the collaboration of the consultant and the designer is the fact that cafeterias devote forty to fifty percent of their space to backroom operations, including food preparation, service, storage, and dishwashing, as compared to twenty-five percent for restaurants. In order to determine the ratio between servery and seating, many designers and consultants begin each project by compiling market research about a particular organization.

Key to the size of a noncommercial foodservice facility is research to determine what hours it will be open, how many shifts of diners must be accommodated, and what percentage of the total employee population is expected to use the facility. Employee usage is often as high as seventy percent, since more corporations have begun to subsidize their foodservices to keep employees at the workplace.

Cafeteria design is also influenced by location of the facility in which it is housed and the availability of nearby restaurants. In organizing a cafeteria, most designers and foodservice consultants agree that a good rule of thumb is to allow 15 square feet per seat in planning the dining area and 5 square feet per seat, respectively, for food prep, storage, and service. Because it is visited every day by employees, the cafeteria must keep pace with the developments in the foodservice business and be designed with enough visual interest—as well as durable materials—to hold up for a long time.

GIVE CAFETERIAS A RESTAURANT AMBIENCE
THREE FACILITIES REFLECT A TREND TOWARD NONINSTITUTIONAL DESIGN

INCREASINGLY, designers are being asked to reflect the elevated status of cafeterias and give them a restaurant ambience rather than institutional character. Menu selection, food display, furnishings, lighting, and finishes are becoming more varied and upscale to serve a larger, more egalitarian cross section of employees.

The cafeteria has gained a position of physical prominence within many organizations. It is no longer relegated to internal, windowless spaces, but ranks alongside the corner office as a desirable place to be. For example, a new cafeteria created by Interior Facilities Associates (IFA) for the Bankers Trust Company's Harborside facility in Jersey City, New Jersey, faces the Hudson River with spectacular views of the New York City skyline.

Whether undertaken for a hospital, museum, or corporation, the planning approach to noncommercial foodservice remains basically the same. The most critical factors are how often the facility will be used and by whom. Calvin Tobin of Loebl Schlossman and Hackl Architects, principal-in-charge of design for the Mount Sinai Dietary Facility in Chicago, recalls that "at Mount Sinai, we tried to create a low-key environment, one that would contrast with the high tension of the hospital. It would be used twenty-four hours a day." To meet this program, he designed a dessert area that doubles as a short order cooking counter at night, and he stipulated a separate vending area.

In planning the public cafeteria for New York City's The Museum of Modern Art, designer Judith Stockman had to gear the facility to a different population of daily users. But like the noncommercial foodservice of a hospital or corporation, it involved the same strategies for achieving the functional adjacencies and efficient circulation required of any cafeteria. Notes Stockman, "A cafeteria is really a type of feeding machine, but it should be designed so that it doesn't feel that way."

While designers are apt to focus most of their efforts on creating a pleasant dining room, foodservice consultants emphasize that the servery and other support functions must not be treated merely as leftover space. Many corporations housed in office towers, for example, require that one kitchen serve both the cafeteria and private or executive dining rooms on adjacent floors.

As the introductory space to any corporate or institutional cafeteria, the servery has become the focus of innovations in noncommercial foodservice and its interior design. Ease of circulation and variety in menu and display are promoted through the "scatter" system, an arrangement of discrete service counters that avoids the delays of conventional, single-line layouts. Under this system, separate counters are organized according to food type; hot food is located nearest the kitchen while self-service foods are placed on islands in the center of the area. Robert Nyman of the George lang Corporation, a New York City–based food consulting firm, says, "The scatter system complements the current boom in health foods and salad bars."

Although this arrangement demands a spacious servery, it creates the effect of separate service areas in the least possible amount of space. For example, the straight line of the MoMA cafeteria servery is articulated by projecting piers to separate each counter with its corresponding food type.

The role of lighting, graphics, and display case design is becoming more important in calling attention to the increasing choice in cafeteria menus. Joseph DeScenza, vice president of Food and Travel Services for the Bankers Trust Company, points out that, to attract employees, the cafeteria servery has become a place for merchandising food. "Restaurants don't feed the same people every day, but we do. If our presentation isn't attractive, we lose those people forever."

The servery of the Mount Sinai Hospital Dietary Facility, for example, highlights each service island with exposed incandescent bulbs. The servery of Bankers Trust's Harborside cafeteria is showcased by computer-inspired graphics and

At the MoMA (above), cafeteria settings are geared to heavy daily use but maintain the look of a tasteful restaurant with views of the museum's sculpture garden. Photography: © Durston Saylor.

As the Bankers Trust Company's Harborside facility (opposite) shows, a well-designed corporate cafeteria can be almost as desirable a perk as the corner office. Photography: © Whitney Cox.

Crucial to the success of any noncommercial cafeteria, especially those accommodating employees on limited lunch hours, are the serving areas. Ranking high among design priorities in those areas are clear diagonal signage, unobstructed traffic patterns, and overall ease of maintenance. Ceiling-mounted "runway" lighting directs diners around curving tray tracks in the Mt. Sinai Dietary Facility servery (above). Photography: © David Clifton.

gleaming white tile, an aesthetic carried into the dining room by a self-service island for utensils and condiments, and for heating food items in microwave ovens. Standard stainless steel–faced service counters, chill pans, and steam tables are being disguised with fascias of natural materials such as wood and stone, the better to display the food.

Beyond the servery, visual variety and comfort have become a matter of course for the design of increasing numbers of cafeteria dining rooms. This effect is being achieved by changes in floor and ceiling heights, a wide range of lighting, seating types, table configurations, and a customized approach to the idiosyncrasies of a particular institution. The colors used and the natural materials are becoming more residential in feeling.

To emphasize a restaurantlike atmosphere, low partitions and lighting variation are utilized to the fullest. The objective is to promote the feeling of intimate spaces, to increase privacy, to separate smoking and nonsmoking areas, and to improve acoustics without resorting to inflexible walls. Carpeting, upholstered seating, baffled ceilings, and fabric-paneled partitions and walls also are used to reduce dining room noise, although in the service areas, hard surfaces are unavoidable.

Because the corporate and institutional cafeteria is increasingly relied upon to serve multipurpose functions for conferences and other social events, flexible furnishings are also required. For example, the Mount Sinai Hospital cafeteria is planned with a main dining room that seats 360, an adjacent conference area that can be subdivided into three smaller rooms, and an enclosed portico that seats 30. Banquettes and tables sized for two or four people that can be grouped together to accommodate larger parties provide flexible yet comfortable ways of conveying "restaurant" atmosphere in a noncommercial setting.

ENERGIZE THE CAFETERIA WITH COLOR

"GAZEBOS," WAIST-HIGH WALLS, AND PALM TREES ANIMATE AN IMPERSONAL SPACE

For the employee cafeteria of a large office park in southern California, project designer Mary Flynn (Merchant Associates, Santa Monica, California) conceived an environment that would be energetic and colorful, yet sophisticated. "We wanted to provide relief from the sterility of the workplace by creating something refreshing, lively, and elegant to the eyes," she recalls.

To achieve such results in 900 square feet of raw space and with a working budget of $95,000, the designers concentrated primarily on color and light. "The colors used are more true than trendy," states Flynn. Blue, green, and orange accents—the chair seats, for example—are scattered throughout the space. Variegated line graphics are painted in shoots and swirls across the walls, lavender knobs crown a zigzag partition, and blue flags hang from the ceiling.

The low level of ambient light helps to create a mood of intimacy. In the servery, a neon tube rims the ceiling, breaking to announce each food offering (salads, deli, beverages) in flowing script. Elsewhere, spots shine down between the rows of ceiling banners and sconces brighten the booth partitions.

"We wanted an international mood here," notes Quinn. To achieve it, menu specialties were used to cue the various service areas: Chinese food is featured in the Far East, Mexican cuisine is available in Peppers, and American fare is served from behind the Grill, which offers such things as bovine burgers and haute dogs.

The designers wanted to keep the space open but also to create some boundarylike divisions so the individual diner would not feel lost among 485 others. To break up the dining area, they raised "gazebos," installed waist-high walls, and anchored 11-foot palms throughout the space, thus creating enclosed sections within the more spacious framework. "We also installed booths along the walls; they're fun as well as functional," notes Flynn. The booths, which have painted cutout partitions alternating with straight-backed gray ones, exemplify the spirit of Park Plaza: a serious eating spot that doesn't take itself too seriously.

PARK PLAZA CAFE El Segundo, California
Owners/Developers: Saga Corporation, Continental Development
Architecture: Noble/White Architects
Interior Design: Merchant/Associates (Mary Flynn)
Photography: © Roland Bishop

Color is everywhere in the Park Plaza cafeteria, from partition knobs to ceiling flags to painted wall graphics. In the servery (above), a bright pink neon tube announces the particular fare from the buffet or the grill: such delicacies as bovine burgers and haute dogs. Stripes of neon repeat in the wall graphics.

BRIDGE OFFICE AREAS WITH A CAFETERIA
SOOTHING DESIGN PROVIDES LUNCHTIME RELIEF FOR COMPUTER-BOUND EMPLOYEES

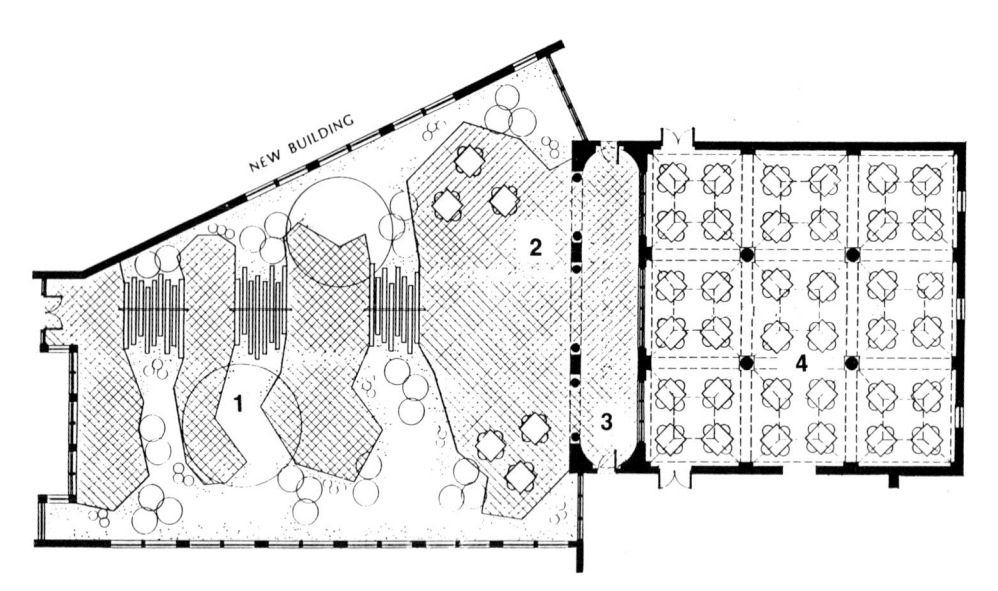

Skylighted grid admits natural light to Emery Air Freight's cafeteria (right). Vending machines are located in a foyer and out of sight. The 1,500-square-foot space accommodates 200 diners at a time. The floorplan illustrates how the cafeteria, fronted by a loggia walkway on a courtyard, bridges old and new office buildings.

WHEN THE YOUNG architectural firm of Leung Hemmler Camayd (Scranton, Pennsylvania) was commissioned to design a 50,000-square foot addition to an existing office structure for Emery Worldwide Air Freight's Accounting Division in nearby Throop, an employee cafeteria was specified as part of the package.

According to LHC's John Kuna, site parameters dictated that the two main buildings be splayed apart, leaving a triangular courtyard in between. The cafeteria itself, part of the new structure, forms a third side of the triangular arrangement.

Fronted by a loggia on the courtyard, the two-story cafeteria serves as a bridge between the old and new office areas. It was planned to provide desk- and computer-bound Emery employees with visual relief—literally, a sight for sore eyes—and with an environment that would refresh and stimulate.

High, coffered ceilings feature skylights that bathe the space in natural light. Clean, cheerful tones of brick, beige, and white, plus accents of green and red, create an atmosphere that is at once comforting and stimulating.

Nine columns section the 1,500-square-foot space into a grid of 16-square-foot coffers that taper to 6-square-foot skylights "like pyramids with their tops cut off," says Kuna. The air distribution system is housed in horizontal louvers within the molding-bordered coffers. The carpet pattern reiterates the grid theme and defines traffic and activity areas.

Kuna acknowledged that the building itself conveys a certain slick, painted quality. To add warmth, he specified natural oak for wainscoting, doorframes, and bases of structural columns. Doors and panels are stained to match. Walls are covered in a durable, linenlike, woven material.

The Emery cafeteria services a staff of 350 employees and accommodates up to 200 diners at a time.

EMERY WORLDWIDE ACCOUNTING HEADQUARTERS CAFETERIA   *Throop, Pennsylvania*

Owner: *Emery Air Freight Corporation*
Architecture: *Leung Hemmler Camayd*
General Contractor: *Breig Brothers*
Furnishings Contractor: *Business Machines Company*
Photography: *© William Mongan*

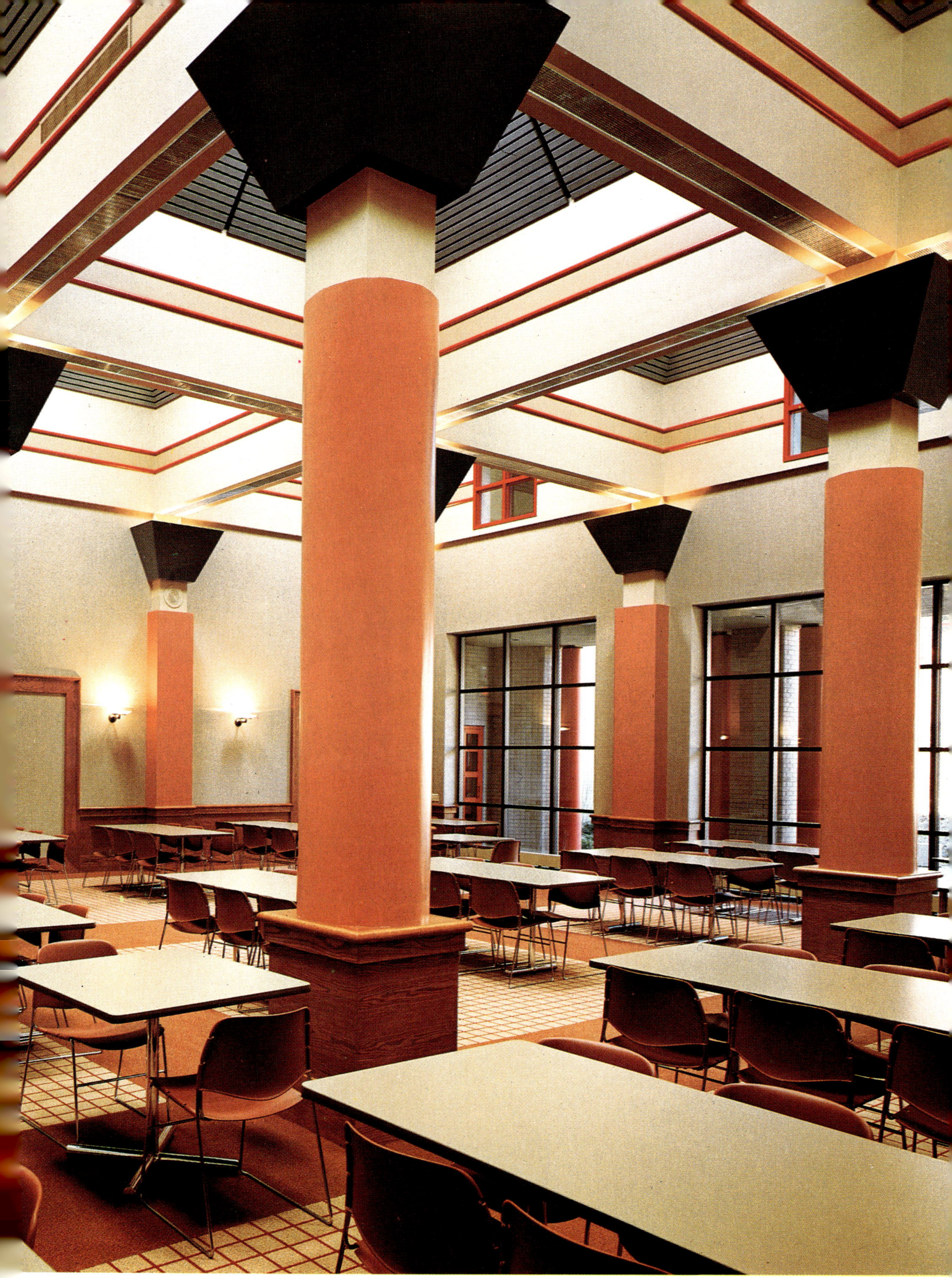

11. RESTAURANTS

WITH VIEWS

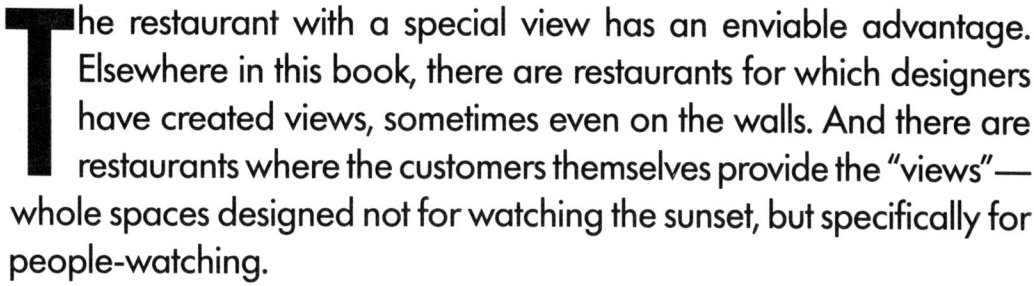

The restaurant with a special view has an enviable advantage. Elsewhere in this book, there are restaurants for which designers have created views, sometimes even on the walls. And there are restaurants where the customers themselves provide the "views"—whole spaces designed not for watching the sunset, but specifically for people-watching.

Setting such broad interpretations aside, however, there is nothing quite like a restaurant with a *real* view of the Pacific Ocean or the Swiss Alps. This chapter includes restaurants that could easily fit in other categories, but it is their views that have made their designs speak.

For example, at Portofino (opposite) in the town of Thalwil near Zurich, Switzerland, architects Kyncl and Arnold found the panoramic view irresistible. It takes in the many church spires of Zurich on one end of the lake and the grand Alpine peaks at the other. So they created a space sheathed in glass. But in a conservative Swiss city where strict codes govern new construction, such a solution was not a simple undertaking. The architects persevered, however, and the magic of their proposal, which places a piece of park under glass, won out.

At Geoffrey's in Malibu, California, owners Geoffrey Etienne and Ron McGuire had a lot to work with in their restoration of a building originally conceived by Richard Neutra. Sculpted into cliffs overlooking the Pacific ocean, the organically designed restaurant has magnificent views. Etienne and McGuire capitalized on the advantages by opening up windows, creating glass sliding doors, and wrapping a deck around the part of the building that commands the sea vista. But their task was complicated by a previous renovation that had nearly deformed the structure.

In planning restaurants to accommodate imposing views, the designer must acknowledge the subtle interaction between the landscape (or seascape) and the interior, for it affects not only the strategic placement of windows, but the selection of colors and materials, the arrangement of tables, and, often, the construction of levels within the space.

BRING THE OUTDOORS IN
A PIECE OF PARK IS SET UNDER GLASS IN A SPLENDID SWISS SETTING

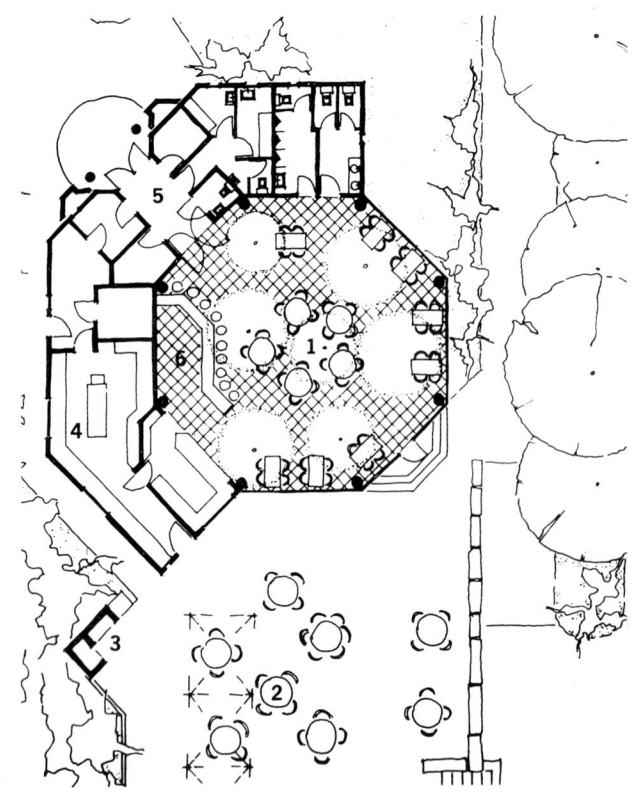

The functional areas of the restaurant—the kitchen, utility rooms, storage, and rest areas shown on the floorplan—provide a buffer that separates the dining area (right) from the parking lot and road, leaving seating completely open to spectacular views of the lake, city, and the Alps. In the glass wall facing the water are doors that open to the outdoor dining area. Floorplan: indoor dining area (1); outdoor dining area (2); outdoor grill (3); kitchen (4); entrance (5); bar (6); utility rooms (7); restrooms (8).

GIVEN AN OUTSTANDING site at the edge of the Lake of Zurich, and with no design restrictions per se from their clients, architects Kyncl & Arnold sought to capitalize on dramatic views. On a clear day the Alps rise up from the lake at the south and the spires of the city of Zurich pierce the sky at the north. Sailboats cut the water in the middle distance.

One specification was firm, however: "The owners insisted that the space be made comfortable for people using the park—sailors and bathers and strollers. That is why we decided to put a glass cover on a piece of the park and to plant trees inside. Even on rainy days, people can sit here and enjoy the views," explains Kyncl. "We wanted the ambience of Italy, of holiday, of free time. For that reason we chose the name Ristorante Portofino, after the Italian town."

The fanciful, hexagonal-shaped steel structure surrounding the dining room is paned entirely in glass; it gleams at the water's edge. But seen from the road, the structure presents a dramatic arched entryway, which both attracts attention and lends privacy to the space inside. They have taken the blues of a changing sky and repeated them in a mosaic of blue tiles that rises to form an arc that is accented in neon. Sturdy, matching blue columns complete the postmodern look. Drawing the eye inward is a circular optical pattern of stripes painted on the glass doors; inside, on a second set of doors, it is repeated in the obverse.

This section of the building, which is closest to the road, houses the kitchen, storage, utility, and restrooms, thus creating a buffer between dining room and street/parking area. When patrons step into the restaurant, all this is behind them. Except for a few trees with delicate foliage, there is nothing to obscure the magnificent view of the lake.

The restaurant seats 80 indoors, plus another 20 at the bar and up to 100 outdoors, weather permitting. The windows do not open in summer; the room is air conditioned. An arched glass door gives access to the outdoor dining area and to an open grill on the north and east sides of the building, which is also accessible to pedestrians and boaters from the walks and docks in the park.

Heating is supplied by hot water pipes in the floor and by baseboard heaters, painted the same turquoise as the structural steel frame. Such functional details double as decoration.

All interior fittings, from the ornate white pedestal tables and bentwood chairs to the blue-and-white napery and the live palm trees, were selected by the architects.

Kyncl and Arnold were able to overcome the project's most formidable challenge when its innovative design, not seen before in this region, passed muster with the conservative town fathers of Zurich. "There are so many building rules in Switzerland and Zurich that it makes creative architecture very difficult," says Kyncl in retrospect.

RISTORANTE PORTOFINO	*Zurich, Switzerland*
Architecture/Interior Design: Kyncl & Arnold Architekten AG, Thalwil, Switzerland	
Budget: $500,000	
Size: 2,600 square feet	
Time: 6 months	
Seating: 60 indoor; 100 outdoor	
Owner: Marcel Capecchi, Kilchberg	
Photography: © Kopp + Vonow, Zurich, Switzerland	

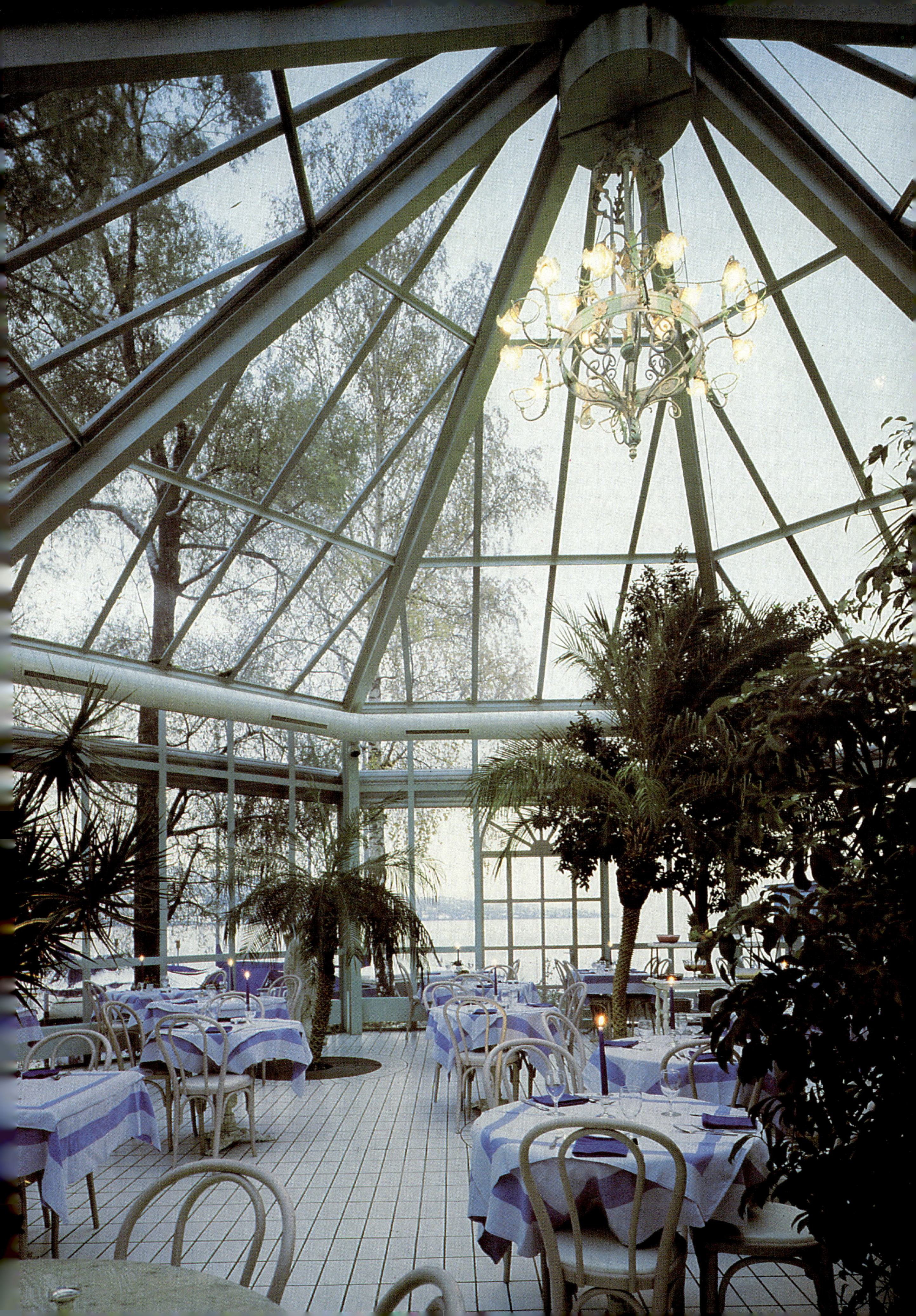

LET THE SEA BE SEEN

A PACIFIC CLIFFSIDE RESTAURANT RECAPTURES THE SIMPLICITY OF RICHARD NEUTRA'S CLASSIC DESIGN

A wraparound deck (above) offers diners a cliffside seat overlooking the Pacific Ocean. The wall of sliding glass doors lets inside-dining patrons enjoy the view, as well. These glass doors were not part of Neutra's original design, but they reinforce the interaction he intended between interior spaces and the natural beauty outside.

ONCE CALLED the Holiday House, a restaurant Richard Neutra sculpted into a cliff overlooking the Pacific Ocean at Malibu, California, is no longer the restrained, organically proportioned structure he designed for producer/director Dudley Murphy in 1949. But thanks to its current owner, Geoffrey Etienne, who renamed the legendary restaurant Geoffrey's, it also is no longer the garish anachronism it had become after being insensitively remodeled several times in the 1960s and 1970s. Today, Neutra might not recognize his creation. But he'd probably approve of it.

"Our entire premise," Etienne says, "was to tone things down and bring back the romance [of the structure] by making the place simple, clean, and unobtrusive again. We wanted to let the natural elements—the ocean and cliff—dominate the entire scene."

Etienne, a graduate of the University of Southern California's School of Marketing and Finance, decided rather spontaneously to buy the former Holiday House after hearing about it from his mentor at USC, Harvey Baskin. The two became partners in the venture.

GEOFFREY'S	*Malibu, California*
Owner:	*Geoffrey Etienne*
Design/Purchasing Team:	*Geoffrey Etienne, Ron McGuire*
Budget:	*$250,000*
Seating:	*150*
Photography:	*© Carlos von Frankenberg/Julius Shulman Associates*

Although he lacked hands-on restaurant experience, Etienne had acquired a taste for fine dining on his extensive travels. He believed a great restaurant should combine "the most romantic and intimate elements of the finest cosmopolitan restaurants and the casual elegance associated with the French Riviera." The vintage Neutra design promised to fulfill his vision.

Acting as his own designer, Etienne soon decided that the restored restaurant should at least recall Neutra's original simplicity. That meant opening the interior to the natural elements of the ocean cliff setting, as well as stripping away layers of ornament, including flashy mirrors and insensitive wallcoverings specified during previous renovations. New plumbing and wiring, as well as a new kitchen, had to be installed.

It was necessary to reverse much of the work done during 1976, when Neutra's double A-frame structure was reconstructed to resemble the hull of a ship, with curved walls and arched ceilings. "Without going into additional major renovation, we tried to work with the forms as they existed," Etienne says, "making them blend into the hillside softly and romantically." His only structural change was to replace a wall of small windows with large sliding glass doors that allow a spectacular view of the ocean, restoring the unique interaction of exterior and interior that Neutra intended. The glass doors now open onto a wraparound deck, which takes the place of an original terrace lost to a rainy-season mud slide.

Etienne also replaced an ugly and broken-down tiered

water fountain on the right side of the dining room with a greenhouse full of flowering plants. The new landscaping ascends an adjacent hill so that patrons in the dining room may look upward into a gardenlike scene.

Etienne wanted the view and the people to be the focal points. Accordingly, he repainted the exterior a soft, sandy hue, then surrounded the building with the deck, on which guests may dine all year long. Wall-mounted portable heaters help thin-blooded Californians tolerate sixty-degree winter nights.

To reach the deck, patrons first pass through coral trees and bougainvillea. Inside, a 60-foot oval bar spreads wide and deep. Textured, sand-colored walls and carpeting echo the natural elements of the seaside perch. Accessories are "sand dollar" white.

To the left of the bar, past the kitchen entrance, is the dining room. The view to the left is dominated by the ocean; to the right, the greenhouse adds a strong element of color. The room's decorative elements subtly complement the dramatic setting. Walls are indigo blue. Table linens and china are white. Sand-colored carpeting is spread underfoot. Tables and chairs are Danish modern.

The $250,000 restoration of Neutra's elegantly simple, subtly organic structure, which seats 80 on the deck and 70 inside, celebrates the best of the California landscape.

GIVE EVERY TABLE A VIEW

IN A WATERSIDE NIGHTCLUB, FLOOR LEVELS ARE CHANGED TO CREATE STAGE SEATING

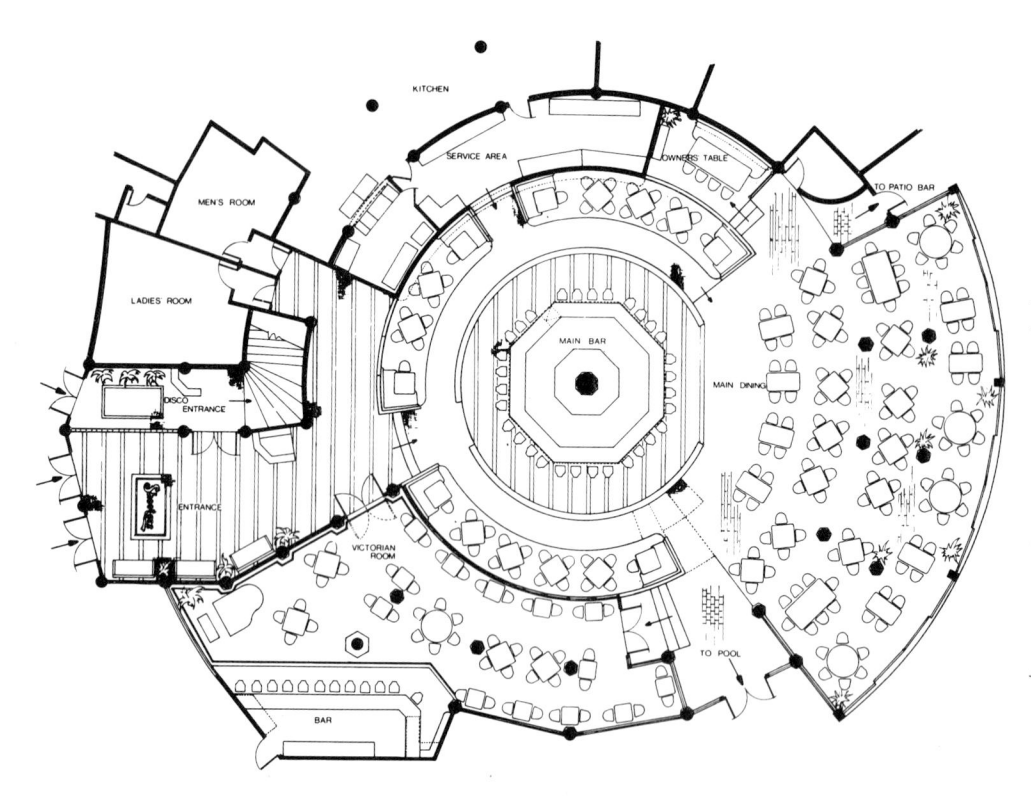

Shooters II was created in an existing circular structure which was extended along the back, facing the water, with an 80-foot-long glass atrium. In good weather the glass doors pocket back, opening the entire area to outdoor dining, a pool, and dockage. To ensure that everyone has a view, mirrors are used on columns, and glass partitions divide dining areas. In the floorplan (left), it is easy to see how the designer utilized the building's circular shape to advantage and reiterated it in the design of the bar, which in turn serves as a focal point for the interior design.

IT IS NOT OFTEN that earth movers go into a building and push dirt around. But to fulfill the design scheme of Susan Welzien (principal, S. W. Wells Design Associates, Fort Lauderdale) for Shooters II in Boynton Beach, Florida, tractors worked inside the existing circular building to change the floor levels.

In Shooters II, Welzien needed the earth movers to create new levels for the stage seating that makes the nearby Intracoastal Waterway visible from just about all of the restaurant/night spot's 380 seats. Where there is not a direct sightline to the outside, Welzien (with senior designer Sylvia Balamut and design assistant Yaly Jones) has installed beveled mirrors on partial walls and columns to reflect the water and the boats at their moorings.

SHOOTERS II	*Boynton Beach, Florida*
Owner:	*Reg Moreau, Mel Burge, Al LaHay, Roland Miranada*
Architecture:	*William L. Osborn*
Interior Design:	*S. W. Wells Design Associates*
Budget:	*$1.3 million*
Time:	*Less than 3 months*
Seating:	*380*
Photography:	*© Martin Fine*

The structure, which had housed a very traditional Italian restaurant, with "lots and lots of velvet" and upholstered booths, was totally gutted, says Welzien, who also designed Shooters I in Fort Lauderdale for owners Reg Moreau, Mel Burge, Al LaHay, and Roland Miranada.

The frame of the building did not change in the designers' plans. In fact, its circular elements are played up to enhance the design. An octagonal bar was built in the middle of the restaurant with traffic radiating around and out from it. The bar repeats the form of the building and makes for easy circulation to all parts of the facility. With its central position, the bar also becomes a focal point for the room. To draw further attention to it, the firm created a circular bar soffit of mirror, etched with the name Shooters II.

To enhance the open feeling of the restaurant and at the same time provide more seating space, the designers added a glass atrium across the back of the building, facing the water. The atrium extends about 10 feet from the original exterior walls and is 80 feet wide. It is constructed of glass doors engineered to pocket back, opening the entire space to the patios, a pool, and dockage.

To keep the sense of openness and the views, Welzien's firm relied on etched glass both to decorate and to create separate areas in the large facility. Level changes also work to divide the different drinking and eating spaces.

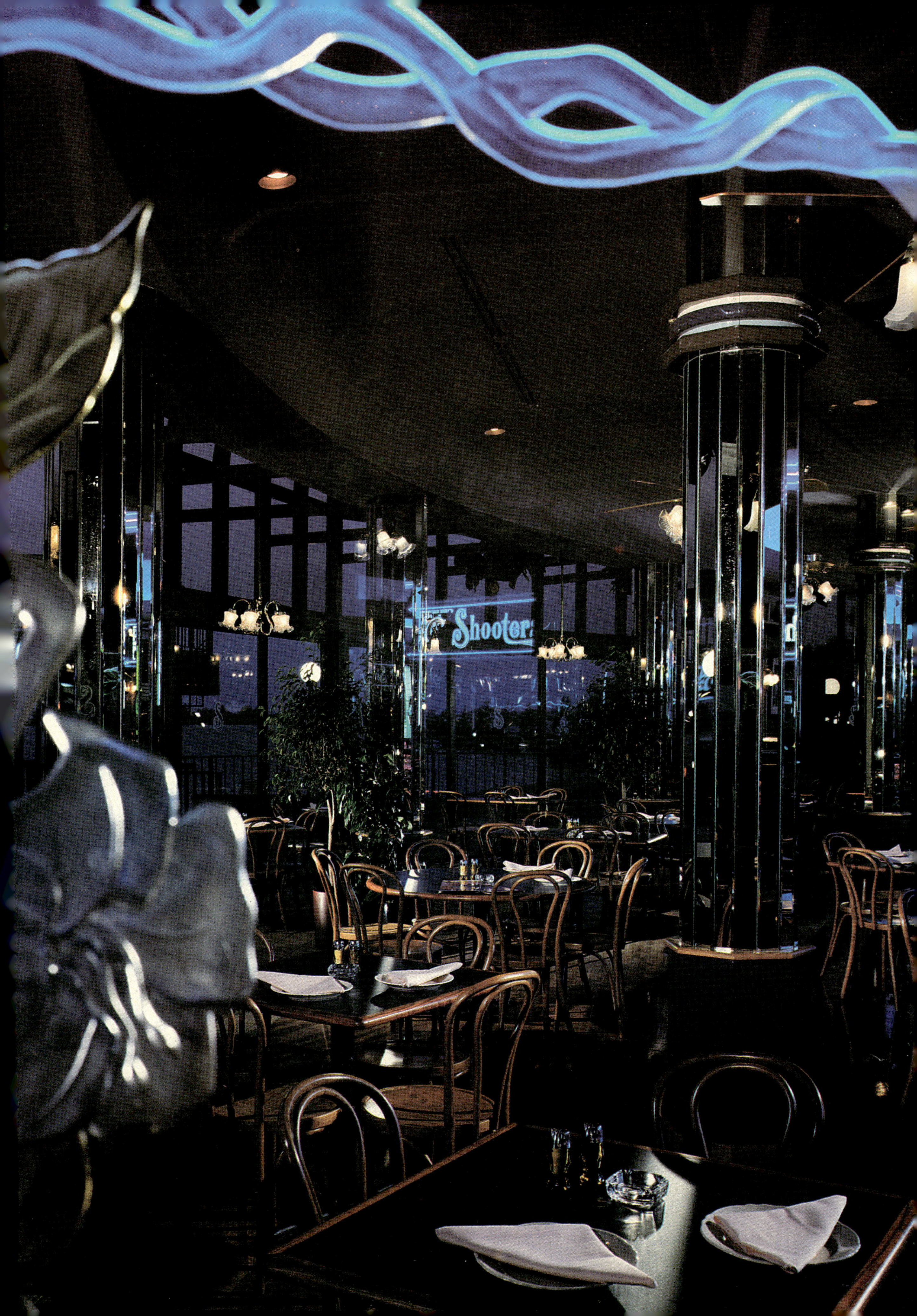
Shooters

MIRROR AN OCEAN PANORAMA
IN THIS SURFSIDE DINING SPOT, EVERY SEAT OVERLOOKS THE PACIFIC

Lavender, peach, and mauve bathe the sky as the sun sinks below the rocky surfline of Morro Bay, California. Nearby, guests enjoy the peaceful view through the windowed walls of The Inn at Morro Bay, where the inn's design reflects the beauty of the famed bay.

Breakfast, lunch, and dinner are served in The Bay Room, which literally holds a series of mirrors up to nature along its back wall. "We wanted the view from every seat to be as good as the next," Shults notes. "The glass partition is not deeply etched; it is almost a mirrored shadow of Morro Rock. We also added a cantilevered deck for outside dining, sheltered by the same style umbrellas repeated elsewhere in the Inn for decoration and creating an intimate, casual mood."

Responding to the muted tones of the evening sky, designer Mabel Shults (Shults & Associates, Goleta, California) recalls that she used the "chalky, almost translucent colors to establish the glow you feel when sunset is here. Unlike the patterned wallpapers our firm typically uses, these colors also helped create the open, spacious feeling we wanted without looking busy or crowded."

Shults worked with associates Paulette Bronstad, project designer, and Suzan Wright, coordinator, to thoroughly renovate and upgrade the 1940s-style restaurant and motel. Few structural changes were necessary: Metal facades and balustrades were replaced with wood inlays and trim, while wooden shutters were added to the inn's many windows and glass doors. "We tried to create a 'California/Cape Cod' feeling," says Shults, "not quite traditional, and very upbeat."

In the lounge, the large canvas umbrellas hide floating light fixtures and create an intimate atmosphere without diminishing the view through original floor-to-ceiling windows. A new faux marble bar, trimmed in brass and wood, enhances the room's understated elegance. Natural wood chairs and blue-gray fabrics echo colors of the sand and sea.

"The greatest challenge," recalls Shults, "was to create elegance with fine components, while maintaining the inn's low-key mood and utilizing its dramatic views."

THE INN AT MORRO BAY	*Morro Bay, California*
Owner:	*Eric Friden*
Architecture:	*Ketzel & Goodman*
Interior Design:	*Shults & Associates*
Photography:	© *Milroy/McAleer*

In the Bay Room (above and opposite), a mirrored wall ensures every diner a magnificent view of Morro Bay and the rocky Pacific coastline that seems to extend from the restaurant's window sills. As part of their renovation of the restaurant and inn, the designers lowered high cathedral ceilings, replacing them with coffered ceilings and indirect lighting. The muted colors of the interior reflect the soft colors of the landscape seen through the many large, expansive windows.

12. ADAPTIVE USE

DESIGNS

Many restaurants today are located in buildings originally intended for some other purpose. Among the restaurants covered in this and other chapters, some have been adapted from such diverse structures as horse stables, movie theaters, private residences, clothing stores, printing plants, auto showrooms, watermills, travel agencies, even mortuaries.

Often, it is the eccentricities of these spaces that lend the character and atmosphere so desirable to today's restaurateurs and their customers. Old loft spaces and factory buildings usually have the wide-open quality conducive to people-watching and noisy activity. Such buildings also offer enough square footage to accommodate different areas and moods: A big bar, an open kitchen, and acres of tables fit easily beneath ceilings expansive enough to suggest the firmament.

While monumental spaces work to an advantage, they must be handled by the designer in a way that relates to human scale. For example, Carlucci's in Chicago is a grandiose space that once was used to stable horses and to warehouse auto parts. To create a place "that everyone uses as a sort of residence when they're not at home," architect Jerome Eastman broke the cavernous space with room dividers, booths, paintings, potted plants, and warm, soft colors.

Not all recycled buildings are large, however. Notable exceptions are former residences, intrinsically intimate and warm, that are made into restaurants through reallocation of rooms for kitchen, prep, and dining use. A good example is Ma Maison in Houston, built in the 1930s as a lodge on rolling countryside overlooking the bayous and transformed in the 1980s into an elegant French restaurant in the shadows of skyscrapers that have sprung up around it.

Architect James Bischoff (Callister Gately and Bischoff, Tiburon, California) asked his clients to consider placing a restaurant (now called Hop Brook) in a historic old mill on their property, rather than erecting a new building. In a sense, all the projects in this chapter plead the same case: Adapt space in an old structure (instead of building new) for a restaurant with special ambience.

GLAZE A FACADE FOR SPARE REFINEMENT
WITH INTERIORS STRIPPED TO THE MINIMUM, SIMPLE FURNISHINGS COMPLETE A DESIGN STATEMENT IN PARIS

A spare interior and an austere glass facade (left) distinguish Coup de Coeur. Its downstairs dining area (opposite, top) seats 22 and offers a more intimate atmosphere than the festive room upstairs (opposite, bottom), which seats 38.

WHEN PATRICK NAMURA and Didier Oudin—both graduates of the hotel school in Nice—decided they wanted to open a restaurant in the French capital city, they bought an unlikely building that housed a travel agency not far from the Paris Opèra. With the help of their friends, Michel Douville and Patrick Garel, the young restaurateurs transformed the space into a restaurant called Coup de Coeur. The interior was stripped, the old staircase was retained, and a glass front was put on the building.

When Coup de Coeur opened, the press labeled this atypical Parisian eatery an "antirestaurant." Everything about it is understated and refined. The two-story glass facade borders on the austere. The interior is also spare: black plastic Philippe Starck chairs, deco-style lighting, classic tables dressed in starched white napery. But the pale-rose–colored walls and gray carpets create a warmth that is heightened when patrons fill the tables.

Linking the intimate and rather sedate 22-seat street-level dining area with the more festive 38-seat space above it is the original staircase, now painted in basic black for contrast. Throughout the 200-square-meter restaurant, counterweighted lights hang over each table; they can be raised for brightness or lowered for a more subdued effect.

By intention, these are rooms that don't feel finished until they are populated. But when patrons fill the restaurant, the effect—in tradition-bound Paris—is remarkably original. Coup de Coeur cost approximately 2 million francs to complete.

COUP DE COEUR	*Paris, France*
Owners:	*Namura, Oudin, Jarl*
Architecture:	*Michel Douville*
Interior Design:	*Patrick Garel*
Seating:	*60*
Photography:	*© Claude Postel*

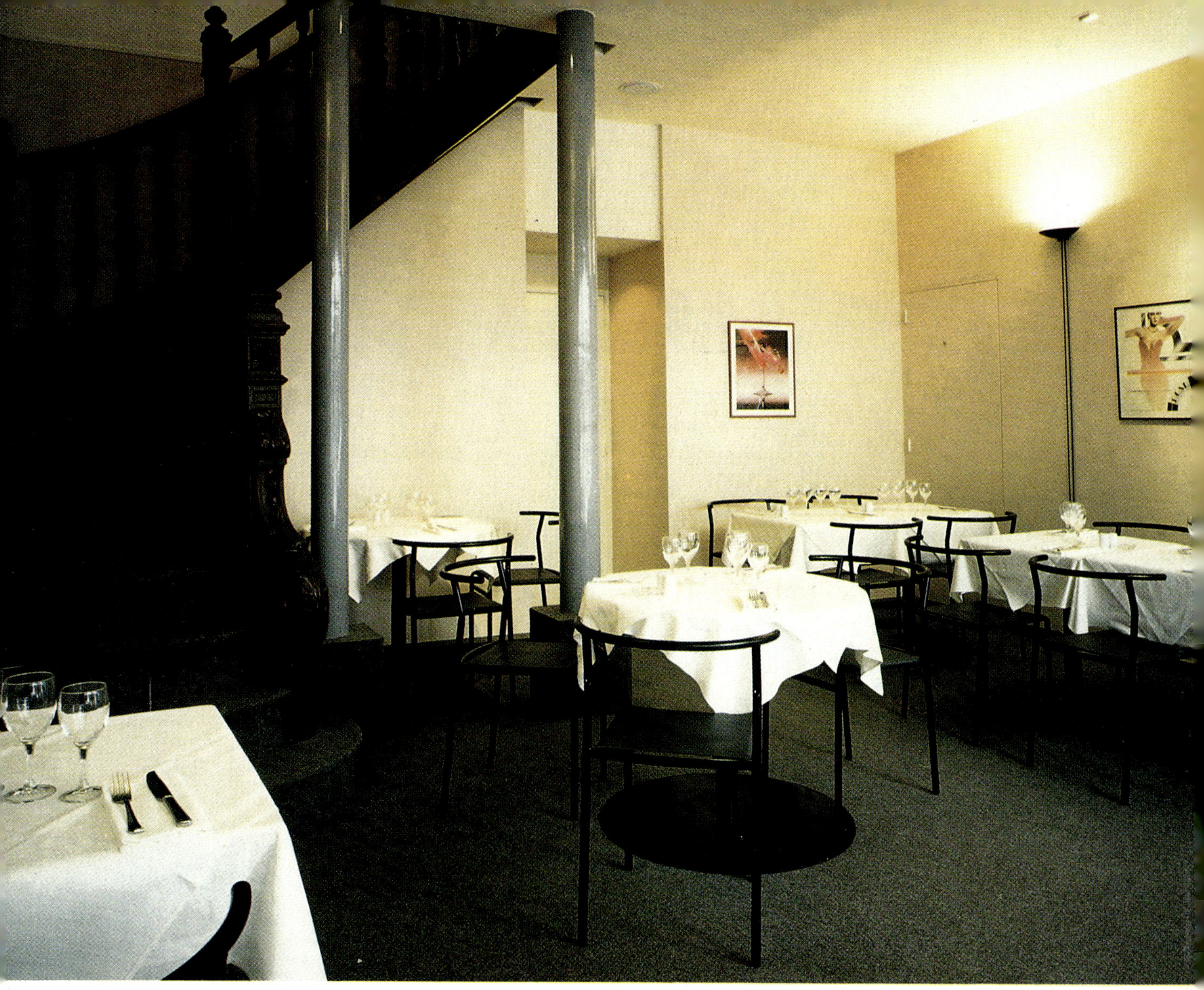

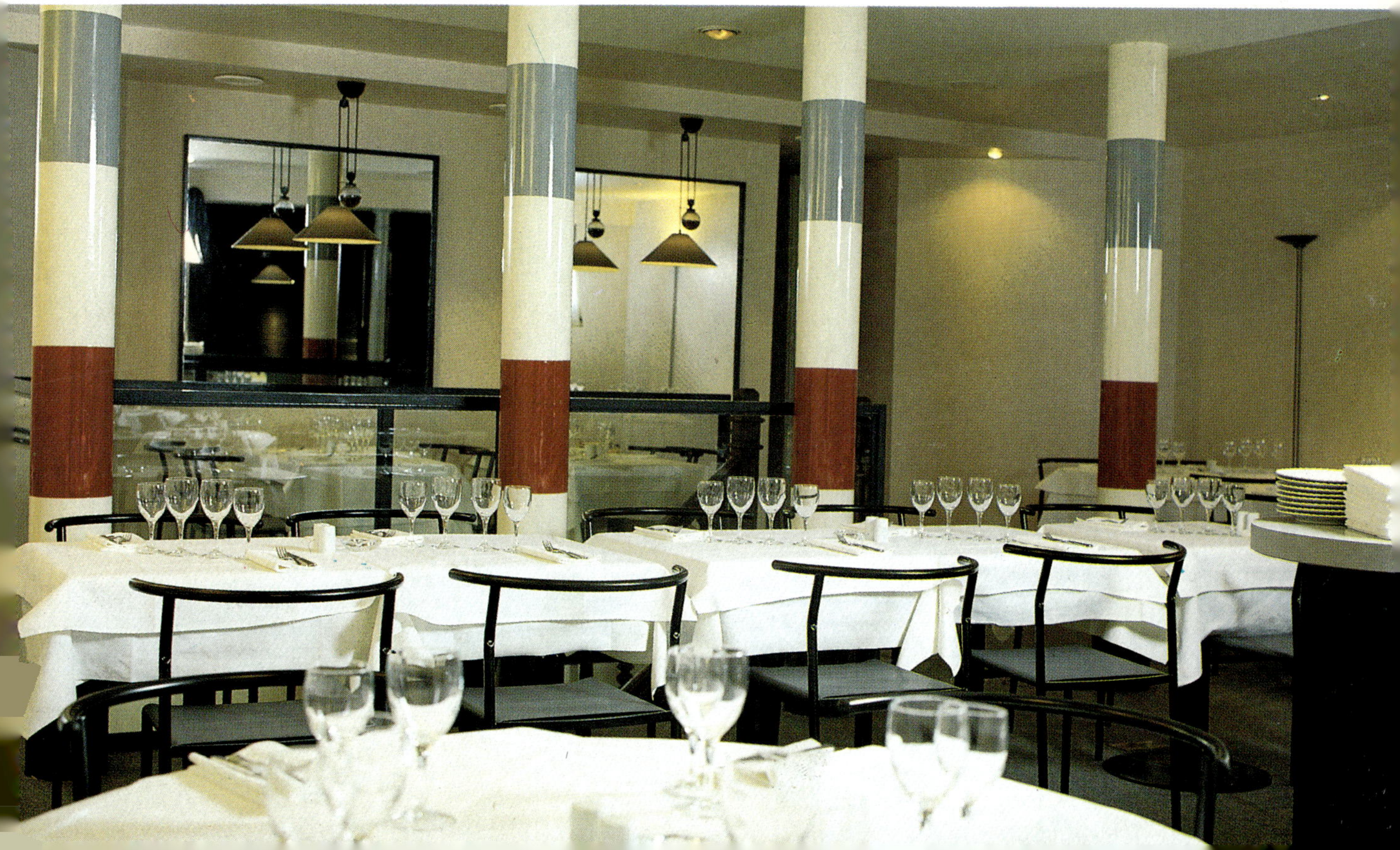

TRANSFORM A RUSTIC LODGE INTO AN URBAN RESTAURANT
AN ELEGANT RESTAURANT WAS ONCE A SIMPLE RESIDENCE

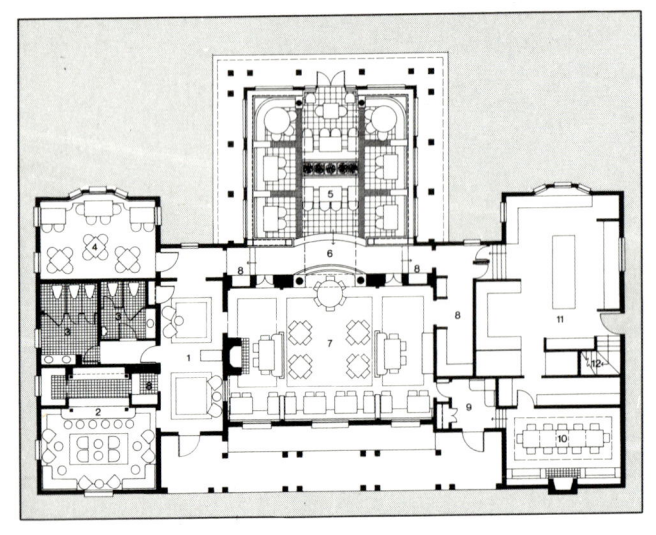

When the James Hill House was originally constructed in 1936 in Houston, the surrounding area was virgin countryside. Today, the rustic one-story country lodge—now the elegant Ma Maison restaurant—sits in the shadows of corporate and residential highrises.

Famed Houston architect William Ward Watkin designed the house in 1936 for Dr. and Mrs. James Hill. Watkin was principal designer for much of Rice Institute (now Rice University) and the Houston Museum of Fine Arts. Clad in white clapboard, the L-shaped structure seems straightforward, but its interior dimensions are surprising: There is a Tudor-style hall inspired by English architect Joseph Kash.

The house remained in the Hill family for almost forty years, while Houston spread outward. Eventually it and the surrounding property were sold to developer Giorgio Borlenghi, head of Interfin Corporation, and the once-charming building stood waiting to be dismantled. In 1979, Michel Lakhdar, looking for a restaurant property, spotted what would become his "maison" and convinced Borlenghi to save the house. It went through several incarnations before the current Ma Maison opened.

Eventually, the house was moved 150 yards to a site among office towers that provides a rare link between the new and the old. Lakhdar, a native of Tunis, worked closely with Chelsea Architects' Sharon Jachmich, AIA, on both of the restaurant's incarnations. In the first remodeling, little was done to alter the character of the house, save for updating the kitchen and inserting a bar and restrooms. The second time around, the developers, realizing the inadequacy of the service area and seating space, brought in Melton Henry Architects to design two additions: a wing containing a large kitchen, offices, and wine room, and an enclosed garden room at the back of the house where the patio had been. A front porch was also added to connect what are now two mirror-image wings.

Ma Maison can seat 155 but is broken up into small rooms that feel manageable and intimate. Given the initial success of Ma Maison during its first, two-year life and a remodeling budget of $350,000, Lakhdar and Jachmich decided to retain the original character of each room. The additions, however, by virtue of their proportions and fenestration, suggested different uses of light and architectural elements. Color was chosen as the means of establishing continuity between old and new: green, rose, and off-white.

A Tudor-style ceiling, original to the former home, dominates Ma Maison's rearranged main dining room (opposite). The scale and warmth of the original home were maintained by architect and designer. A coffered ceiling and walls upholstered in pale pearl-colored fabric mark the wine room (top), designed for private parties. Floorplan: main entry (1); bar and lounge (2); restrooms (3); bay room (4); garden room (5); promenade (6); main dining room (7); waiter's station (8); reception area (9); wine room (10); kitchen (11); stair (12).

MA MAISON   Houston, Texas
Owner: *Interfin Corporation*
Original Architecture: *William Ward Watkin*
Exterior Architecture: *Melton Henry Architects (1983 additions)*
Interior Architecture: *Chelsea Architects*
Seating: *155*
Photography: *© Paul Hester*

237

INSTALL A RESTAURANT IN A STABLE
PAINTINGS, PARTITIONS, AND PLANTS
BRING INTIMACY TO A CAVERNOUS SPACE

At the termination of Carlucci's dramatic vaulted entry passage, a dark-stained, open colonnade sets off the bar and 120-seat dining area (left). The large room is dominated by a 72-foot-long skylight.

WHEN UPSCALE redevelopment hits a neglected city neighborhood, it often creates special problems for restaurant owners in these neighborhoods. More often than not, hitching on to such a trend can mean having to install a complex operation in a space originally designed for something very different.

This was the case when three Chicago restaurateurs first approached veteran designer Jerome Eastman about creating interiors for a café/bistro they planned to open on Chicago's booming North Halsted Street. Joe Carlucci, Nick Novich, and Tim Glascott had in mind a big, informal, European-style place with lots of purely American activity. They planned to serve a combination of Italian regional dishes. And they wanted to install the whole thing in a cavernous one-time stable then operating as an auto parts warehouse.

As in most successful adaptations, the foundation of Eastman's interior scheme, the space plan, was largely dictated by the eccentricities of the existing structure. After providing for two separate shops on the front of the building, and convincing the owners to create an outdoor dining garden on its south side, Eastman allowed the dining room/bar area to be, at 52 feet, virtually as wide as the building itself. He placed the operation's primary internal axis along an existing, 72-foot-long skylight.

Though the resulting 52-foot by 72-foot space fit the owner's prescription for a combination bar/dining area where people-watching would be a major part of the experience (making an hour wait seem only half as long), it created a potential problem as well. Nick Novich, a managing partner of the restaurant, puts it succinctly: "Our fear was that it would be like eating dinner in a bank lobby."

"The idea," says Eastman, "was to create one of those public spaces that everyone uses as a sort of residence when they're not at home." So he set about creating elements that give the barnlike space a comfortable human scale. Inside the main door, which is flanked by the two street-side shops, Eastman's opening gambit was a long *faux marbre* vault in direct line with the succeeding interior skylight. The vault, Eastman says, both provides an architectural transition from street to dining room and establishes the requisite quasi-European atmosphere from the start.

Inside, the spatial volume is "broken down" by a series of

CARLUCCI	Chicago, Illinois
Owners:	Joe Carlucci, Nick Novich, Tim Glascott
Architecture:	Jerome Eastman
Engineers:	Design 21
Graphics:	William Vargas Design
Acoustics:	R. Lawrence Kirkegaard & Associates
Contractor:	Jensen Mechanical Contractors
Seating:	120, plus 66 at bar and seasonal outdoor dining
Budget:	$700,000
Photography:	© Jim Norris

In the dining room (top), paintings commissioned from Chicago artist Charles Voris help reduce the room's cavernous scale while balancing large windows on the opposite wall. A band of mirror, installed around the room's entire circumference, allows patrons seated facing the wall to view the restaurant's activity. With the opening of the dining garden in the spring, the 66-seat bar (above), which has open views of the dining areas, will become the center of the operation. Floorplan: entry (1); vaulted entry corridor (2); foyer (3); dining area (4); booth dining area (5); bar (6); garden dining area (7); retail shop (8); gelateria (9); restrooms (10); service corridor/food pick-up (11); kitchen (12).

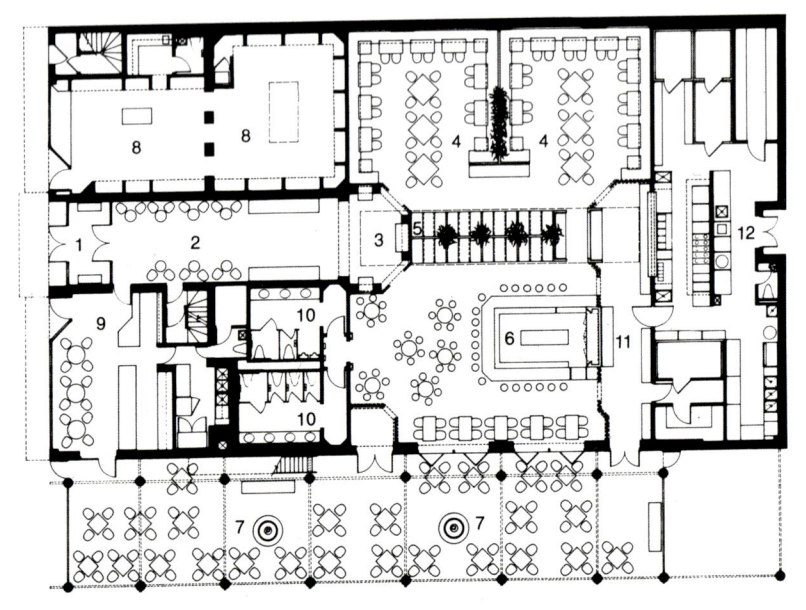

specific architectural intrusions: An open colonnade just beyond the vaulted entry passage demarcates the foyer; against the rear wall, a Chippendale-inspired cupboard serves as a food pick-up station and focal point; the bar features a gradually stepped facade; and, centered on and directly opposite the bar, the doorway to the restrooms lies beyond a crown-molded portico.

Furthering Eastman's campaign for a human scale within the outsized space is a row of potted palms placed on a low wall separating rows of booths in the room's center. A row of ivy plants marks yet another division within the dining room. Crown moldings around the room repeat the 18-inch by 18-inch dimensions of the skylight's grille. Perhaps most important of all, a series of lively paintings lines the dining room's north wall, balancing French doors that open onto the south-side garden.

Colors and materials throughout the room are warm and soft. The rough-coat plaster walls are painted taupe, and the ceiling—including the striking geometric skylight—is a warm ivory color. The floor is sheathed variously in squares of quarry tile (bar and corridors) and gray carpet (main dining area). All the architectural elements were stained dark, Eastman says, "simply because we used several different kinds of wood."

Opened for less than its $700,000 budget, Carlucci's improvised location, heterogeneous design vocabulary, and easy-going ambience make it a quintessentially American restaurant.

STRIP AWAY ACCRETIONS AND LET THE LOBBY SHINE

TILE FLOORS, 18-FOOT CEILINGS, AND MARBLE COLUMNS LEND
PERIOD AUTHENTICITY TO AN INDIANAPOLIS RESTAURANT

Leaded-glass casement windows on the mezzanine level of the Majestic Oyster Bar and Grill (above) open above the grand dining room, housed in the lobby of the former Indianapolis Gas Company.

AFTER THE ARCHITECTURAL firm of Woollen, Molzan and Partners bought the ten-story Majestic Building, located in downtown Indianapolis, its partners were not quite sure what to expect when they began restoring the ground floor and mezzanine. "It was a process of discovery," notes principal Lynn Molzan, "involving more subtraction than addition." What they quickly uncovered was a glorious, circa 1895 interior.

Immediately, the design team sought outside investors, formed a corporation, and planned a $500,000 restoration/rehabilitation for a restaurant. The result is the unique 225-seat, two-level Majestic Oyster Bar and Grill.

Above the 9-foot dropped ceilings were the 18-foot originals. Inspired by this discovery, the architects also removed interior walls that had chopped the 7,700-square-foot space into many drab cubicles, and they unblocked southern windows. What remained was the original banklike lobby of the Indianapolis Gas Company, where customers at the turn of the century (during the heyday of Indiana's natural gas boom) paid their gas bills. Beneath the makeshift modernization, the lobby's opulent architectural features—including a colorful ceramic tile floor, marble-sheathed Corinthian columns, plate-glass windows, and 18-foot ceilings—were intact.

After stripping the lobby to its original state, the designers began the intricate processes of repair and restoration, and the planning of an addition necessary to transform the space into a restaurant. For the ground-floor interior, they carefully selected both materials and forms to complement the existing architecture. A new 20-seat beverage bar and a 15-seat oyster bar across the room were custom-designed in marble-topped oak.

The grand 10-foot-wide entry, with oak doors, side lights, and fan/light crown, is a "fairly accurate replica" of the original, according to Molzan. The semicircular form of the oyster bar echoes the shapes of the mirrored, arched alcove behind it (originally a window and the entry). The gas company vault, complete with pediment, is now the wine cellar.

To separate the beverage area from the 120-seat dining room and to define the entry as well, the designers installed a custom metal railing resembling "turn-of-the-century New Orleans wrought iron," says Molzan. Made of steel and painted light blue, this railing also climbs the new oak-tread staircase connecting the main floor and mezzanine. (The original staircase is in the back of the house.) As a trio, the railing, staircase, and colonnade help divide and organize space.

MAJESTIC OYSTER BAR AND GRILL   Indianapolis, Indiana
Interior Architecture: *Woollen, Molzan and Partners*
Exterior Architecture: *Oscar Bohlen*
Photography: © *Wilbur Montgomery*

What is now the 70-seat dining mezzanine was added in the 1920s to hold the offices of gas company officials and clerks. With original leaded-glass casement windows opening out over the main dining room, the mezzanine offers a perfect setup for an intimate dining area, as well as a 20-seat private dining room. A gray-green patterned carpet and wall sconces complete the mezzanine decor.

Both mezzanine and main dining areas feature burgundy-upholstered bentwood armchairs and white-linen–covered tables. Small marble tables and cane-backed armchairs informally surround a piano in the lounge. By the beverage bar, the designers encircled the columns supporting the mezzanine with rings of marble to provide additional counter space.

The original green and yellow ceramic tile floor on the main dining level perfectly suited the oyster house ambience the architects sought. After sending a supplier around the country in search of tile to match the 100-year-old tile pattern, the architects discovered several boxes of it right in the building. They supplemented this with new tile in a matching color for repairs and finished the rest of the ground floor in hardwood.

A cream-and-tan color scheme, chosen to complement the floors, also divides the space. By painting the plaster-encased ceiling beams and decorative plasterwork a tan darker than that of the recessed ceiling areas, the planners both highlighted details and established orderly spatial division corresponding to the placement of windows and columns.

Yellow diamonds in the floor tile are picked up by several bright yellow, palm-filled planters, placed along the windows. These yellow planters, the blue rails, the burgundy upholstery, and the light wall colors—all bathed in natural light from the large windows—complete the "light, bright, and cheerful" color scheme Molzan and the design team sought.

By day, the bright sun from the south and west windows is controlled by Austrian shades with a period look. Daylight also filters through the windows' transoms. Most contain original lead-and-bevel work bearing the Indianapolis Gas Company logo, which repeats on old doorknobs. By night, period chandeliers and wall sconces offer soft illumination.

Installing the kitchen and HVAC was the costliest part of the project. A mechanical engineer helped plan HVAC; an equipment supplier served as kitchen consultant. A former tailor's shop houses a prep kitchen and a mechanical room is tucked away upstairs.

The decorative wrought-iron staircase (a new addition) links the main floor with the mezzanine dining area; it also serves as a room divider. Just beyond the staircase (left), a long bar was custom designed of oak and marble to coordinate with existing architectural features.

ADAPT A PRINTING PLANT TO A PRIVATE CLUB
EXPOSED BRICK AND WOOD RETAIN ORIGINAL CHARACTER

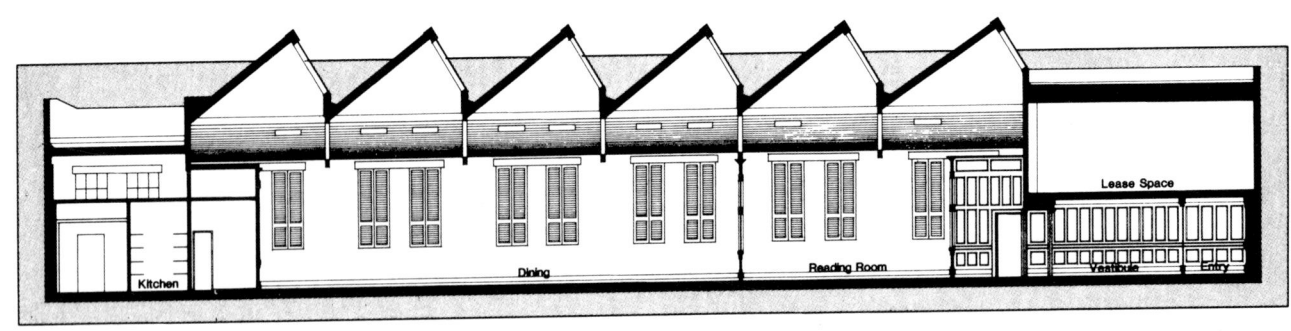

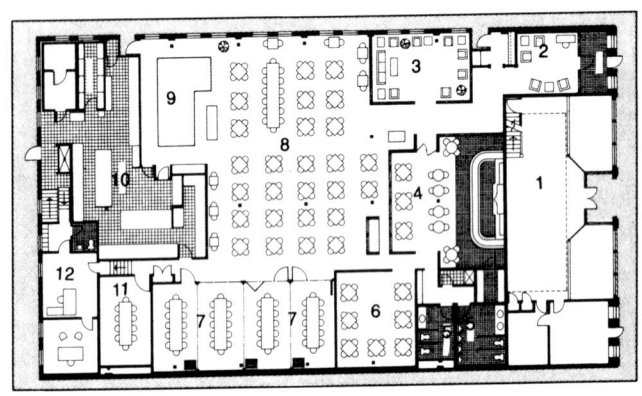

Floorplan: leasable space (1); entry (2); reading room (3); bar (4); restrooms (5); gaming room (6); private dining rooms (7); dining area (8); press (9); kitchen (10); boardroom (11); offices (12).

THE IMAGINATIVE adaptation of commercial/industrial space for hospitality use has an honorable place in the annals of American restaurant design. San Francisco's Ghiradelli Square, Boston's Faneuil Hall, and New York's South Street Seaport all illustrate how dormant, often decaying structures can find new life, once restored. In Fresno, California, architect William Patnaude (Allen Lew & William Patnaude) adapted a crumbling printing plant into the Downtown Club, a private luncheon spot catering to professionals.

The structure was designed in 1919 by Glass & Butner for The Fresno Republican Printery, which turned out college yearbooks and small-circulation newspapers. The printery functioned with diminishing regularity until the mid-1960s.

By 1979, when the Downtown Club first became interested in the space, the building had deteriorated so much that it was red-tagged by the city. Its unreinforced, three-brick-thick walls, sealed with lime mortar, were crumbling (an earthquake had, in fact, cracked them perilously); and the roof, a series of six saw-toothed skylights, had been leaking "apparently since the beginning of time," says John Edward Powell. Water damage had rotted the truss system and the walls were bearing the roof weight.

Even on the verge of collapse, the printery was not without appeal, and indeed, was listed on the National Register of Historic Places. Its high ceilings (14 feet below the truss line) and generous 16,000-square-foot interior afforded an airiness further enhanced by the play of light from skylights. Its role in Fresno's commercial history bestowed additional distinction.

Because the building was in an advanced state of deterioration—and because its historic designation required fidelity to the original structure—the undertaking "became a major reconstruction project," says Patnaude. Two layers of brick were removed in some areas, and steel was used to reinforce the remaining walls. The roof was removed completely and replaced by a sturdy duplicate.

"The real strength of the whole solution," says Patnaude, "is

---

DOWNTOWN CLUB   *Fresno, California*

Owner: *Printery Partners*

Architecture: *Allen Y. Lew & William E. Patnaude (Sandra Muratore)*

Exterior Architecture: *Terry Jones*

Historic Design Consultant: *John Edward Powell*

Photography: *© Hanna Barsam*

the way the light floats through it." To maintain this effect, the architect let no new construction intrude above the truss line. The roughhewn character of the structural brick and wood was carried through in the shutters, casework, and trim of redwood and oak. Wooden chairs in the dining room complete the motif.

To separate the drinking and dining areas, Patnaude used stained-glass panels to create a "pavilion" that gives coziness to the contained bar area and sheds a warm glow on the dining space outside. The nineteenth-century mirror behind the bar was found rotting in a field in Fresno's Chinatown and was restored by Powell and Patnaude, who stripped it on weekends and evenings.

Such a gesture characterizes the care that went into the project. An American Institute of Architects award attests to the quality of the restoration.

An old printing press helps retain the building's original flavor, as do the exposed brick walls and exposed structural beams.

SALVAGE A MILL FOR A MULTILEVEL RESTAURANT
THREE-CENTURY-OLD STONE WALLS AND ORIGINAL
ROOF'S BEAMS RECALL THE SEVENTEENTH CENTURY

From the outside, the cluster of red-clad buildings (left) nestles perfectly along the Hop Brook, just as the gristmill and sawmill once did. Inside, an open staircase (opposite) cascades from level to level, affording fine views of the waterfall outside. The architects left the sprinkler pipes exposed along the ceiling. Brass stair rails reinforce the rustic look.

WATER HAD WORKED its way through the stone walls of the three-century-old gristmill and sawmill along the Hop Brook in Simsbury, Connecticut, and wind whistled through the rafters. That was before architects Callister, Gately and Bischoff of Tiburon, California, were engaged to work on the restoration. Under their direction, the entire structure was taken apart and then attentively put back together to create a successful 210-seat restaurant named for the brook.

Ensign-Bickford Realty Corporation, the owners, wanted a restaurant in the 500-acre parcel they were developing as an office park. As architects for the master plan, Callister, Gately and Bischoff persuaded its clients to make use of existing historic structures that sat so beautifully in the landscape.

"We took our clients to a similar restored building that had been turned into a restaurant, so they could see that restoration would be the right move," says James Bischoff, head of the project team. "We proposed integrating the mill's three stories to create six levels. Now, patrons cross the Hop Brook on foot over a covered bridge to enter the building on the third level. The main dining room flows down to the bar through a progression of half-levels so that the activities of drinking and dining are combined naturally. The existing bridge provided a natural entrance to the restaurant and afforded dramatic views of Hop Brook's waterfall."

Wherever possible, rotten ends of old beams were sawed off and the good wood was reused. And a new roof was built over the old one, allowing for an insulated airspace between the roofs, plus a ceiling that looks unchanged.

"One of our major problems was creating a multilevel dining facility with an open staircase that would satisfy all the building codes," says Bischoff. "We solved it by installing a water curtain around the stairwell." Another potentially sticky situation that went smoothly for the architects: Two contractors were hired to complete the project in sequence. Ensign-Bickford was the contractor for the first phase, which entailed getting the shell up to code. Then The Stout Company took the project to completion for The Restaurant Group of Hartford, restaurant leaseholders.

The $1.4 million, 9,000-square-foot restoration project (the footage includes a new kitchen wing) retains the poetry of the old mill while assimilating the modern conveniences necessary for a successful restaurant.

HOP BROOK Simsbury, Connecticut
Owners: *The Restaurant Group, Ensign-Bickford Realty Corporation*
Architecture: *Callister, Gately and Bischoff*
  (James Bischoff, Joseph O. Newberry)
Interior Design: *Jay DuMond*
Contractors: *Ensign-Bickford, The Stout Company*
Landscape Architecture: *Johnson and Richter*
Photography: *© James Bischoff*

247

SOURCES AND CREDITS

1. DESTINATION RESTAURANTS

LE TRIANGLE (pages 17–19)
CHAIRS AND BAR STOOLS Beylerian, Janus et Cie; DINING ROOM TABLES Waukegan Cafe Tables, Intrex; MILLWORK Stanley Felderman, Northwestern Showcase; TRACK LIGHTING Halo, Capri; FLOOR Consolidated Terrazzo; LOUNGE CHAIRS Stanley Felderman (International Restaurant Equipment fabrication, Donghia fabric); LOUNGE TABLES Hoffmann, ICF; BAR STOOLS Stanley Felderman (Maharam fabric). CARPET Sun West, Paul Singer Floorcovering; TABLES Stanley Felderman, Oliver & Company; BANQUETTE FABRIC Sunar/Hauserman; MILLWORK Northwestern Showcase; CHAIRS Stanley Felderman (International Restaurant Equipment fabrication, Maharam fabric); ELEVATOR PANELS Alaim Paul Sevilla; ART GLASS Ken Sequine Glass; PAVILION Pietro Studios. *Contributing writer: Michael Webb.*

HISTORIC BRYAN HOMES RESTAURANT (pages 20–23)
TABLES Falcon; GLASSWARE Mason; CHINA Jackson; CUSTOM MILLWORK Architectural Antiques Exchange; CHAIRS Hickory (p. 22), Henry Trellis (p. 23); TABLES Falcon; CARPETING Couristan; DRAPERIES Jack Miller; UPHOLSTERY FABRICS Lee Jofa, Brickel. *Contributing writer: Jerry Cooper.*

ARCADIA (pages 24, 25)
CHAIRS Stendig; LIGHTING Edison Price; BAR STOOLS Beaver Furniture; BAR Theo J. Svalgard Inc. Architectural Woodwork (custom); UPHOLSTERY Lee Jofa. *Contributing writer: Mark Kristal.*

VERDI (pages 26, 28)
TILE Cerbuati; CARPET Fabrica; CHAIRS Loewenstein; BAR STOOLS Thonet; LAMINATES Formica; LIGHTING Halo, Marco, Theatrical; FABRIC Metropolitan. *Contributing writer: Michael Webb.*

SPIAGGIA (pages 28, 29)
MILLWORK AND FIXTURES Equipment Manufacturing Company; FURNITURE Shelby Williams; LIGHTING FIXTURES Atelier International, Halo, Capri; ENTRYWAY RUG Edward Fields; CARPETING Alexander Smith; WALLCOVERINGS AND FABRICS Thomas Decorative Fabrics, Design-Tex, Jack Lenor Larsen, Gretchen Bellinger. *Contributing writer: Mary Jean Madigan.*

LE CYGNE (pages 30–32)
MARBLE FLOORS Miller Druck; ACOUSTIC TILE CEILING Johns-Manville Corp.; PERFORATED METAL CEILING Harrington & King; CHAIRS Empire State Chair; UPHOLSTERY FABRICS Ward Bennett; GRAY SILK WALLCOVERING Wolf/Gordon. *Contributing writer: Barbara Knox.*

AURORA (page 33)
Contributing writer: Susan Colgan.

2. CAFES, GRILLES, AND BRASSERIES

CASUAL QUILTED GIRAFFE (pages 36–39)
CUSTOM LIGHTING FIXTURES J. Woodson Rainey Jr.; CUSTOM METAL FABRICATION (LIGHTING FIXTURES, HANDRAILS, BAR LEGS, GLASS CABINET) Fayston Iron & Steel, Waitsfield, Vermont; METAL WALL PANELS F.W. Werner Inc.; TERRAZZO D. Magnan Company; GRANITE BAR AND TABLETOPS Granite Importers; TITANIUM TABLE INSERTS Tomico Ferguson; CABINETRY Cozzolino Furniture; CHAIRS Bieffeplast imported by Gullans International; LEATHER BANQUETTE AND CHAIR UPHOLSTERY Rollhaus Brothers; CARPET Harmony. *Contributing writer: Mary Jean Madigan.*

ANCORA (pages 40–43)
FLOORING Buckingham Slate; WINDOWS, DOORS, SUNSCREEN J. Zeluck Inc.; LIGHTING Edison Price, Lightolier, Stonco; MILLWORK Art Fabricators; TABLE BASES L & B Contract Industries; CHAIRS Shelby Williams; UPHOLSTERY Design Tex; LAMINATE Formica; PAINT Benjamin Moore, PPG; ALUMINUM STOREFRONT Kawneer; HARDWARE Rixon, Stanley, Schlage, Baldwin; TILE American Olean. *Contributing writer: Deborah Dietsch.*

TWENTY/TWENTY (pages 44, 45)
TABLES L & B Contract Industries, Alta Woodwork; DINING CHAIRS Deutsch Wicker; ELECTRICAL INSTALLATION Light-Up Electric; DOWNLIGHTS Edison Price; NEON Alan Banks; DECORATIVE WINDOWS AND FIRE ESCAPES Bruce & Bruce Stage Scenery; CARPENTRY Transformer; WALL SURFACES IN NICHES Plextone; FLOORCOVERINGS Top Grade by N.Y. Carpet; SLATE FLOOR John Savittieri; UPHOLSTERY Mira-X; BAR Alta Woodwork. *Contributing writer: Susan Colgan.*

UNION SQUARE CAFE (pages 46–48)
CHAIRS, TABLE STANDS Falcon; TILE American Olean; PLATES Sterling China (pattern designed by Philip Johnson); FLATWARE Oneida; GENERAL LIGHTING Halo. *Contributing writer: Maureen Picard.*

GOTHAM BAR AND GRILL (pages 49–51)
BAR custom by Rathe Production; CAST STONE ORNAMENTS Cusano Bros.; SHEET RUBBER FLOORING American Flooring Products; TRACK LIGHTING Lightolier; UPHOLSTERY Naco Fabrics; CHAIRS Shelby Williams; GLASSWARE Cardinal International, Schott Zweisel; FLATWARE D. J. Industries, Alfredo Zanger; CHINA Hall China, Villeroy and Boch. *Contributing writer: Maureen Picard.*

72 MARKET (pages 52, 53)
CHAIRS Jacky Pecheron; TABLE BASES L & B Contract Industries; LIGHTING Halo; CARPET Fabrika; GLASS BLOCK PPG. *Contributing writer: Michael Webb.*

CHAYA BRASSERIE (pages 54, 55)
TABLES AND BAR STOOLS Gold Coast Industries; CHAIRS, TABLETOP WARES, FABRICS Sazaby (Tokyo); SPOTLIGHTS Halo; BAR Alwy Visschedyic (custom); WINDOW FRAMES Torrence Windows; SIGNAGE Ampersand. *Contributing writer: Michael Webb.*

WINNETKA GRILL (pages 56–59)
COLUMNS Omni Craft; CHAIRS Shelby Williams; WOOD FLOORING Hallmark Floors; MURAL FLOOR STENCIL Elise Kapnick; CEILING FIXTURES Joyce Culkin; CARPETING Lees; DRAPERY Bards Decorating. *Contributing writer: Philip Mazzurco.*

RED'S (pages 60, 61)
TABLES, TABLE BASES Falcon; CHAIRS Loewenstein; BAR STOOLS Ron Nunn (custom); BAR Imbolloni Construction; LOUNGE SEATING Stendig, Kinetics; FLOORCOVERING Armstrong, Forms & Surfaces; LIGHTING Halo, Ron Rezek Lighting; UPHOLSTERY Maharam; SIGNAGE Neon Neon; ARTWORK Museum of Modern Art, San Francisco (on loan). *Contributing writer: Kim Johnson Devins.*

L'EXPRESS (pages 62, 63)
FLOOR Kentile; BAR TOP, TABLES, TABLE BASES, BAR STOOLS L & B Contract Industries; BAR S & S Cabinets; VINYL UPHOLSTERY Naugahyde; GENERAL LIGHTING Halo; TASK LIGHTING Artemide, Ron Rezek; NEON Brite-lite Neon; DINING ROOM CHAIRS Atelier International; GREENHOUSE CHAIRS Artemide; BOOTHS Barry Volk; METAL BENCHES Forms & Surfaces; CARPET Bentley Mills; BOOTH FABRIC DesignTex; WINDOWS Torrance Windows; SLIDING DOORS, PARTITIONS S & S Cabinets. *Contributing writer: Michael Webb.*

3. FAST FOOD ESTABLISHMENTS

MRS. GARCIA'S (pages 66, 67)
STOOLS Georgia Chair Company; TABLE BASES Gary Kaplan & Associates; TABLETOPS, COUNTER custom; TILE American Olean, Metro; LIGHTING Halo, Lightolier; EQUIPMENT Surfas, Incorporated; PAINT Pittsburgh Paint; NEON Elro Manufacturing; CONDIMENT BOWLS Nelson McCoy. *Contributing writer: Michael Webb.*

CITY SPIRIT CAFE (pages 68, 69)
TILE Duro Bath & Tile, Design Materials; CARPET Colman Kahn; CHAIRS Contract and Leisure Seating Inc.; FIXTURES recycled. *Contributing writer: Jill Fox.*

JACKETS (pages 70, 71)
Contributing writer: Rachel Long.

ANGELI (pages 72, 73)
TABLE BASES L & B Contract Industries; CHAIRS Chair Factory; RECESSED LIGHTING Halo; WALL SCONCES Morphosis. *Contributing writer: Michael Webb.*

RISTORANTE REPLAY
(pages 74, 75)
LIGHTING Technolyte; CHAIRS, TABLES Tonon; STUCCO Sikkens. Contributing writer: Adriana Spazzoli.

PIZZAPIAZZA (pages 76, 77)
CHINA Jackson; GLASSWARE Arcoroc, Cardinal; FLATWARE Stanley Roberts; LINENS TAG Associates; CHAIRS Empire; VETTER STONE TABLETOP, BAR TOP Domestic Marble; TABLE BASES L & B Contract Industries; UPHOLSTERY Naugahyde; WALLCOVERING, WAINSCOTING Formica ColorCore; FLOORING Worthwood. Contributing writer: Maureen Picard.

MAMA MIA! PASTA
(pages 78, 79)
FLOOR TILE Monocuttura; CARPET TILE Interface; CEILING TILE U.S. Gypsum; DOWNLIGHTS Halo, Lightolier; LAMINATE Formica; BAR Custom Equipment Manufacturing Company; BOOTH BACK UPHOLSTERY DesignTex; BOOTH SEAT UPHOLSTERY Naugahyde; CHAIRS Empire State Chair Company; SOUND Musicall. Contributing writer: Barbara J. Knox.

DINE-O-MAT (pages 80, 81)
LAMINATES Laminart; FLOOR TILE American Olean; STAINLESS STEEL PANELS Parlamis Construction; CEILING Simplex; LIGHTING Kurt Versen; BELT LIGHTING Litelab; GLASS BLOCK PPG; FABRIC J. M. Lynn; ARTWORK John Baeder; PORCELAIN ENAMEL STEEL PANELS Greensteel Products, Inc. Contributing writer: Jerry Cooper.

EATS (pages 82, 83)
FLOOR TILES Kentile; CABINETRY Formica; NEON Hollywood Neon; CHAIRS Emu; PIE CASE Schmidt; INDUSTRIAL LIGHTS Hubbell; LIGHT TROUGHS custom. Contributing writer: Barbara J. Knox.

4. CHAIN RESTAURANTS

THE BIG SPLASH (pages 86–88)
LIGHTING Litelab-Ken Lewis, Rambusch; CHAIRS Shelby Williams; TABLES custom of DuPont Corian; WALL SURFACE Plextone. Contributing writer: Susan Colgan.

CHARLEY O'S (pages 89–91)
CHAIRS, LIGHT SCONCES Atelier International; BAR STOOLS L & B Contract Industries; RAILINGS Ship'N Out; BANQUETTE FABRIC DesignTex; WALLCOVERING Zolatone. Contributing writer: Maureen Picard.

CASA LUPITA (pages 92, 93)
BANQUETTES/BOOTHS Jenson Manufacturing; CHAIRS Shelby Williams; TABLETOPS Custom by Sikeston Woodworking; UPHOLSTERY Brunschwig & Fils, Shelby Williams; TABLE BASES Falcon Products; WALLCOVERINGS, REEDED CEILING MAT, PAINT Construction Associates; COLUMNS, CAPITALS, CHANDELIERS, WALL SCONCES, ARTIFACTS, ACCESSORIES Arte De Mexico; ARCHITECTURAL MILLWORK, WOOD CEILING BEAMS Starlite Cabinets & Construction; FLOOR TILE Dal-Tile; CARPET Durkan; TRACK, RECESSED LIGHTING Halo; PLANTS P & G Plants; CHINA Hall China; FLATWARE Oneida; GLASSWARE Libbey; SILK FLOWER ARRANGEMENTS custom by designer. Contributing writer: Susan Colgan.

KNOWLWOOD'S (pages 94, 95)
TABLES West Coast Industries; CHAIRS L & B Contract Industries, Shafer Commercial Seating; LIGHTING Hubbel Industrial Lighting; FLOORCOVERING Armstrong. Contributing writer: Jerry Cooper.

McDONALD'S (pages 96, 97)
CUSTOM MILLWORK, LAMINATION Jerry Adams; LAMINATE Wilsonart; CHAIRS Shelby Williams; CHAIR UPHOLSTERY Herschell's Fabrics; TILE American Olean; CEILING COVERING Acousticord by Eurotex; NEON Paradise Neon; LIGHTING Halo; CUSTOM RAILS Lawrence Metal Products; BANQUETTE FABRIC Pindler & Pindler; PLANTERS Architectural Supplies; MIRROR Pritchard Glass; PLANT MATERIALS Plantscapes Inc.; VINTAGE WHEEL COVERS Hubcap Annie. Contributing writer: Kim Johnson Devins.

PIZZERIA UNO
(pages 98–100)
(New York City) TABLES, BASES, CHAIRS, BAR STOOLS L & B Contract Industries; TILE Nemo, American Olean; CEILING SURFACE W. F. Norman; HALOPHANE LIGHTS American Glass Light Co.; RECESSED LIGHTS Lightolier; GLASSWARE Mason; FLATWARE Shenango. (Secaucus) TABLES, BASES, CHAIRS, BAR STOOLS L & B Contract Industries; TILE U.S. Ceramic; TRACK LIGHTS Lite Lab; HALOPHANE LIGHTS American Glass Light; RECESSED LIGHTS Lightolier; UPHOLSTERY Naugahyde, DesignTex. Contributing writer: Kim Johnson Devins.

A & W ROOT BEER (page 101)
TABLES Huber Manuel; CUSTOM CHAIRS Arnold Industries. Contributing writer: Mary Jean Madigan.

ARBY'S (page 102)
CHAIRS Lowenstein; TABLES Johnson Industries; PLANTERS Architectural Supplements; FABRIC Carnegie, Baumann; BLINDS Levolor; BANQUETTES Falcon Products; HIGH CHAIRS Decor Concepts; CUSTOM CABINETWORK Star Cabinet; CARPETING Harbinger; GRAPHICS AND AND MENU American Sign. Contributing writer: Mary Jean Madigan.

COFFEE WORKS (page 103)
SIGNAGE Maury Lasky (Associated Display); MILLWORK Ted Hanenburg; LIGHTING FIXTURES American Glass Light; BANNERS Abacrombe; BRASS Ship'N Out; LAMINATES Formica; FLOORING Hoboken Wood Floor; TRACK LIGHTING Halo; PAINT Pratt & Lambert; CEILING Armstrong. Contributing writer: Mary Jean Madigan.

CHOICES (page 104)
PENDANT LIGHTS Abolite, Design Gallery; KIOSK LAMINATES Formica; SIGNAGE, MILLWORK, CASES Babcock & Schmid (custom); BLINDS Flexalum Decor Blinds; LAMINATES Wilsonart; CARPET Durkan; WALLCOVERING Collins & Aikman; BOOTH FABRIC Maharam; ART Paragon Pictures; AWNING Boyle Awnings (custom). Contributing writer: Mary Jean Madigan.

WENDY'S (page 105)
CHAIRS Thonet; FLOORS Associated Flooring Contractors; WALL PANELING Marlite by Masonite; NEON Pat Tomasso; SUSPENDED LIGHTING Lighting Center; BUD VASES Lew Dolin, Keith Knops. Contributing writer: Justin Henderson.

SGT. PEPPERONI'S (page 106)
TABLETOPS RAMCO; TABLE BASES West Coast Industries; CHAIRS Casual Dining of California; TILE American Olean, Franciscan; CARPETING Milliken; PANELING Marlite by Masonite; WALL GRAPHICS Brent Harder; AWNINGS Parrish Canvas; CABINETRY Orien Fadler; LIGHTING Halo; ENERGY MANAGEMENT CONTROL Tork. Contributing writer: Justin Henderson.

FRANKS FOR THE MEMORY
(page 107)
TABLES, CHAIRS, BASES, LIGHTING custom by Mirich Developments; FLOORCOVERINGS Ammoco Turf. Contributing writer: Justin Henderson.

5. THEMATIC DESIGNS

CURLY'S GARAGE
(pages 110, 111)
TABLES KF; CHAIRS Corry Jamestown, Thonet; PHOTO MURAL Photographic Specialties; TILE Pirelli; CARPETING Harbinger; NEON CAR MURAL David Marel; TASK LIGHTING Abolite Pendant; UPHOLSTERY Schumacher, Unika-Vaev. Contributing writer: Susan Colgan.

LIBERTY CAFE (pages 112–115)
SEAGULL SCULPTURE SLAJ; MAHOGANY BAR Alpine Store Equipment; FLOOR TILE Nemo Tile; OAK CHAIRS Jasper; BRASS RAIL Brunson & Berleth; BAR TRAIN CONSULTANT Gordon's; MURAL MGS Architects with EverGreene Studios; EPOXY TERRAZZO D. Magnan & Co.; OAK CHAIRS Jasper; SWIVEL CHAIRS L & B Contract Industries; TRACK ACCENT LIGHTING Litelab Corporation; MENU DESIGN Dale Glasser. Contributing writer: Mary Jean Madigan.

WILLOW TEA ROOM
(pages 116, 117)
CARPET Pacific Crest Carpets; CUSTOM IRONWORK Robert Horn, John Hudson; CUSTOM SCONCES Carl Hacock; WINDOW TREATMENTS The Drapery Connection; ENTRY WALLCOVERING SJW Design; SALON WALLCOVERING, FABRICS Pindler & Pindler; DINING ROOM WALLCOVERING Deschemaker; DINING ROOM UPHOLSTERY, SHADES Clarence House; DINING TABLES West Coast Industries; DINING WINDOW SHEERS Pindler & Pindler. Contributing writer: Rachael Long.

RUBY'S BALBOA DINER
(pages 118, 119)
GLASS BLOCK Pittsburgh Corning; UPHOLSTERY VINYL Gilford; TABLE LAMINATE Formica; WALLCOVERING Marlite; FLOOR VINYL Flexco; TASK LIGHTING Halo; STAINLESS STEEL BANDING E. B. Bradley; STOOLS Paul Dodd (Los Angeles). Contributing writer: Jerry Cooper.

249

FOG CITY DINER
(pages 120, 121)
LIGHT FIXTURES, SCONCES, BOOTHS, BAR custom by Kuleto Consulting & Design; OVERHEAD LIGHTS Jim Lundberg, Lundberg Studios; BACK BAR LIGHTS Kim Hicks/Near Future Traders; BOOTH UPHOLSTERY Congers Seat Co.; OYSTER BAR Andrew Christie; BAR STOOL BASES California Casting (custom by Kuleto Consulting & Design). *Contributing writer: Michael Webb.*

CAFE BA-BA-REEBA
(pages 122–125)
TOREADOR JACKETS Unique Boutique; REFRIGERATION UNITS Custom Bar-Crafters; TILE, MARBLE Acorn Tile; CHROME TUBE STOOLS Vitro; WOODEN STOOLS L & B Contract Industries; FAN-BACK CHAIRS Shelby Williams; LIGHT FIXTURES A-Lamp & Fixture; CHINA Homer Laughlin; FLATWARE Meridional; GLASSWARE Arcoroc; MURALS AND ARTWORK Made in Chicago (Paul Punke & Corkie Neuhaus), Vicki Tessmer, Mark Wingo/Grambauer, Tom Zoroya. *Contributing writer: Maureen Picard.*

EXTRA!EXTRA! (pages 126–129)
CABINETRY AND BAR Crown River Inc.; BAR STOOLS PML, The Furniture Group; MURALS Serpentine Studio, Ltd.; CARTOONS CONCEPT Gene Meyers; CARTOON EXECUTION Serpentine Studio, Ltd.; TABLES, CHAIRS Lebensfeld Top Equipment Corp. *Contributing writer: Mary Jean Madigan.*

BUBBLES (pages 130–133)
DINING CHAIRS Images of America; CARPETING Brintons Carpet Ltd.; LINOLEUM D.L.W. by D.M.B. Associates; BAR TABLES, CHAIRS Falcon Products; URNS, BAR LOUNGE, LOVESEATS Jadis Moderne; WALL TREATMENT Frazee Paints; LIGHTING Halo; BUBBLE COLUMN custom by Cavanaugh Development; BAR STOOLS Paul Dodd. *Contributing writer: Michael Webb.*

6. ETHNIC RESTAURANTS

CUISINE DES CHEFS
(pages 136–138)
CARPET Kemos Carpets International; WALLCOVERING Sunwall of America; MILLWORK Whitefire Studio; TABLES Falcon; CHAIRS Shelby Williams, with Arc-Com fabric; STOOLS Falcon, with Arc-Com fabric; BAR STOOLS Shelby Williams, with Stroheim & Romann fabric; BANQUETTES Artcraft Booth, with Duralee and Knoll International fabrics and with Arc-Com and Stroheim & Roman fabrics; CARPET Navan; CHANDELIERS Chapman; DRAPERY FABRIC Vieille Provence; LACE CURTAINS Rue de France; TABLES, CHAIRS Mona Liza Fine Furniture; ARMOIRE DOORS House of France; WALL-MOUNTED SHELF Hickory Manufacturing Co.; artwork: Fine Art Ltd., FLOORCOVERING Merida Meridian; SCONCES Contract Fabricators; MARBLE TABLETOPS Elliott's Stone & Marble; BENT-METAL CHAIRS Molla. *Contributing writer: Rachael Long.*

FRANK FATS (pages 139–141)
TABLES, TABLE BASES, BAR STOOLS, BAR BANQUETTE, UPHOLSTERY West Coast Industries; CHAIRS Stendig International; WALLCOVERING Wolf Gordon; CARPETING Patrick Carpet Mills (custom pattern by Anthony Machado); CEILING Charles Gracie; LIGHTING Artemide; CHANDELIER Dick Sylvia (custom design by Anthony Machado). *Contributing writer: Michael Webb.*

KIIROIHANA (pages 142–145)
FURNITURE, LIGHTING custom by architects; FLOOR TILE Gail; WALL TILE American Olean, Dillon Tile; LAMINATE Wilsonart, Nevamar, ABET; PAINT Fuller O'Brien; HARDWARE Forms & Surfaces; CARPETING Hollytex Carpets. *Contributing writer: Michael Webb.*

INDIAN OVEN (pages 146–148)
CHAIRS, TABLES Bon Marche; FLOORING The Structural Slate Corporation; LIGHTING Bowery Lighting; FIXTURES Progress; CHINA, GLASSWARE Balter Sales; FABRICS handloomed batik from George Wheeler Imports. *Contributing writer: Susan Colgan.*

SHILLA (pages 149–151)
TABLES, TABLE BASES Falcon; KOREAN-STYLE TABLES Contemporary Mica (custom); CHAIRS, UPHOLSTERY Oggo/Loewenstein; WALLCOVERING Genon/Midwest Wallcoverings, FlexiWall; FLOORING Tarkett; CARPETING Charleston Carpet, Lees Carpet; CEILING Armstrong; LIGHTING LPI, George Kovacs, Halo; WINDOW BLINDS Glover Shade Company; SCREENING ON GLASS Howard Lindquist; RUBBINGS DeHaan Collection; PICTURE FRAMES Seaburg Picture Framing Inc.; LINENS Artex; GLASSWARE Libbey Glass Company; FLATWARE Oneida Silversmiths; CHINAWARE Homer Laughlin. *Contributing writer: Diana M. Aceti.*

SHAMIANA (pages 152, 153)
TABLES Barrco, Empire State; CHAIRS Shelby Williams, Empire State; WALLPAPER BORDER Bradbury & Bradbury; FLOOR TILE American Olean; GENERAL LIGHTING Lightolier; TASK LIGHTING Norbert Belfer; UPHOLSTERY Arc-Com, Wolf-Gordon Vinyls; TEAK SCREEN, BRASS K&K Imports; WALL SCONCES Sirmos. *Contributing writer: Diana M. Aceti.*

LES TUILERIES (pages 154, 155)
BAR/MAITRE D' POST Premier Woodworking Company (custom); FLOORING Tellini Terrazzo; LIGHTING Lightolier; BAR STOOLS Bar Mart; BANQUETTE FABRIC Gretchen Bellinger; CHAIRS Atelier International; PAINT Glidden Professional Colors; MARBLE TABLETOPS Rico Tile & Marble; TABLE BASES L & B Contract Industries. *Contributing writer: Justin Henderson.*

AOKI (pages 156, 157)
WALL LAMINATES Wilsonart; GRANITE TILE Forms & Surfaces; LIGHTING FIXTURES Tronconi; CHAIRS Loewenstein; KITCHEN EQUIPMENT Bowers & Associates. *Contributing writer: Mary Jean Madigan.*

7. EAT-IN/TAKE-OUT ESTABLISHMENTS

DDL FOODSHOW
(pages 160–163)
(*Beverly Hills*)—FLOORS Cerebatti Tile; LIGHTING Litelab; BAR Ganhal (custom); TABLES, TABLE BASES, CHAIRS, BAR STOOLS Empire State; FABRIC Schumacher; WALLPAPER Clarence House. (*New York*)—TABLES Capitol Cabinet; TABLE BASES Empire State; BAR Capitol Cabinet (custom); MARBLE FLOORS Peter Bratti; CEILING SYSTEM AND SURFACE Regency Tile, lighting Capri; FABRICS Schumacher. *Contributing writer: Barry H. Slinker.*

LAKESIDE DELICATESSEN
(pages 164–166)
FLOORING All American Terrazzo; GRAPHIC DESIGN Frances Butler of Poltroon Press, Kristin Meuser; CHAIRS Flyline/Limn Contract; TABLES Emu; PLYWOOD Louisiana Pacific; LIGHTING Halo; CASEWORK Creative Spaces; COUNTERTOPS DuPont Corian; FIGURATIVE WALL PAINTING Judy Choi, Lucia Howard, Joseph Ruffatto, David Weingarten. *Contributing writer: Michael Webb.*

POLCARI & SONS
(pages 167–169)
DISPLAY CASES Royal Store Fixtures; FLOOR TILE Frontenac; LIGHTING Lightolier, Plugmold, Koch + Lowy; EXTERIOR AWNING Peterson Products; NEON C. W. Williams; WALL TILE Hastings; CHAIRS, BAR STOOLS Loewenstein; BAR custom; WALL TILE Hastings; CARPET Patrick Carpets; FLOOR TILE Frontenac; GLASS BLOCK Pittsburgh Corning UPHOLSTERY DesignTex; FISHTANKS Lobster Market Co.; LINENS Artex; GLASSWARE Libbey; FLATWARE World Tableware; CHINA Royal Doulton. *Contributing writer: Susan Colgan.*

PIRET'S (pages 170, 171)
FLOOR TILE Emser Tile; CARPET Hallmark; SCONCES, PENDANT FIXTURES Ron Rezek; TRACK LIGHTING Halo; WHITE CIRCULAR SCONCES ON SOFFIT custom designed by CRHO, fabricated by Light Gallery; RED VINYL STRIPE VPI Tile; LAMINATE Nevamar; BOOTH UPHOLSTERY Naugahyde; CHAIRS Thonet; NAPERY Marko; RAILING custom designed by Mark Spatz, fabricated by Vicorp; ARTWORK Nancy Kay; EXIT SIGNS Lithonia; FLORAL ARRANGEMENTS Glenn

Hadel; REFRIGERATION DISPLAY CASE fabricated by Royal Food Display Systems; OVERHEAD SHELVING custom designed by CRHO and Vicorp; NEON ART custom designed by Mark Spatz, fabricated by Signtech. *Contributing writer: Maureen Picard.*

TUTTI'S (pages 172, 173)
FLOORING Flexco; SEATING Atelier International; TABLES, BOOTHS West Coast Industries; LIGHTING Capri, Ron Rezek; FIXTURES Royal Fixtures; RAILINGS Hewi; HARDWARE Ironmonger. *Contributing writer: Justin Henderson.*

DUCK AND DECANTER
(pages 174, 175)
FLOOR TILE American Universal; WALL TILE INA; LAMINATES Wilsonart, Formica; REFRIGERATION EQUIPMENT Hussman; PAINT Dunn Edwards; LIGHTING Prescolite, Halo, Georgian Art Lighting Designs, Inc. *Contributing writer: Mary Jean Madigan.*

PANACHE (pages 176, 177)
CASEWORK Gunanl; KITCHEN EQUIPMENT Alcon Design; MARBLE AND TILE Bayshore Tile; NEON SUPPLY AND INSTALLATION Comet Signs; LIGHTING PRODUCTS Capri Lighting; UMBRELLAS Terra; HANGING LIGHTS G. J. Neville; TABLE BASES West Coast Industries. *Contributing writer: Mary Jean Madigan.*

SOUTH STREET SEAPORT
(pages 178, 179)
Contributing writer: Maureen Picard.

8. RESTAURANTS IN HOTELS

CAMPTON PLACE
(pages 182, 183)
TABLE BASES L & B Contract Industries; CHAIRS, BAR STOOLS Traditional Imports; WALLCOVERING Manuel Canovas; CARPETING Brintons; LIGHTING Lightolier, ELA Lighting, Cal Lighting; UPHOLSTERY S. Harris; ETCHED GLASS Faralon Glass Studios; ARTWORK Nancy Graves, Stanley Boxer, Mary Ellen Long; ART REPRESENTATION Joyce Hunsaker & Associates; ART FRAMING Jerry Solomon; MARBLE CONTRACTOR Clervi Marble Company; CHINAWARE Wedgwood; GLASSWARE Mid-Atlantic Glass Company, Schott-Zwiesel; FLATWARE DJ Tableware; LINEN Baker (J. P. Stevens), James G. Hardy & Company. *Contributing writer: Barbara J. Knox.*

MORRISON HOUSE
(pages 184, 185)
MILLWORK Arlington Woodworking; FABRIC Stroheim & Romann, Grayson; DRAPERY Lee Jofa; CHAIRS Donghia, IPF; TABLES IPF; SIDEBOARD Smith & Watson; PAINT Benjamin Moore; CARPETING custom by Regency Textiles; LIGHTING King's Chandelier; MIRROR Friedman Brothers. *Contributing writer: Richard Sasanow.*

LE PARIS RESTAURANT
(pages 186, 187)
CUSTOM DOORS Fancelli; CHAIRS Rosello; CHANDELIER custom by Slavik, fabricated by Kobis Lorence & Midiplex; CHINA Bernardaud Limoges. *Contributing writer: Florence Bruin.*

THE IMPERIAL HOTEL
(pages 188, 189)
CHAIRS Kimball Furniture Reproductions; CHAIR FABRICS Bergamo, Thorpe; DRAPERY Payne Fabrics, Duralee, Schumacher; LACE PANELS Stroheim & Romann; SHEERS Cohama; TABLE BASES Falcon; TABLETOPS D. J. Price Co. (custom); LIGHTING FIXTURES Scott Lamps; WALLCOVERING Schumacher; ARTWORK Graphic Arts. *Contributing writer: Mary Jean Madigan.*

THE SCHOONERS
(pages 190, 191)
SEATING Stendig; UPHOLSTERY FABRIC Knoll; FLOORCOVERING Wellco Polo; CUSTOM FURNITURE Thomas Moser; WINDOW TREATMENT Hunter Douglas; LIGHTING Koch + Lowy. *Contributing writer: Rachael Long.*

RITZ-CARLTON (pages 192–194)
(*The Grill*)—BRONZE CASTING OF "HUNTSMAN AND HOUNDS" (after Pierre Jules Mené, 1810–1879), from Northgate Galleries; "THE HUNT," unsigned eighteenth-century Swiss School painting; "WHITE HORSE AND SQUIRE" by William Barrand (England, 1810–1850) from Barrie A. Wright; FRENCH EIGHTEENTH-CENTURY TERRA ROSA MARBLE FIREPLACE from Connoisseur Antiques; REPRODUCTION FOO DOGS from Lloyd Paxton; NINETEENTH-CENTURY TERRA COTTA BUST by Paul F. Berthand from Didier Aaron; "HORSE AND JOCKEY" bronze cast after Isidore Jules Bonheur (France, 1827–1901) from Northgate Galleries; TABLES Trouvailles; CHAIRS Shelby Williams with fabrics by Ametex and Brunschwig & Fils; CHINA Hutschewnreuther; SILVER Gebr. Hepp.; CRYSTAL Schott Zwiesel; FLOORCOVERING Weavercraft; ANTIQUE STANDS Kentshire Galleries. (*Dining room*) STAFFORDSHIRE AND OLD IRONSTONE PLATES from Rothschilds fill a circa 1780 English secretaire from Clements Antiques; PAINTINGS, from left are "PORTRAIT OF MISS ELLEN SMITH" by Sir William Beechy (England, 1753–1839) from Stair & Company; unsigned "COUNTRY ROAD WITH TWO BOYS" (nineteenth-century Dutch school), and "THE SOUTH DORSET HUNT" by Frederick W. N. Whitehead (England, 1853–1938) from Kurt E. Schoen Gallery; WALLCOVERING Lee Jofa; CHANDELIERS Bruce Eicher; CHAIRS Shelby Williams with Clarence House fabric; BANQUETTES Rob Jones with Ametex fabric; FLOORCOVERING Weavercraft; CHINA Rosenthal; SILVER Gebr. Hepp.; CRYSTAL Schott Zwiesel. *Contributing writer: Mary Jean Madigan.*

THE PLAZA ATHÉNÉE
(page 195)
CARPET Tai Ping; CUSTOM BANQUETTES Chairmasters with fabric by Decorators Walk; SIDE CHAIRS Artistic Frames Int'l, with leather upholstery by Gilford; CHAIR FINISHING Trouvailles; TABLES Edward Pashayan; CHANDELIERS, SCONCES Delisle; PAINTED LUNETTES Pierre-Marie Rudelle (Paris); CUSTOM MIRRORS Bartolozzi & Maioli (Italy); CEILING MURAL Robert Jackson; SCREENS Edward Pashayan with fabric by Decorators Walk; WALLCOVERING IN PASSAGE Columbus Coated Fabrics. *Contributing writer; Mary Jean Madigan.*

9. NIGHTSPOTS

PULSATIONS (pages 198, 199)
CARPETING Mira-X, Floorgraphix, Inc.; ARTIFICIAL FOLIAGE The Flower Works, Perma Plant, Great Leighton Inc.; CEILING custom by Southern Aluminum Finishing Co.; CEILING LAMINATE Laminators Inc.; FABRIC Valley Forge, Danzian's Inc., McMannus Enterprises; GLASS ENTRY Virginia Glass Products; LAMINATES, METAL Wilsonart through Paco Distributors; LIGHTING O. J. Productions, Litelab, McMannus Enterprises, Altemose Construction; MIRRORS Rohm Glass & Glazing; PAINT Sherwin Williams; NEON City Lights; RAILINGS General Copper & Brass; SEATING Shelby Williams; SOUND Richard Long Associates; TABLETOPS custom by Frank J. Bompadre & Son Inc.; TABLE BASES L & B Contract Industries; WALLCOVERING Collins & Aikman; L. E. Carpenter. *Contributing writer: Jill Fox.*

ZAKIE'S (pages, 200–203)
DANCE FLOOR Zickgraf; CARPETING Commercial Design; COUNTERS, TABLETOPS Nevamar; LIGHTING Conran's, Times Square, Progress Lighting; CHAIRS, STOOLS, TABLE BASES L & B Contract Industries; FACADE WOODWORK Grant Street Woodworking; EXTERIOR HARDWARE Baldwin; AWNING Custom. *Contributing writer: Jill Fox.*

FIZZ (pages 204, 205)
TABLES, TABLE BASES Berco; CHAIRS Globe Business Furniture; CHAIR UPHOLSTERY Wolf Gordon; BAR STOOLS Shelby Williams; BOOTHS Steinmann Interests (custom); BANQUETTE UPHOLSTERY Waverly, Pindler & Pindler, Maharam; FLOORCOVERING Armstrong Tile, Durkan Carpet; TASK LIGHTING Stage Lighting Inc. *Contributing writer: Teresa Byrne-Dodge.*

OVERTURES LOUNGE
(pages 206, 207)
CHAIRS, BAR STOOLS Albert Martin Company; CHAIR, BAR STOOL FABRIC Valley Forge; MARBLE Marvin L. Walker; TABLE BASES Falcon Products; CUSTOM LAMINATE TABLES John Walden; WALL SCONCES Winona Studio of Lighting; CARPETING The Scott Group; WALLCOVERING Innovations, HGH; ARTWORK Teri Muse/Beverly Gordon Fine Art; LIGHTING/SOUND EQUIPMENT London Towne Associates; MILLWORK Cederquist, Inc. *Contributing writer: Rachael Long.*

PETE & MARTY'S
(pages 208, 209)
FENCE, BRICK BAR, NEON custom; BAR STOOLS Richardson Seating Corporation; UPHOLSTERY Wolf Gordon; TILE Tiles International; LIGHTING Litelab, G. J. Neville Lighting, Stonco Inc.; CEILINGS A. A. Abbingdon Affiliates; FABRICS DesignTex, Duralee; CARPET Monterey Carpets; CEILING FANS Robbins Meyers/Hunter; TABLES Liberty Woodcraft; TABLETOPS Cork-O-Plast; CHAIRS Beylerian, Falcon. *Contributing writer: Betsy Lippy.*

SNUGGERY (pages 210, 211)
TILE Kentile; LIGHTING Tech Lighting; SEATING, BANQUETTES Waco Mfg.; TABLES Johnson Industries; TABLE BASES CSI; WALL ART Orlandi Studios; NEON FABRICATOR Lightwriters; COLUMN TILE Brann Clay Tile Co.; VITREOUS TILE American Olean; WALLCOVERING David & Dash, Innovations; BAR STOOLS Waco Mfg.; FLOORING Kentile; BAR Surman Construction; LAMINATES Wilsonart; UPHOLSTERY DesignTex, Naugahyde. *Contributing writer: Jay Pridmore.*

RASCALS (pages 212, 213)
BAR STOOLS West Coast Industries with Naugahyde upholstery; PLANTERS Architectural Supplements; PLANTS Dalmarko; SCULPTURE Niedermaier; TABLES West Coast Industries; DANCE FLOOR CHAIRS Loewenstein; BOOTH BACK FABRIC California Dropcloth; BOOTH SEAT FABRIC S. Harris; LIGHTING FIXTURES Aurora; ENTERTAINMENT, BAR ACCENT LIGHTING Litelab; TABLETOPS AND BASES West Coast Industries; CARPETING Harbinger; WINDOW COVERINGS Flexalum Vertical. *Contributing writer: Mary Jean Madigan.*

10. CAFETERIAS

BANKERS TRUST (page 216)
SIGNAGE Spandex Inc.; LIGHTING Edison Price, Rambusch; CEILING Simplex; WALLCOVERING Vicrtex; TILE Orion.

MOMA (page 217)
LIGHTING Lightolier; FLOORCOVERING Marazzi; TABLETOPS International Store Fixtures; CHAIRS General Fireproofing.

MOUNT SINAI DIETARY FACILITY (page 218)
TABLES Richard Winter & Associates; CHAIRS Claude Bunyard, Westin-Nielsen; WALLCOVERING Genon; FLOORCOVERING American Olean; CARPETING Milliken; CEILING Armstrong; LIGHTING Metalux, Gibson, Marco, Daray; UPHOLSTERY DesignTex; PAINT Benjamin Moore; MILLWORK Altman Modern Woodwork; OPERABLE WALL Kwik Wall; PROJECTION SCREENS Draper. *Contributing writer: Mary Jean Madigan.*

PARK PLAZA CAFE (page 219)
CARPET Harbinger; CHAIRS Loewenstein; BOOTHS, TABLES, BASES Falcon Products; GRAPHICS, NEON GEOMETRIC PARTITIONS Windsor Display. *Contributing writer: Dion Birney.*

EMERY WORLDWIDE ACCOUNTING HEADQUARTERS CAFETERIA (pages 220, 221)
CARPET J&J; WALLCOVERING Polaris Mills Division of Amoco; SKYLIGHTS Bohem Skylights; TABLES Falcon; CHAIRS Shaw Walker. *Contributing writer: Maureen Picard.*

11. RESTAURANTS WITH VIEWS

RISTORANTE PORTOFINO
(pages 224, 225)
CHINA Rosenthal; SILVER Berndorf; GLASSWARE Riedel. *Contributing writer: Susan Colgan.*

GEOFFREY'S (pages 226, 227)
CHAIRS Hagen International; FABRIC Rogers & Waters; WALLCOVERING Forms + Surfaces; FLOORCOVERING International Tile; PAINT Dunn-Edwards; GLASSWARE Schott-Zwiesel, Gourmet France; FLATWARE Towle Silver. *Contributing writer: Kim Johnson Devins.*

SHOOTERS II (pages 228, 229)
FLOORTILE Dal-tile, Peliop, Grigio-National Ceramics of Florida; OAK FLOORING Adams Flooring; CARPETS Bentley, Carpet Systems; WALLCOVERING Sante Fe-Wallco, Wolf-Gordon; WALLPAPERING AND PAINTING Jerry DeLapp Inc.; CEILING TILE Armstrong-Accousti Engineering Company of Florida; LIGHTING Fans & Filers by Edward Inc., Flowers Lighting, Irving Borton, Hill Lighting, Astro Lite, D'Lights; NEON Max Wheeler; ATRIUM Atlantic Glass; ETCHED GLASS, MIRRORS, STAINED GLASS, GLASS BLOCK Carved Glass Inc.; MILLWORK W. I. Gibbs; BRASS/CHROME RAILINGS, FITTINGS Classic Brass Inc.; SIGNAGE Bishop Signs; TABLES Woodsmiths; CHAIRS, BAR STOOLS L & B Contract Industries; OUTDOOR FURNITURE Pompeii Casual Furniture; UPHOLSTERY Quality Custom-Made, Dot-Lon Standard Fabrics. *Contributing writer: Susan Colgan.*

THE INN AT MORRO BAY
(pages 230, 231)
CARPETING Bentley; MARBLE FLOORING Marbles Unlimited; LIGHTING Ron Rezek; BLINDS M & B Manufacturers; UMBRELLAS Basta Sole; BAR AND TABLETOP GW Surfaces (DuPont Corian with brass and wood inlay); CHAIRS Lewittes; TABLES Custom Craft; TABLE BASES L & B Contract Industries; LAMPS Chapman. *Contributing writer: Jill Fox.*

12. ADAPTIVE USE DESIGNS

COUP DE COEUR
(pages 234, 235)
CHAIRS Driade, designed by Philippe Starck; TABLES custom designed by Michel Douville and Patrick Garel; WALLCOVERINGS Nobilis; CARPETING Bigelow Heuga; LIGHTING Hallogene, Gilles Derain, Artemide; CHINA Schoenwald; SILVER Christofle; GLASSWARE Luminarc. *Contributing writer: Susan Colgan.*

MA MAISON (pages 236, 237)
CHAIR FABRIC Brunschwig & Fils; CUSTOM MILLWORK Renaissance Builders (Houston) WALL UPHOLSTERY Clarence House; SUSPENDED LIGHT FIXTURES Boyd Lighting; BACK BAR LIGHTING Tivoli; ARCHITECTURAL LIGHTING Lightolier; CARPETING Campbell Collection, Bentley Carpet Mills; GLASS RACKS Texas Custom Brass; CHAIRS Falcon; CHAIR UPHOLSTERY Stroheim & Romann; DRAPERY FABRIC TRIM Brunswig & Fils; TABLES L & B Contract Industries; TABLE SKIRT FABRIC Pindler & Pindler; CHANDELIERS, SCONCES custom by Alcon (Houston); SLATE HEARTH American Olean. *Contributing writer: Teresa Byrne-Dodge.*

CARLUCCI (pages 238–241)
TABLES Johnson Industries; CHAIRS Empire State; TROMPE L'OEIL PAINTING William Wagenaar Associates; TILE American Olean; CARPETING Watson Smith; LIGHTING Lang Levin, Capitol Hardware; BOOTH, BANQUETTE UPHOLSTERY Naugahyde; LINENS Steiner; FLATWARE Hinricks; GLASSWARE Libbey; CHINA Jackson; BAR RAILINGS Gallery Brass. *Contributing writer: Jerry Cooper.*

MAJESTIC OYSTER BAR AND GRILL (pages 242, 243)
TABLE BASE Berco; CHAIRS, UPHOLSTERY Shelby Williams; BAR STOOLS Empire State Chair Company; LIGHTING D'Lites; WINDOW SHADES Aero Drapery (custom); LINEN Morgan Linen Company; GLASSWARE Libbey; FLATWARE World Tableware; CHINA Shenango. *Contributing writer: Justin Henderson.*

DOWNTOWN CLUB
(pages 244, 245)
CHAIRS Bunyard; WALLCOVERING DesignTex; FLOORCOVERING American Olean; CARPETING Berven Carpets; LIGHTING Halo, Capri, Robert Long Lighting; WINDOW SHUTTERS Pinecrest; CHINA Shenango; STEMWARE Libbey Glass. *Contributing writer: Mark Kristal.*

HOP BROOK (pages 246, 247)
CHAIRS Nichols and Stone; TABLES, BAR custom by the Stout Company; CARPETING Wellco Carpet (supplied by David Rosenthal Associates); LIGHTING Abolite Lighting Inc. *Contributing writer: Susan Colgan.*

INDEX

Ace Architects, 164–166
A&D Mercantile, New York City, 178
Altemose, Arthur, 198–99
Altemose Architects and Engineers, 198–99
Amick Harrison Architects, 142–45
Ancora, New York City, 40–43
Anderson, Craig, 92–93
Angeli, Los Angeles, Cal., 72–73
Aoki, Seattle, Wash., 156–57
Arai, Kiyokazu, 52–53
Arby's, Atlanta, Ga., 102
Arby's, Louisville, Ky., 102–3
Arcadia, New York City, 14, 15, 24–25
Arlen, Samuel S., 70–71
Arlen/Fox Architects, 70–71
Ashworth, Warren, 46–48
Associated Space Design of Atlanta, 102
Aumiller, Bill, 122–25
Aumiller/Yonquist P. C., 122–25
Aurora, New York City, 33
A&W, Short Hills, N.J., 101, 103

Babcock, Bill, 101–2, 103
Babcock & Schmid Associates, 101, 103, 104
Baehler, Hans J., 86–87
Bairley, Dan, 184–85
Bairley & Maginniss, 184–85
Balamut, Sylvia, 228–29
Banik, Jane, 110
Banik-Cumby, 110–11
Bankers Trust Co. Harborside Cafeteria, Jersey City, N.J., 216–18
Banks, John, 78–79
Banks/Eakin Architects, 64–65, 78–79
Beckham/Eisenman Commercial Design and Furnishings, 94–95
Bennett, Charles, 122–25
Berkley (Lawrence) & Associates, Inc. 78–79
Berman, David, 60–61
Bertaux + Copley and Associates, 190–91
Betts, John, 167–69
Biber, James, 49–51
Big Splash, The, North Miami Beach, Fla., 85, 86–87, 101
Binder, Rebecca L., 82–83
Bischoff, James, 233, 246–47
Bitici, Sergio, 8

Bogdanow, Larry, 46–48
Bogdanow (L.) & Associates, 46–48
Bohlen, Oscar, 242–43
Boivin, Alan, 62–63
Bolton, Michael, 176–77
Bolton (Michael) Designs, 176–77
Boxenbaum, Charles, 40–43, 76–77, 101, 103
Branham, Deborah, 160–63
Bronstad, Paulette, 230–31
Brown, Scott, 118–19
Brown (J. S.) Design, 118–19
Bubbles, Balboa, Cal., 109, 130–33
Burgee, John, 8
Burson, Rodgers, 206–7
Burson & Cox, 206–7

Cafe Ba-Ba-Reeba, Chicago, Ill., 122–25
Cafe du Triangle, Beverly Hills, Cal., 16–17
Caffey, Ben, 26–27
Callister, Gately and Bischoff, 233, 246–47
Cameron, David, 208–9
Campton Place, San Francisco, Cal., 181–83
Cannon, John, 56–59
Cannon/Davis Interiors, 56–59
Carlucci, Chicago, Ill., 233, 238–41
Carman, Rodney D., 96–97
Casa Lupita, Totem Lake, Wash., 85, 92–93
Case, G. D., 116–17
Casual Quilted Giraffe, New York City, 35–39
Chambers (H.) Company, 188–89
Charley O's, New York City, 85, 89–91
Chaya Brasserie, West Hollywood, Cal., 54–55
Chelsea Architects, 236–37
Chesapeake Associated Architects Inc., 188–89
Chesser, Lynda E., 136–38
Chi, Tony, 98–100
Chilla, Chicago, Ill., 135
City Spirit Cafe, Denver, Col., 65, 68–69
Coffee Works, Morristown, N.J., 102, 103–4
Colwell Ray Hornacek Okinaka (CRHO), 170–71
Compton, Christopher, 154–55
Compton Architects, 154–55
Costa, Wendy, 20–23
Costa & Kline Interiors, 20–23

Coup de Coeur, Paris, France, 234–35
Croxton, Randolph, 15, 24–25
Croxton Collaborative, 24–25
Cuisine des Chefs, Orlando, Fla., 136–38
Curley's Garage, Salisbury, Md., 110–11
Cygne, Le, New York City, 30–32

Daniels, Jeffrey, 54–55
DDL Foodshow, Beverly Hills, Cal.; New York City, 160–63
DeHaan, Norman, 135, 149–51
DeHaan (Norman) Associates, Inc., 149–51
Dermady, Martin, 49–51
Designworks, 172–73
Dethlefs, Gary, 92–93
DiLeonardo International, 208–9
Dine-O-Mat, New York City, 65, 80–81
Dodge, Kathy, 208–9
Dolin, Lew, 104, 105
Dorf, Martin, 102–4
Dorf Associates, 103–4
Douglas, Mike, 104, 106
Douville, Michael, 234–35
Downtown Club, Fresno, Cal., 244–45
Drysdale, Mary, 184–85
Drysdale Design Associates, 184–85
Duck and Decanter, Scottsdale, Ariz., 174–75
DuMond, Jay, 246–47
Duncan Design Associates, 204–5
Dunn, John Paul, 86–87
Dunnette, Lee, 36–39

Eakin, Garret, 78–79
Eastman, Jerome, 233, 238–41
Eats, El Segundo, Cal., 82–83
Emerson, Brad, 172–73
Emery Air Freight Corp. Cafeteria, Throop, Pa., 220–21
Etienne, Geoffrey, 226–27
Everett, Jeff, 122–25
Express, L', Los Angeles, Cal., 62–63
Extra! Extra!, New York City, 109, 126–29

253

FABRAP Architects, 102–3
Felderman, Stanley, 15, 16–19
Felderman & Associates, 16–19
Fizz, Houston, Texas, 204–5
Flack, Robert, 167–69
Flack (Robert) & Associates, Inc., 167–69
Flynn, Mary, 219
Fog City Diner, San Francisco, Cal., 120–21
Forman, Fran, 167–69
Forrest, Deborah Lloyd, 206–7
Four Seasons Restaurant, New York City, 15
Fox, Frederick B., Jr., 70–71
Frank Fat's, Sacramento, Cal., 139–41
Franks for the Memory, Vancouver, Canada, 106–7
Frapwell, Larry, 130–33
Friend, William, 96–97
Fritz, Marsha, 188
Fujikawa Johnson and Associates, Inc., 78–79
Fulton Market Building, New York City, 178–79

Garel, Patrick, 234–35
Gelardi, Anthony and Paul, 190–91
Geoffrey's, Malibu, Cal., 223, 226–27
George, Philip, 33
Glaser, Milton, 33, 76–77
Gotham Bar and Grill, New York City, 49–51
Grammenopoulous, Anthony, 112–15
Grandberg, Ira, 80–81
Grandesign Architects, 80–81
Granoff, Richard, 86–87
Grenon, Nathalie, 8, 11
Grinstein, Elyse, 54–55
Grinstein/Daniels, Inc., 54–55

Hanson, George, 92–93
Harrison, H. Lynn, 135, 142–45
Harvey Houses, 10, 85
Hausler, Andreas, 36–39
Haverson, Jay, 44–45, 85–87
Haverson/Rockwell Architects, 35, 44–45, 86–87, 101
Hellmuth, Obata & Kassabaum (HOK), 206–7
Henle, John, 49–51
Henning, Randolph, 15, 20–23
Hess, Elvin, 200–3
Hickey, Carol, 200–3
Hickey/Hess Architecture & Design, 200–3
Hill Partnership, The, 130–33
Hirsch/Bedner & Associates, 182–83
Historic Bryan Homes Restaurant, Fort Lauderdale, Fla., 15, 20–23

Hop Brook, Simsbury, Conn., 233, 246–47
Hornacek, Robert J., 170–71
Howard, Lucia, 164–66
Howell, Andrew N., 206–7
Hricak, Michael, 66–67

Imperial Hotel, The, Chestertown, Md., 188–89
Indian Oven, New York City, 134–35, 146–48
Inn at Morro Bay, The, Morro Bay, Cal., 230–31
Interior Facilities Associates (IFA), 216–18

Jachmich, Sharon, 236–37
Jackets, New York City, 70–71
Johnson, Philip, 8
Jones, Terry, 244–45
Jones, Yaly, 228–29

Kato, Cindi, 92–93
Ketzel & Goodman, 230–31
Kiiroihana, San Francisco, Cal., 135, 142–45
Kipelainen, T. L., 172–73
Kline, Paula, 20–23
Knowlwood's, Santa Ana, Cal., 94–95
Korbin, Jay, 152–53
Kuhn, Frederick, 167–69
Kuleto, Patrick E., 120–21
Kuna, John, 220
Kyncl & Arnold Architekten, 223, 224–25

Lacayo, Norman, 197, 212–13
Lacayo, Pam, 212–13
Lakeside Delicatessen, Oakland, Cal., 159, 164–66
Lamb, Linda, 116–17
LaRoche, David, 208–9
Larson, Bill, 174–75
Laufer, R., 112–15
Le Cygne, New York City, 30–32
Le Paris, Paris, France, 181, 186–87
Le Triangle, Beverly Hills, Cal., 15–19
Lee, Sarah Tomerlin, 181
Lee (Tom) Ltd., 181
Leggitt, John, 172–73
Les Tuileries, New York City, 135, 154–55
Leung Hemmler, Camayd, 220–21
Lew (Allen Y.) & Patnaude (William E.), 244–45
Lewis, Diane, 154–55
L'Express, Los Angeles, Cal., 62–63
Liberty Cafe, New York City, 109, 112–15
Limone Thomas, 208–9
Littenberg, Barbara, 146–48
Loebl Schossman and Hackl Architects, 216

Lokensgaard, Ole, 40–43
Loomis, John, 94–95
Lopata, Sam, 109, 126–29

McClintock, Libby, 112–15
McCree Inc., 136–38
McCulloch, Barnett, 149–51
McDonald's, Raleigh, N.C., 84–85, 96–97
McDonough, William A., 36–39
McDonough Nouri Rainey & Associates, 35–39
McFarlane, Maureen, 122–25
McGuire, Ron, 226–27
Machado, Anthony, 139–41
Majestic Oyster Bar and Grill, Indianapolis, Ind., 242–43
Ma Maison, Houston, Texas, 233, 236–37
Mama Mia! Pasta, Chicago, Ill., 64, 65, 78–79
Marmount Design Associates, 152–53
Marshand, Mike, 44–45
Max au Triangle, Beverly Hills, Cal., 17, 18–19
Mayne, Thom, 26–27, 52–53, 72–73
Mazzola, Holly, 198–99
Meisel, Joseph A. III, 28–29
Meisel Associates, Ltd., 28–29
Melman, Richard, 122–25
Melton Henry Architects, 236–37
Merchant Associates, 219
Merchant's Coffee Tea and Spice, New York City, 178
MGS Architects, 109, 112–15
Mickle, Peter, 154–55
Micunis, Gordon, 152–53
Micunis (Gordon) Designs, 152–53
Middleton, Doug, 160–63
Miller, Joan and Don, 116–17
Mirich, Shelly, 107
Mirich Developments, 107
Mittelstaedt Kesler Ltd., 174–75
Molzan, Lynn, 242–43
Montaine, Richard, 152–53
Moore, Charles, 164
Morphosis, 26–27, 52–53, 72–73
Morris, John, 130–33
Morrison House, Alexandria, Va., 184–85
Mount, Charles Morris, 98–100
Mount Sinai Hospital Dietary Facility, Chicago, Ill., 216, 217, 218
Mrs. Garcia's, Los Angeles, Cal., 66–67
Murata, Kazuyuki, 156–57
Murray, Christopher, 156–57
Museum of Modern Art Cafeteria, New York City, 216, 217

Nathanson, Morris, 98
Neal, Michael, 36–39
Nelson, Gregory, 62–63
Neutra, Richard, 223, 226–27
Newberry, Joseph O., 246–47
Newmark, Judith, 26–27
Nicholson, Frank, 192–94
Noble/White Architects, 219
Norris, David, 40–43
Northcutt, James, 182–83
Nouri, Hamid R., 36–39
Nunes, George, 208–9
Nunn, Ron, 60–61
Nunn (Ron) Associates, Inc., 60–61

Obelenus, John, 24–25
Orsini, Susan Francesca, 85, 89–91
Orsini Design Associates, 89–91
Osborn, William L., 228–29
Overtures Lounge, Birmingham, Ala., 197, 206–7
Owen (Louis) Inc., 92–93

Paehler, Hans, 44–45
Panache, Fullerton, Cal., 175, 176–77
Paris, Le, Paris, France, 181, 186–87
Park Plaza Cafe, El Segundo, Cal., 219
Pate (Milton) & Associates, 192–94
Patnaude, William E., 244–45
Paxton & Whitfield, New York City, 179
Perry & Plummer Design Associates, 85, 96–97
Pete & Marty's, Toronto, Canada, 208–9
Peterson, Steven K., 146–48
Peterson, Littenberg Architects, 135, 146–48
Pheasant (Michelle) Design, Inc., 116–17
Pheasant-Angelo, Michelle, 116–17
Piret's, Beverly Hills, Cal., 159, 170–71
Pizzapiazza, New York City, 76–77
Pizzeria Uno, New York City; Secaucus, N.J., 98–100
Plaza Athénée, New York City, 195
Plummer, D. Gordon, 96–97
Poeschl, Robert, 68–69
Polcari & Sons, Boston, Mass., 158–59, 167–69
Portland Design Team, 190–91
Provisions, New York City, 179
Pulsations, Glen Mills, Pa., 197, 198–99

Rainey, J. Woodson, Jr., 35, 36–39
Raleigh, Christopher P., 136–38
Raleigh & Associates, 136–38
Rascals, Honolulu, Hawaii, 196–97, 212–13

Red's, San Francisco, Cal., 60–61
Reiss, David, 167–69
Richardson, Janet, 188–89
Ristorante Portofino, Zurich, Switzerland, 223–25
Ristorante Replay, Milan, Italy, 74–75
Ritz-Carlton Hotel Naples, Fla., 192–94
Rizzo, Charles, 210–11
Rockefeller, Darrell, 66–67
Rockefeller/Hricak Architects, 66–67
Rockwell, David S., 44–45, 85–87
Rodrigues, Nancy, 208–9
Rose, S., 112–15
Rotondi, Michael, 26–27, 52–53, 72–73
Ruby's Balboa Diner, Balboa, Cal., 109, 118–19, 130, 132
Rutter, Jeff, 210–11
Rybar, Valerian, 195
Rybar (Valerian) & Daigre Design, 195
Rykiel, Sonia, 186–87
Rylander, Mark, 36–39

Saie, Michele, 72–73
Sartogo, Piero, 8, 11
Savany Associates, 30–32
Schauer, Carol, 208–9
Schmid, Jurig, 104
Schooners, The, Kennebunkport, Me., 181, 190–91
Schwedfeger, Jane, 89–91
Segal, Paul, 49–51
Segal (Paul) Associates, 49–51
72 Market, Venice, Cal., 52–53
Sgt. Pepperoni's, Irvine, Cal., 104, 106
Shamiana, Stamford, Conn., 152–53
SHAPE, Inc., 190–91
Shilla, Chicago, Ill., 149–51
Shooters II, Boynton Beach, Fla., 228–29
Shults, Mabel, 230–31
Shults & Associates, 230–31
Skidmore, Owings & Merrill (SOM), 28–29
Skyline Design of Chicago, 210–11
Slavik, 186–87
Sloan, Eva, 170–71
Smith, Christopher, 44–45
Snuggery, Northbrook, Ill., 210–11
Soloway, Bill, 112–15
Spatz, Mark A., 170–71
Speer, Madeline, 178
Spiaggia, Chicago, Ill., 28–29
Stafford, James G., 82–83
Stockman, Judith, 179, 216
Stubbe, Lee, 156–57
Sui-Sheng Chang, 78–79

Tanaka, George, 54
Thirtieth Street Architects, 94–95, 118–19

Thompson (Benjamin) and Associates, 178, 179
Tihany, Adam D., 160–63
Tihany (Adam) International, 160–63
Timm, Mary, 122–25
Tobin, Calvin, 216
Tolson (Fred) Associates, 96–97
Toscana Ristorante, New York City, 8–12
Triangle, Le, Beverly Hills, Cal., 15–19
Tuileries, Les, New York City, 135, 154–55
Tutti's, Montecito, Cal., 172–73
Twenty/Twenty, New York City, 35, 44–45
2S2M Architects, 156–57
Tyson, Burt, 36–39

Ullo, Tom, 210–11
Union Square Cafe, New York City, 46–48

Van Pelt, Ron, 130–33
Van Tilburg, Johannes, 62–63
Van Tilburg (Johannes) & Partners, 62–63
Velsor, Richard, 32
Verdi, Santa Monica, Cal., 26–27
Vignelli, Lella and Massimo, 8
Voith, Jerry, 102–3
Voorsanger & Mills Associates, 30–32

Warnecke, John Carl, 195
Watkin, William Ward, 236–37
Webster, David, 190
Weingarten, David, 164–66
Wells (S. W.) Design Associates, 228–29
Welzien, Susan, 228–29
Wendy's, New York City, 104, 105
Westin Hotel, Washington, D.C., 180–81
Wick, Susan, 68–69
Willow Tea Room, Carmel, Cal., 116–17
Wimberly, Whisenand, Allison, Tong & Goo, 192–94
Winnetka Grill, Winnetka, Ill., 56–59
Woolen, Molzan and Partners, 242–43
Wright, Suzan, 230–31
WTR Studio, 116–17
Wynn, Joyce K., 206–7
Wynn (Joyce K.), Inc., 206–7

Zakie's, York, Pa., 197, 200–203
Zerbi, Pupa and Georgia, 74–75

Senior Editor: Julia Moore
Associate Editor: Victoria Craven-Cohn
Designer: Bob Fillie
Production Manager: Ellen Greene
Set in 10-point Berkeley Old Style Book